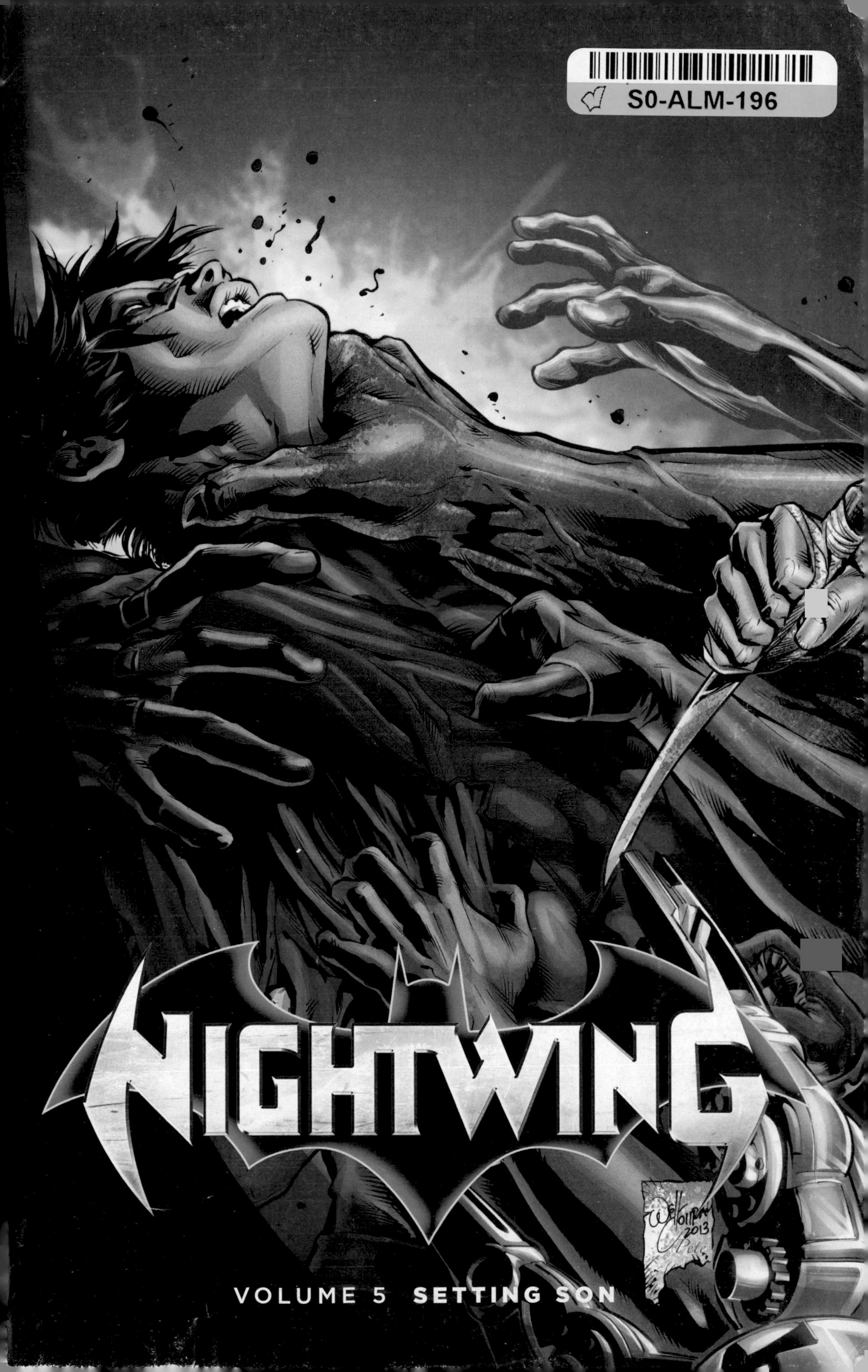

NIGHTWING

VOLUME 5 SETTING SON

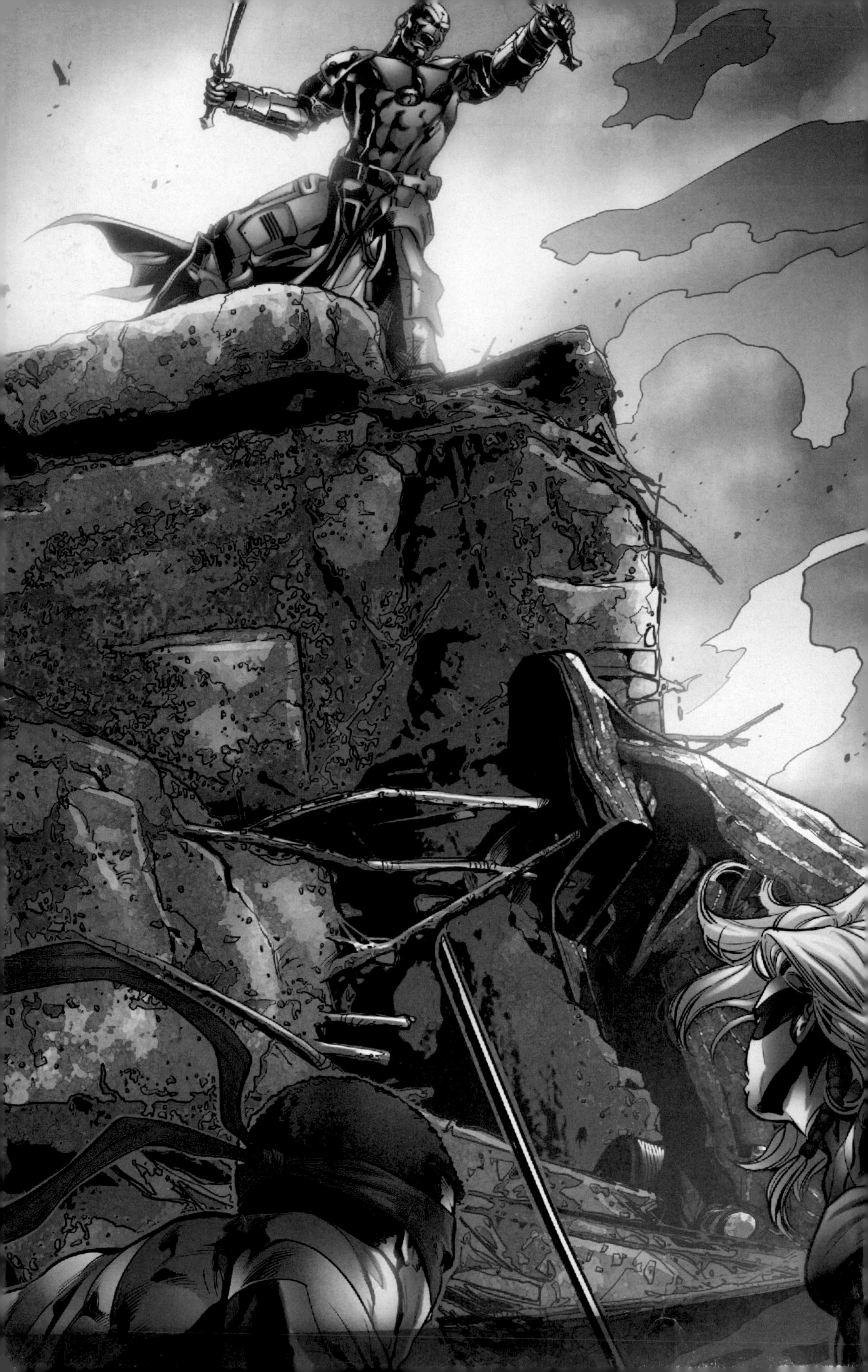

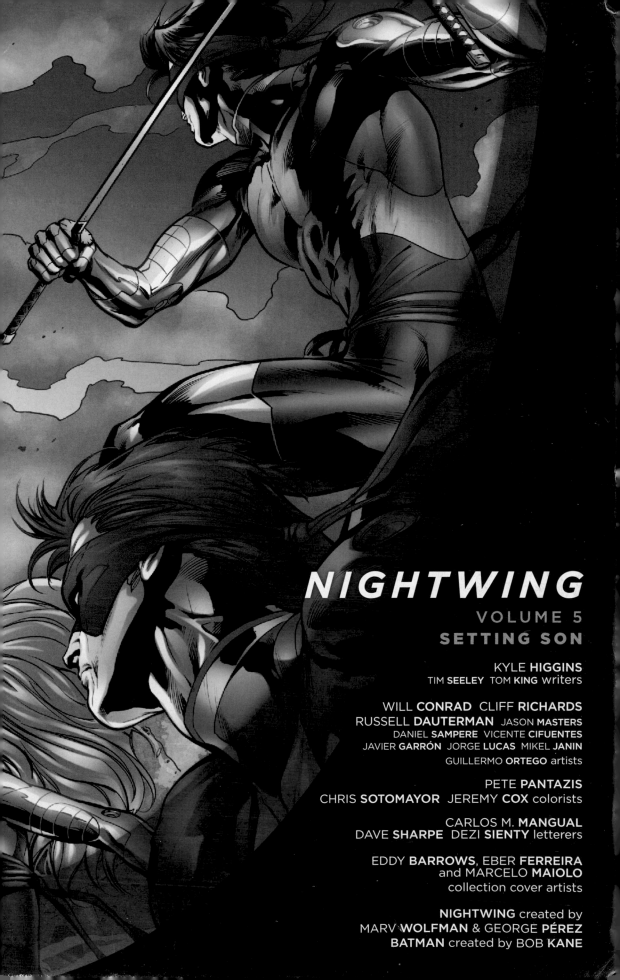

NIGHTWING

VOLUME 5
SETTING SON

KYLE **HIGGINS**
TIM **SEELEY** TOM **KING** writers

WILL **CONRAD** CLIFF **RICHARDS**
RUSSELL **DAUTERMAN** JASON **MASTERS**
DANIEL **SAMPERE** VICENTE **CIFUENTES**
JAVIER **GARRÓN** JORGE **LUCAS** MIKEL **JANIN**
GUILLERMO **ORTEGO** artists

PETE **PANTAZIS**
CHRIS **SOTOMAYOR** JEREMY **COX** colorists

CARLOS M. **MANGUAL**
DAVE **SHARPE** DEZI **SIENTY** letterers

EDDY **BARROWS**, EBER **FERREIRA**
and MARCELO **MAIOLO**
collection cover artists

NIGHTWING created by
MARV **WOLFMAN** & GEORGE **PÉREZ**
BATMAN created by BOB **KANE**

RACHEL GLUCKSTERN KATIE KUBERT Editors – Original Series
DARREN SHAN MATT HUMPHREYS Assistant Editors – Original Series LIZ ERICKSON Editor
ROBBIN BROSTERMAN Design Director – Books ROBBIE BIEDERMAN Publication Design

BOB HARRAS Senior VP – Editor-in-Chief, DC Comics

DIANE NELSON President DAN DIDIO and JIM LEE Co-Publishers GEOFF JOHNS Chief Creative Officer
AMIT DESAI Senior VP – Marketing and Franchise Management
AMY GENKINS Senior VP – Business and Legal Affairs NAIRI GARDINER Senior VP – Finance
JEFF BOISON VP – Publishing Planning MARK CHIARELLO VP – Art Direction and Design
JOHN CUNNINGHAM VP – Marketing TERRI CUNNINGHAM VP – Editorial Administration
LARRY GANEM VP – Talent Relations and Services ALISON GILL Senior VP – Manufacturing and Operations
HANK KANALZ Senior VP – Vertigo and Integrated Publishing JAY KOGAN VP – Business and Legal Affairs, Publishing
JACK MAHAN VP – Business Affairs, Talent NICK NAPOLITANO VP – Manufacturing Administration SUE POHJA VP – Book Sales
FRED RUIZ VP – Manufacturing Operations COURTNEY SIMMONS Senior VP – Publicity BOB WAYNE Senior VP – Sales

NIGHTWING VOLUME 5: SETTING SON

Published by DC Comics. Copyright © 2014 DC Comics. All Rights Reserved.

Originally published in single magazine form in NIGHTWING 25-30; NIGHTWING ANNUAL 1 © 2013, 2014 DC Comics.
All Rights Reserved. All characters, their distinctive likenesses and related elements featured in this publication are trademarks of DC Comics.
SCRIBBLENAUTS and all related characters and elements are trademarks of and © Warner Bros. Entertainment Inc.
ROBOT CHICKEN, the logo and all related elements are trademarks of and copyright by Cartoon Network. (s2014)
MAD and Alfred E. Neuman © and ™ E. C. Publications, Inc. The stories, characters and incidents featured in this publication
are entirely fictional. DC Comics does not read or accept unsolicited ideas, stories or artwork.

DC Comics, 1700 Broadway, New York, NY 10019
A Warner Bros. Entertainment Company.
Printed by RR Donnelley, Owensville, MO, USA. 11/28/14 First Printing.
ISBN: 978-1-4012-5011-9

Certified Chain of Custody
20% Certified Forest Content,
80% Certified Sourcing
www.sfiprogram.org
SFI-01042
APPLIES TO TEXT STOCK ONLY

Library of Congress Cataloging-in-Publication Data

Higgins, Kyle, 1985- author.
Nightwing. Volume 5, Setting son / Kyle Higgins, Will Conrad.
pages cm. — (The New 52!)
ISBN 978-1-4012-5011-9 (paperback)
1. Graphic novels. I. Conrad, Will, illustrator. II. Title. III. Title: Setting son.

PN6728.N55H58 2014
741.5'973—dc23

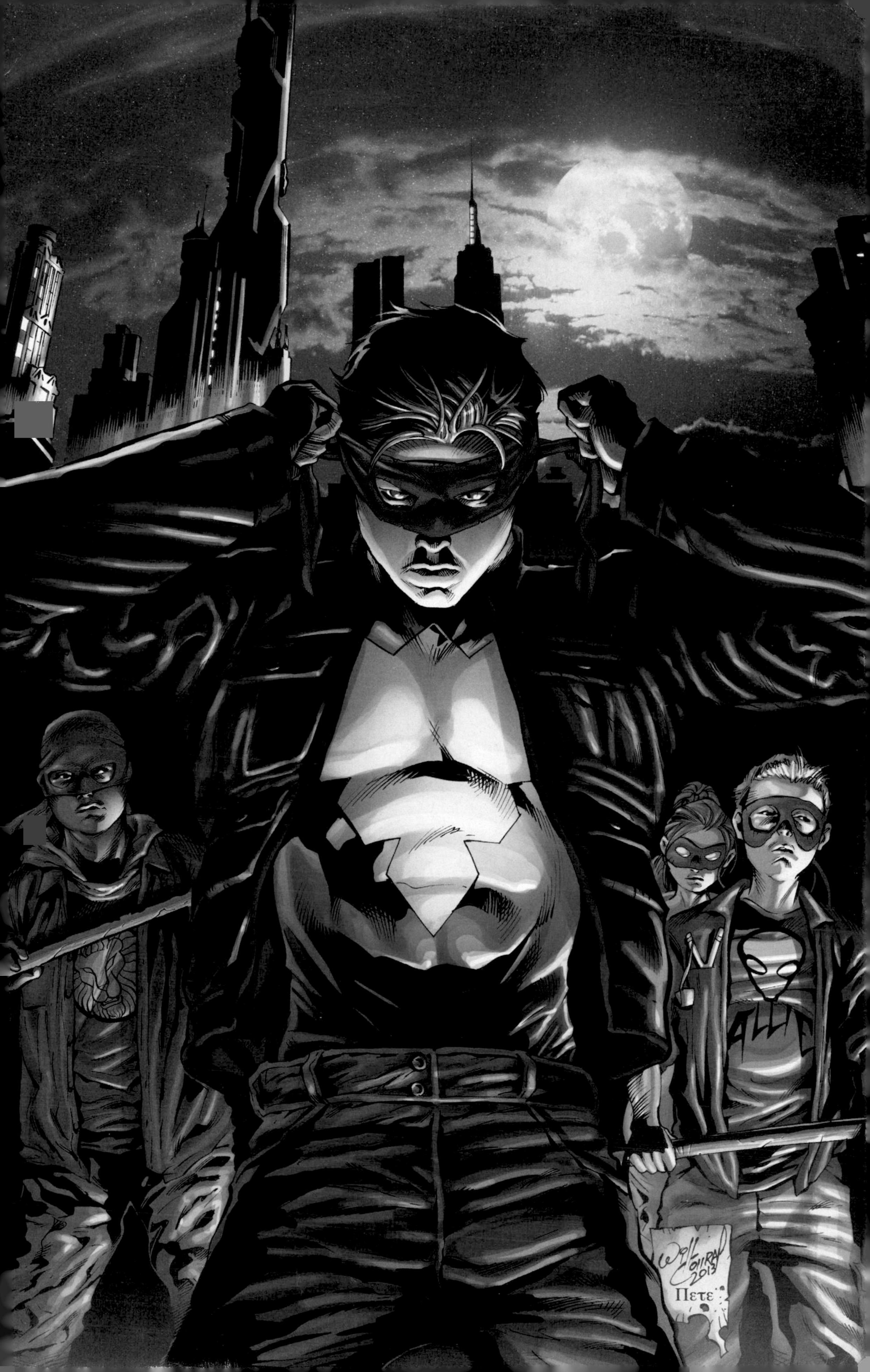

ONE DARK CITY NIGHT

KYLE HIGGINS writer **WILL CONRAD & CLIFF RICHARDS** artists **PETE PANTAZIS** colorist
CARLOS M. MANGUAL letterer cover art by **WILL CONRAD** and **PETE PANTAZIS**

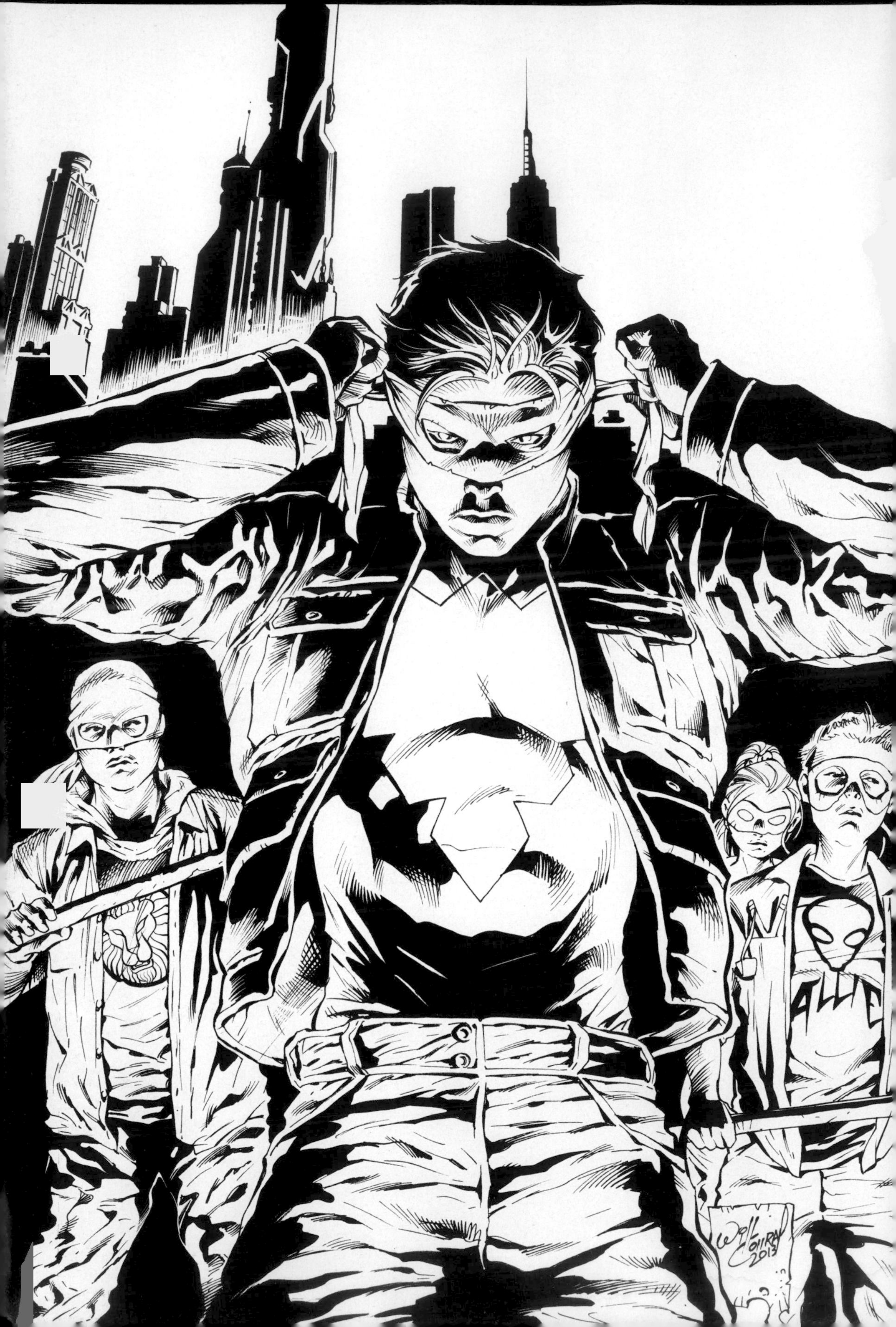

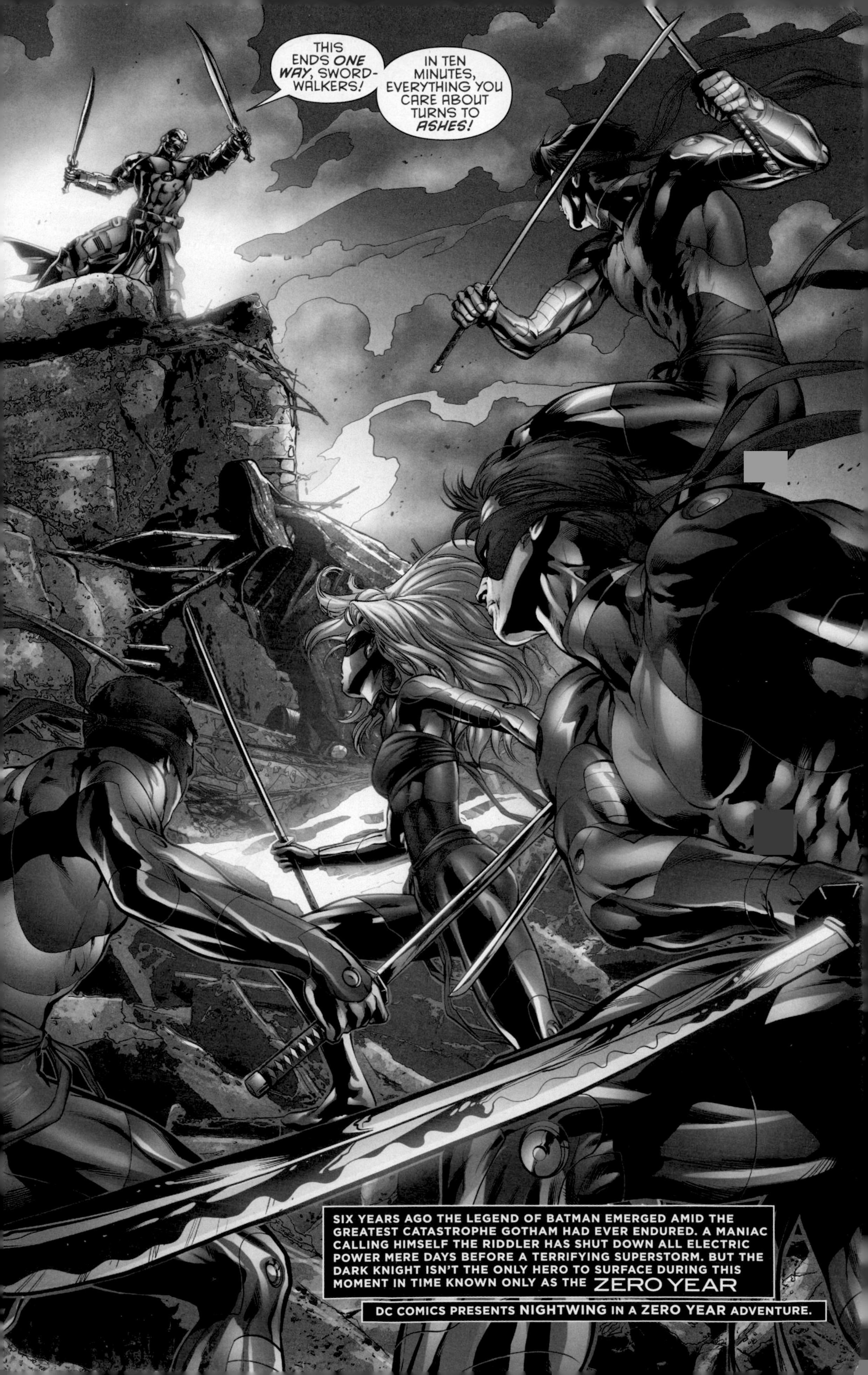

THIS ENDS *ONE WAY*, SWORD-WALKERS!
IN TEN MINUTES, EVERYTHING YOU CARE ABOUT TURNS TO *ASHES!*
SIX YEARS AGO THE LEGEND OF BATMAN EMERGED AMID THE GREATEST CATASTROPHE GOTHAM HAD EVER ENDURED. A MANIAC CALLING HIMSELF THE RIDDLER HAS SHUT DOWN ALL ELECTRIC POWER MERE DAYS BEFORE A TERRIFYING SUPERSTORM. BUT THE DARK KNIGHT ISN'T THE ONLY HERO TO SURFACE DURING THIS MOMENT IN TIME KNOWN ONLY AS THE ZERO YEAR
DC COMICS PRESENTS NIGHTWING IN A ZERO YEAR ADVENTURE.

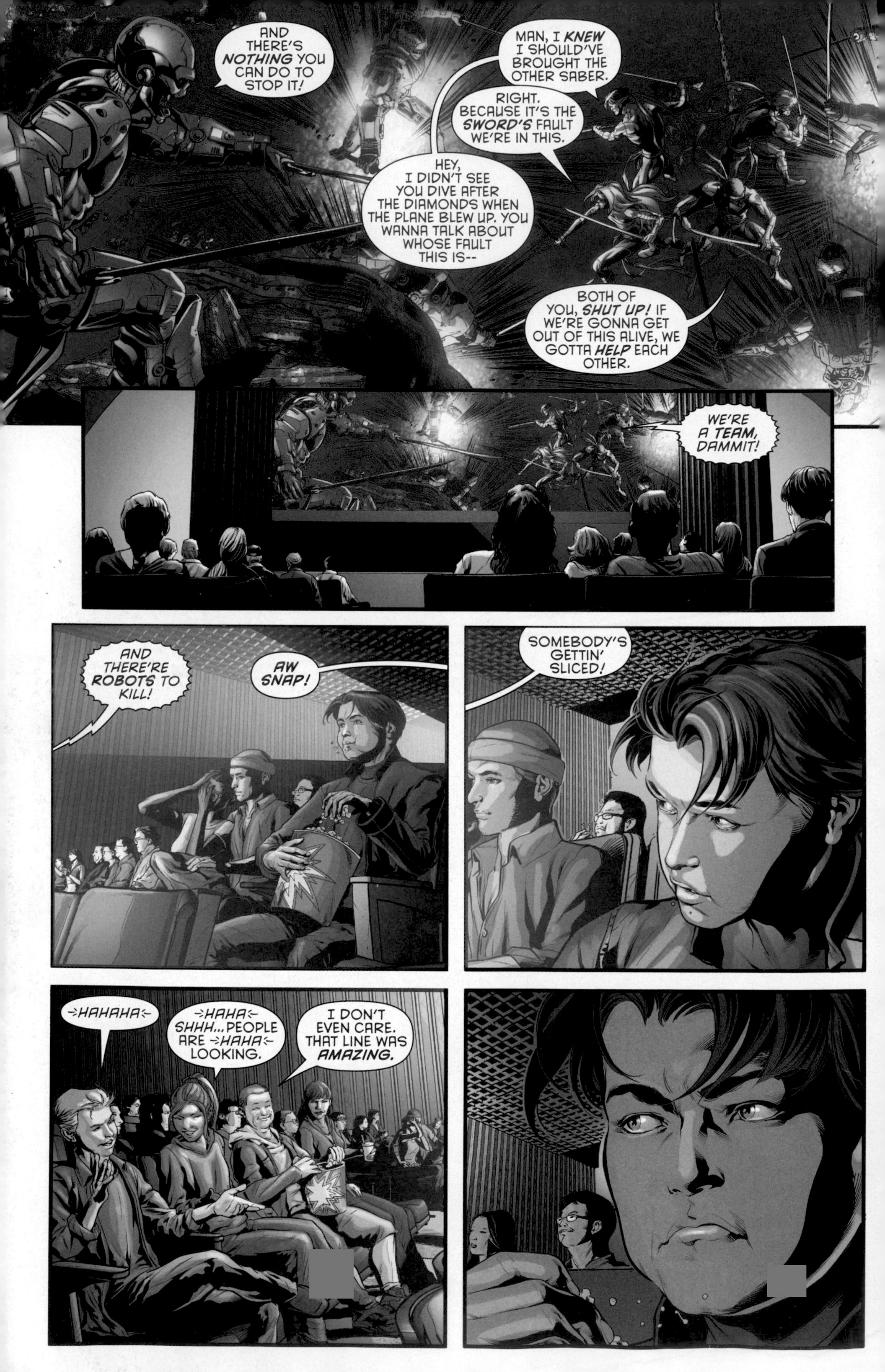
AND THERE'S NOTHING YOU CAN DO TO STOP IT!
MAN, I KNEW I SHOULD'VE BROUGHT THE OTHER SABER.
RIGHT. BECAUSE IT'S THE SWORD'S FAULT WE'RE IN THIS.
HEY, I DIDN'T SEE YOU DIVE AFTER THE DIAMONDS WHEN THE PLANE BLEW UP. YOU WANNA TALK ABOUT WHOSE FAULT THIS IS--
BOTH OF YOU, SHUT UP! IF WE'RE GONNA GET OUT OF THIS ALIVE, WE GOTTA HELP EACH OTHER.
WE'RE A TEAM, DAMMIT!
AND THERE'RE ROBOTS TO KILL!
AW SNAP!
SOMEBODY'S GETTIN' SLICED!
HAHAHA
HAHA SHHH... PEOPLE ARE HAHA LOOKING.
I DON'T EVEN CARE. THAT LINE WAS AMAZING.

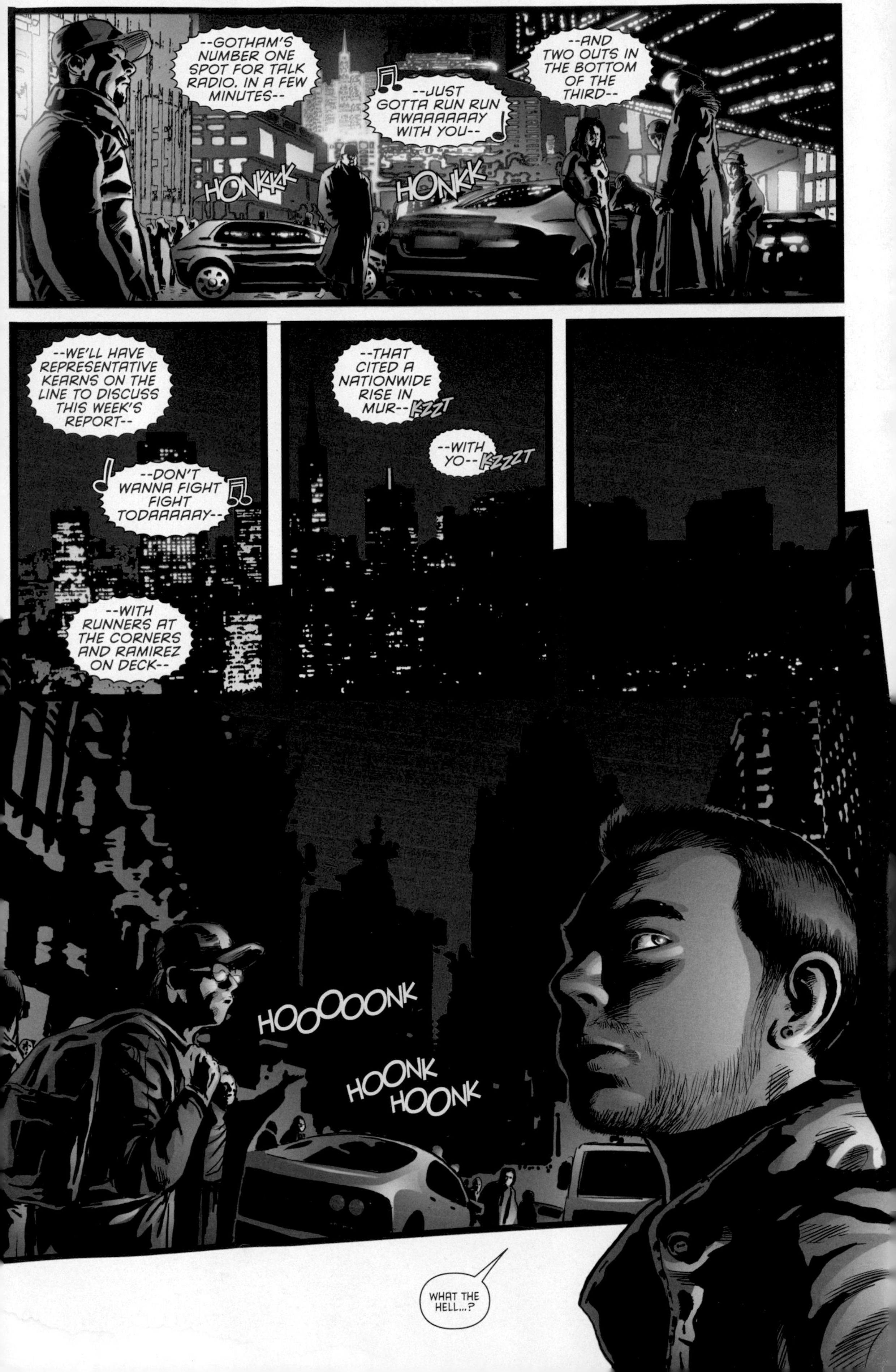
--GOTHAM'S NUMBER ONE SPOT FOR TALK RADIO. IN A FEW MINUTES--
--JUST GOTTA RUN RUN AWAAAAAAY WITH YOU--
--AND TWO OUTS IN THE BOTTOM OF THE THIRD--
HONKKK
HONKK
--WE'LL HAVE REPRESENTATIVE KEARNS ON THE LINE TO DISCUSS THIS WEEK'S REPORT--
--DON'T WANNA FIGHT FIGHT TODAAAAAAY--
--WITH RUNNERS AT THE CORNERS AND RAMIREZ ON DECK--
--THAT CITED A NATIONWIDE RISE IN MUR--KZZT
--WITH YO--KZZZZT
HOOOOONK
HOONK HOONK
WHAT THE HELL...?

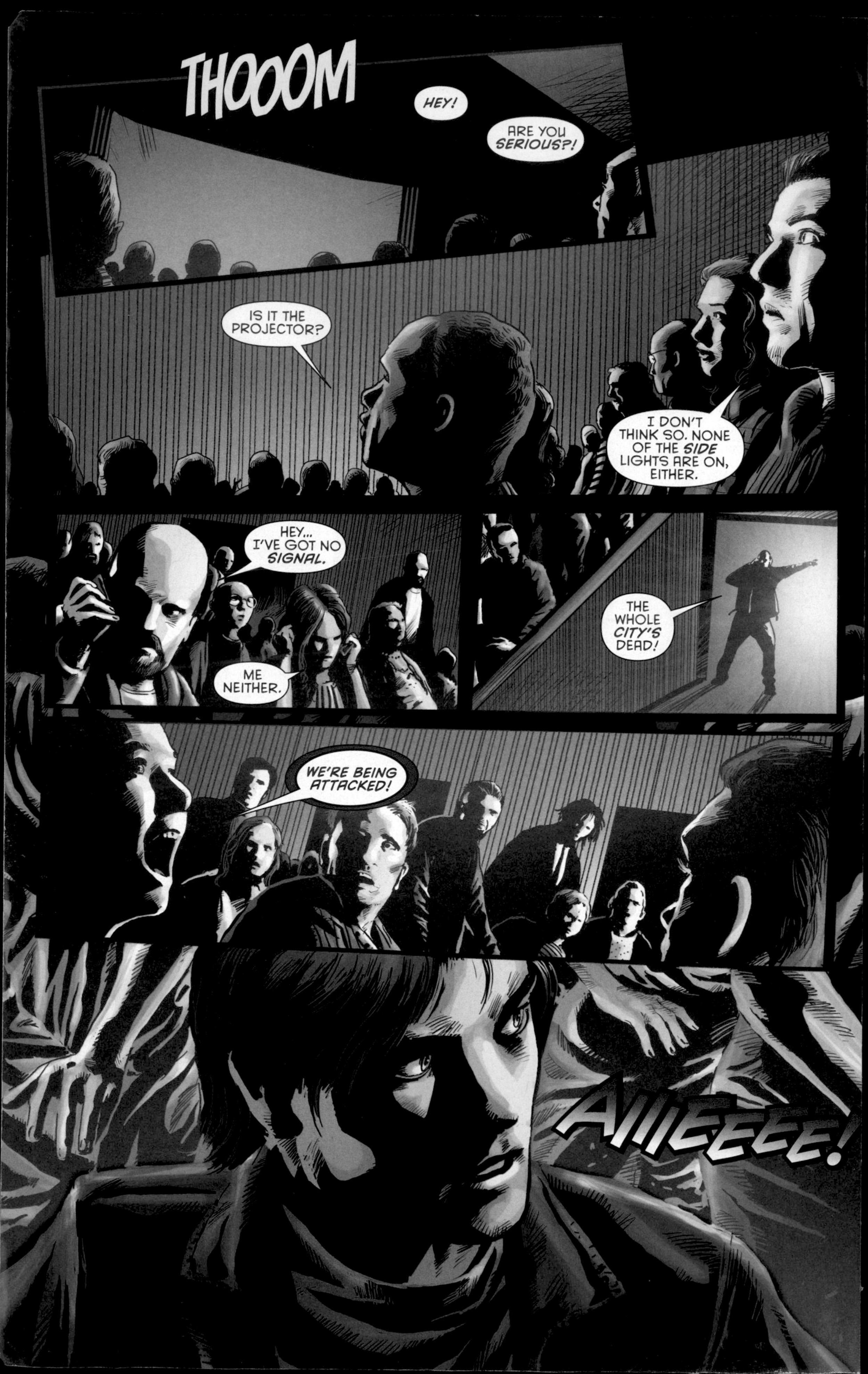
THOOOM
HEY!
ARE YOU SERIOUS?!
IS IT THE PROJECTOR?
I DON'T THINK SO. NONE OF THE SIDE LIGHTS ARE ON, EITHER.
HEY... I'VE GOT NO SIGNAL.
ME NEITHER.
THE WHOLE CITY'S DEAD!
WE'RE BEING ATTACKED!
AIIEEEE!

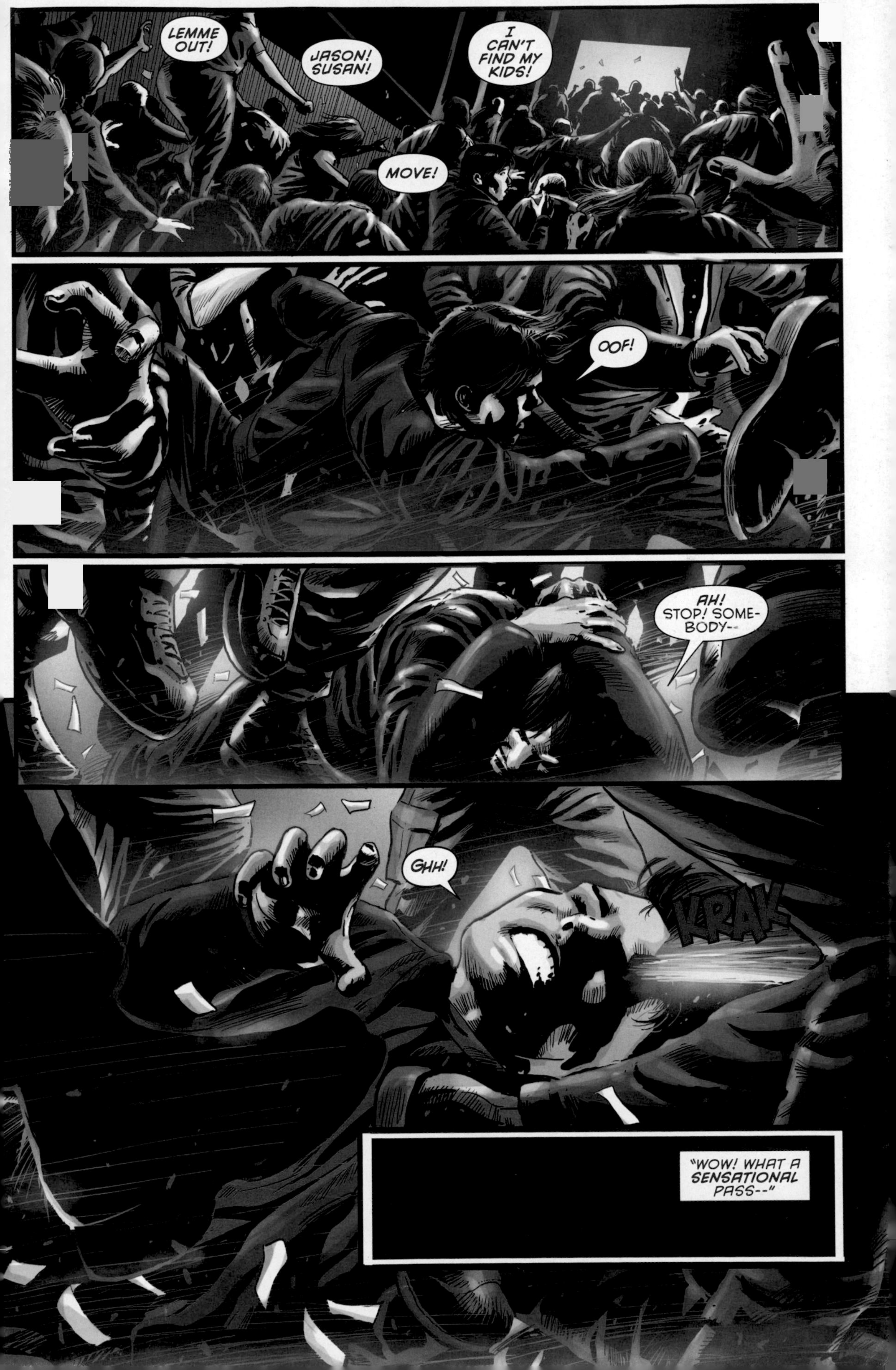
LEMME OUT!
JASON! SUSAN!
I CAN'T FIND MY KIDS!
MOVE!
OOF!
AH! STOP! SOME-BODY--
GHH!
KRAK
"WOW! WHAT A SENSATIONAL PASS--"

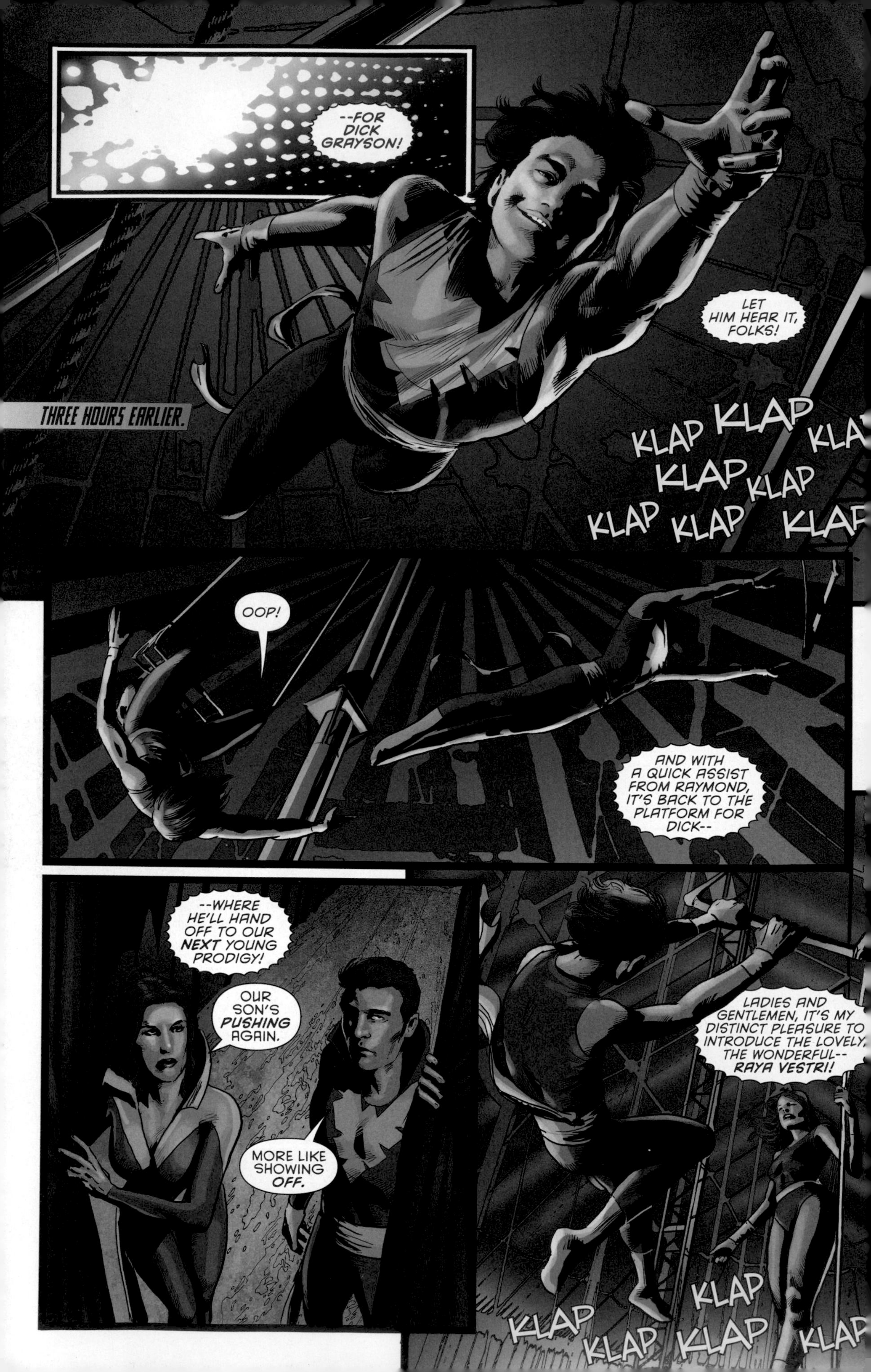
--FOR DICK GRAYSON!
LET HIM HEAR IT, FOLKS!
THREE HOURS EARLIER.
KLAP KLAP KLAP KLAP KLAP KLAP KLAP
OOP!
AND WITH A QUICK ASSIST FROM RAYMOND, IT'S BACK TO THE PLATFORM FOR DICK--
--WHERE HE'LL HAND OFF TO OUR NEXT YOUNG PRODIGY!
OUR SON'S PUSHING AGAIN.
MORE LIKE SHOWING OFF.
LADIES AND GENTLEMEN, IT'S MY DISTINCT PLEASURE TO INTRODUCE THE LOVELY, THE WONDERFUL-- RAYA VESTRI!
KLAP KLAP KLAP KLAP

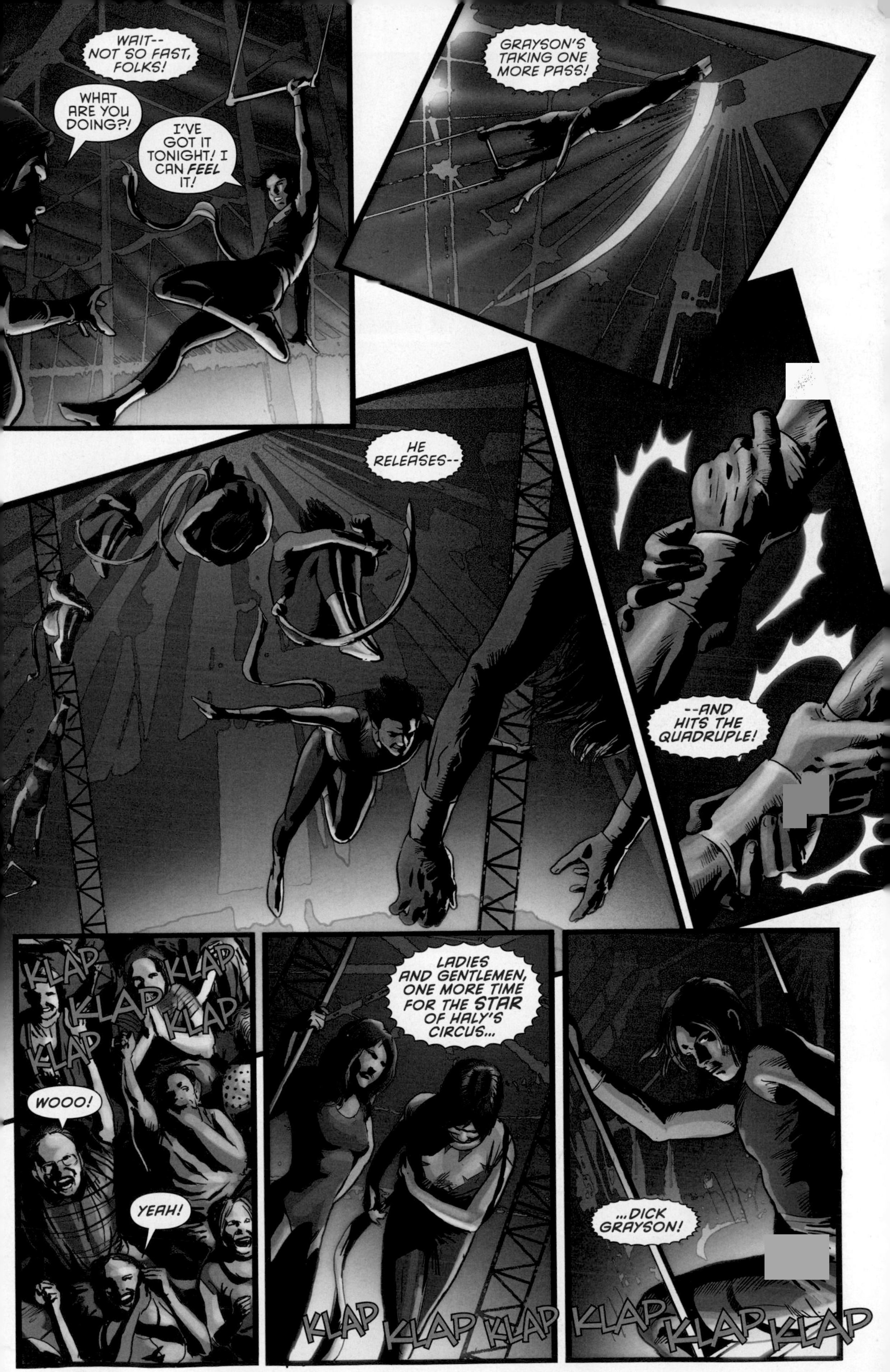
WAIT-- NOT SO FAST, FOLKS!
WHAT ARE YOU DOING?!
I'VE GOT IT TONIGHT! I CAN FEEL IT!
GRAYSON'S TAKING ONE MORE PASS!
HE RELEASES--
--AND HITS THE QUADRUPLE!
KLAP KLAP KLAP KLAP KLAP
WOOO!
YEAH!
LADIES AND GENTLEMEN, ONE MORE TIME FOR THE STAR OF HALY'S CIRCUS...
...DICK GRAYSON!
KLAP KLAP KLAP KLAP KLAP KLAP

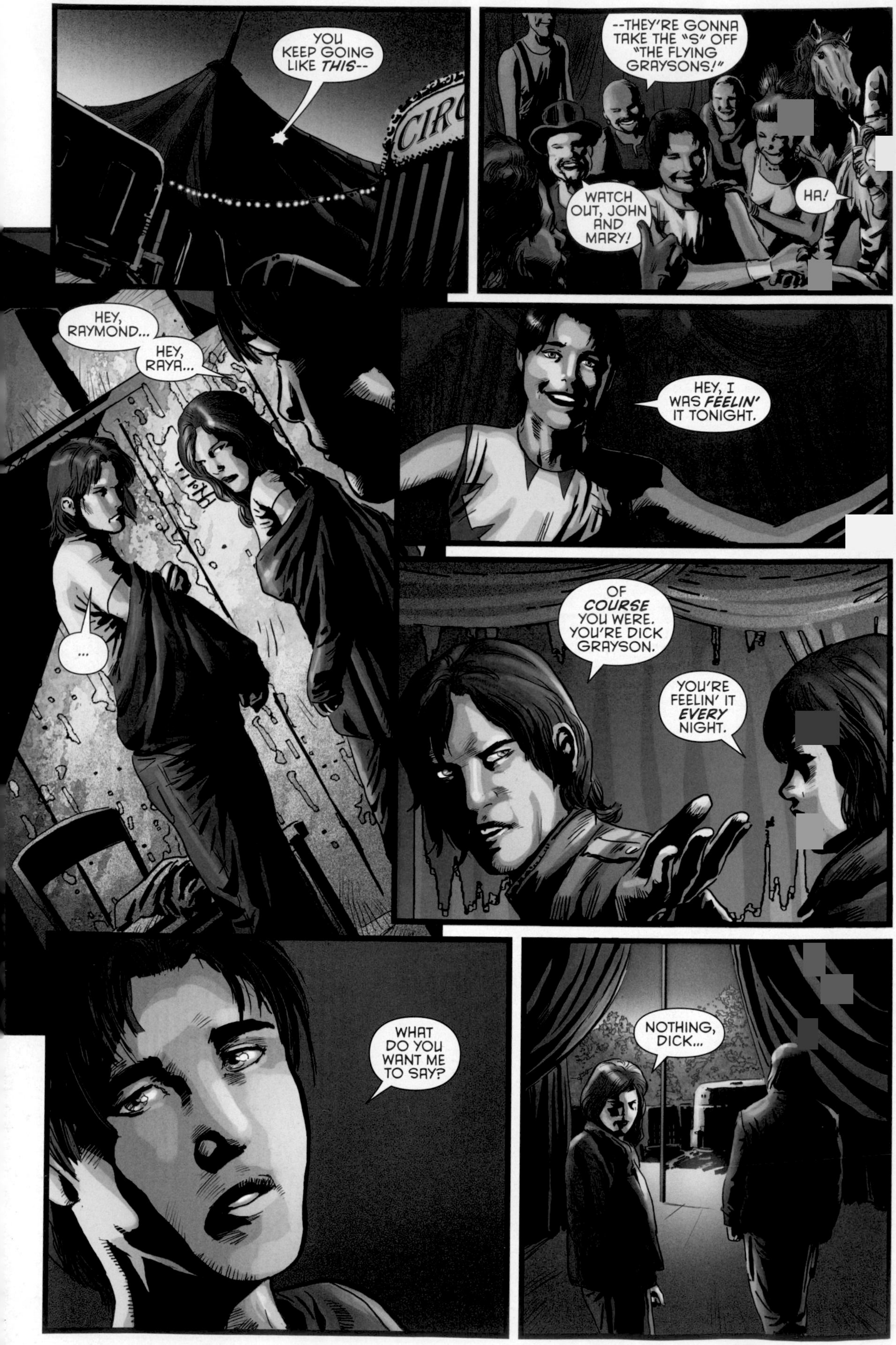

YOU KEEP GOING LIKE THIS--
--THEY'RE GONNA TAKE THE "S" OFF "THE FLYING GRAYSONS!"
WATCH OUT, JOHN AND MARY!
HA!
HEY, RAYMOND...
HEY, RAYA...
...
HEY, I WAS FEELIN' IT TONIGHT.
OF COURSE YOU WERE. YOU'RE DICK GRAYSON.
YOU'RE FEELIN' IT EVERY NIGHT.
WHAT DO YOU WANT ME TO SAY?
NOTHING, DICK...

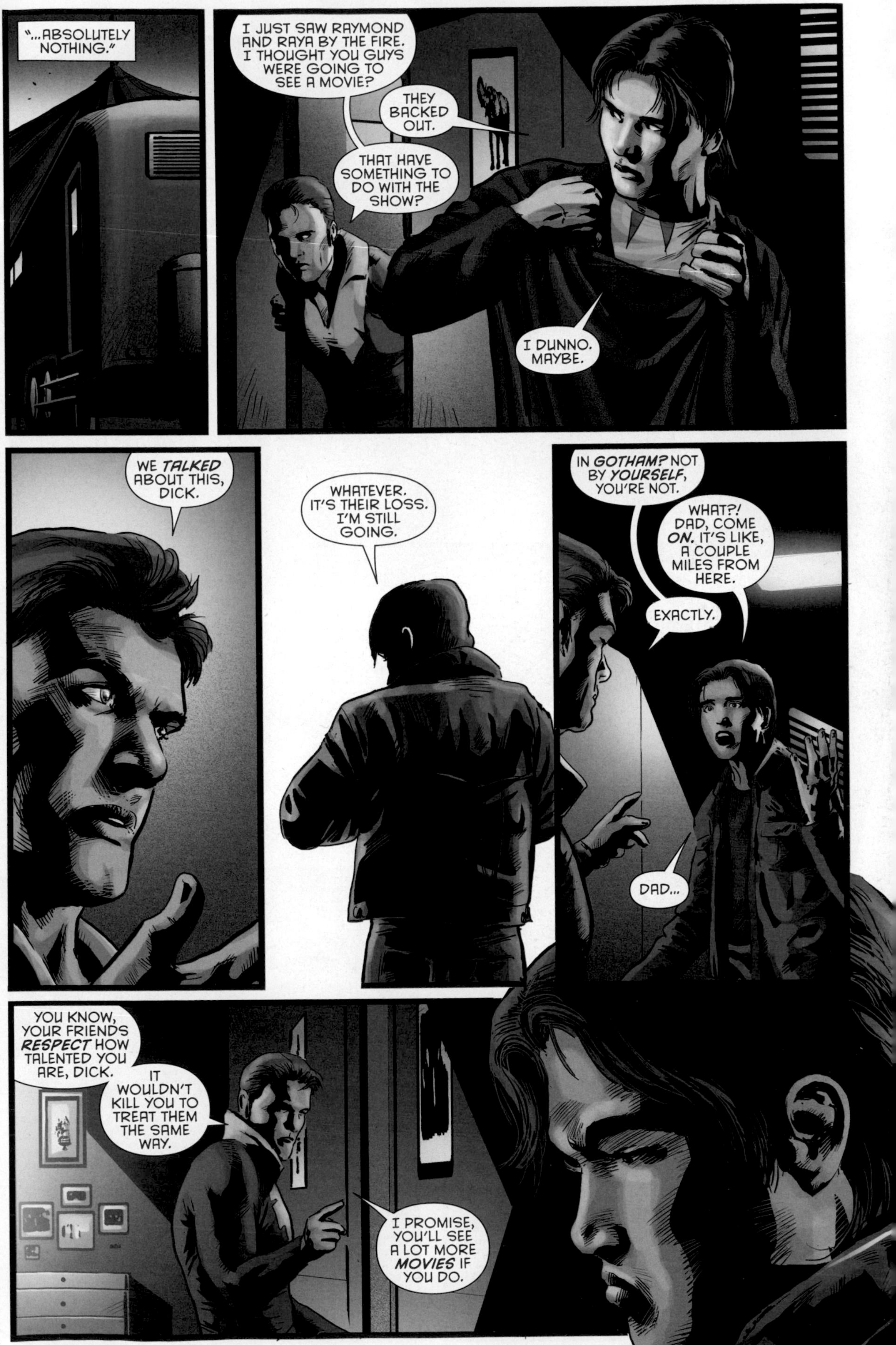
"...ABSOLUTELY NOTHING."
I JUST SAW RAYMOND AND RAYA BY THE FIRE. I THOUGHT YOU GUYS WERE GOING TO SEE A MOVIE?
THEY BACKED OUT.
THAT HAVE SOMETHING TO DO WITH THE SHOW?
I DUNNO. MAYBE.
WE *TALKED* ABOUT THIS, DICK.
WHATEVER. IT'S THEIR LOSS. I'M STILL GOING.
IN *GOTHAM?* NOT BY *YOURSELF*, YOU'RE NOT.
WHAT?! DAD, COME *ON.* IT'S LIKE, A COUPLE MILES FROM HERE.
EXACTLY.
DAD...
YOU KNOW, YOUR FRIENDS *RESPECT* HOW TALENTED YOU ARE, DICK.
IT WOULDN'T KILL YOU TO TREAT THEM THE SAME WAY.
I PROMISE, YOU'LL SEE A LOT MORE *MOVIES* IF YOU DO.

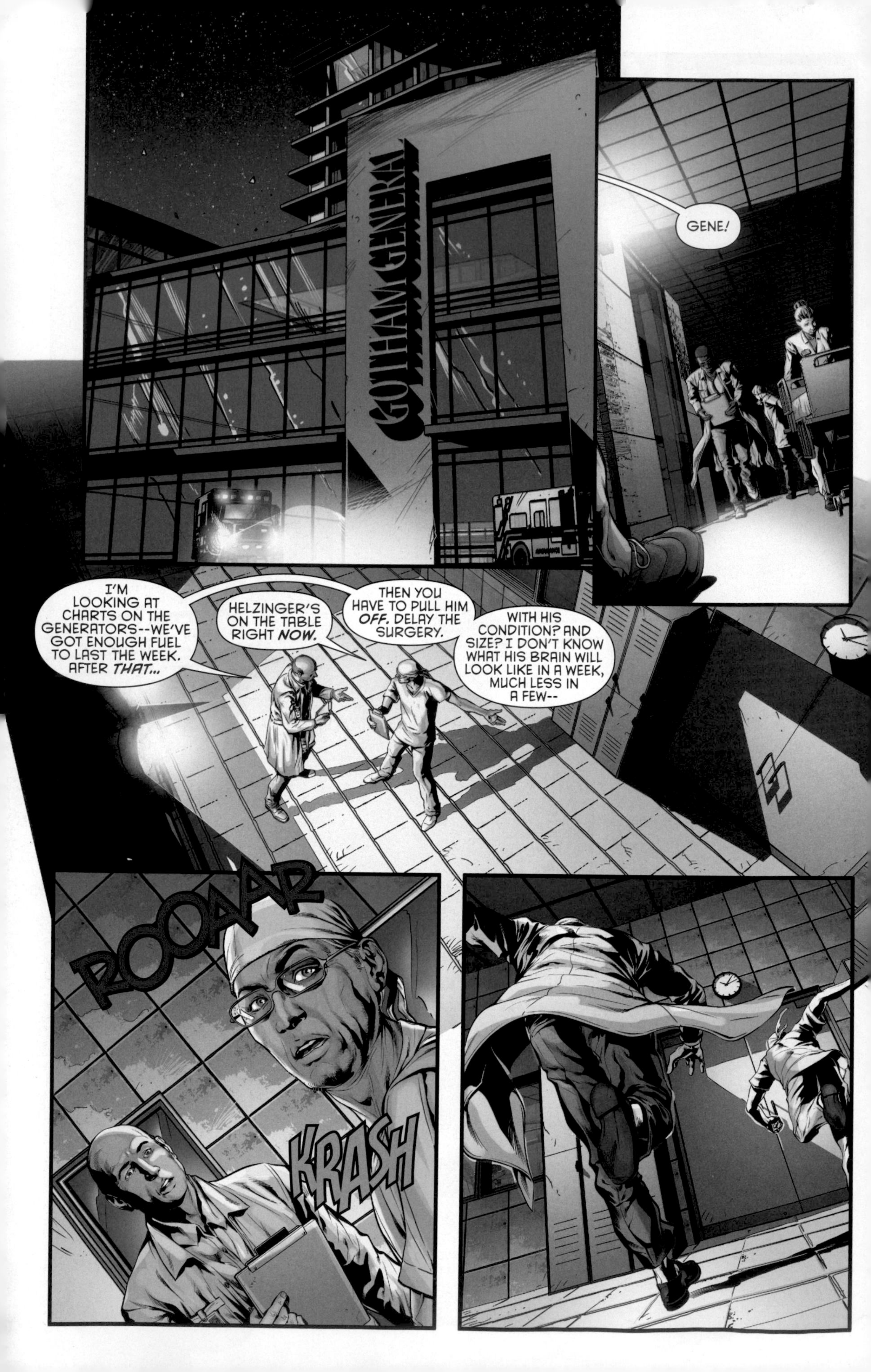
GOTHAM GENERAL
GENE!
I'M LOOKING AT CHARTS ON THE GENERATORS--WE'VE GOT ENOUGH FUEL TO LAST THE WEEK. AFTER THAT...
HELZINGER'S ON THE TABLE RIGHT NOW.
THEN YOU HAVE TO PULL HIM OFF. DELAY THE SURGERY.
WITH HIS CONDITION? AND SIZE? I DON'T KNOW WHAT HIS BRAIN WILL LOOK LIKE IN A WEEK, MUCH LESS IN A FEW--
ROOAAR
KRASH

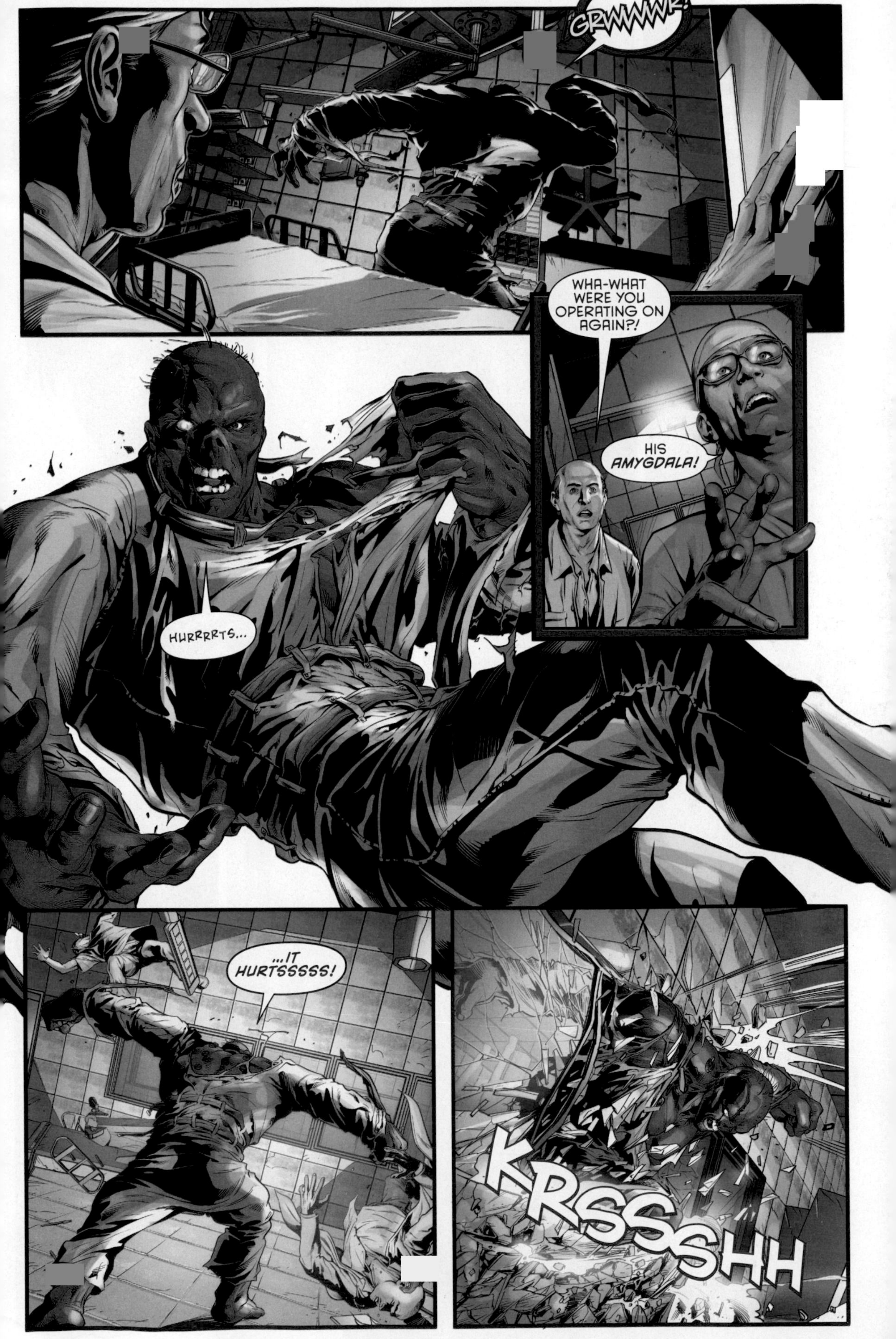
GRWWWR!
WHA-WHAT WERE YOU OPERATING ON AGAIN?!
HIS AMYGDALA!
HURRRRTS...
...IT HURTSSSSS!
KRSSSSHH

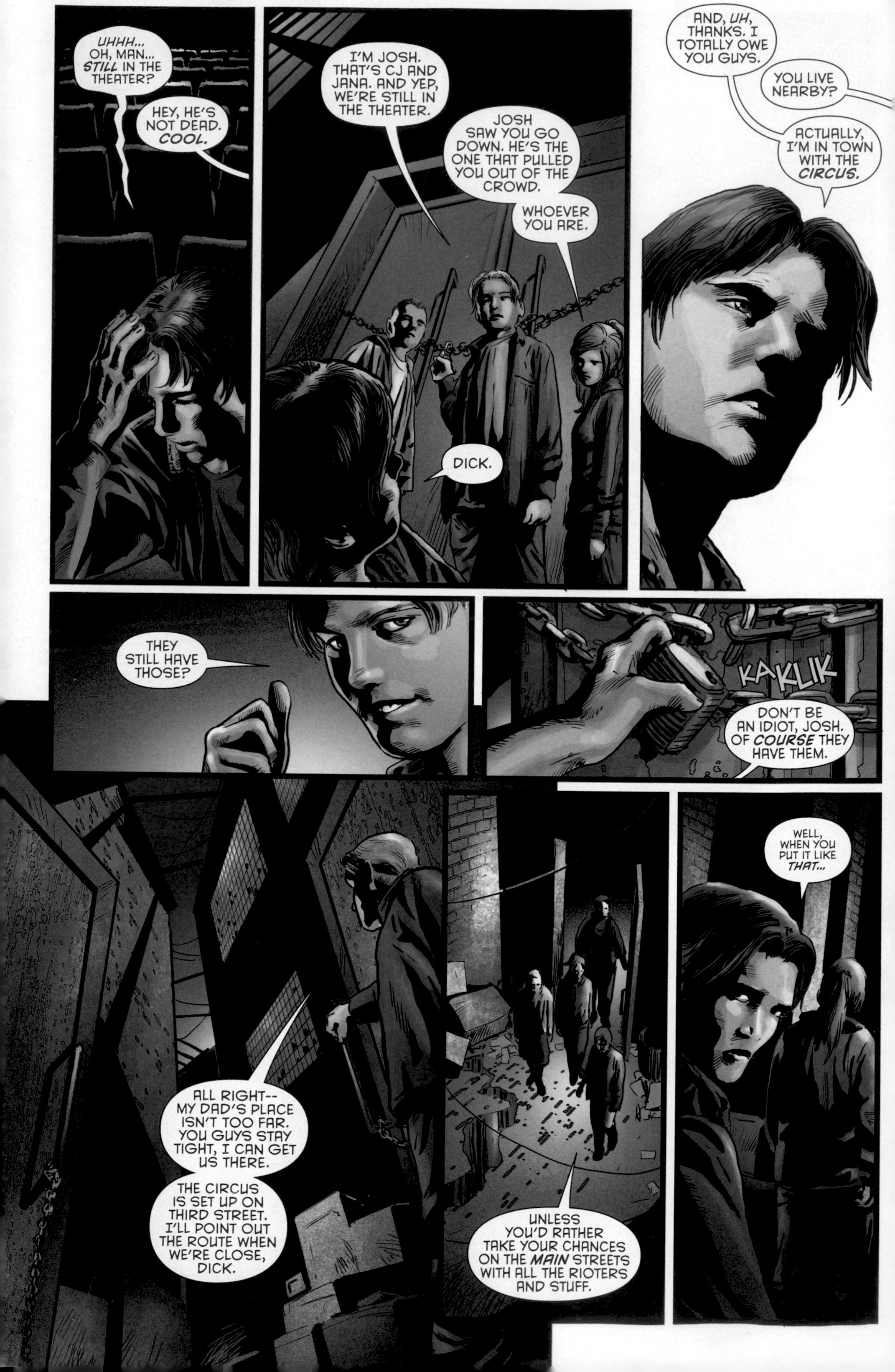
UHHH... OH, MAN... STILL IN THE THEATER?
HEY, HE'S NOT DEAD. COOL.
I'M JOSH. THAT'S CJ AND JANA. AND YEP, WE'RE STILL IN THE THEATER.
JOSH SAW YOU GO DOWN. HE'S THE ONE THAT PULLED YOU OUT OF THE CROWD.
WHOEVER YOU ARE.
DICK.
AND, UH, THANKS. I TOTALLY OWE YOU GUYS.
YOU LIVE NEARBY?
ACTUALLY, I'M IN TOWN WITH THE CIRCUS.
THEY STILL HAVE THOSE?
KAKLIK
DON'T BE AN IDIOT, JOSH. OF COURSE THEY HAVE THEM.
ALL RIGHT-- MY DAD'S PLACE ISN'T TOO FAR. YOU GUYS STAY TIGHT, I CAN GET US THERE.
THE CIRCUS IS SET UP ON THIRD STREET. I'LL POINT OUT THE ROUTE WHEN WE'RE CLOSE, DICK.
UNLESS YOU'D RATHER TAKE YOUR CHANCES ON THE MAIN STREETS WITH ALL THE RIOTERS AND STUFF.
WELL, WHEN YOU PUT IT LIKE THAT...

EVERY-THING'S LOCKED DOWN.

WE CAN'T GET ANYWHERE *NEAR* THE THEATER. THE ONLY THING WE CAN DO IS *WAIT*, MARY.

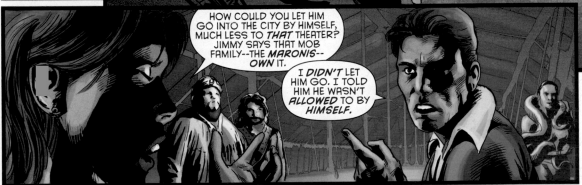

HOW COULD YOU LET HIM GO INTO THE CITY BY HIMSELF, MUCH LESS TO *THAT* THEATER? JIMMY SAYS THAT MOB FAMILY--THE *MARONIS*--OWN IT.

I *DIDN'T* LET HIM GO. I TOLD HIM HE WASN'T *ALLOWED* TO BY HIMSELF.

GOD, WHEN HE GETS BACK HERE HE'S *SO* GROUNDED...

IF HE GETS BACK...

HE *WILL*, MARY. DICK'S A SMART KID. I'M SURE HE'S OKAY...

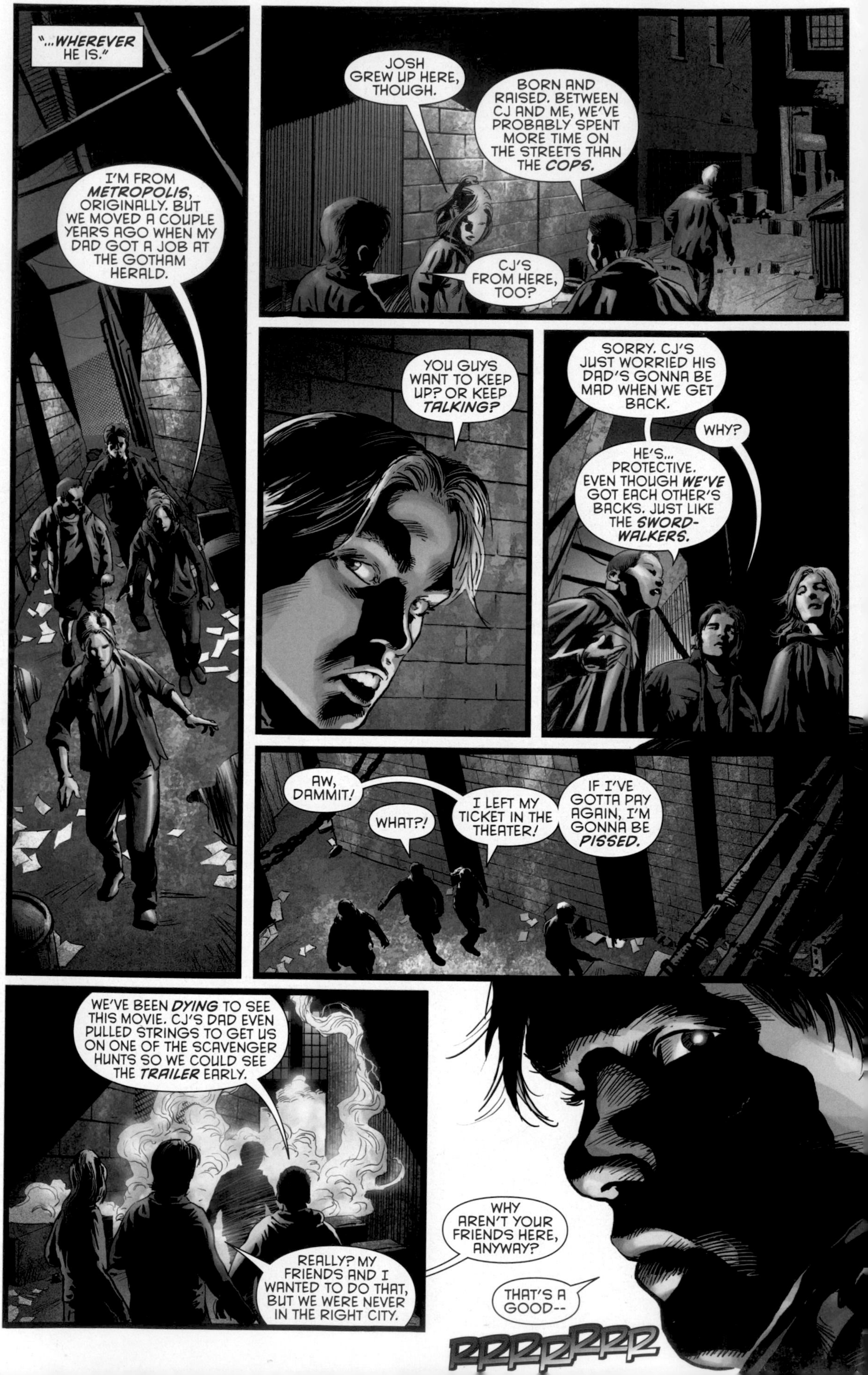
"...WHEREVER HE IS."
I'M FROM METROPOLIS, ORIGINALLY. BUT WE MOVED A COUPLE YEARS AGO WHEN MY DAD GOT A JOB AT THE GOTHAM HERALD.
JOSH GREW UP HERE, THOUGH.
BORN AND RAISED. BETWEEN CJ AND ME, WE'VE PROBABLY SPENT MORE TIME ON THE STREETS THAN THE COPS.
CJ'S FROM HERE, TOO?
YOU GUYS WANT TO KEEP UP? OR KEEP TALKING?
SORRY. CJ'S JUST WORRIED HIS DAD'S GONNA BE MAD WHEN WE GET BACK.
WHY?
HE'S... PROTECTIVE. EVEN THOUGH WE'VE GOT EACH OTHER'S BACKS. JUST LIKE THE SWORD-WALKERS.
AW, DAMMIT!
WHAT?!
I LEFT MY TICKET IN THE THEATER!
IF I'VE GOTTA PAY AGAIN, I'M GONNA BE PISSED.
WE'VE BEEN DYING TO SEE THIS MOVIE. CJ'S DAD EVEN PULLED STRINGS TO GET US ON ONE OF THE SCAVENGER HUNTS SO WE COULD SEE THE TRAILER EARLY.
REALLY? MY FRIENDS AND I WANTED TO DO THAT, BUT WE WERE NEVER IN THE RIGHT CITY.
WHY AREN'T YOUR FRIENDS HERE, ANYWAY?
THAT'S A GOOD--
RRRRRRRR

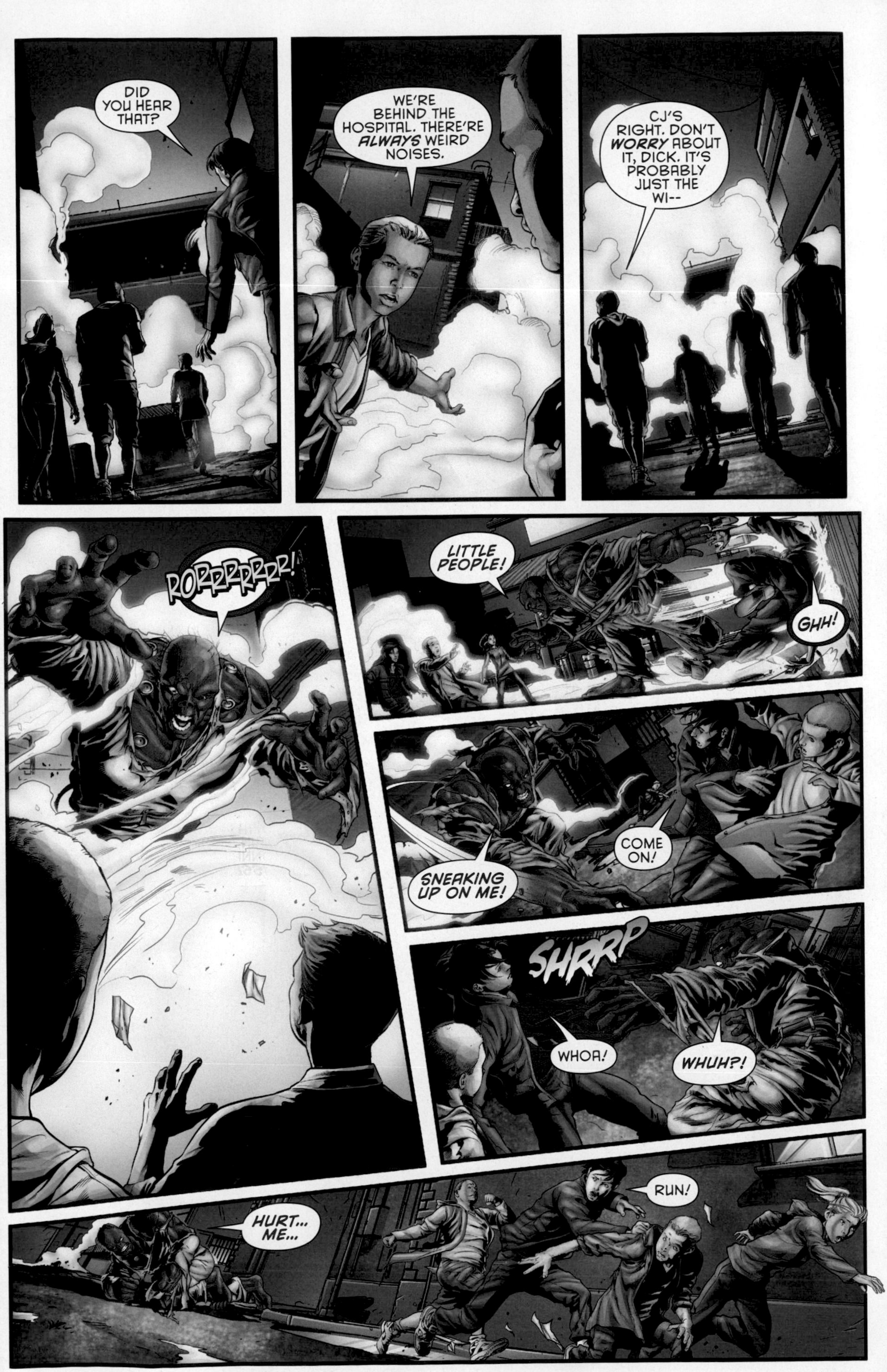
DID YOU HEAR THAT?
WE'RE BEHIND THE HOSPITAL. THERE'RE ALWAYS WEIRD NOISES.
CJ'S RIGHT. DON'T WORRY ABOUT IT, DICK. IT'S PROBABLY JUST THE WI--
RORRRRRRR!
LITTLE PEOPLE!
GHH!
SNEAKING UP ON ME!
COME ON!
SHRRP
WHOA!
WHUH?!
RUN!
HURT... ME...

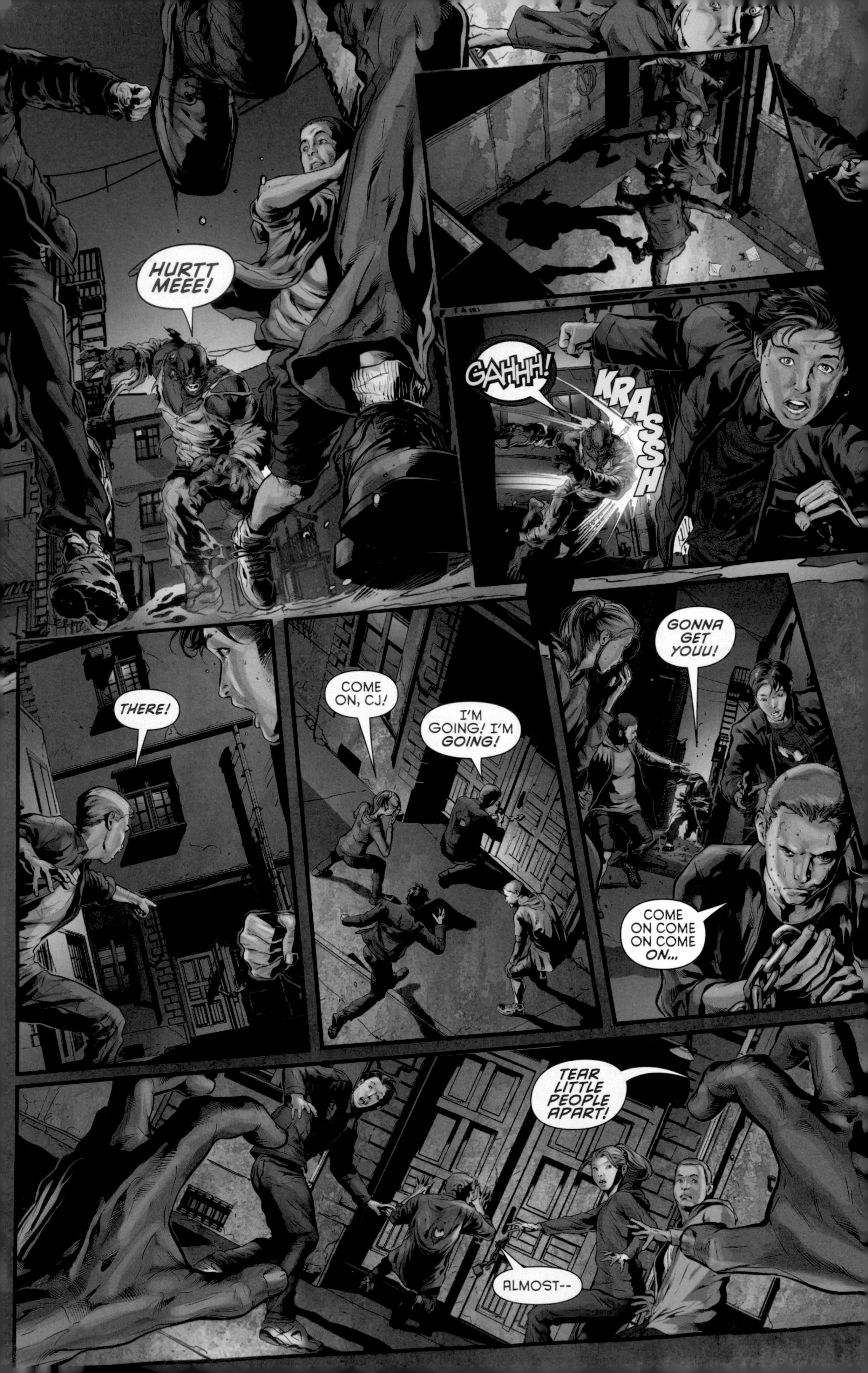
HURTT MEEE!
GAHHH!
KRASSH
THERE!
COME ON, CJ!
I'M GOING! I'M GOING!
GONNA GET YOUU!
COME ON COME ON COME ON...
TEAR LITTLE PEOPLE APART!
ALMOST--

--THERE!

RAAARRRR!

SLAM

EVERY →PANT← BODY →PANT← OKAY?

WHA-WHAT THE HELL *IS* THAT THING?!

NO...NO IDEA...

DID IT *GET* YOU?

JUST MY *SHIRT*. I'M *FINE*.

SLAM SLAM

RRRRRR!

SLAM BOOM SLAM

WHAT DO WE DO *NOW?*

IS THERE ANOTHER WAY OUT?

THERE'S A SIDE DOOR--INTO THE OTHER ALLEY. IF WE HURRY, WE CAN GET TO IT BEFORE HE STARTS LOOKING FOR ANOTHER WAY IN!

UH, GUYS?

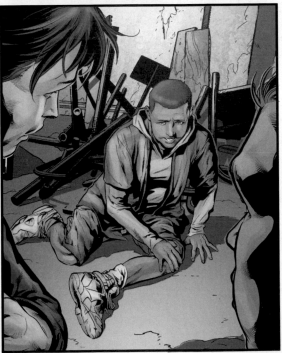

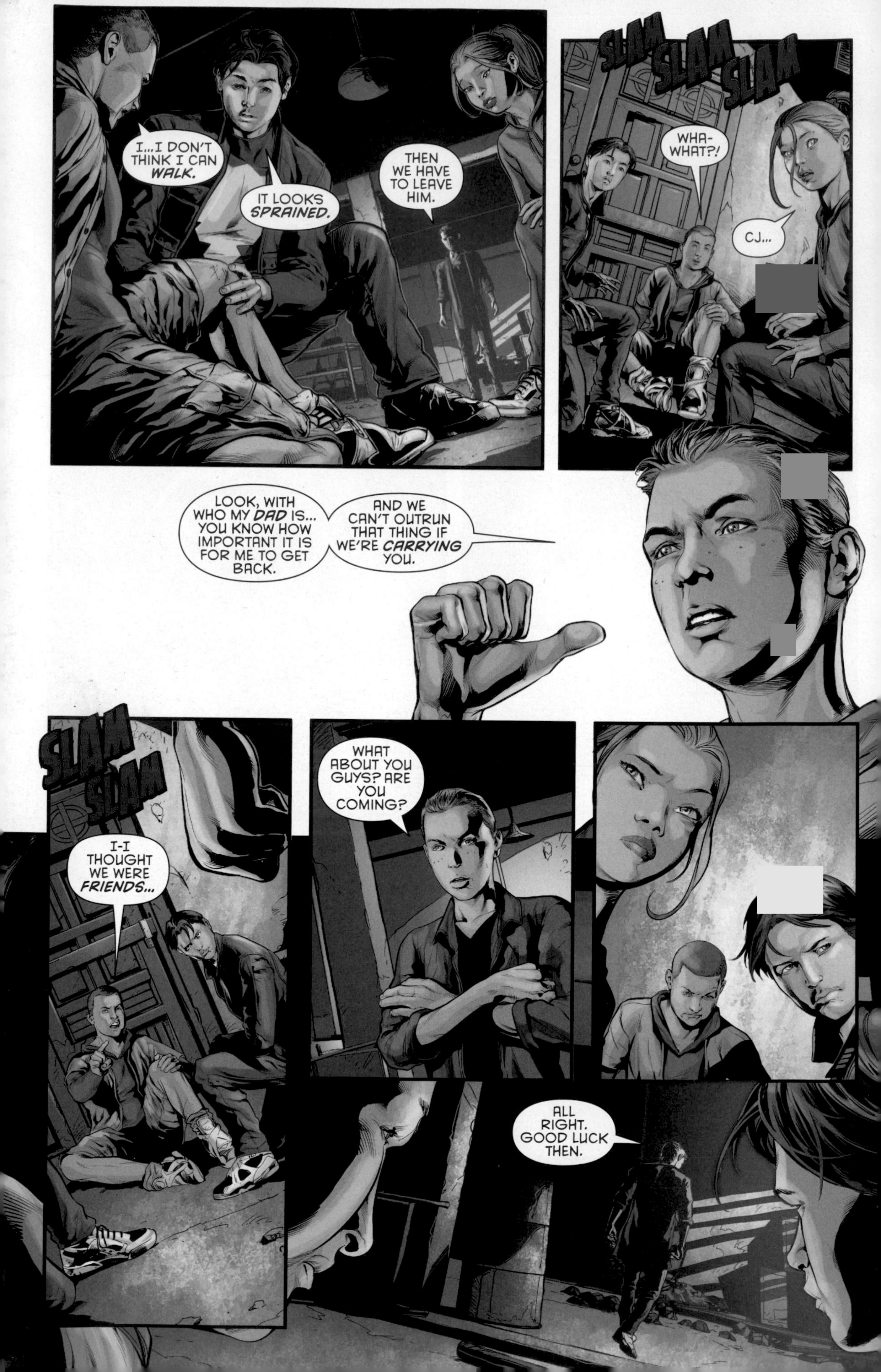
I...I DON'T THINK I CAN WALK.
IT LOOKS SPRAINED.
THEN WE HAVE TO LEAVE HIM.
SLAM SLAM SLAM
WHA-WHAT?!
CJ...
LOOK, WITH WHO MY DAD IS... YOU KNOW HOW IMPORTANT IT IS FOR ME TO GET BACK.
AND WE CAN'T OUTRUN THAT THING IF WE'RE CARRYING YOU.
SLAM SLAM
I-I THOUGHT WE WERE FRIENDS...
WHAT ABOUT YOU GUYS? ARE YOU COMING?
ALL RIGHT. GOOD LUCK THEN.

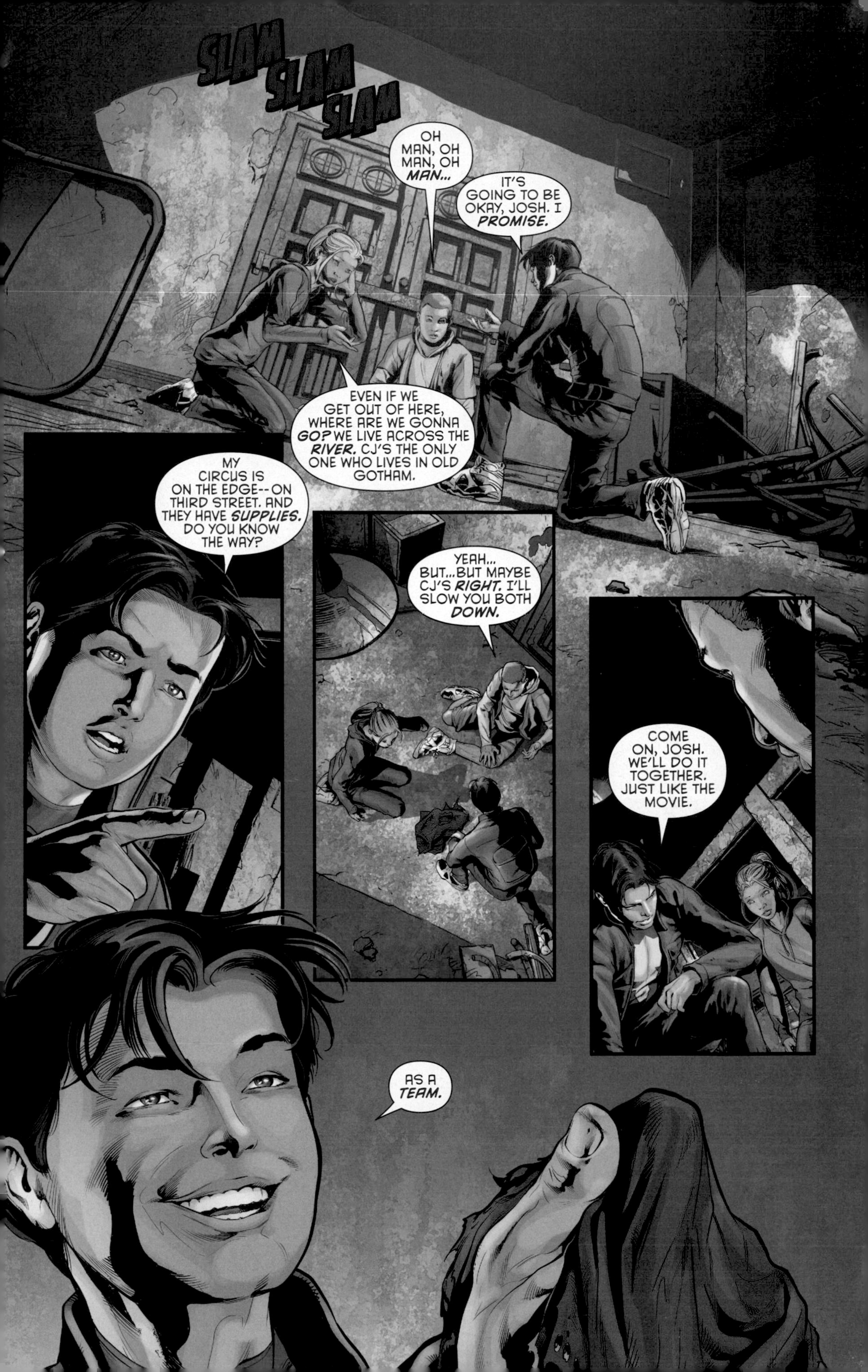
SLAM SLAM SLAM
OH MAN, OH MAN, OH MAN...
IT'S GOING TO BE OKAY, JOSH. I PROMISE.
EVEN IF WE GET OUT OF HERE, WHERE ARE WE GONNA GO? WE LIVE ACROSS THE RIVER. CJ'S THE ONLY ONE WHO LIVES IN OLD GOTHAM.
MY CIRCUS IS ON THE EDGE--ON THIRD STREET. AND THEY HAVE SUPPLIES. DO YOU KNOW THE WAY?
YEAH... BUT...BUT MAYBE CJ'S RIGHT. I'LL SLOW YOU BOTH DOWN.
COME ON, JOSH. WE'LL DO IT TOGETHER. JUST LIKE THE MOVIE.
AS A TEAM.

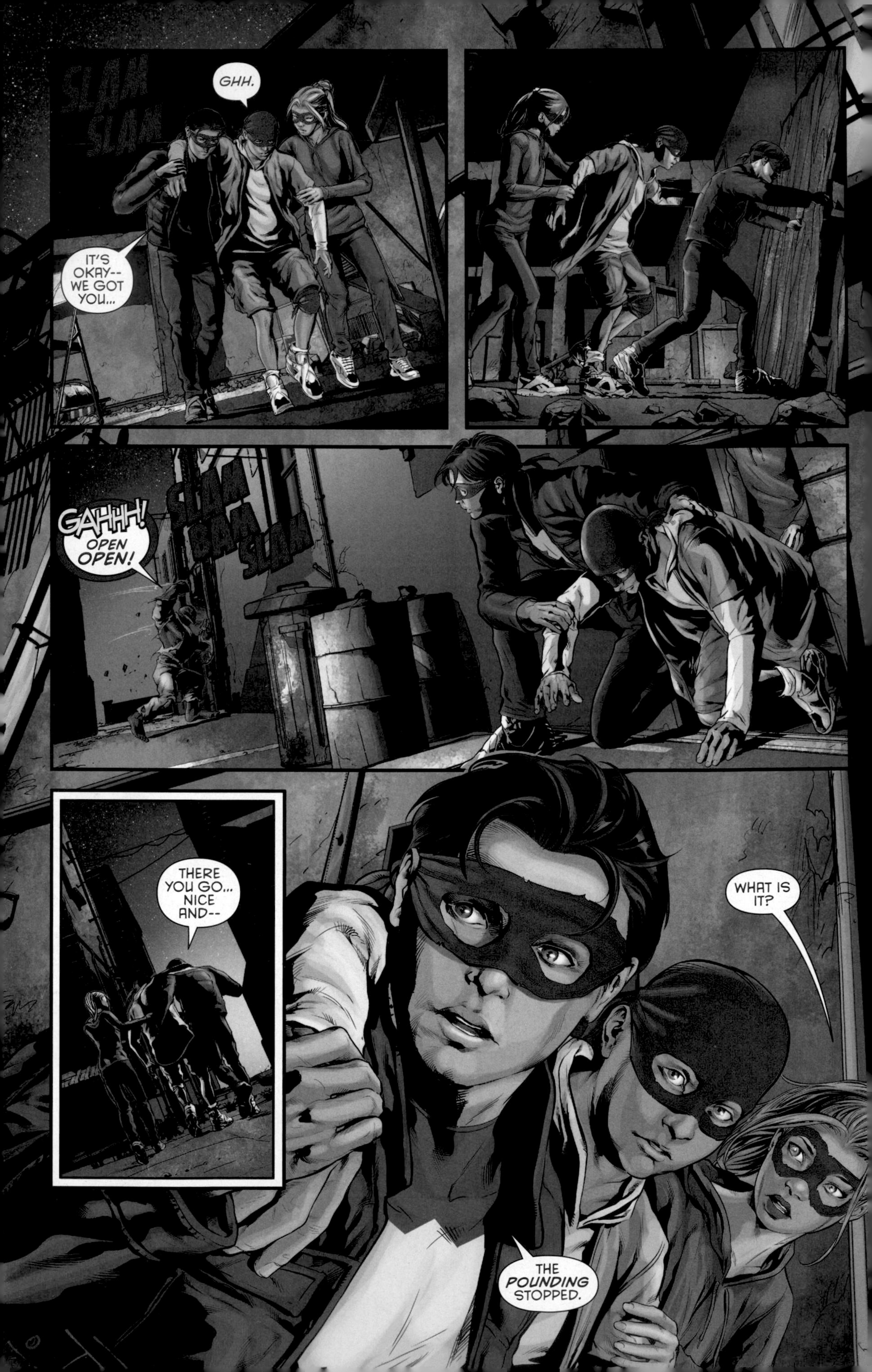
SLAM
SLAM
GHH.
IT'S OKAY-- WE GOT YOU...
SLAM SLAM SLAM
GAHHH! OPEN OPEN!
THERE YOU GO... NICE AND--
WHAT IS IT?
THE *POUNDING* STOPPED.

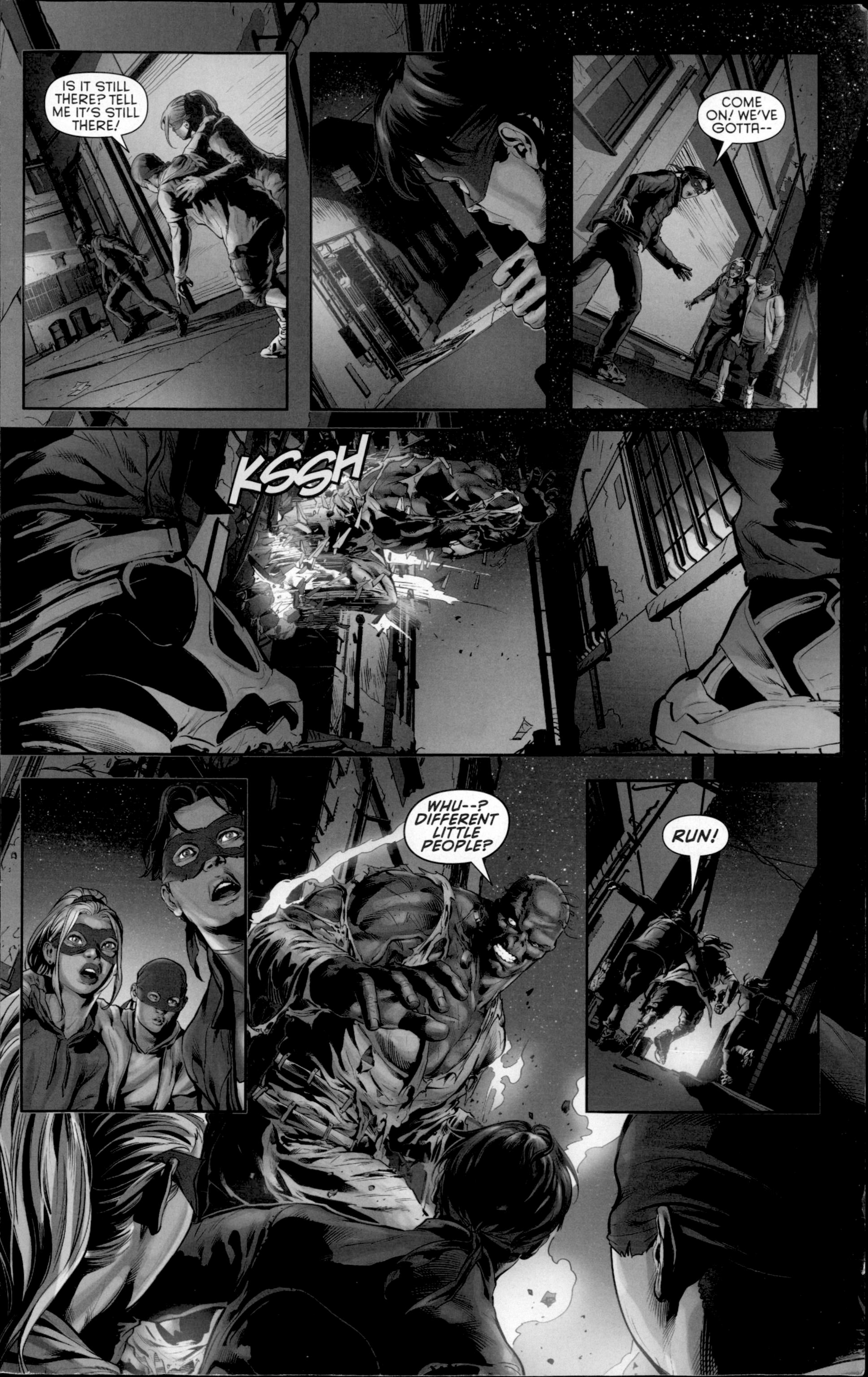
IS IT STILL THERE? TELL ME IT'S STILL THERE!
COME ON! WE'VE GOTTA--
KSSH
WHU--? DIFFERENT LITTLE PEOPLE?
RUN!

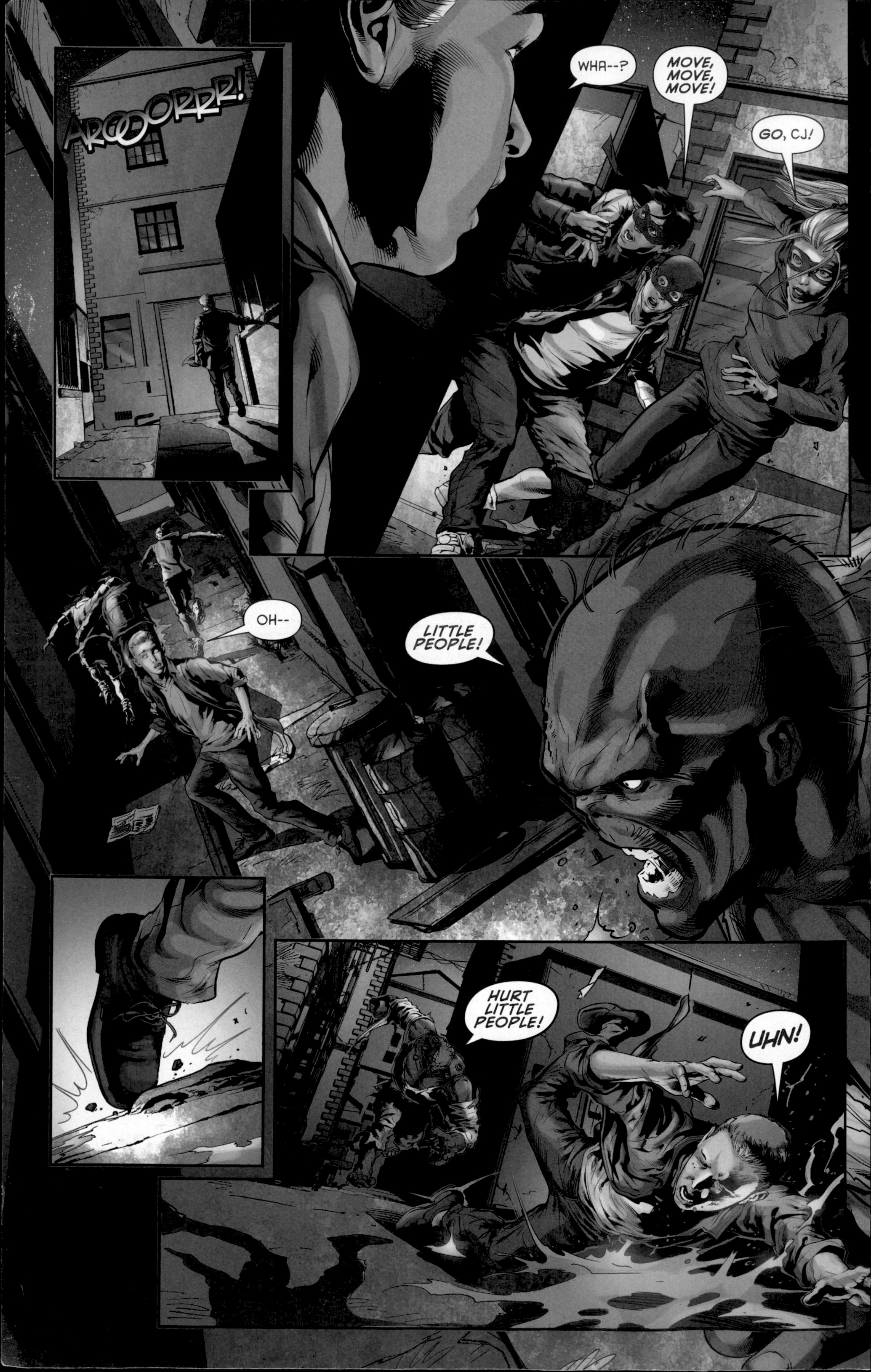
ARGOORRR!
WHA--?
MOVE, MOVE, MOVE!
GO, CJ!
OH--
LITTLE PEOPLE!
HURT LITTLE PEOPLE!
UHN!

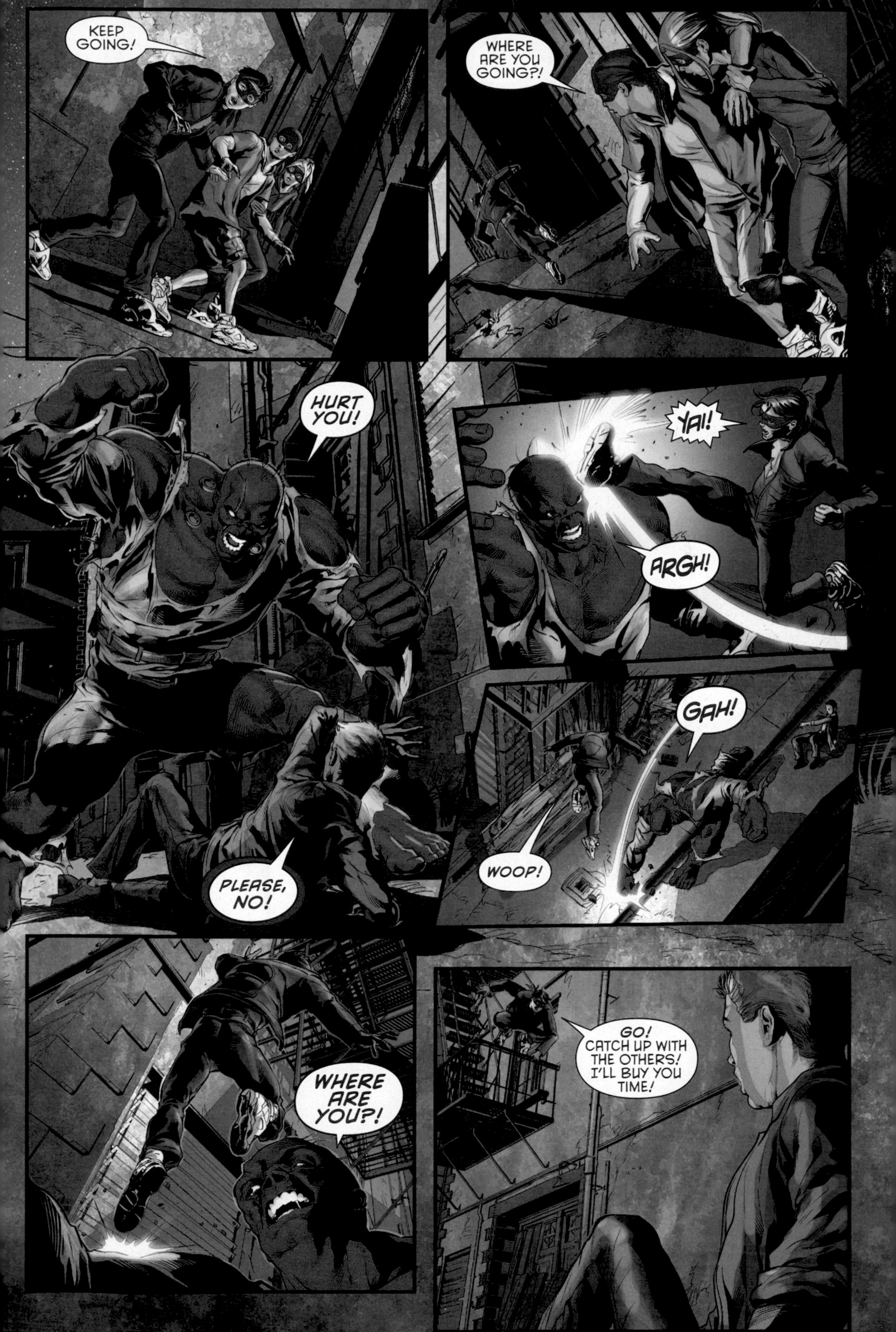
KEEP GOING!
WHERE ARE YOU GOING?!
HURT YOU!
YAI!
ARGH!
PLEASE, NO!
GAH!
WOOP!
WHERE ARE YOU?!
GO! CATCH UP WITH THE OTHERS! I'LL BUY YOU TIME!

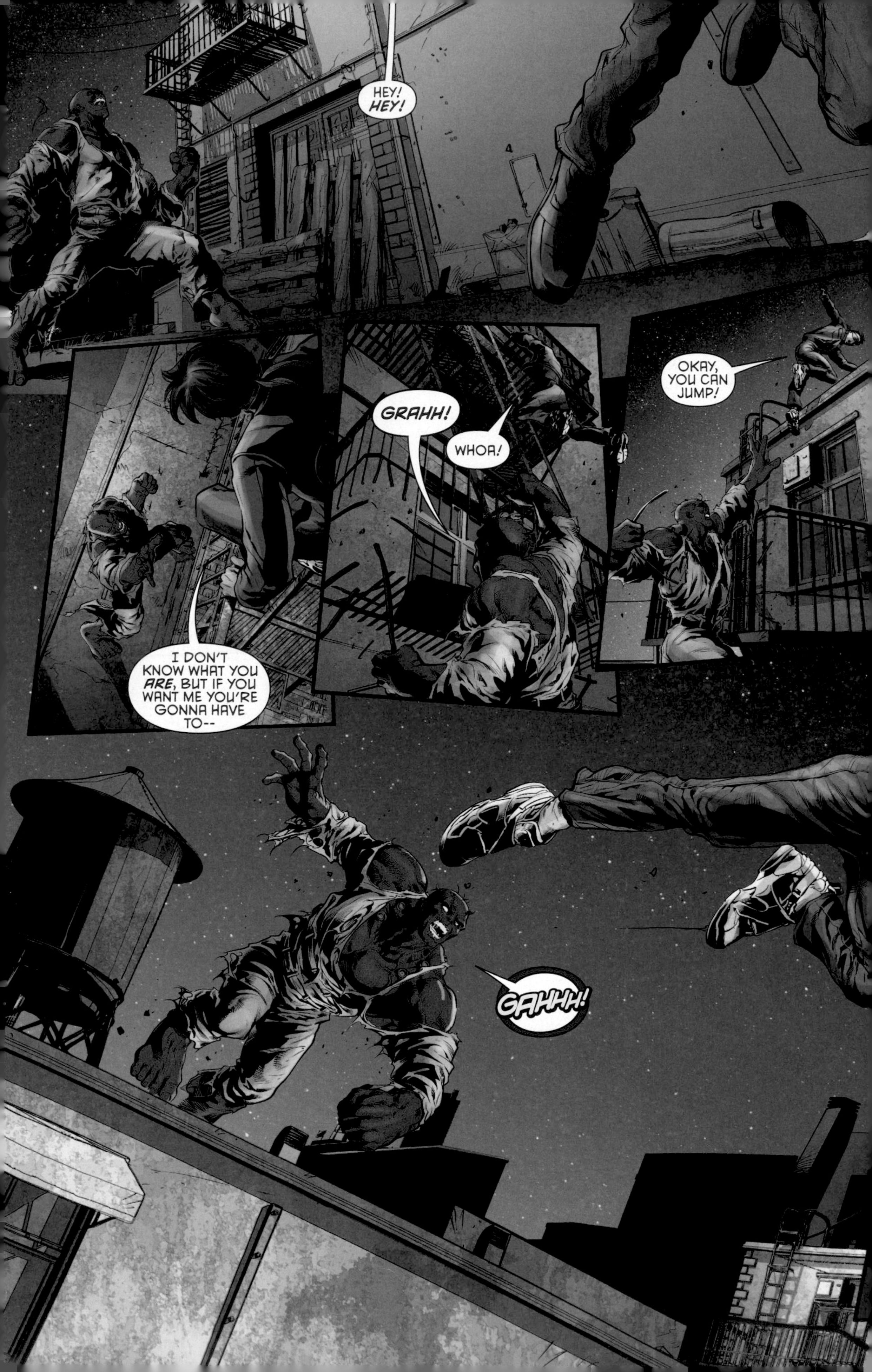
HEY! HEY!
I DON'T KNOW WHAT YOU ARE, BUT IF YOU WANT ME YOU'RE GONNA HAVE TO--
GRAHH!
WHOA!
OKAY, YOU CAN JUMP!
GAHHH!

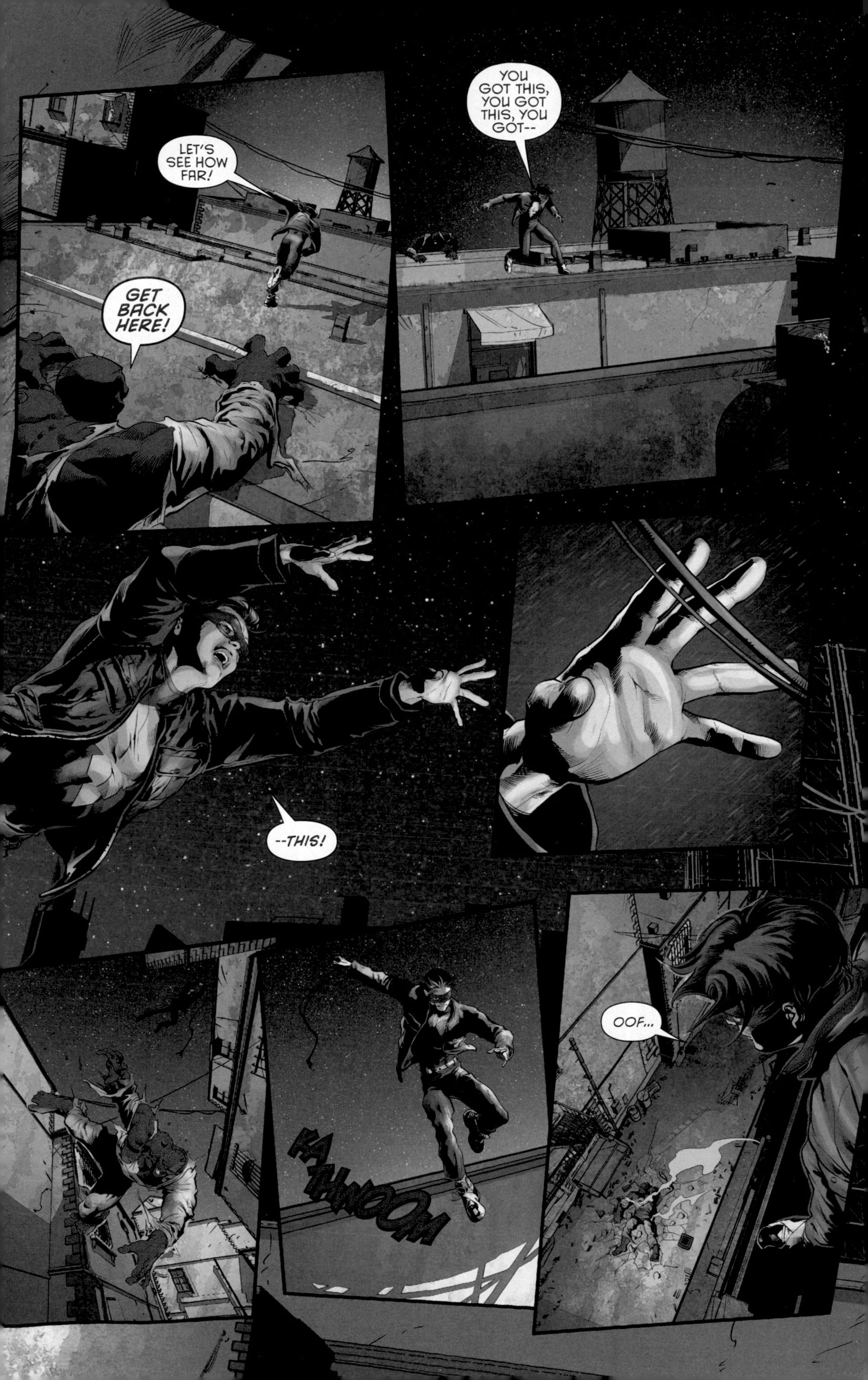
LET'S SEE HOW FAR!
GET BACK HERE!
YOU GOT THIS, YOU GOT THIS, YOU GOT--
--THIS!
KA-THWOOM
OOF...

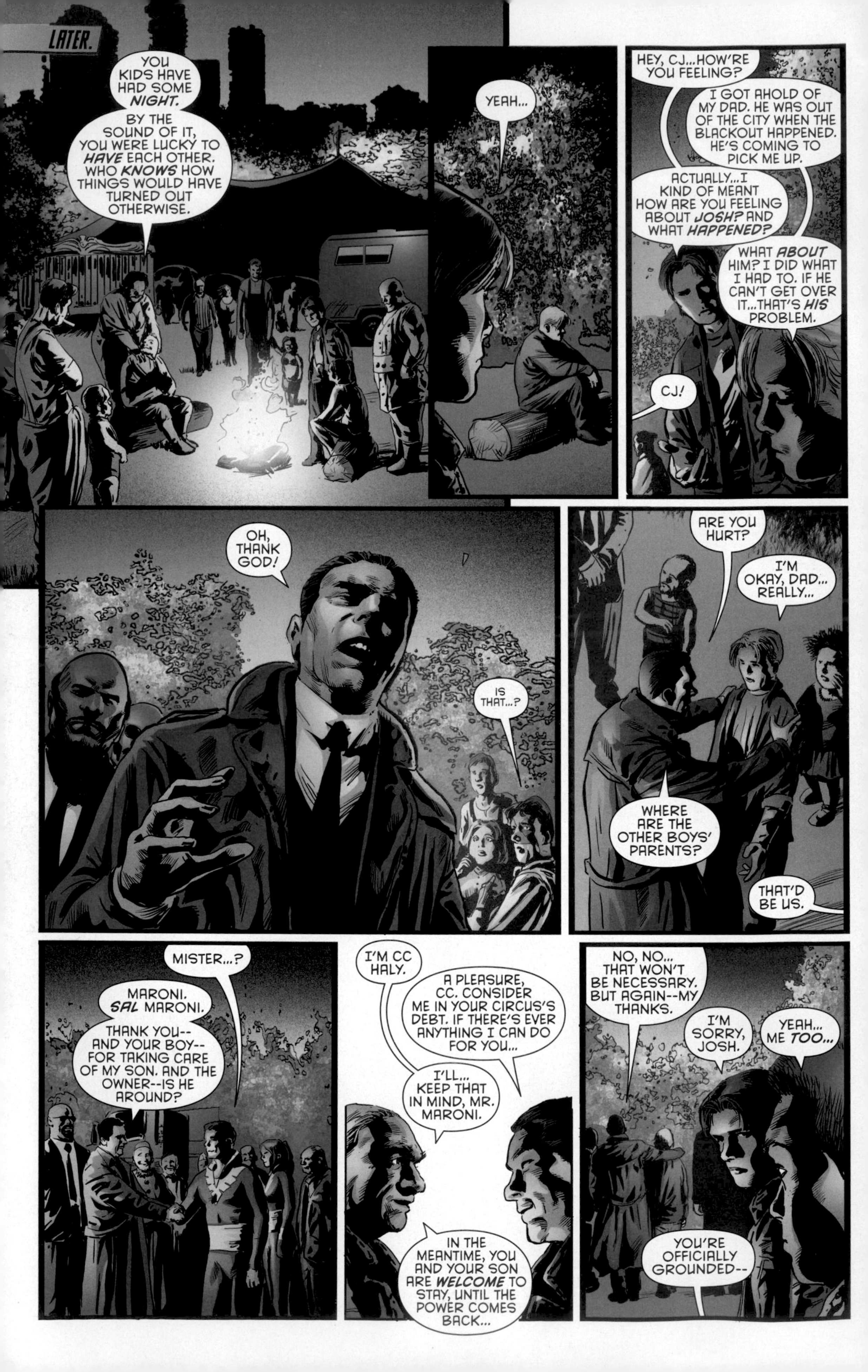
LATER.
YOU KIDS HAVE HAD SOME NIGHT.
BY THE SOUND OF IT, YOU WERE LUCKY TO HAVE EACH OTHER. WHO KNOWS HOW THINGS WOULD HAVE TURNED OUT OTHERWISE.
YEAH...
HEY, CJ...HOW'RE YOU FEELING?
I GOT AHOLD OF MY DAD. HE WAS OUT OF THE CITY WHEN THE BLACKOUT HAPPENED. HE'S COMING TO PICK ME UP.
ACTUALLY...I KIND OF MEANT HOW ARE YOU FEELING ABOUT JOSH? AND WHAT HAPPENED?
WHAT ABOUT HIM? I DID WHAT I HAD TO. IF HE CAN'T GET OVER IT...THAT'S HIS PROBLEM.
CJ!
OH, THANK GOD!
IS THAT...?
ARE YOU HURT?
I'M OKAY, DAD... REALLY...
WHERE ARE THE OTHER BOYS' PARENTS?
THAT'D BE US.
MISTER...?
MARONI. SAL MARONI.
THANK YOU-- AND YOUR BOY-- FOR TAKING CARE OF MY SON. AND THE OWNER--IS HE AROUND?
I'M CC HALY.
A PLEASURE, CC. CONSIDER ME IN YOUR CIRCUS'S DEBT. IF THERE'S EVER ANYTHING I CAN DO FOR YOU...
I'LL... KEEP THAT IN MIND, MR. MARONI.
IN THE MEANTIME, YOU AND YOUR SON ARE WELCOME TO STAY, UNTIL THE POWER COMES BACK...
NO, NO... THAT WON'T BE NECESSARY. BUT AGAIN--MY THANKS.
I'M SORRY, JOSH.
YEAH... ME TOO...
YOU'RE OFFICIALLY GROUNDED--

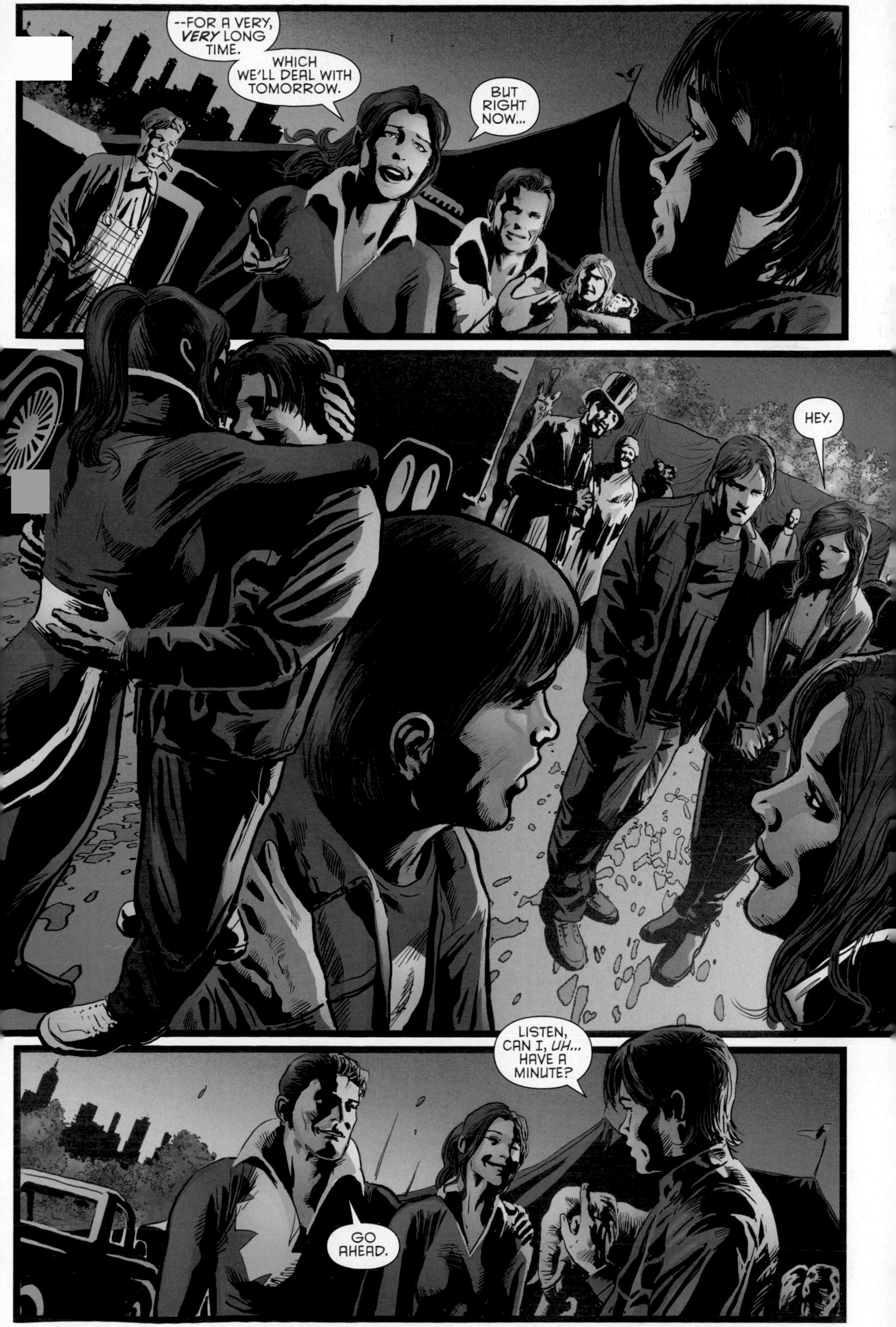
--FOR A VERY, VERY LONG TIME.
WHICH WE'LL DEAL WITH TOMORROW.
BUT RIGHT NOW...
HEY.
LISTEN, CAN I, UH... HAVE A MINUTE?
GO AHEAD.

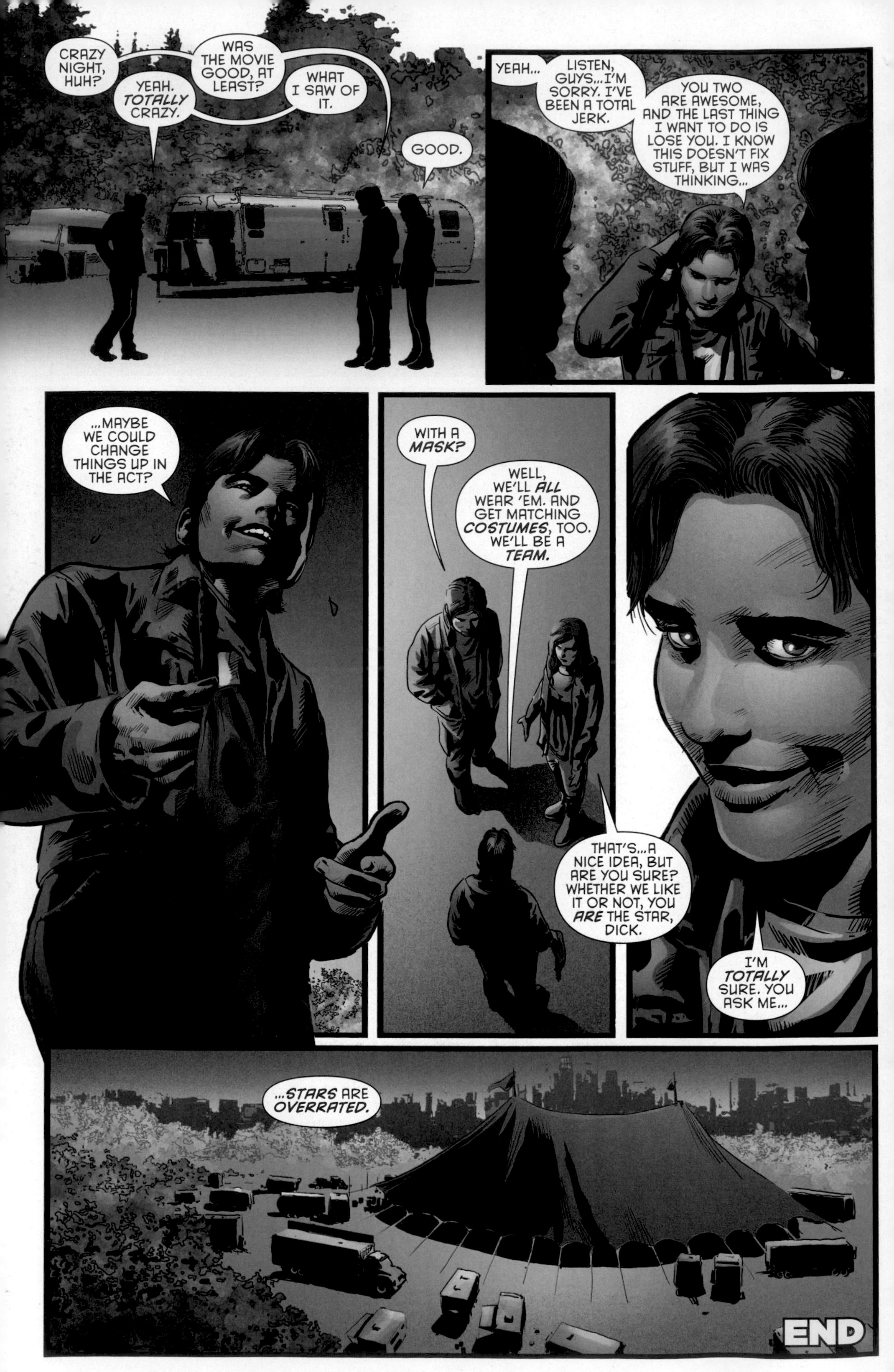
CRAZY NIGHT, HUH?
YEAH. *TOTALLY* CRAZY.
WAS THE MOVIE GOOD, AT LEAST?
WHAT I SAW OF IT.
GOOD.
YEAH...
LISTEN, GUYS...I'M SORRY. I'VE BEEN A TOTAL JERK.
YOU TWO ARE AWESOME, AND THE LAST THING I WANT TO DO IS LOSE YOU. I KNOW THIS DOESN'T FIX STUFF, BUT I WAS THINKING...
...MAYBE WE COULD CHANGE THINGS UP IN THE ACT?
WITH A *MASK?*
WELL, WE'LL *ALL* WEAR 'EM. AND GET MATCHING *COSTUMES*, TOO. WE'LL BE A *TEAM.*
THAT'S...A NICE IDEA, BUT ARE YOU SURE? WHETHER WE LIKE IT OR NOT, YOU *ARE* THE STAR, DICK.
I'M *TOTALLY* SURE. YOU ASK ME...
...*STARS* ARE *OVERRATED.*
END

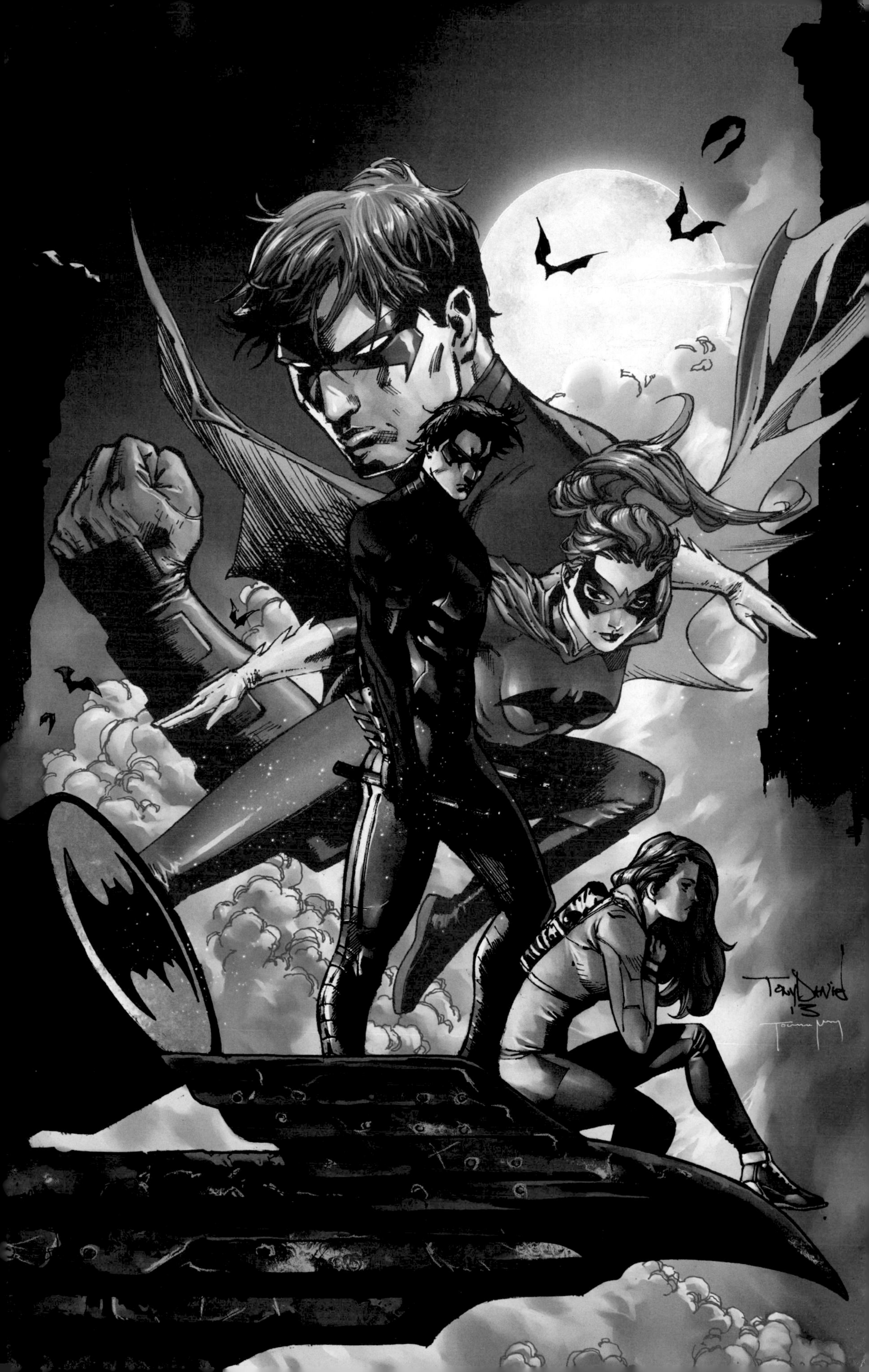

EMBERS

KYLE HIGGINS writer **JASON MASTERS** with **DANIEL SAMPERE & VICENTE CIFUENTES** artists **CHRIS SOTOMAYOR** colorist
DAVE SHARPE letterer cover art by **TONY DANIEL** and **TOMEU MOREY**

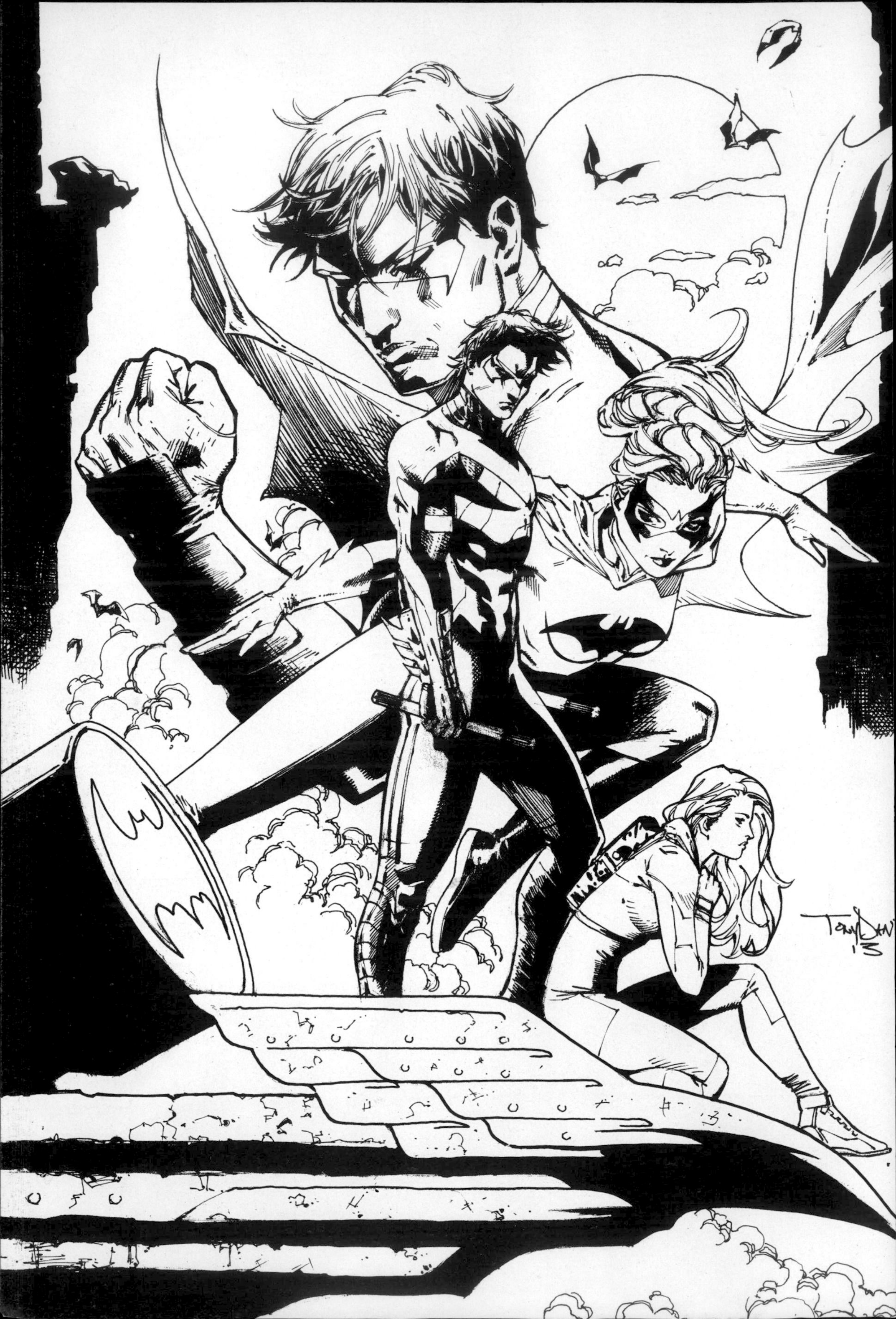

GOTHAM CITY. TED CARSON'S APARTMENT.

NOTHING ABOUT THIS IS IDEAL, I *KNOW.*

BUT FOR WHAT IT'S WORTH...

...I WISH YOU HADN'T FORCED ME TO *BEAT* YOU.

IT WOULD HAVE BEEN BETTER IF YOU COULD *SMELL* THE GASOLINE. I THINK YOU WOULD HAVE *LIKED* THAT.

MMHM! MHMM!

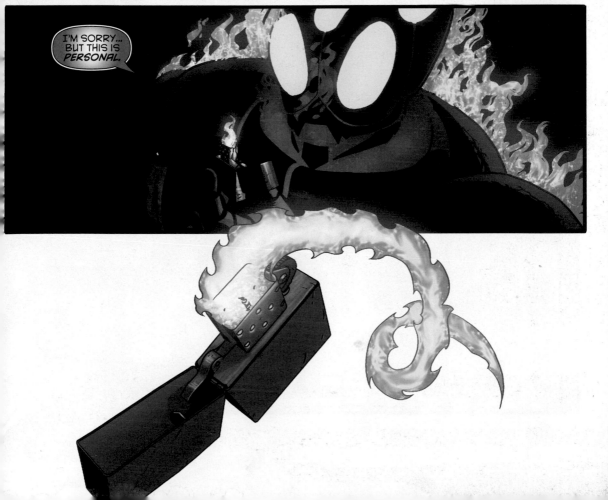

I'M SORRY... BUT THIS IS *PERSONAL.*

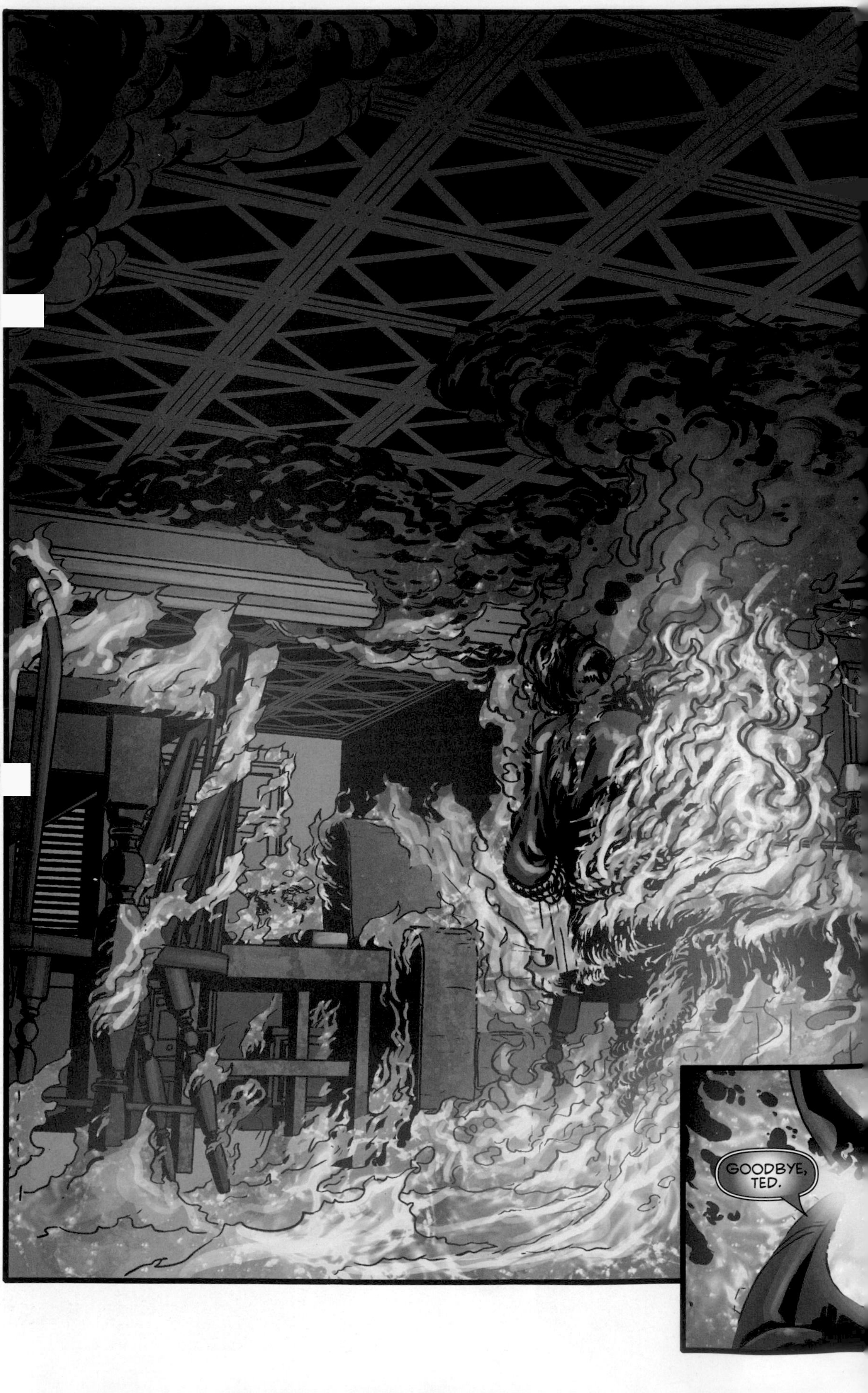
GOODBYE, TED.

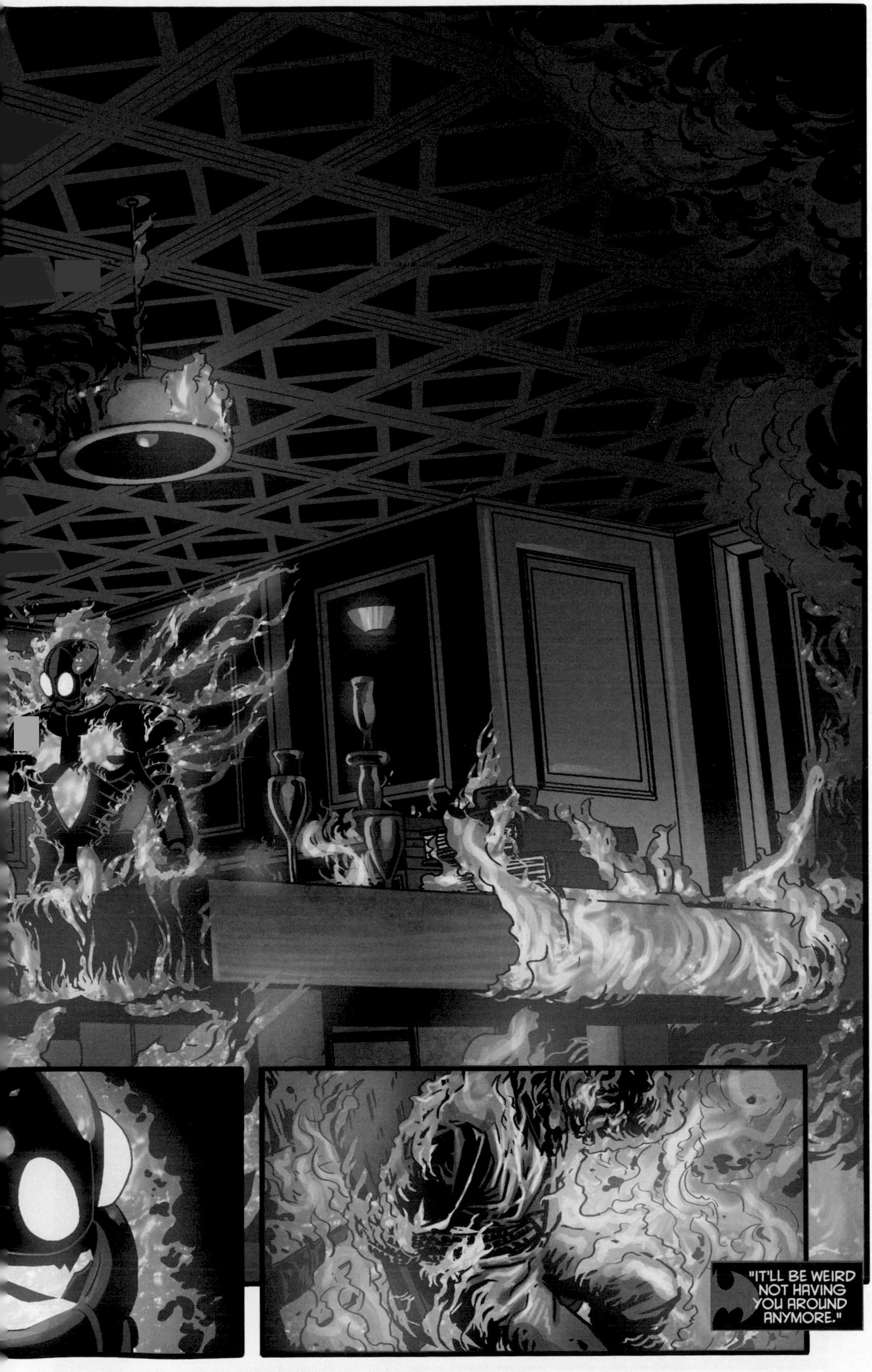
"IT'LL BE WEIRD NOT HAVING YOU AROUND ANYMORE."

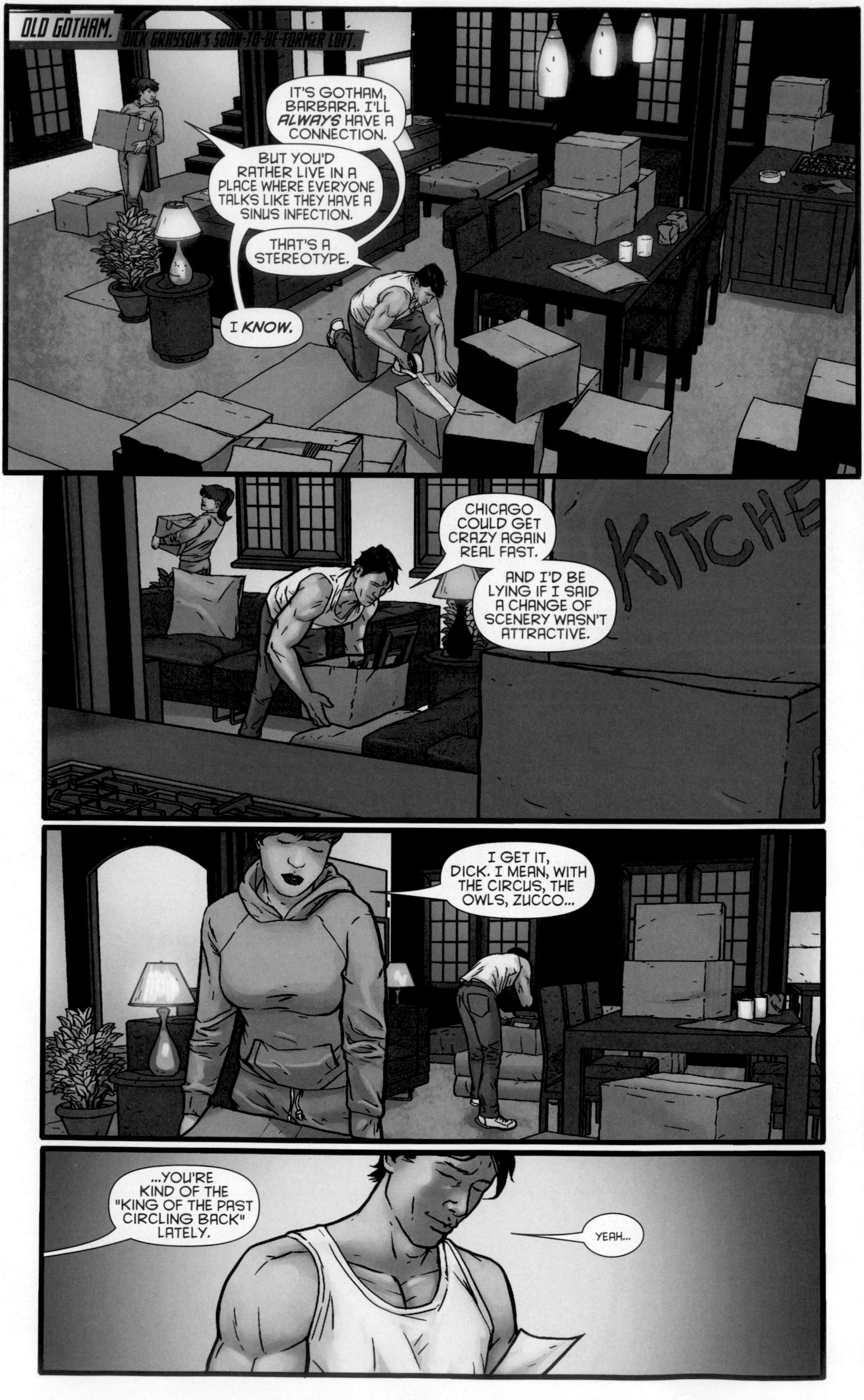
OLD GOTHAM.
DICK GRAYSON'S SOON-TO-BE-FORMER LOFT.
IT'S GOTHAM, BARBARA. I'LL ALWAYS HAVE A CONNECTION.
BUT YOU'D RATHER LIVE IN A PLACE WHERE EVERYONE TALKS LIKE THEY HAVE A SINUS INFECTION.
THAT'S A STEREOTYPE.
I KNOW.
CHICAGO COULD GET CRAZY AGAIN REAL FAST.
AND I'D BE LYING IF I SAID A CHANGE OF SCENERY WASN'T ATTRACTIVE.
I GET IT, DICK. I MEAN, WITH THE CIRCUS, THE OWLS, ZUCCO...
...YOU'RE KIND OF THE "KING OF THE PAST CIRCLING BACK" LATELY.
YEAH...

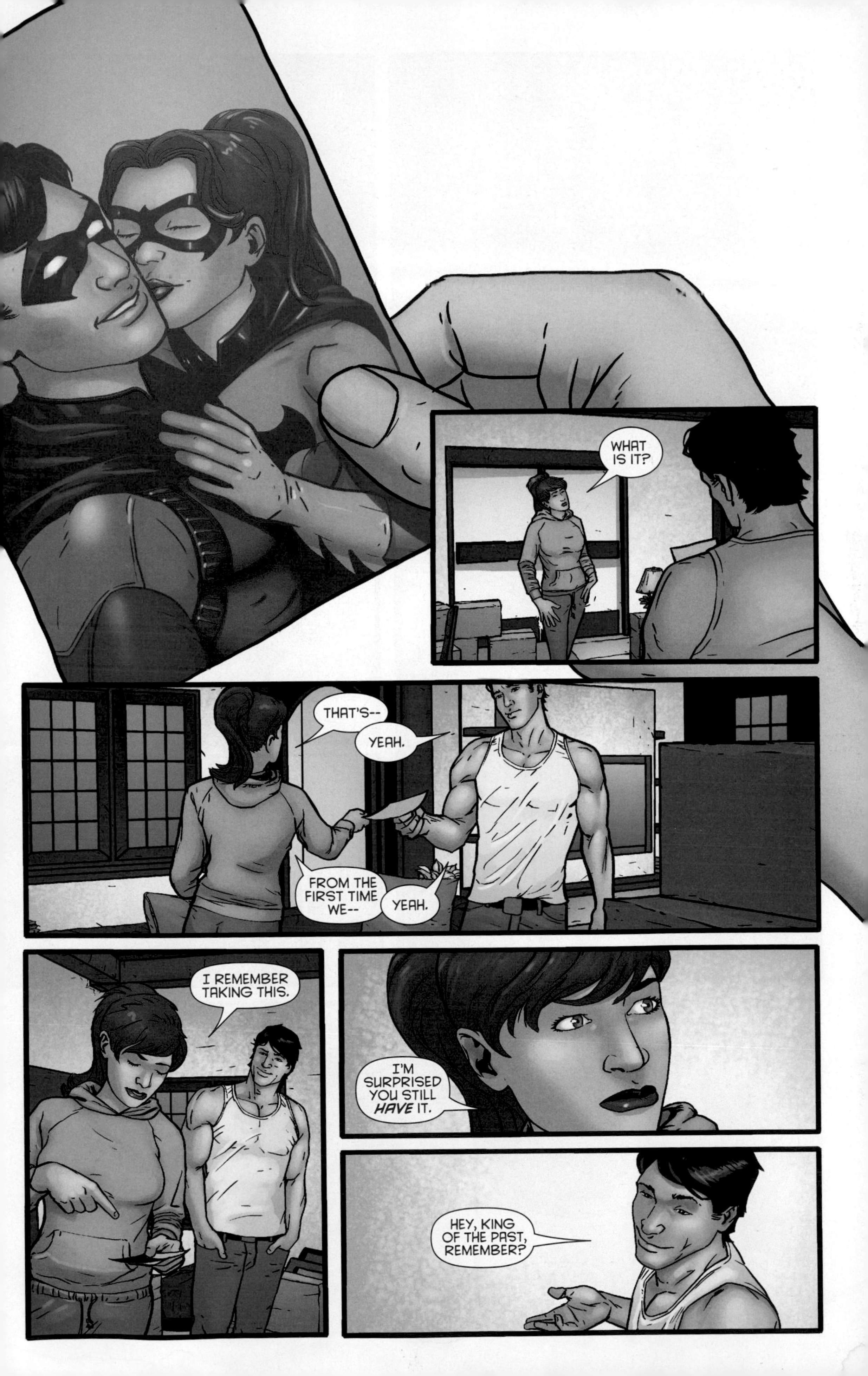
WHAT IS IT?
THAT'S--
YEAH.
FROM THE FIRST TIME WE--
YEAH.
I REMEMBER TAKING THIS.
I'M SURPRISED YOU STILL HAVE IT.
HEY, KING OF THE PAST, REMEMBER?

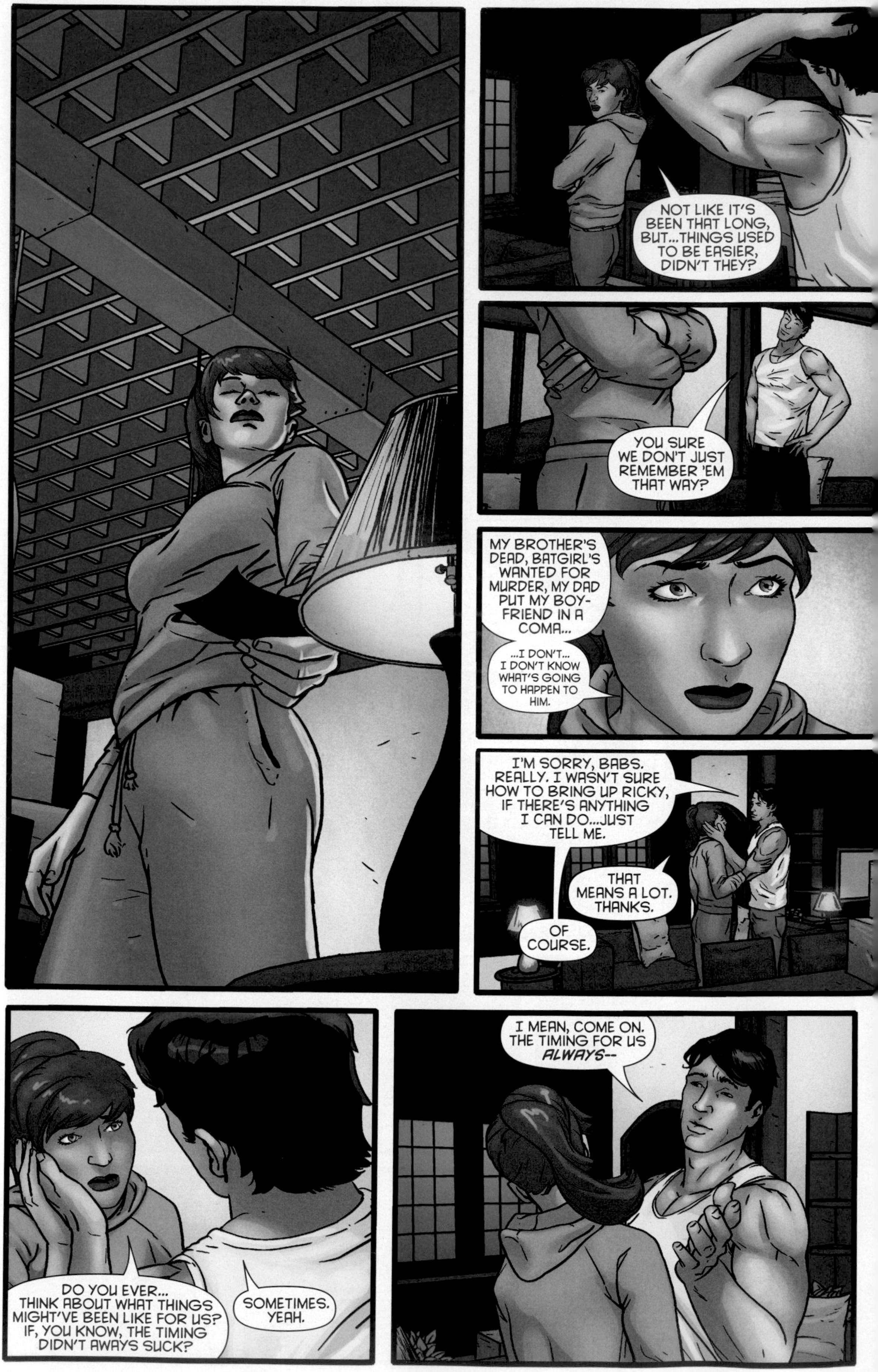
NOT LIKE IT'S BEEN THAT LONG, BUT...THINGS USED TO BE EASIER, DIDN'T THEY?
YOU SURE WE DON'T JUST REMEMBER 'EM THAT WAY?
MY BROTHER'S DEAD, BATGIRL'S WANTED FOR MURDER, MY DAD PUT MY BOY-FRIEND IN A COMA...
...I DON'T... I DON'T KNOW WHAT'S GOING TO HAPPEN TO HIM.
I'M SORRY, BABS. REALLY. I WASN'T SURE HOW TO BRING UP RICKY, IF THERE'S ANYTHING I CAN DO...JUST TELL ME.
THAT MEANS A LOT. THANKS.
OF COURSE.
DO YOU EVER... THINK ABOUT WHAT THINGS MIGHT'VE BEEN LIKE FOR US? IF, YOU KNOW, THE TIMING DIDN'T AWAYS SUCK?
SOMETIMES. YEAH.
I MEAN, COME ON. THE TIMING FOR US *ALWAYS*--

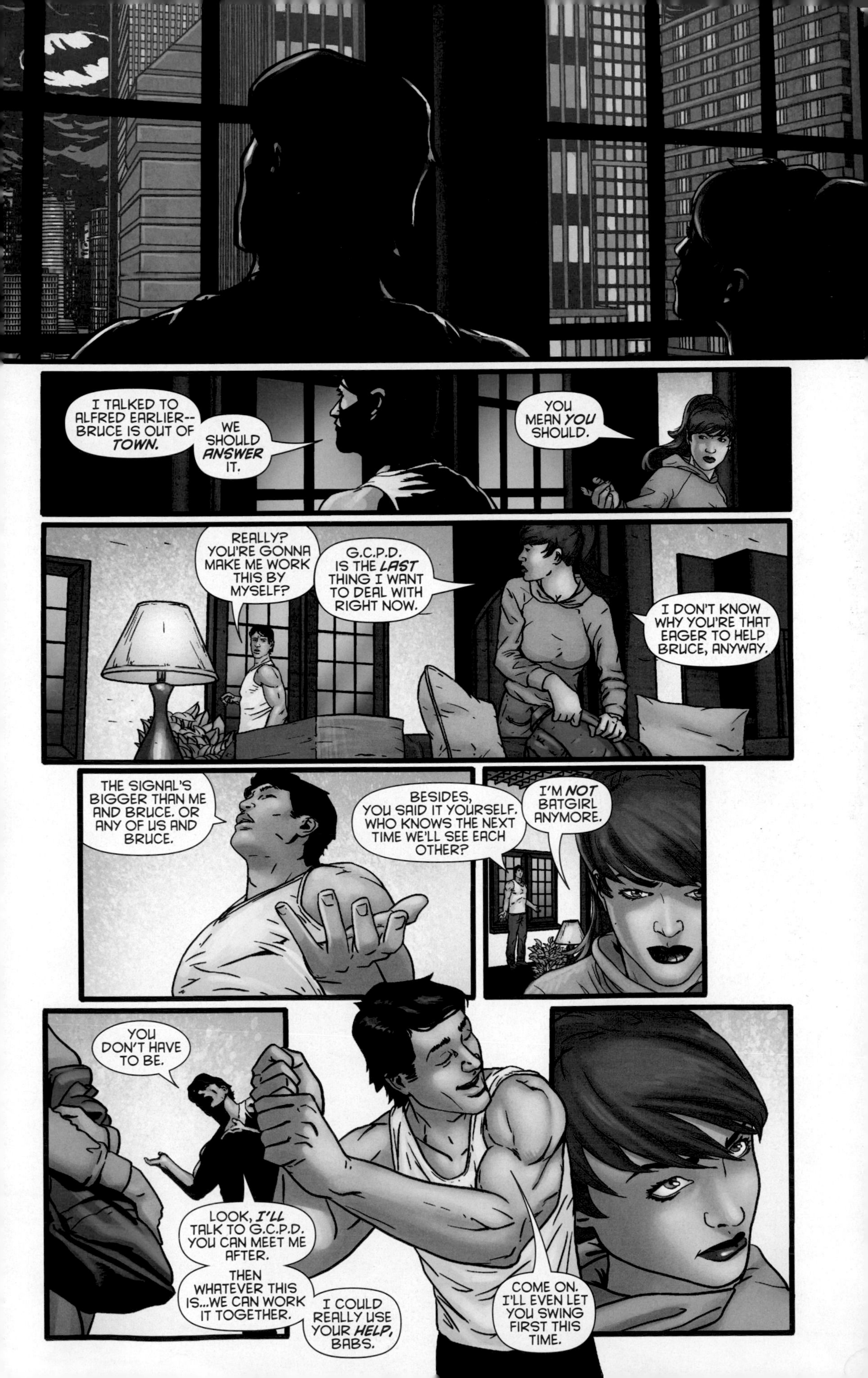
I TALKED TO ALFRED EARLIER-- BRUCE IS OUT OF *TOWN.*
WE SHOULD *ANSWER* IT.
YOU MEAN *YOU* SHOULD.
REALLY? YOU'RE GONNA MAKE ME WORK THIS BY MYSELF?
G.C.P.D. IS THE *LAST* THING I WANT TO DEAL WITH RIGHT NOW.
I DON'T KNOW WHY YOU'RE THAT EAGER TO HELP BRUCE, ANYWAY.
THE SIGNAL'S BIGGER THAN ME AND BRUCE. OR ANY OF US AND BRUCE.
BESIDES, YOU SAID IT YOURSELF. WHO KNOWS THE NEXT TIME WE'LL SEE EACH OTHER?
I'M *NOT* BATGIRL ANYMORE.
YOU DON'T HAVE TO BE.
LOOK, *I'LL* TALK TO G.C.P.D. YOU CAN MEET ME AFTER.
THEN WHATEVER THIS IS...WE CAN WORK IT TOGETHER.
I COULD REALLY USE YOUR *HELP,* BABS.
COME ON. I'LL EVEN LET YOU SWING FIRST THIS TIME.

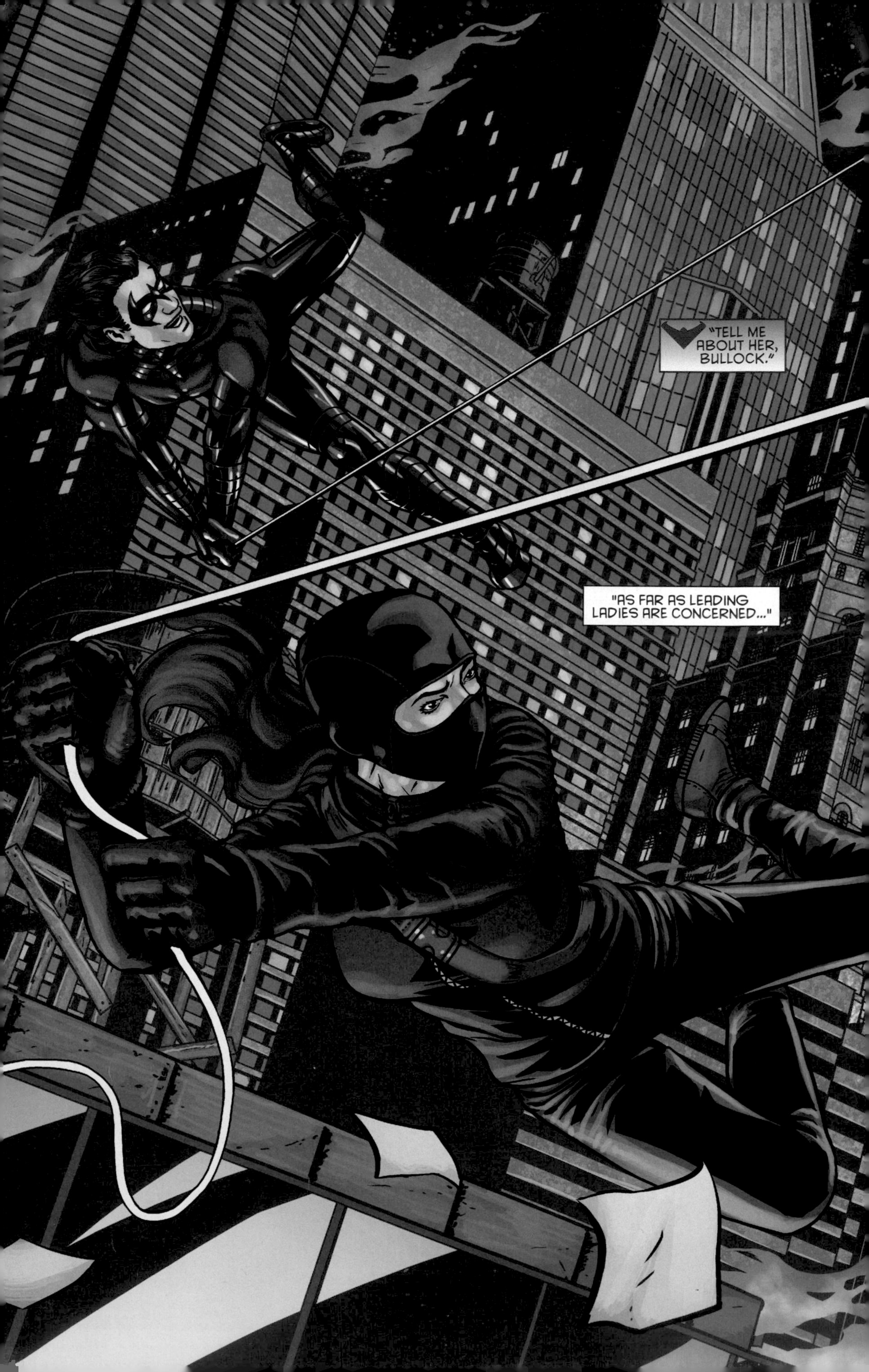
"TELL ME ABOUT HER, BULLOCK."
"AS FAR AS LEADING LADIES ARE CONCERNED..."

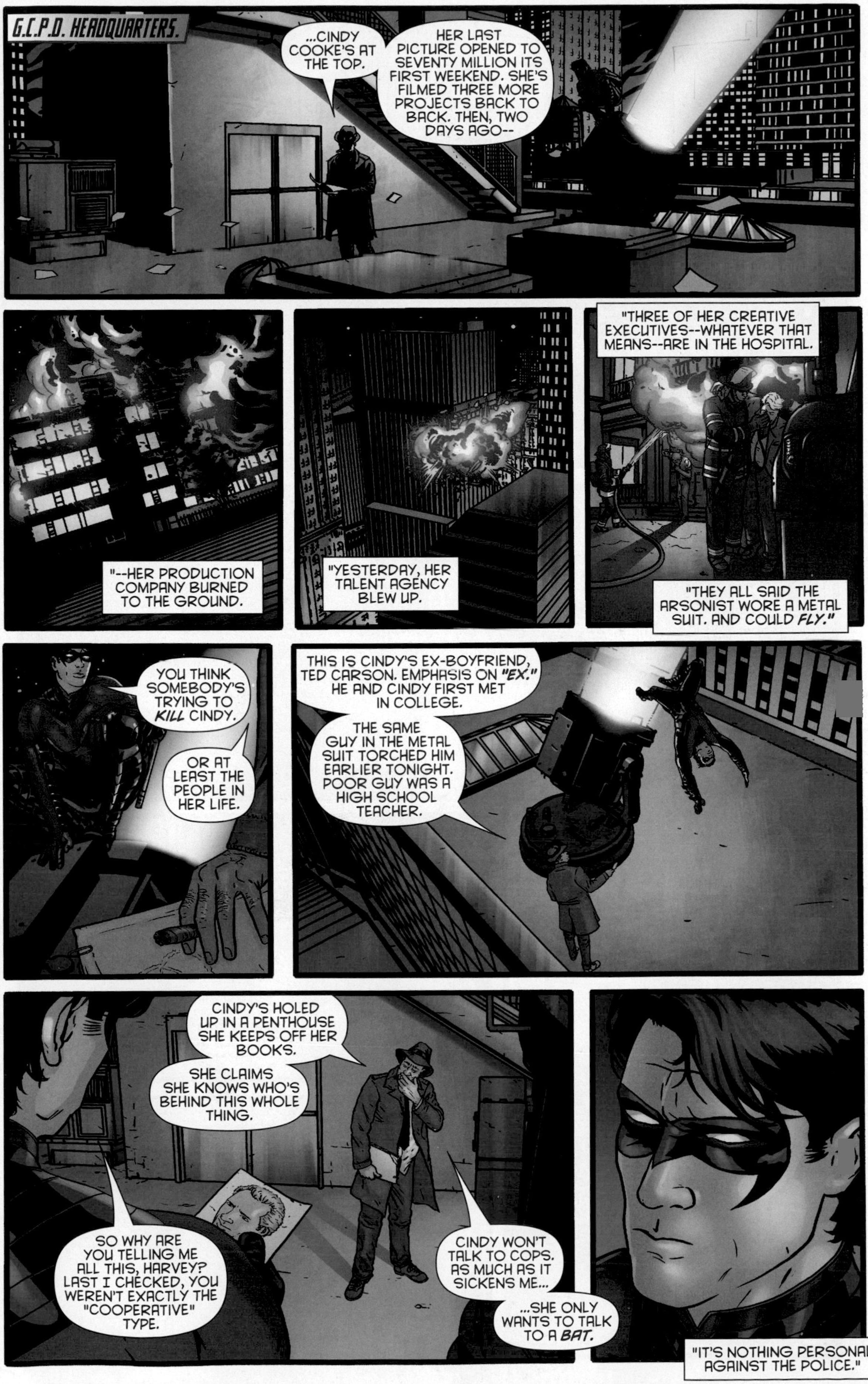
G.C.P.D. HEADQUARTERS.
...CINDY COOKE'S AT THE TOP.
HER LAST PICTURE OPENED TO SEVENTY MILLION ITS FIRST WEEKEND. SHE'S FILMED THREE MORE PROJECTS BACK TO BACK. THEN, TWO DAYS AGO--
"--HER PRODUCTION COMPANY BURNED TO THE GROUND.
"YESTERDAY, HER TALENT AGENCY BLEW UP.
"THREE OF HER CREATIVE EXECUTIVES--WHATEVER THAT MEANS--ARE IN THE HOSPITAL.
"THEY ALL SAID THE ARSONIST WORE A METAL SUIT. AND COULD FLY."
YOU THINK SOMEBODY'S TRYING TO KILL CINDY.
OR AT LEAST THE PEOPLE IN HER LIFE.
THIS IS CINDY'S EX-BOYFRIEND, TED CARSON. EMPHASIS ON "EX." HE AND CINDY FIRST MET IN COLLEGE.
THE SAME GUY IN THE METAL SUIT TORCHED HIM EARLIER TONIGHT. POOR GUY WAS A HIGH SCHOOL TEACHER.
CINDY'S HOLED UP IN A PENTHOUSE SHE KEEPS OFF HER BOOKS.
SHE CLAIMS SHE KNOWS WHO'S BEHIND THIS WHOLE THING.
SO WHY ARE YOU TELLING ME ALL THIS, HARVEY? LAST I CHECKED, YOU WEREN'T EXACTLY THE "COOPERATIVE" TYPE.
CINDY WON'T TALK TO COPS. AS MUCH AS IT SICKENS ME...
...SHE ONLY WANTS TO TALK TO A BAT.
"IT'S NOTHING PERSONAL AGAINST THE POLICE."

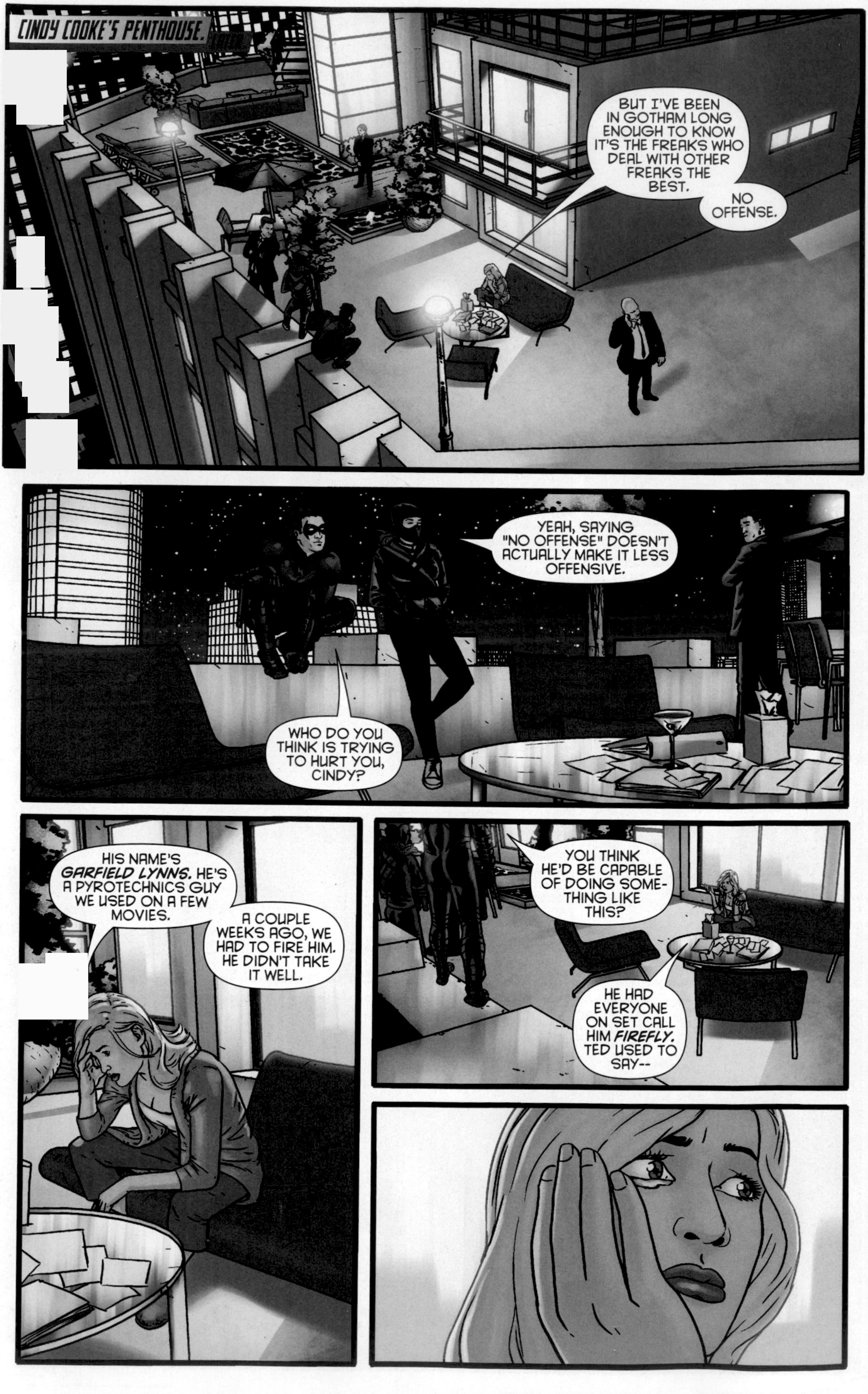
CINDY COOKE'S PENTHOUSE.
BUT I'VE BEEN IN GOTHAM LONG ENOUGH TO KNOW IT'S THE FREAKS WHO DEAL WITH OTHER FREAKS THE BEST.
NO OFFENSE.
YEAH, SAYING "NO OFFENSE" DOESN'T ACTUALLY MAKE IT LESS OFFENSIVE.
WHO DO YOU THINK IS TRYING TO HURT YOU, CINDY?
HIS NAME'S *GARFIELD LYNNS.* HE'S A PYROTECHNICS GUY WE USED ON A FEW MOVIES.
A COUPLE WEEKS AGO, WE HAD TO FIRE HIM. HE DIDN'T TAKE IT WELL.
YOU THINK HE'D BE CAPABLE OF DOING SOMETHING LIKE THIS?
HE HAD EVERYONE ON SET CALL HIM *FIREFLY.* TED USED TO SAY--

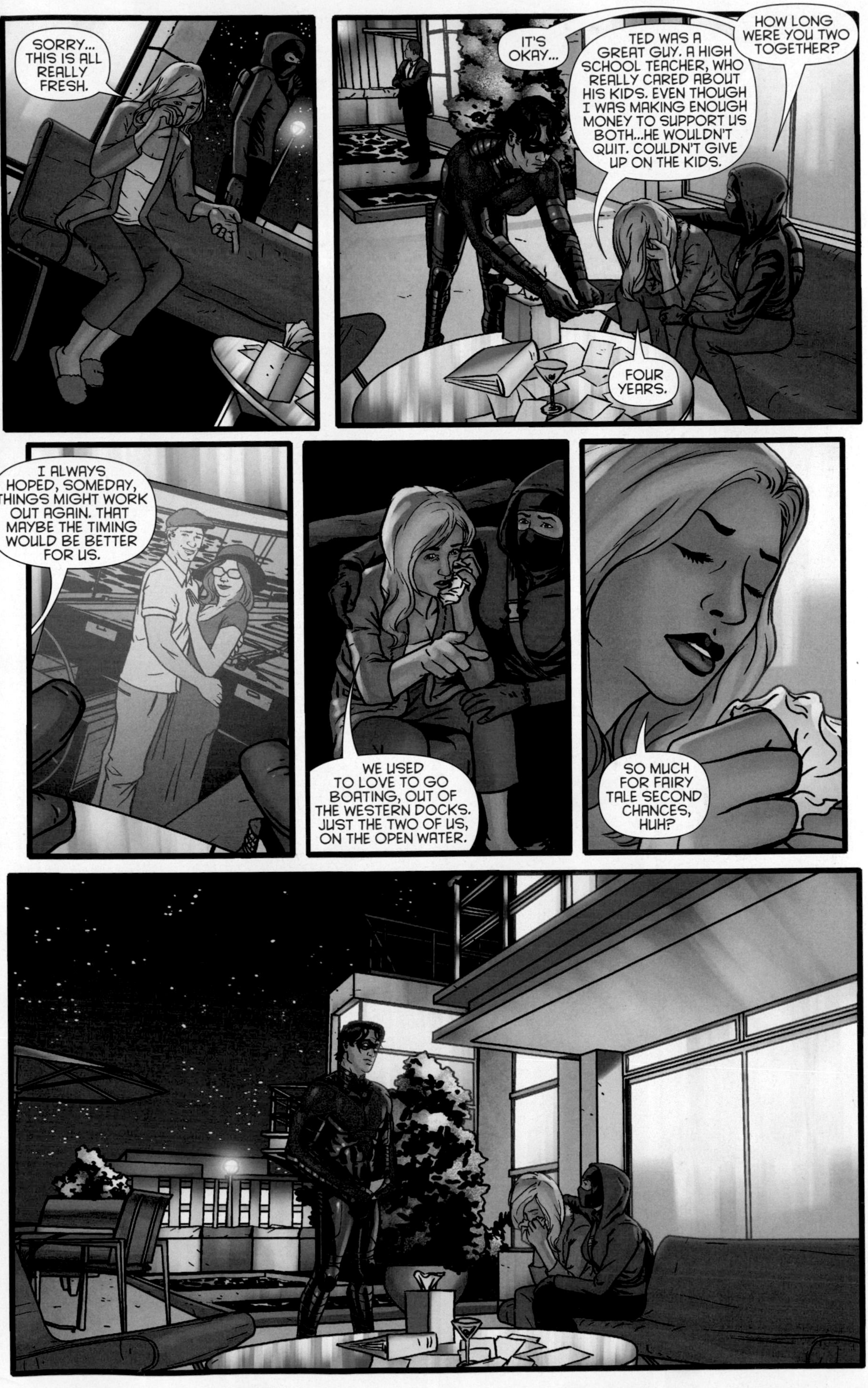

SORRY... THIS IS ALL REALLY FRESH.
IT'S OKAY...
HOW LONG WERE YOU TWO TOGETHER?
TED WAS A GREAT GUY. A HIGH SCHOOL TEACHER, WHO REALLY CARED ABOUT HIS KIDS. EVEN THOUGH I WAS MAKING ENOUGH MONEY TO SUPPORT US BOTH...HE WOULDN'T QUIT. COULDN'T GIVE UP ON THE KIDS.
FOUR YEARS.
I ALWAYS HOPED, SOMEDAY, THINGS MIGHT WORK OUT AGAIN. THAT MAYBE THE TIMING WOULD BE BETTER FOR US.
WE USED TO LOVE TO GO BOATING, OUT OF THE WESTERN DOCKS. JUST THE TWO OF US, ON THE OPEN WATER.
SO MUCH FOR FAIRY TALE SECOND CHANCES, HUH?

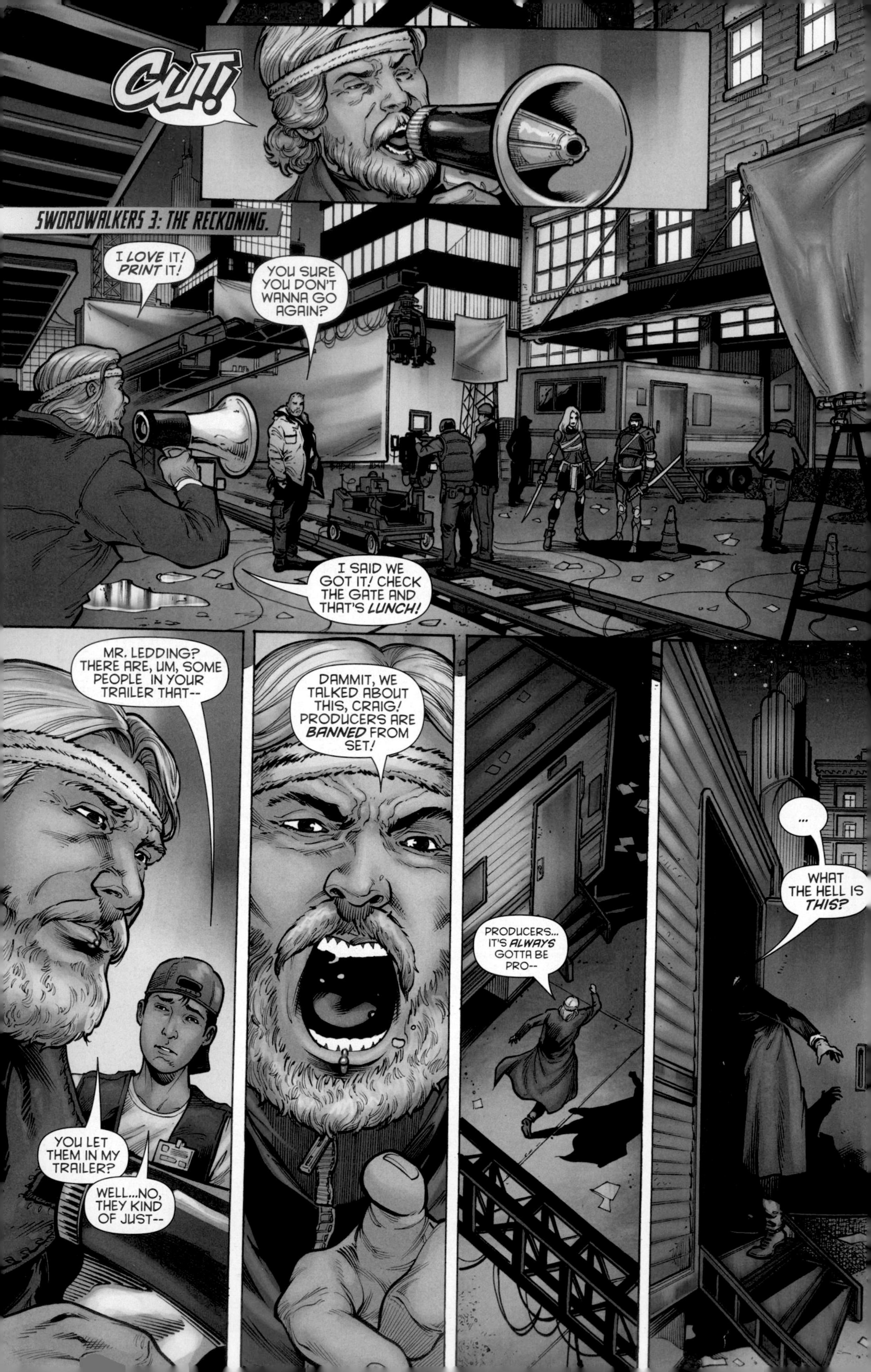
CUT!
SWORDWALKERS 3: THE RECKONING.
I LOVE IT! PRINT IT!
YOU SURE YOU DON'T WANNA GO AGAIN?
I SAID WE GOT IT! CHECK THE GATE AND THAT'S LUNCH!
MR. LEDDING? THERE ARE, UM, SOME PEOPLE IN YOUR TRAILER THAT--
YOU LET THEM IN MY TRAILER?
WELL...NO, THEY KIND OF JUST--
DAMMIT, WE TALKED ABOUT THIS, CRAIG! PRODUCERS ARE BANNED FROM SET!
PRODUCERS... IT'S ALWAYS GOTTA BE PRO--
...
WHAT THE HELL IS THIS?

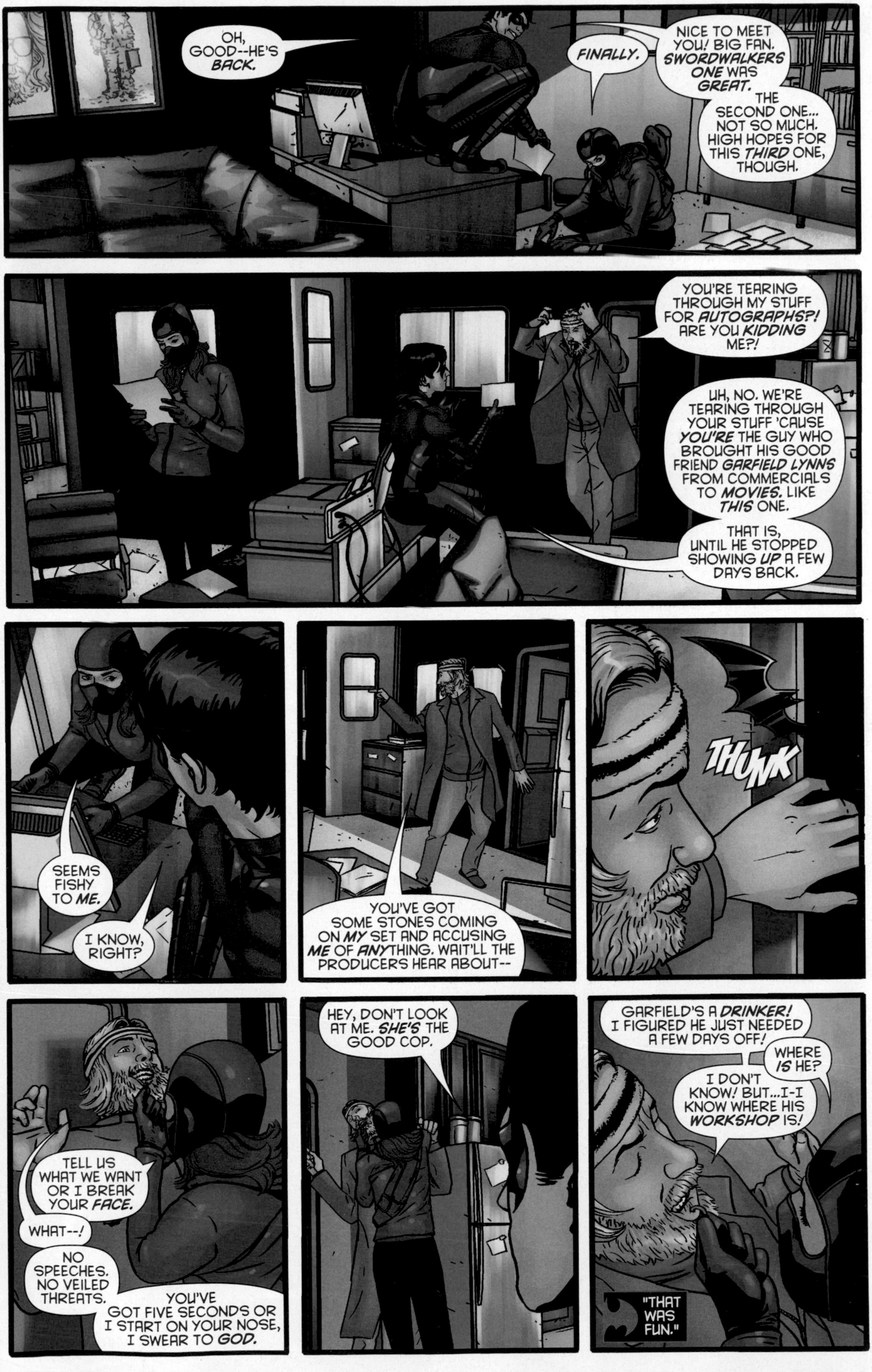
OH, GOOD--HE'S BACK.
FINALLY.
NICE TO MEET YOU! BIG FAN. SWORDWALKERS ONE WAS GREAT.
THE SECOND ONE... NOT SO MUCH. HIGH HOPES FOR THIS THIRD ONE, THOUGH.
YOU'RE TEARING THROUGH MY STUFF FOR AUTOGRAPHS?! ARE YOU KIDDING ME?!
UH, NO. WE'RE TEARING THROUGH YOUR STUFF 'CAUSE YOU'RE THE GUY WHO BROUGHT HIS GOOD FRIEND GARFIELD LYNNS FROM COMMERCIALS TO MOVIES. LIKE THIS ONE.
THAT IS, UNTIL HE STOPPED SHOWING UP A FEW DAYS BACK.
SEEMS FISHY TO ME.
I KNOW, RIGHT?
YOU'VE GOT SOME STONES COMING ON MY SET AND ACCUSING ME OF ANYTHING. WAIT'LL THE PRODUCERS HEAR ABOUT--
THUNK
TELL US WHAT WE WANT OR I BREAK YOUR FACE.
WHAT--!
NO SPEECHES. NO VEILED THREATS.
YOU'VE GOT FIVE SECONDS OR I START ON YOUR NOSE, I SWEAR TO GOD.
HEY, DON'T LOOK AT ME. SHE'S THE GOOD COP.
GARFIELD'S A DRINKER! I FIGURED HE JUST NEEDED A FEW DAYS OFF!
WHERE IS HE?
I DON'T KNOW! BUT...I-I KNOW WHERE HIS WORKSHOP IS!
"THAT WAS FUN."

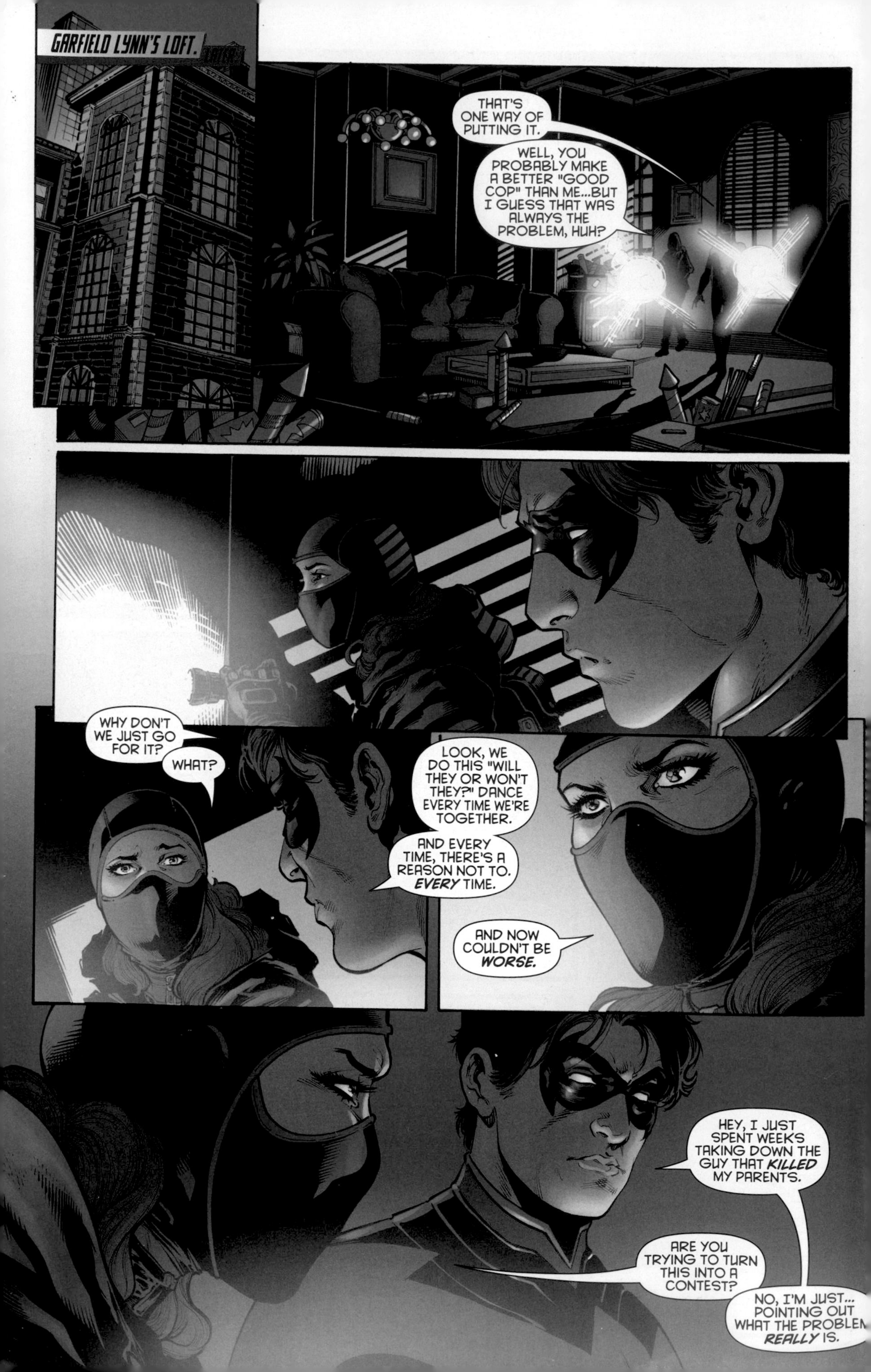
GARFIELD LYNN'S LOFT.
THAT'S ONE WAY OF PUTTING IT.
WELL, YOU PROBABLY MAKE A BETTER "GOOD COP" THAN ME...BUT I GUESS THAT WAS ALWAYS THE PROBLEM, HUH?
WHY DON'T WE JUST GO FOR IT?
WHAT?
LOOK, WE DO THIS "WILL THEY OR WON'T THEY?" DANCE EVERY TIME WE'RE TOGETHER.
AND EVERY TIME, THERE'S A REASON NOT TO. EVERY TIME.
AND NOW COULDN'T BE WORSE.
HEY, I JUST SPENT WEEKS TAKING DOWN THE GUY THAT KILLED MY PARENTS.
ARE YOU TRYING TO TURN THIS INTO A CONTEST?
NO, I'M JUST... POINTING OUT WHAT THE PROBLEM REALLY IS.

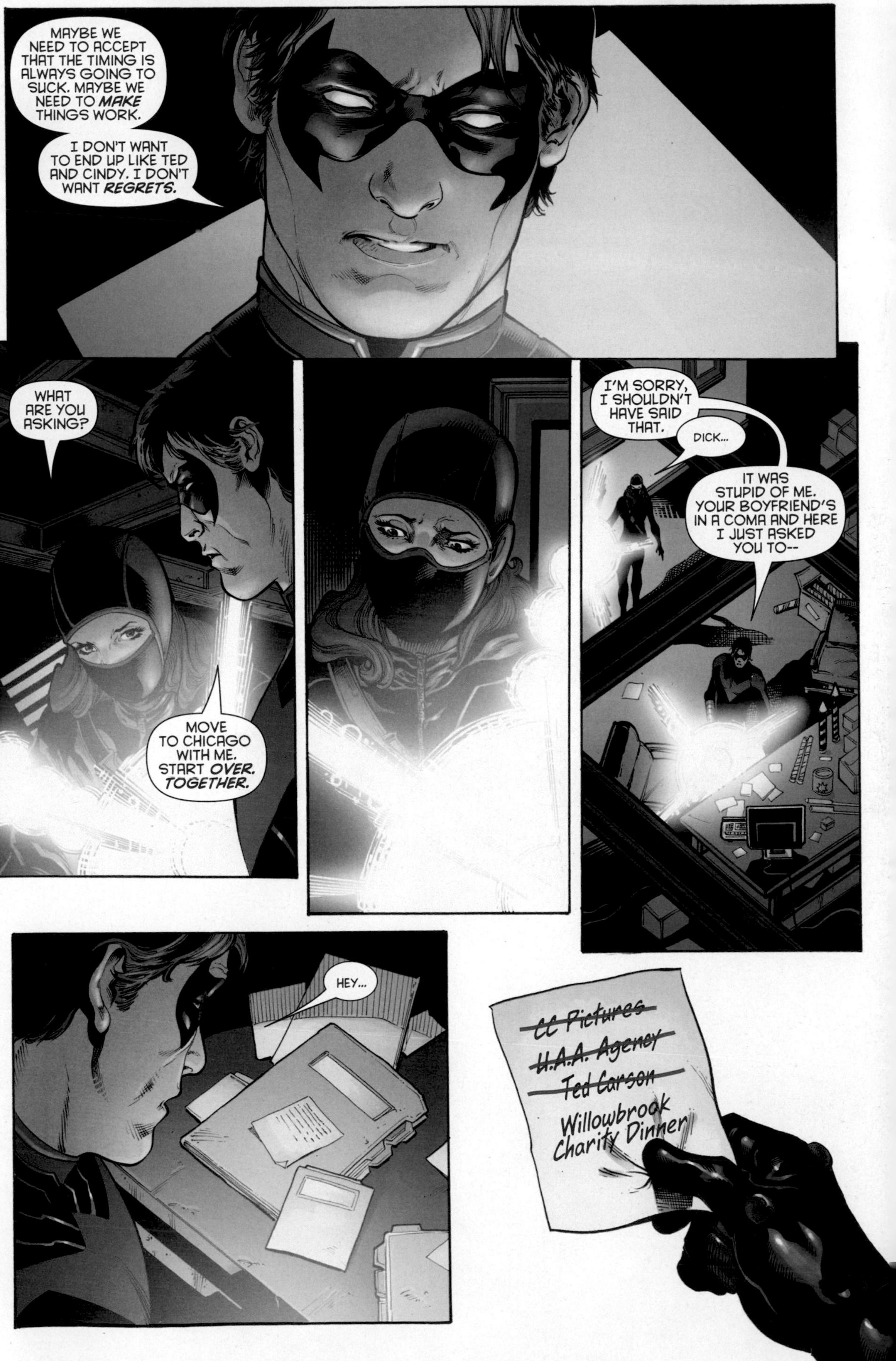

MAYBE WE NEED TO ACCEPT THAT THE TIMING IS ALWAYS GOING TO SUCK. MAYBE WE NEED TO *MAKE* THINGS WORK.
I DON'T WANT TO END UP LIKE TED AND CINDY. I DON'T WANT *REGRETS.*
WHAT ARE YOU ASKING?
MOVE TO CHICAGO WITH ME. START *OVER. TOGETHER.*
I'M SORRY, I SHOULDN'T HAVE SAID THAT.
DICK...
IT WAS STUPID OF ME. YOUR BOYFRIEND'S IN A COMA AND HERE I JUST ASKED YOU TO--
HEY...
CC Pictures
U.A.A. Agency
Ted Carson
Willowbrook
Charity Dinner

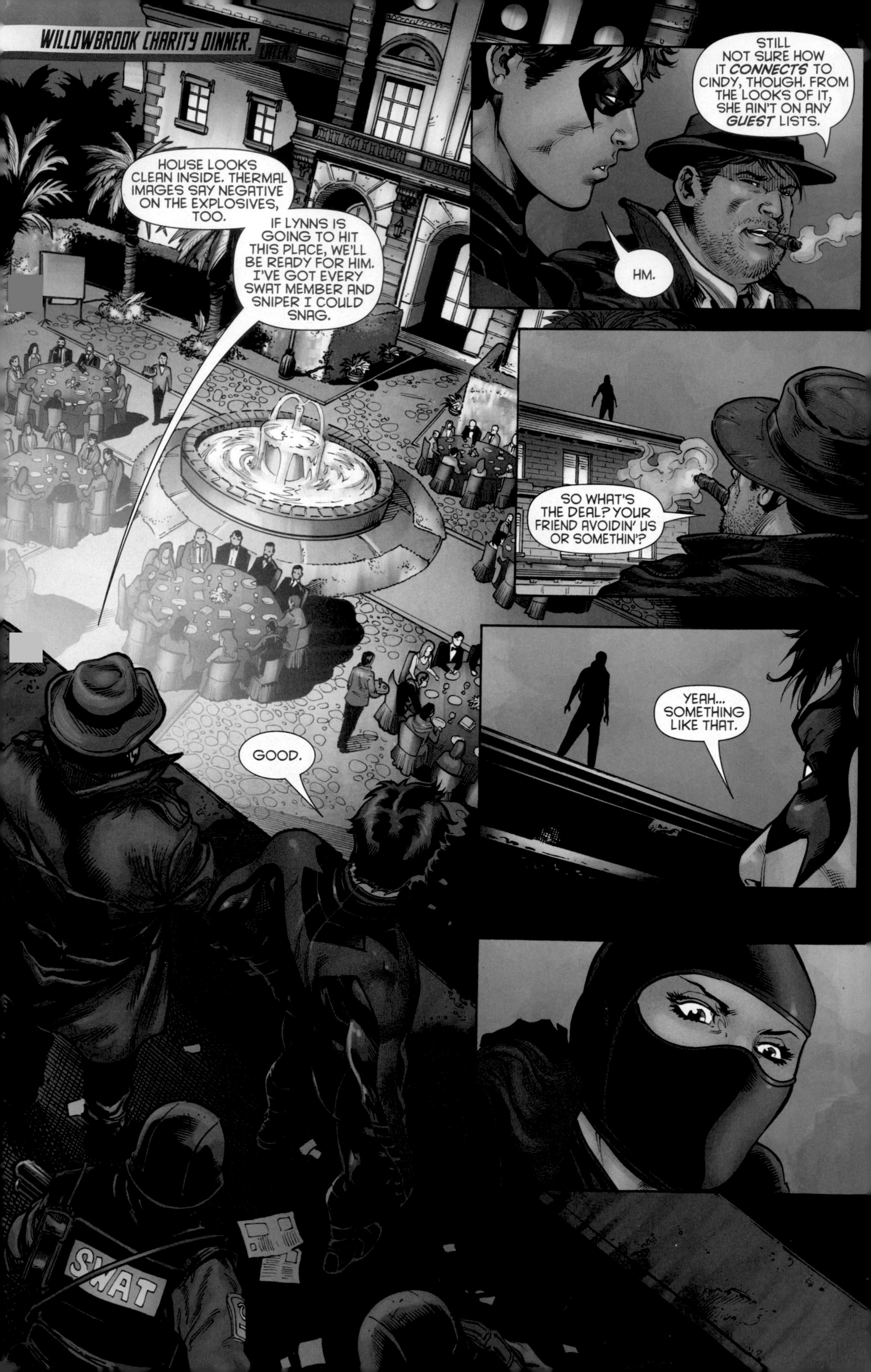
WILLOWBROOK CHARITY DINNER.
LATER.
HOUSE LOOKS CLEAN INSIDE. THERMAL IMAGES SAY NEGATIVE ON THE EXPLOSIVES, TOO.
IF LYNNS IS GOING TO HIT THIS PLACE, WE'LL BE READY FOR HIM. I'VE GOT EVERY SWAT MEMBER AND SNIPER I COULD SNAG.
GOOD.
STILL NOT SURE HOW IT CONNECTS TO CINDY, THOUGH. FROM THE LOOKS OF IT, SHE AIN'T ON ANY GUEST LISTS.
HM.
SO WHAT'S THE DEAL? YOUR FRIEND AVOIDIN' US OR SOMETHIN'?
YEAH... SOMETHING LIKE THAT.
SWAT

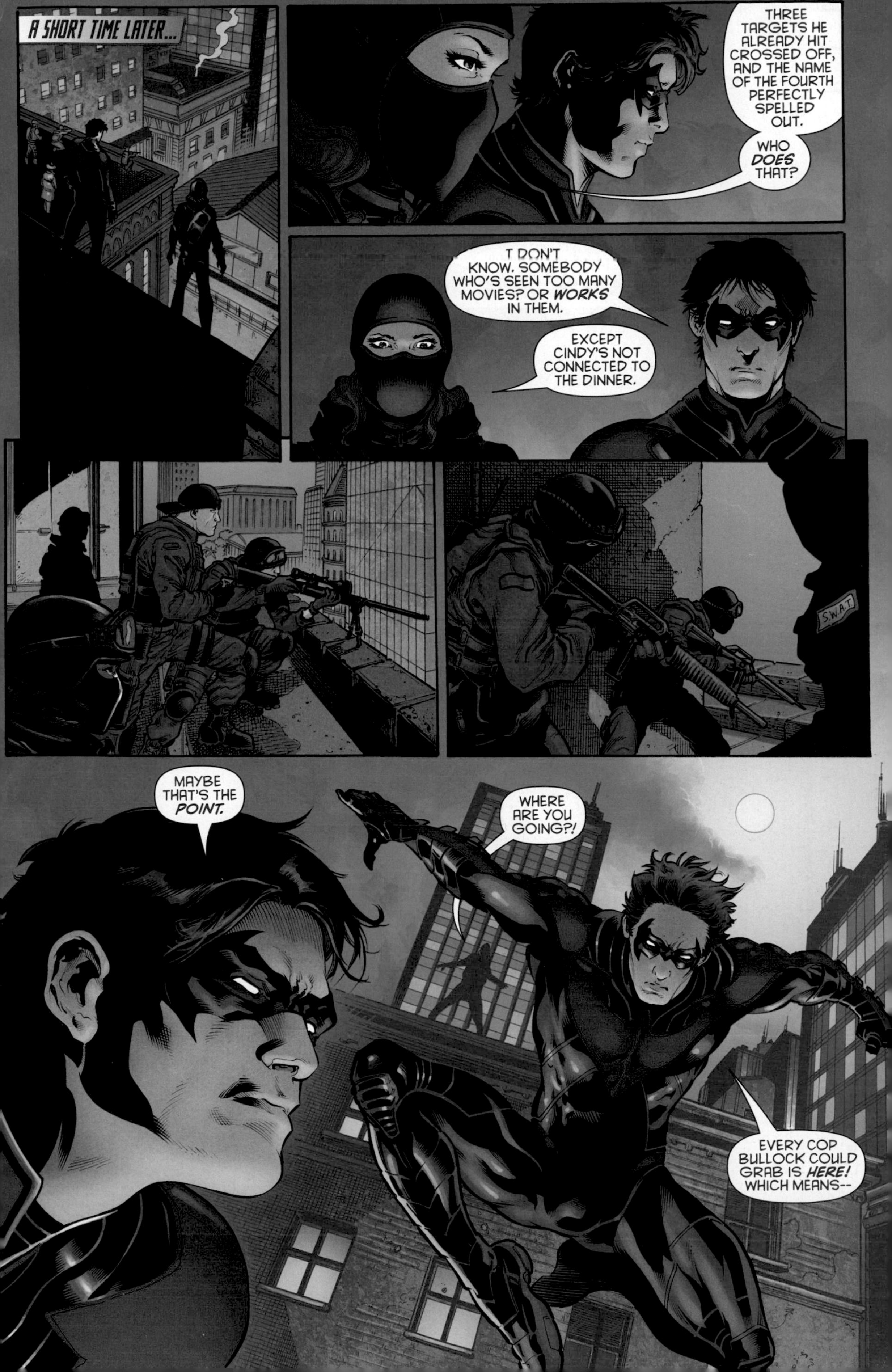
A SHORT TIME LATER...
THREE TARGETS HE ALREADY HIT CROSSED OFF, AND THE NAME OF THE FOURTH PERFECTLY SPELLED OUT.
WHO DOES THAT?
I DON'T KNOW. SOMEBODY WHO'S SEEN TOO MANY MOVIES? OR WORKS IN THEM.
EXCEPT CINDY'S NOT CONNECTED TO THE DINNER.
S.W.A.T.
MAYBE THAT'S THE POINT.
WHERE ARE YOU GOING?!
EVERY COP BULLOCK COULD GRAB IS HERE! WHICH MEANS--

--THEY'RE NOT WITH CINDY!"

STAY AWAY FROM ME!

THAT'S HOW YOU WANT TO PLAY IT?

SUIT YOURSELF!

SHOOOM

AHH!

HEY! SHE SAID--

TNK

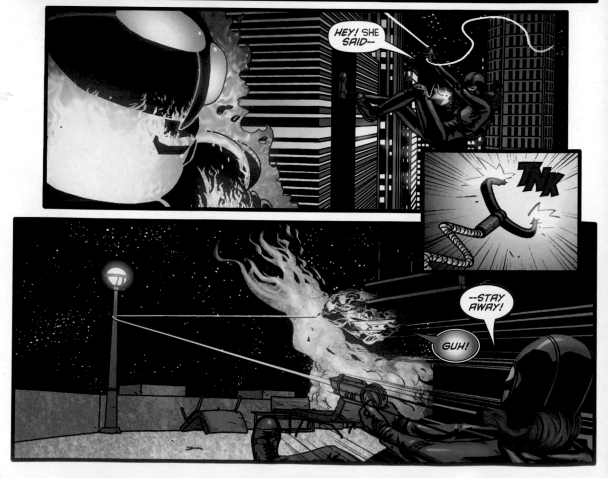

--STAY AWAY!

GUH!

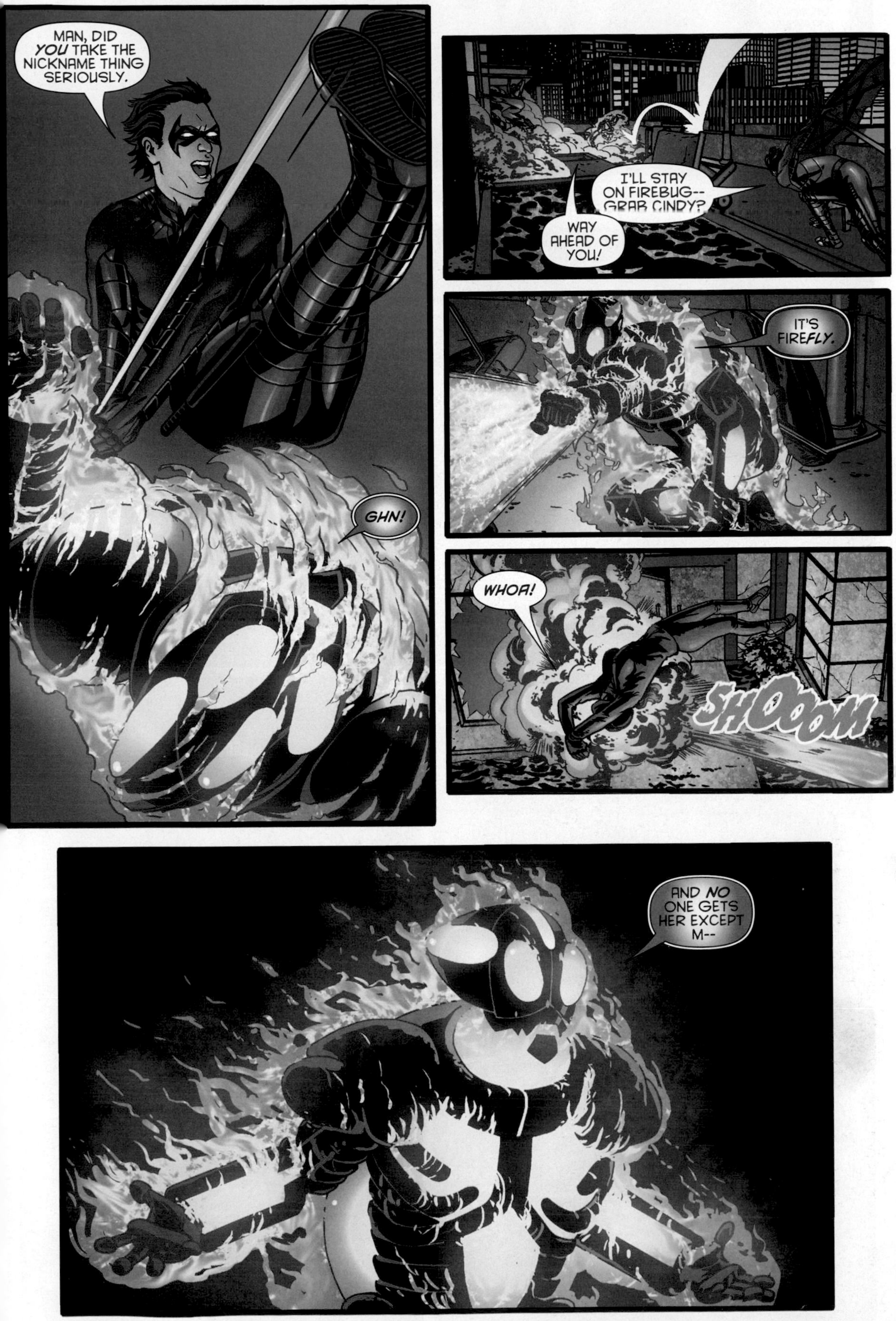
MAN, DID YOU TAKE THE NICKNAME THING SERIOUSLY.
GHN!
I'LL STAY ON FIREBUG-- GRAB CINDY?
WAY AHEAD OF YOU!
IT'S FIREFLY.
WHOA!
SHOOOOM
AND NO ONE GETS HER EXCEPT M--

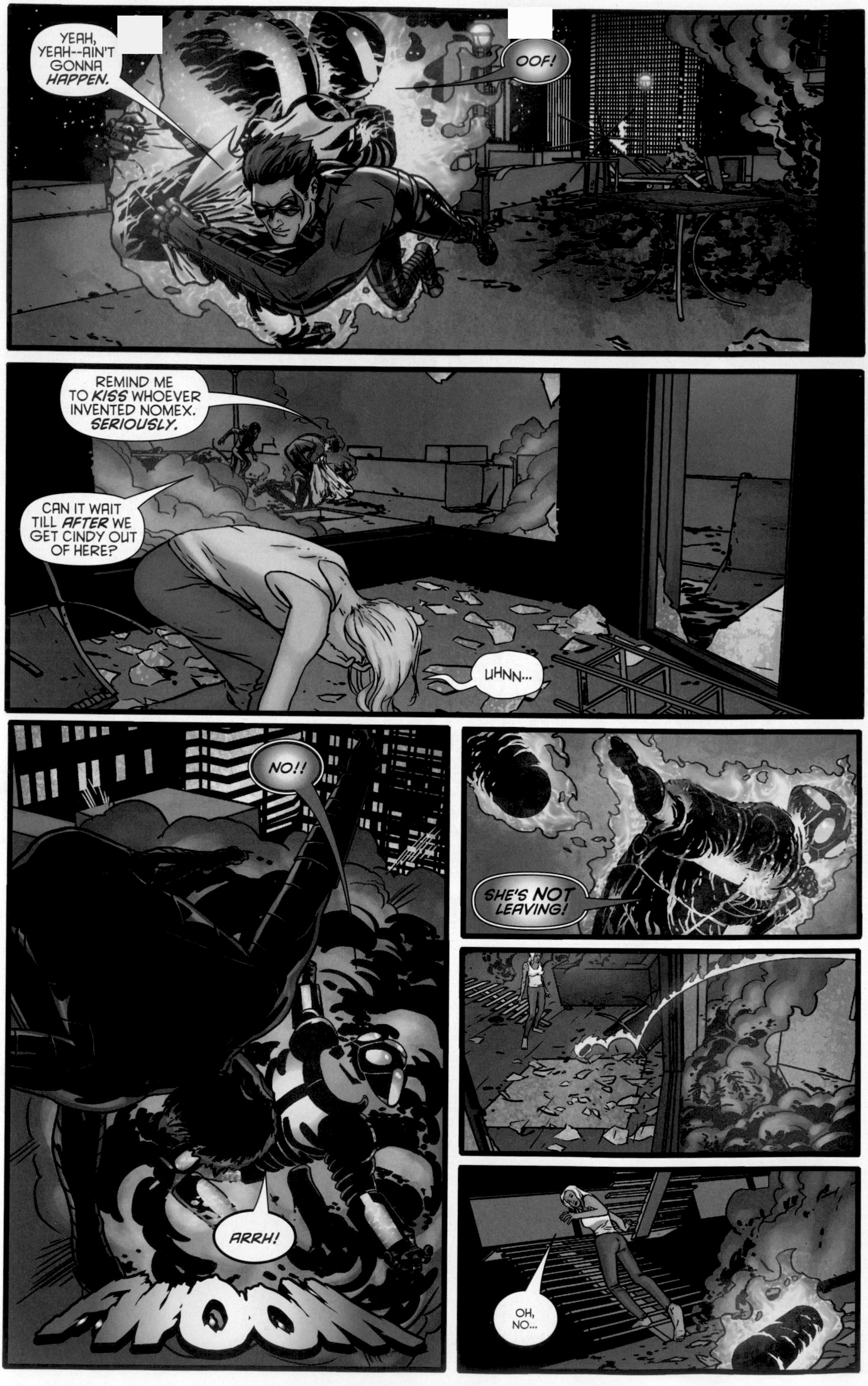
YEAH, YEAH--AIN'T GONNA HAPPEN.
OOF!
REMIND ME TO KISS WHOEVER INVENTED NOMEX. SERIOUSLY.
CAN IT WAIT TILL AFTER WE GET CINDY OUT OF HERE?
UHNN...
NO!!
ARRH!
FWOOM
SHE'S NOT LEAVING!
OH, NO...

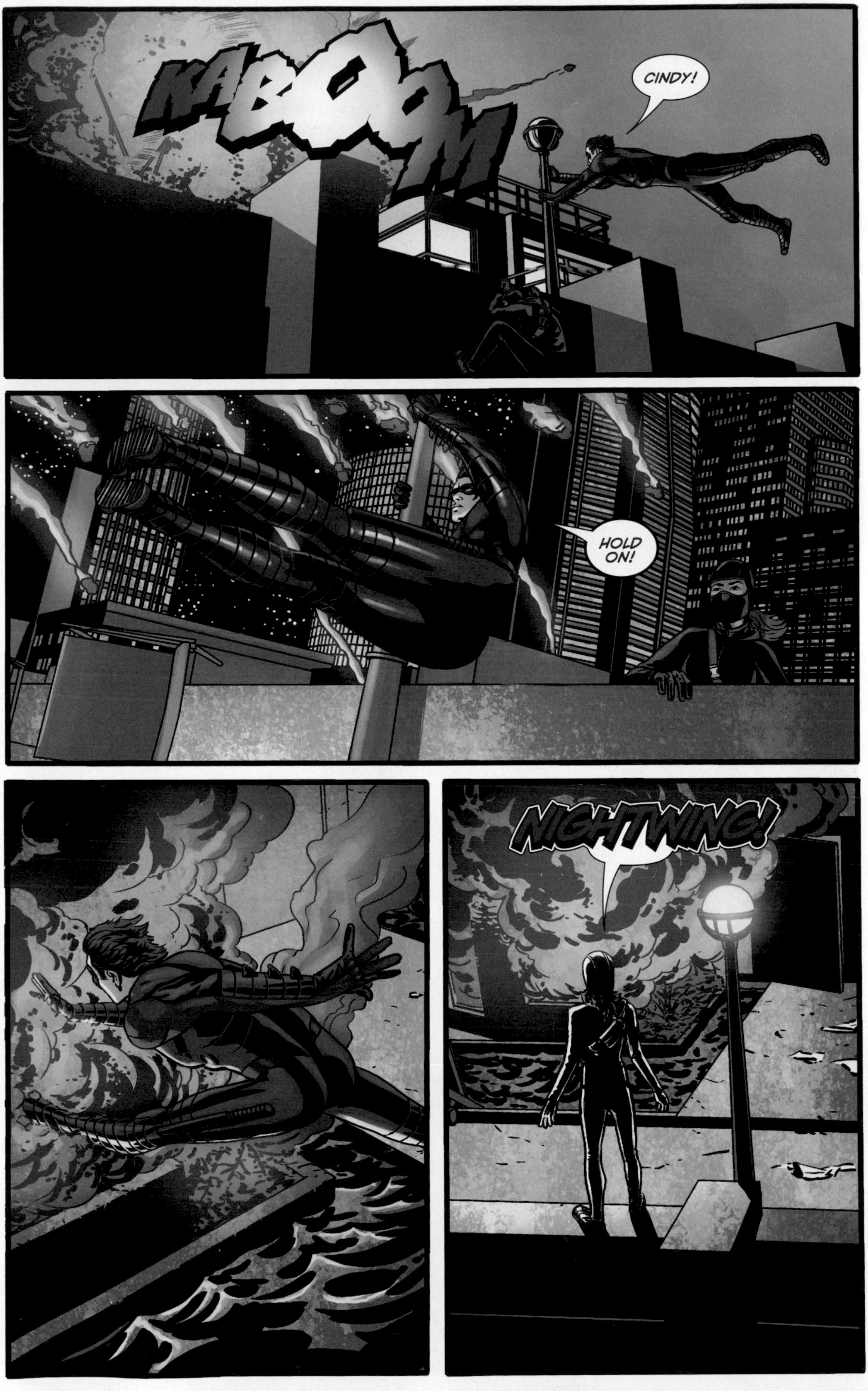
KABOOM
CINDY!
HOLD ON!
NIGHTWING!

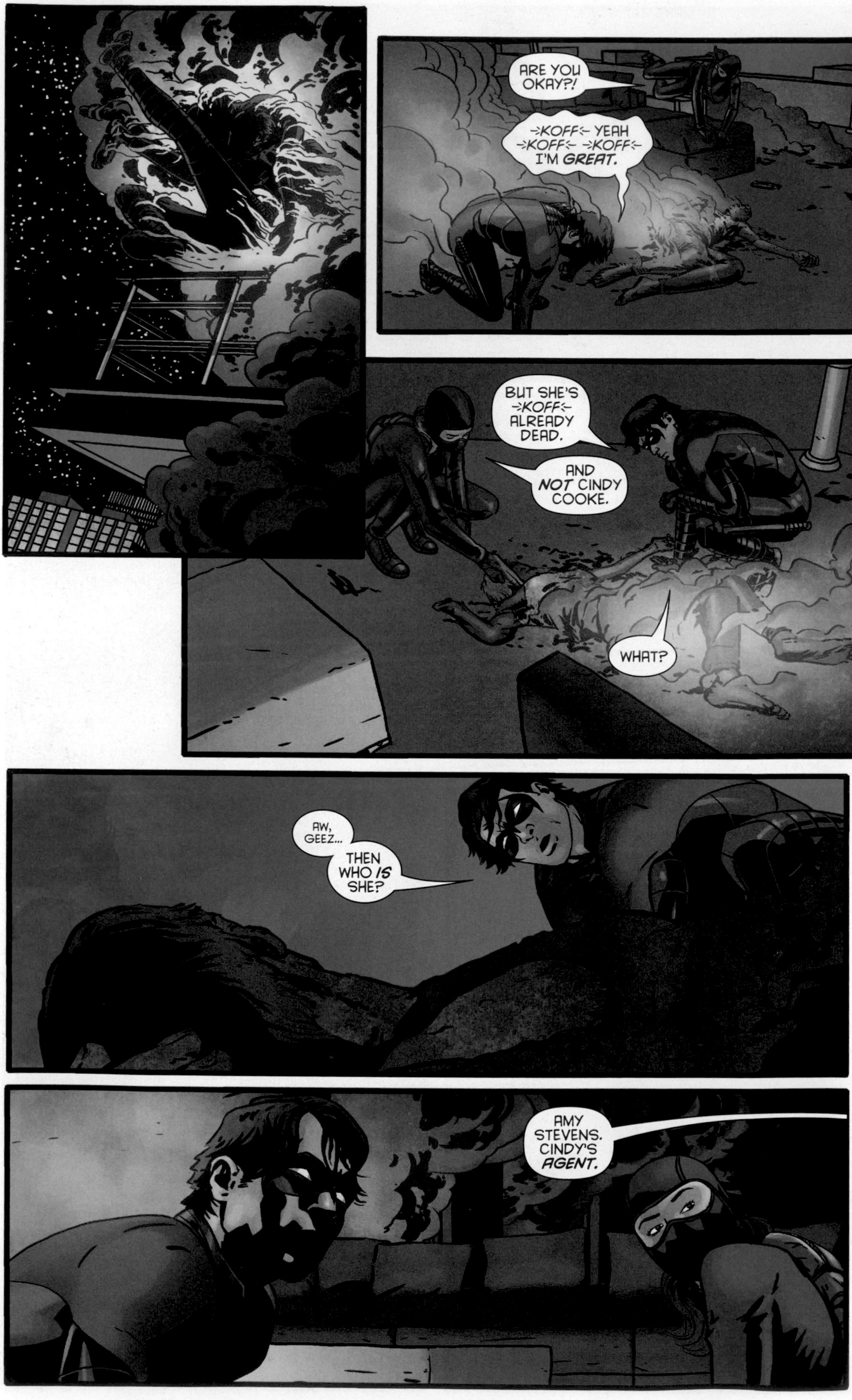
ARE YOU OKAY?!
-KOFF- YEAH -KOFF- -KOFF- I'M GREAT.
BUT SHE'S -KOFF- ALREADY DEAD.
AND NOT CINDY COOKE.
WHAT?
AW, GEEZ...
THEN WHO IS SHE?
AMY STEVENS. CINDY'S AGENT.

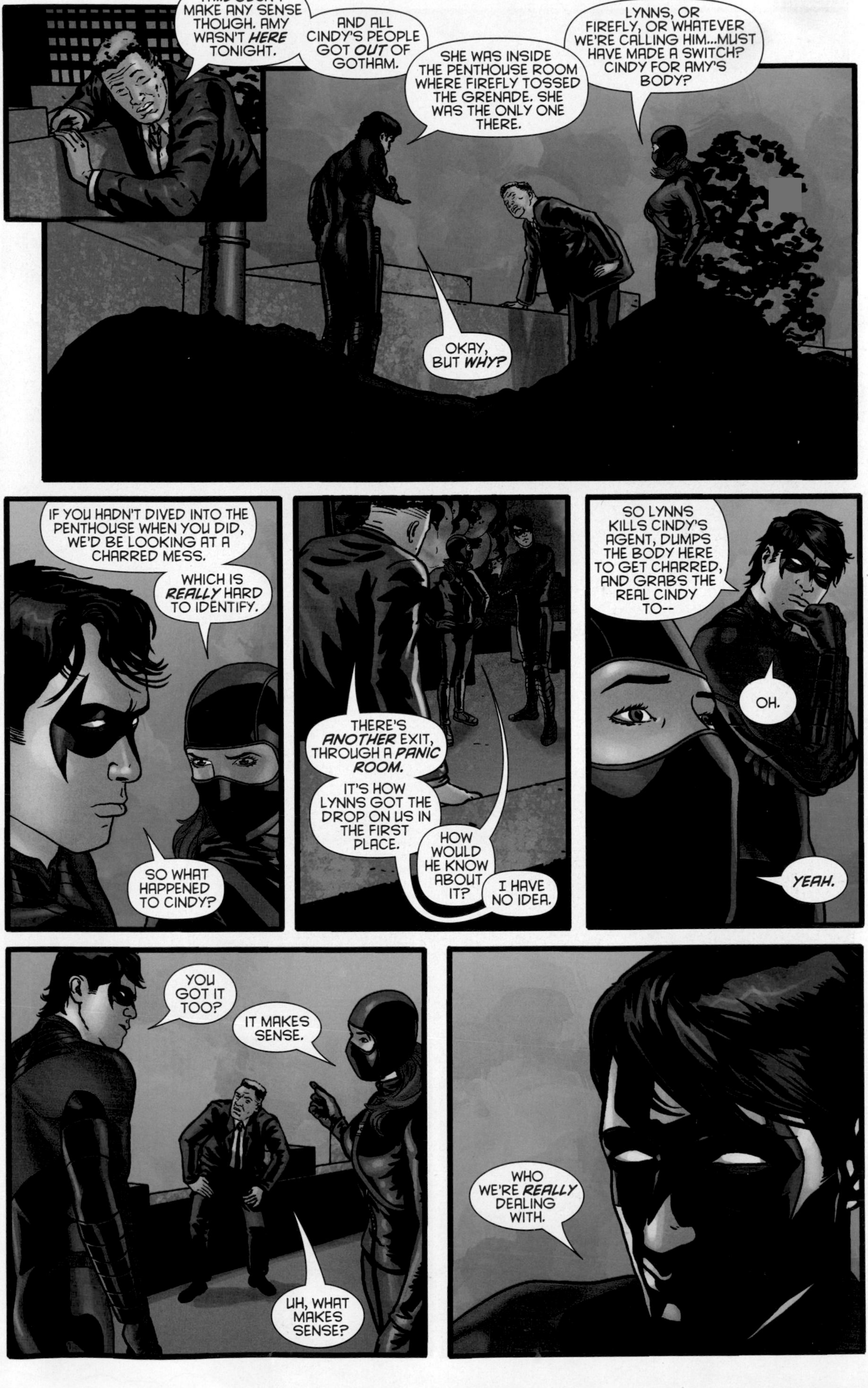

IT...DOESN'T MAKE ANY SENSE THOUGH. AMY WASN'T HERE TONIGHT.
AND ALL CINDY'S PEOPLE GOT OUT OF GOTHAM.
SHE WAS INSIDE THE PENTHOUSE ROOM WHERE FIREFLY TOSSED THE GRENADE. SHE WAS THE ONLY ONE THERE.
LYNNS, OR FIREFLY, OR WHATEVER WE'RE CALLING HIM...MUST HAVE MADE A SWITCH? CINDY FOR AMY'S BODY?
OKAY, BUT WHY?
IF YOU HADN'T DIVED INTO THE PENTHOUSE WHEN YOU DID, WE'D BE LOOKING AT A CHARRED MESS.
WHICH IS REALLY HARD TO IDENTIFY.
SO WHAT HAPPENED TO CINDY?
THERE'S ANOTHER EXIT, THROUGH A PANIC ROOM.
IT'S HOW LYNNS GOT THE DROP ON US IN THE FIRST PLACE.
HOW WOULD HE KNOW ABOUT IT?
I HAVE NO IDEA.
SO LYNNS KILLS CINDY'S AGENT, DUMPS THE BODY HERE TO GET CHARRED, AND GRABS THE REAL CINDY TO--
OH.
YEAH.
YOU GOT IT TOO?
IT MAKES SENSE.
UH, WHAT MAKES SENSE?
WHO WE'RE REALLY DEALING WITH.

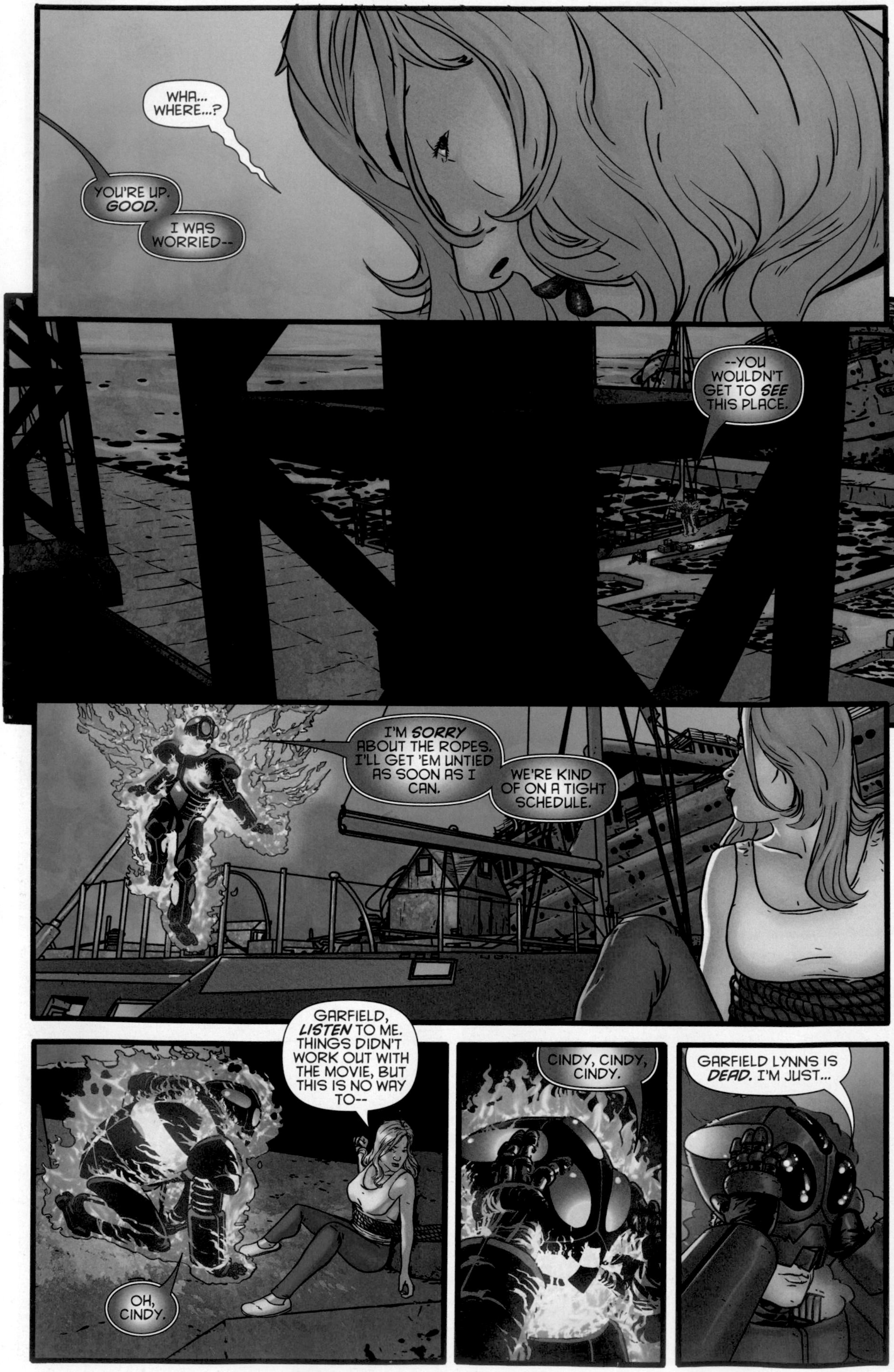
WHA... WHERE...?
YOU'RE UP. GOOD.
I WAS WORRIED--
--YOU WOULDN'T GET TO SEE THIS PLACE.
I'M SORRY ABOUT THE ROPES. I'LL GET 'EM UNTIED AS SOON AS I CAN.
WE'RE KIND OF ON A TIGHT SCHEDULE.
GARFIELD, LISTEN TO ME. THINGS DIDN'T WORK OUT WITH THE MOVIE, BUT THIS IS NO WAY TO--
OH, CINDY.
CINDY, CINDY, CINDY.
GARFIELD LYNNS IS DEAD. I'M JUST...

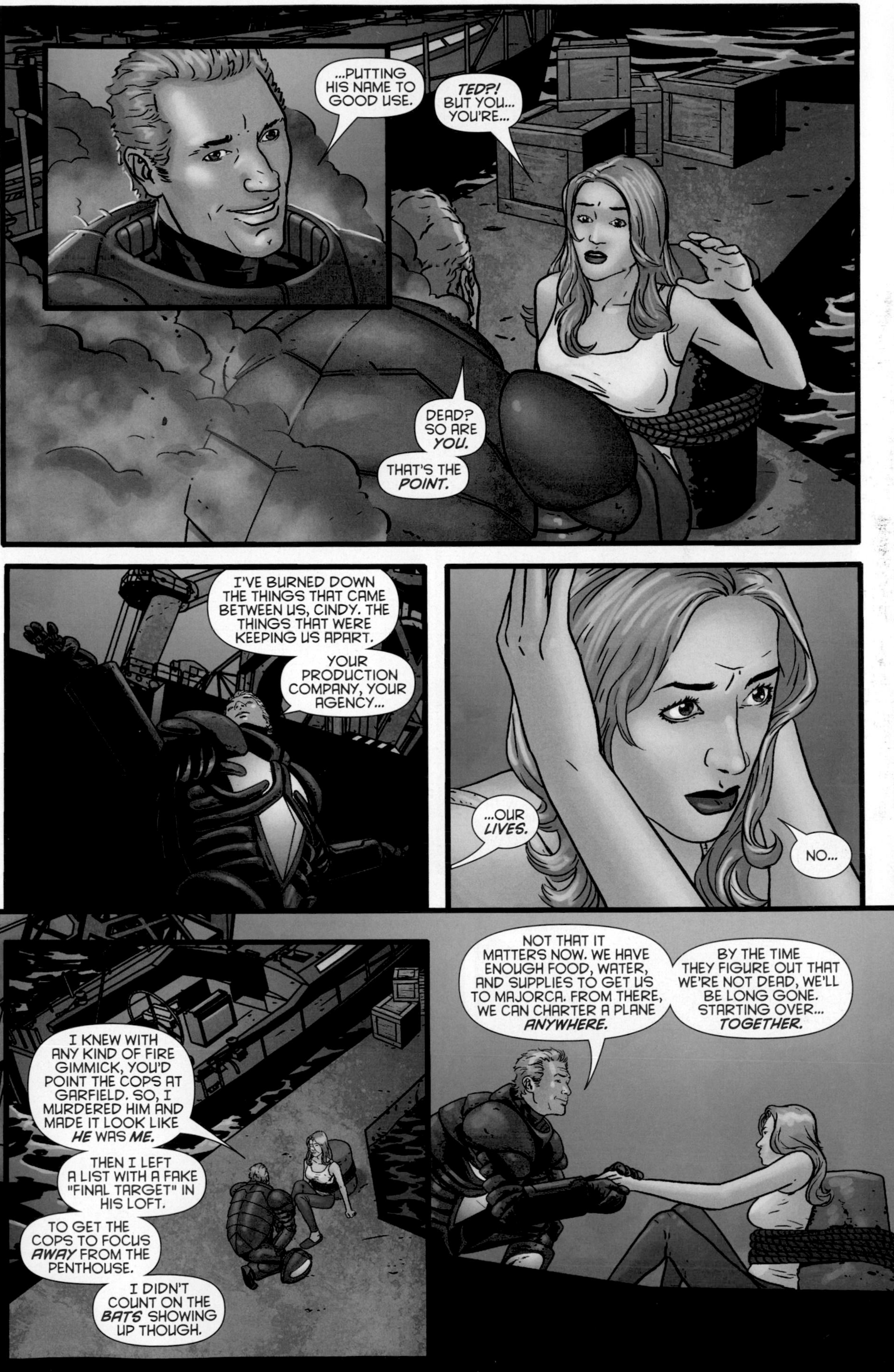
...PUTTING HIS NAME TO GOOD USE.
TED?! BUT YOU... YOU'RE...
DEAD? SO ARE YOU.
THAT'S THE POINT.
I'VE BURNED DOWN THE THINGS THAT CAME BETWEEN US, CINDY. THE THINGS THAT WERE KEEPING US APART.
YOUR PRODUCTION COMPANY, YOUR AGENCY...
...OUR LIVES.
NO...
I KNEW WITH ANY KIND OF FIRE GIMMICK, YOU'D POINT THE COPS AT GARFIELD. SO, I MURDERED HIM AND MADE IT LOOK LIKE HE WAS ME.
THEN I LEFT A LIST WITH A FAKE "FINAL TARGET" IN HIS LOFT.
TO GET THE COPS TO FOCUS AWAY FROM THE PENTHOUSE.
I DIDN'T COUNT ON THE BATS SHOWING UP THOUGH.
NOT THAT IT MATTERS NOW. WE HAVE ENOUGH FOOD, WATER, AND SUPPLIES TO GET US TO MAJORCA. FROM THERE, WE CAN CHARTER A PLANE ANYWHERE.
BY THE TIME THEY FIGURE OUT THAT WE'RE NOT DEAD, WE'LL BE LONG GONE. STARTING OVER... TOGETHER.

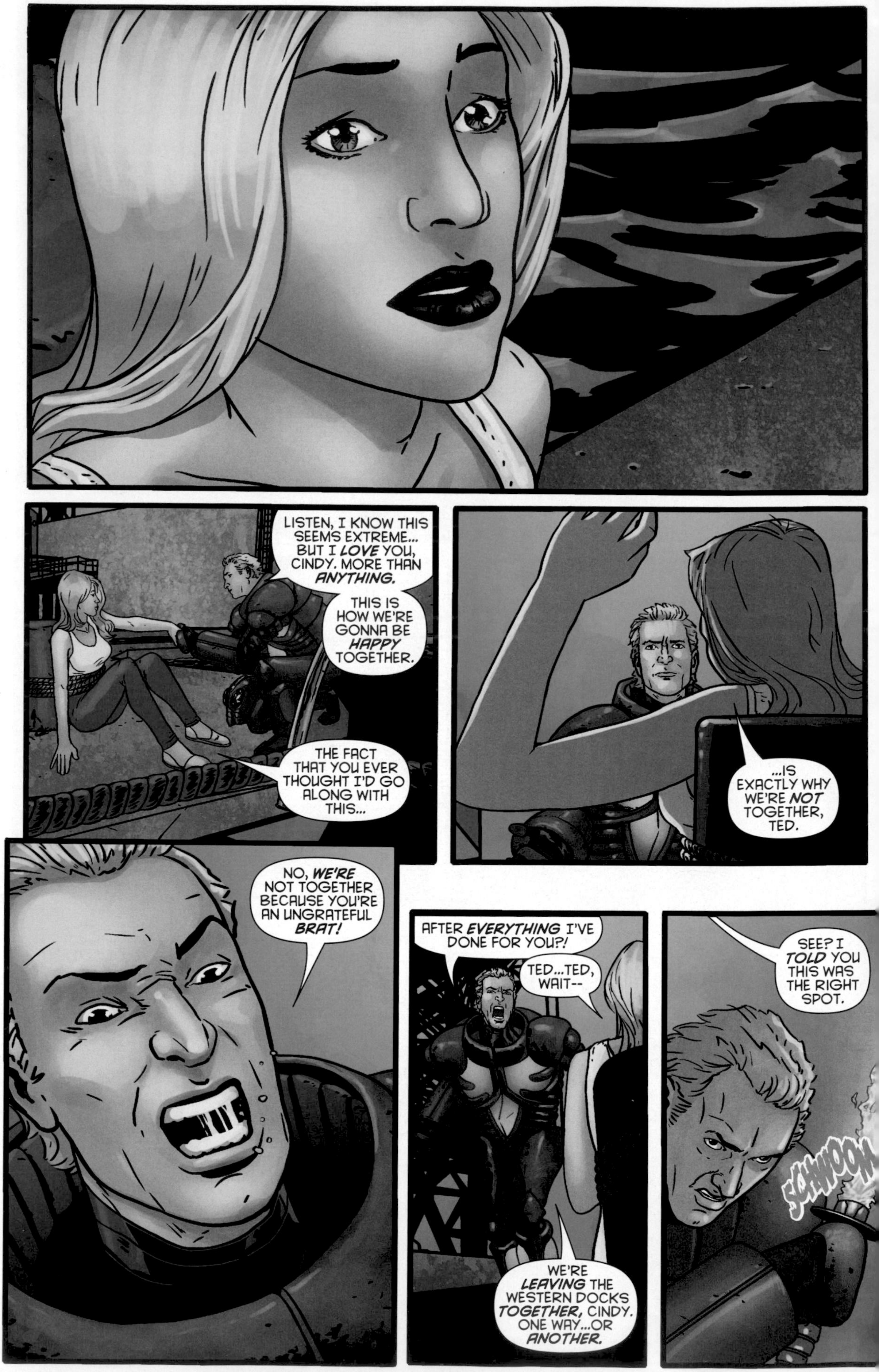
LISTEN, I KNOW THIS SEEMS EXTREME... BUT I LOVE YOU, CINDY. MORE THAN ANYTHING.
THIS IS HOW WE'RE GONNA BE HAPPY TOGETHER.
THE FACT THAT YOU EVER THOUGHT I'D GO ALONG WITH THIS...
...IS EXACTLY WHY WE'RE NOT TOGETHER, TED.
NO, WE'RE NOT TOGETHER BECAUSE YOU'RE AN UNGRATEFUL BRAT!
AFTER EVERYTHING I'VE DONE FOR YOU?!
TED...TED, WAIT--
WE'RE LEAVING THE WESTERN DOCKS TOGETHER, CINDY. ONE WAY...OR ANOTHER.
SEE? I TOLD YOU THIS WAS THE RIGHT SPOT.
SCHWOOM

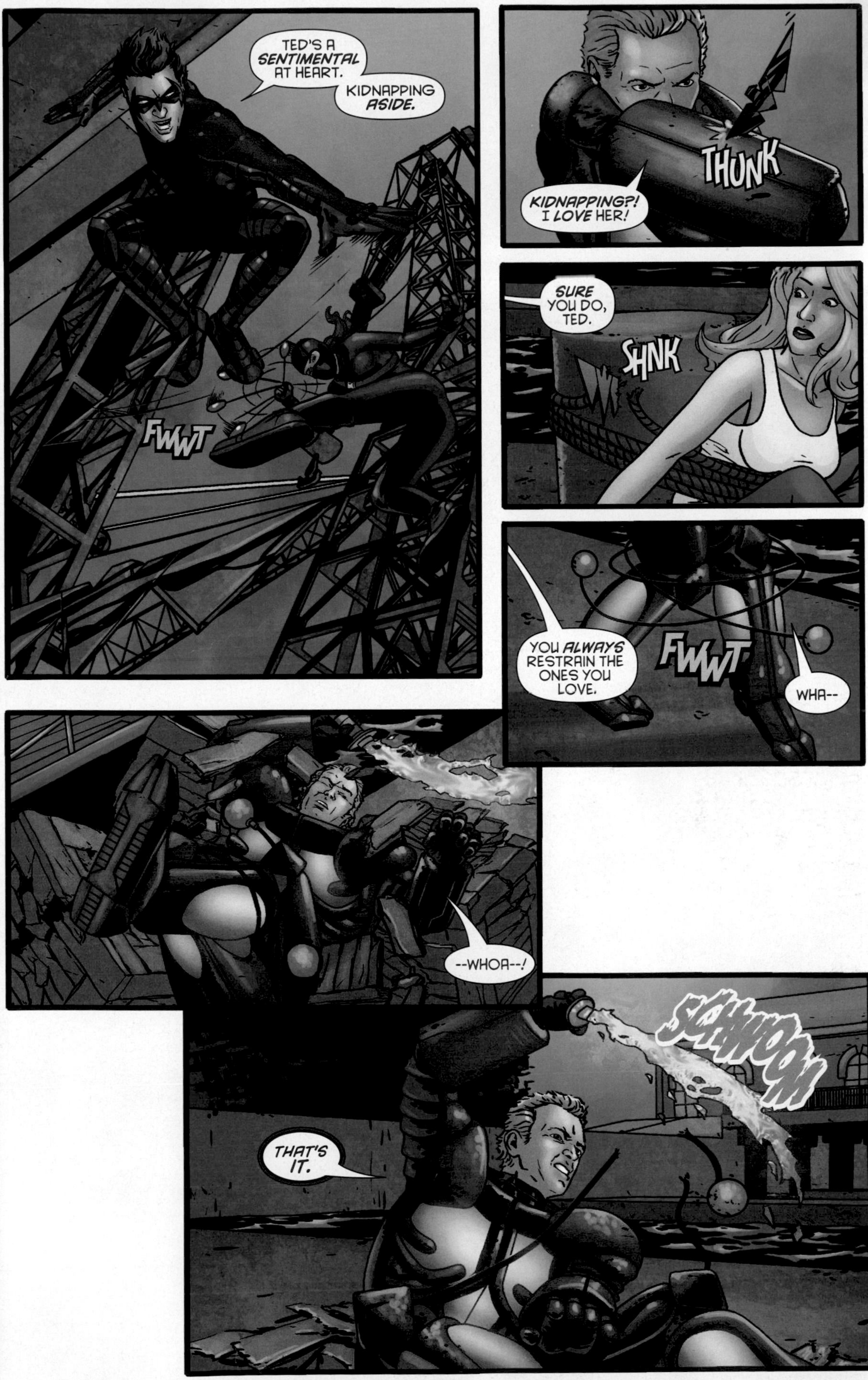
TED'S A SENTIMENTAL AT HEART.
KIDNAPPING ASIDE.
FWWT
THUNK
KIDNAPPING?! I LOVE HER!
SURE YOU DO, TED.
SHNK
YOU ALWAYS RESTRAIN THE ONES YOU LOVE.
FWWT
WHA--
--WHOA--!
SCHWOOM
THAT'S IT.

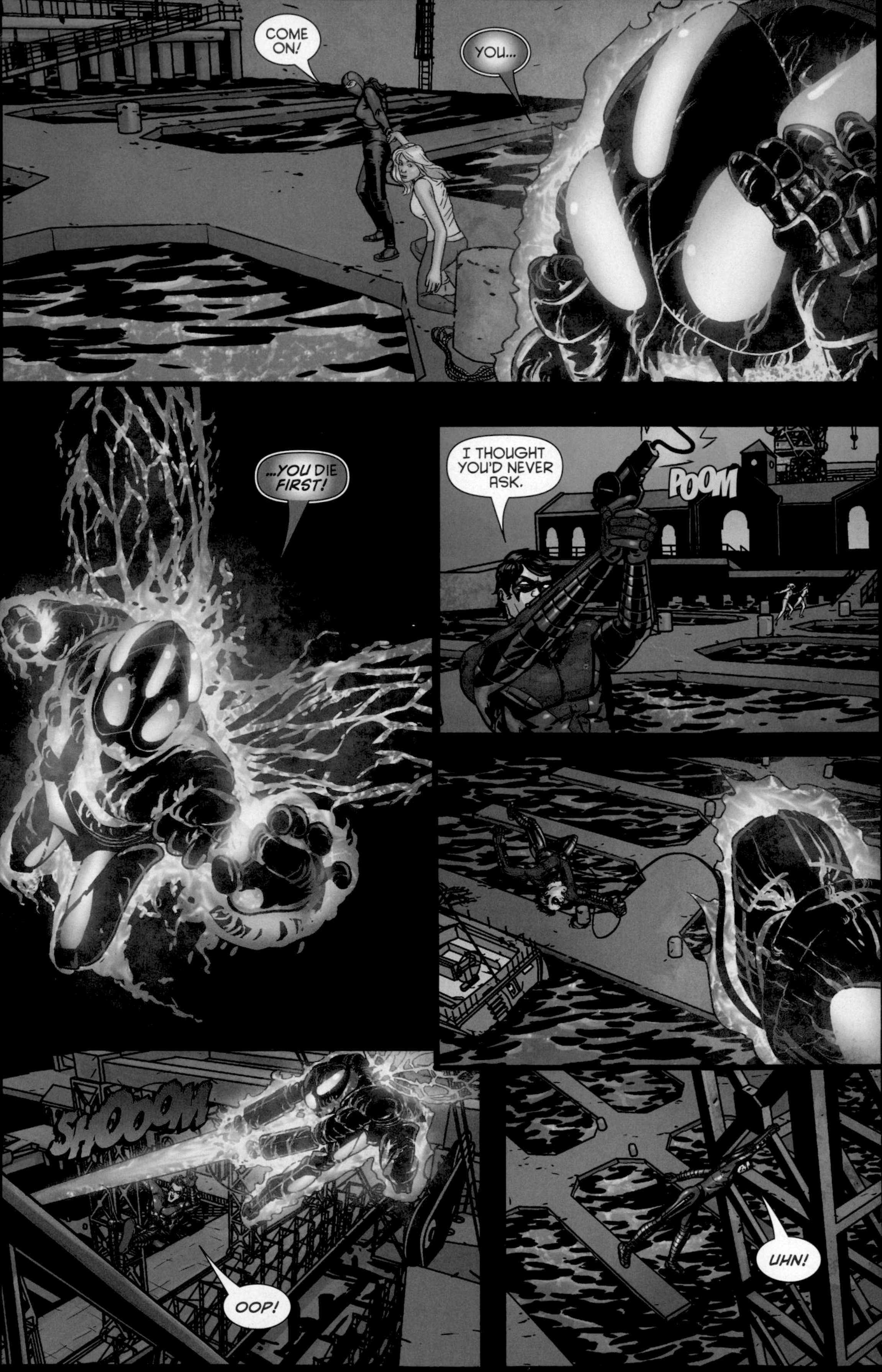
COME ON!
YOU...
...YOU DIE FIRST!
I THOUGHT YOU'D NEVER ASK.
POOM
SHOOOM
OOP!
UHN!

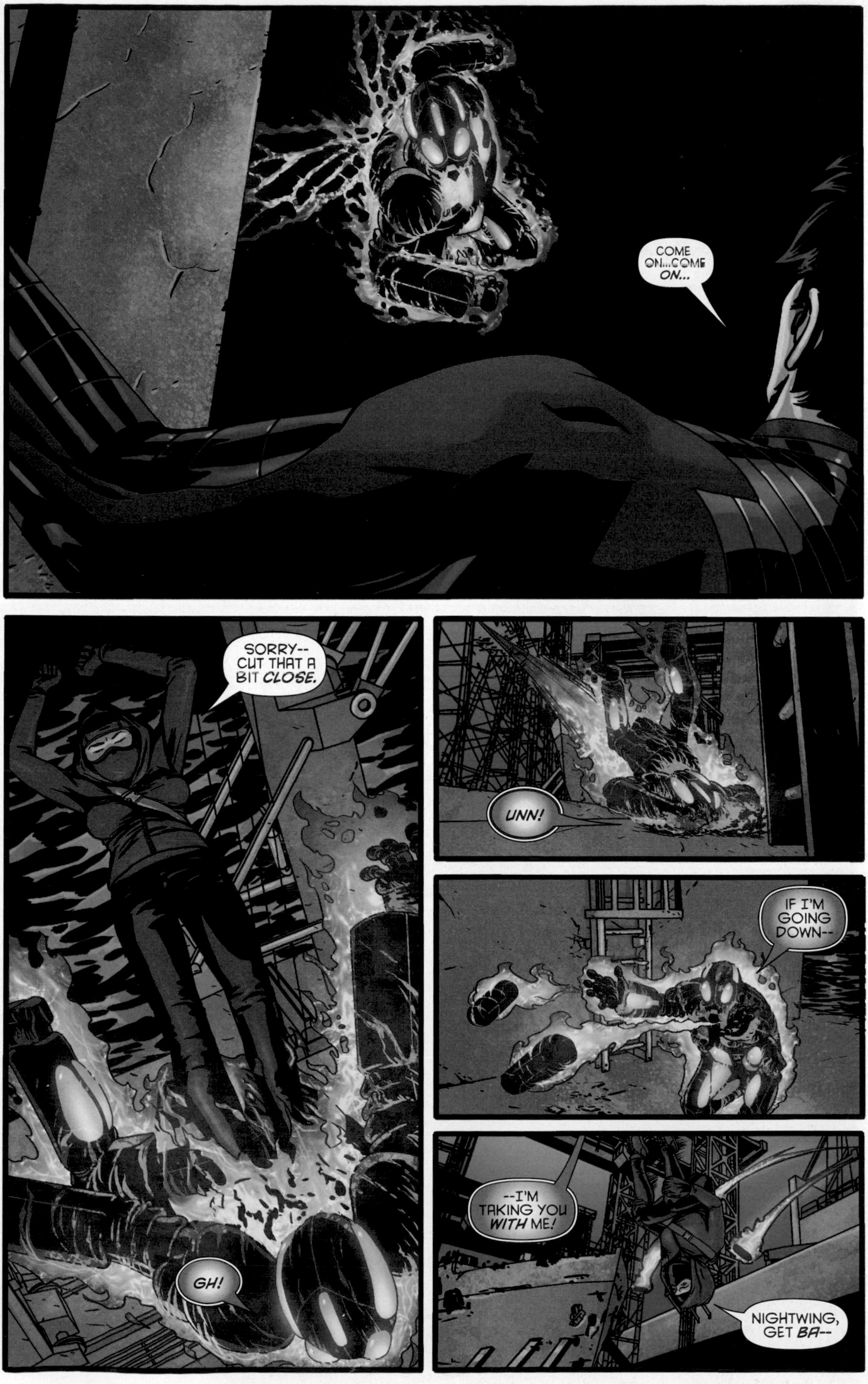
COME ON...COME ON...
SORRY-- CUT THAT A BIT CLOSE.
GH!
UNN!
IF I'M GOING DOWN--
--I'M TAKING YOU WITH ME!
NIGHTWING, GET BA--

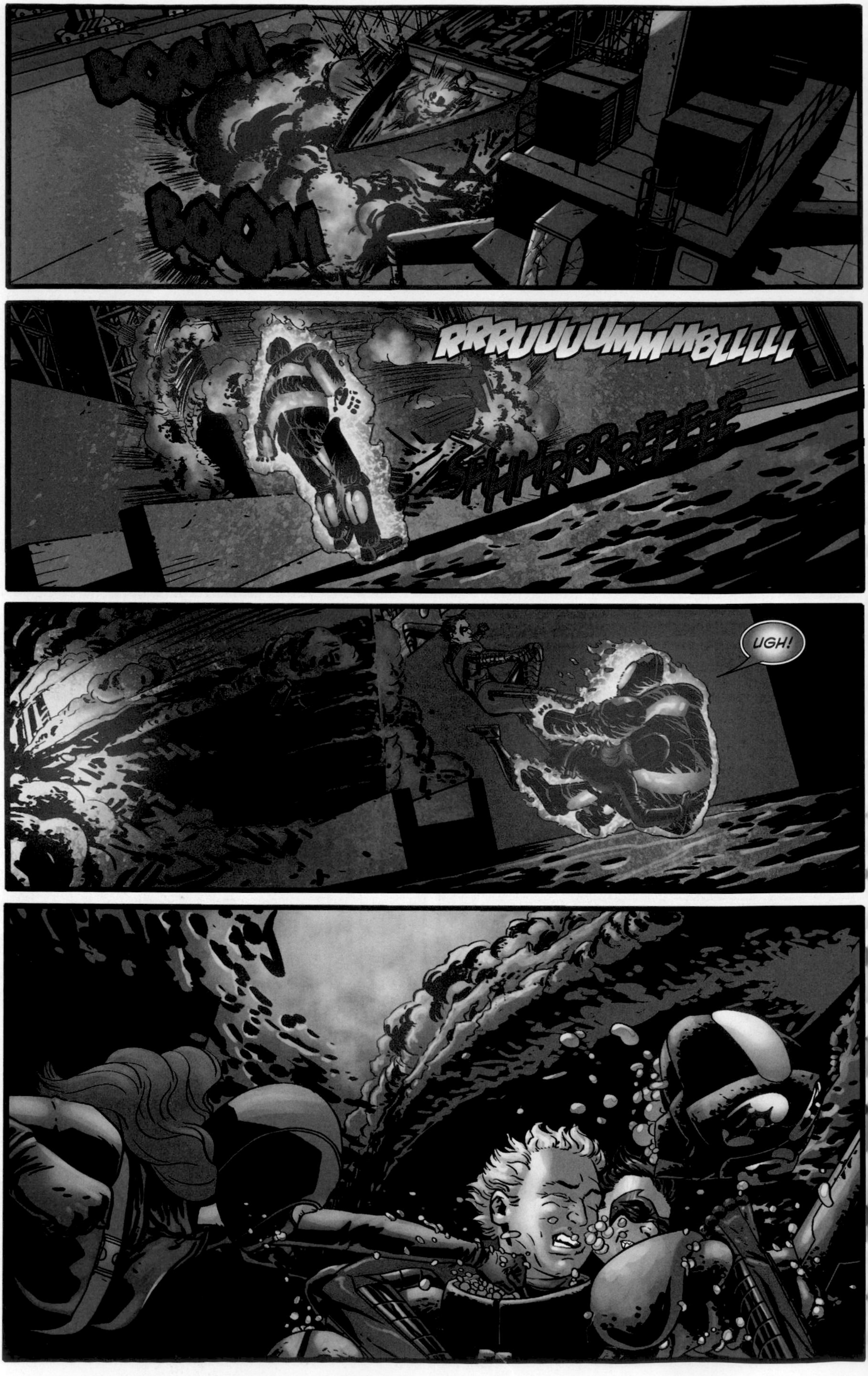
BOOM
BOOM
RRRUUUUMMMBLLLLL
SHHHRRRREEEEE
UGH!

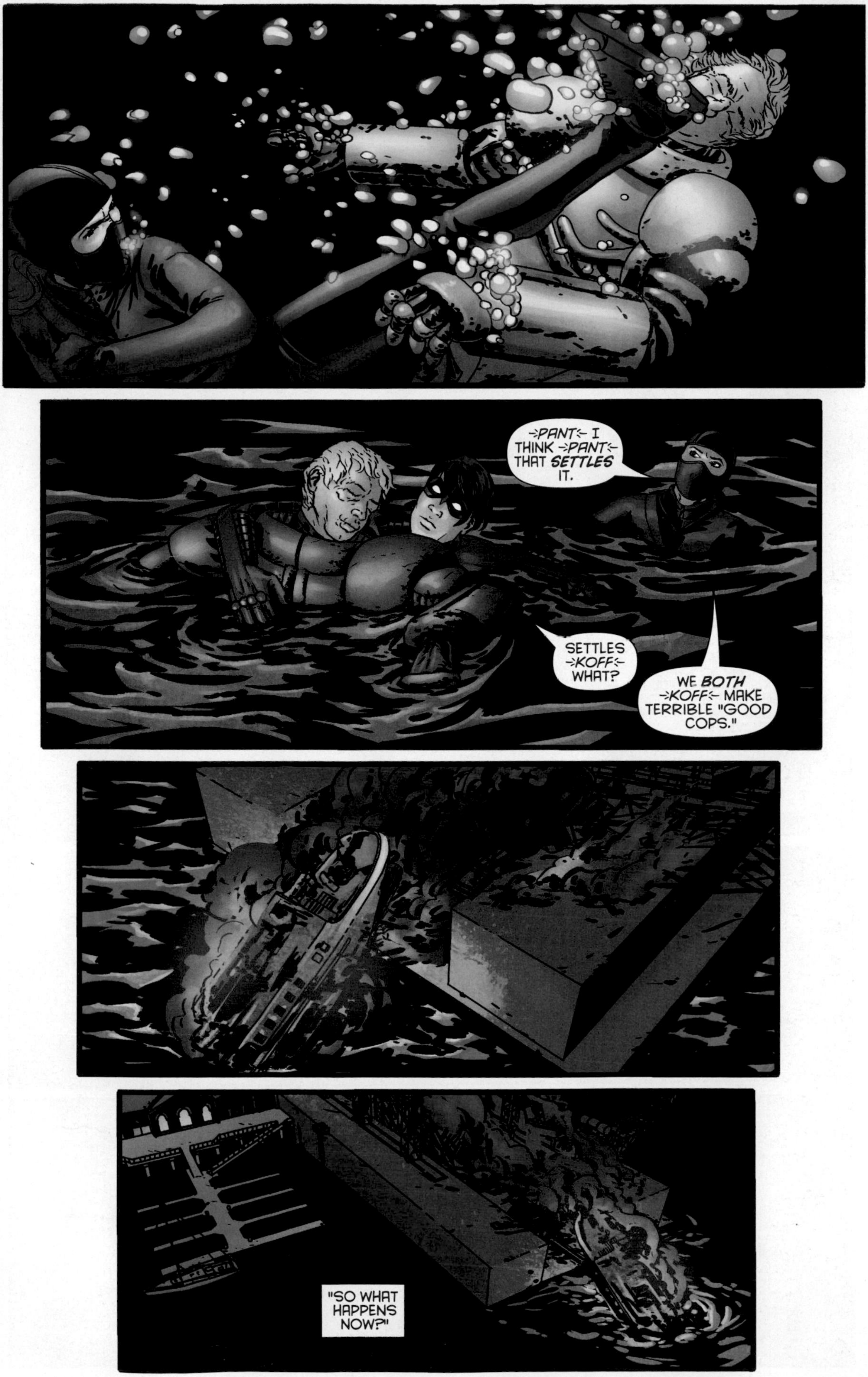

-PANT- I THINK -PANT- THAT *SETTLES* IT.
SETTLES -KOFF- WHAT?
WE *BOTH* -KOFF- MAKE TERRIBLE "GOOD COPS."
"SO WHAT HAPPENS NOW?"

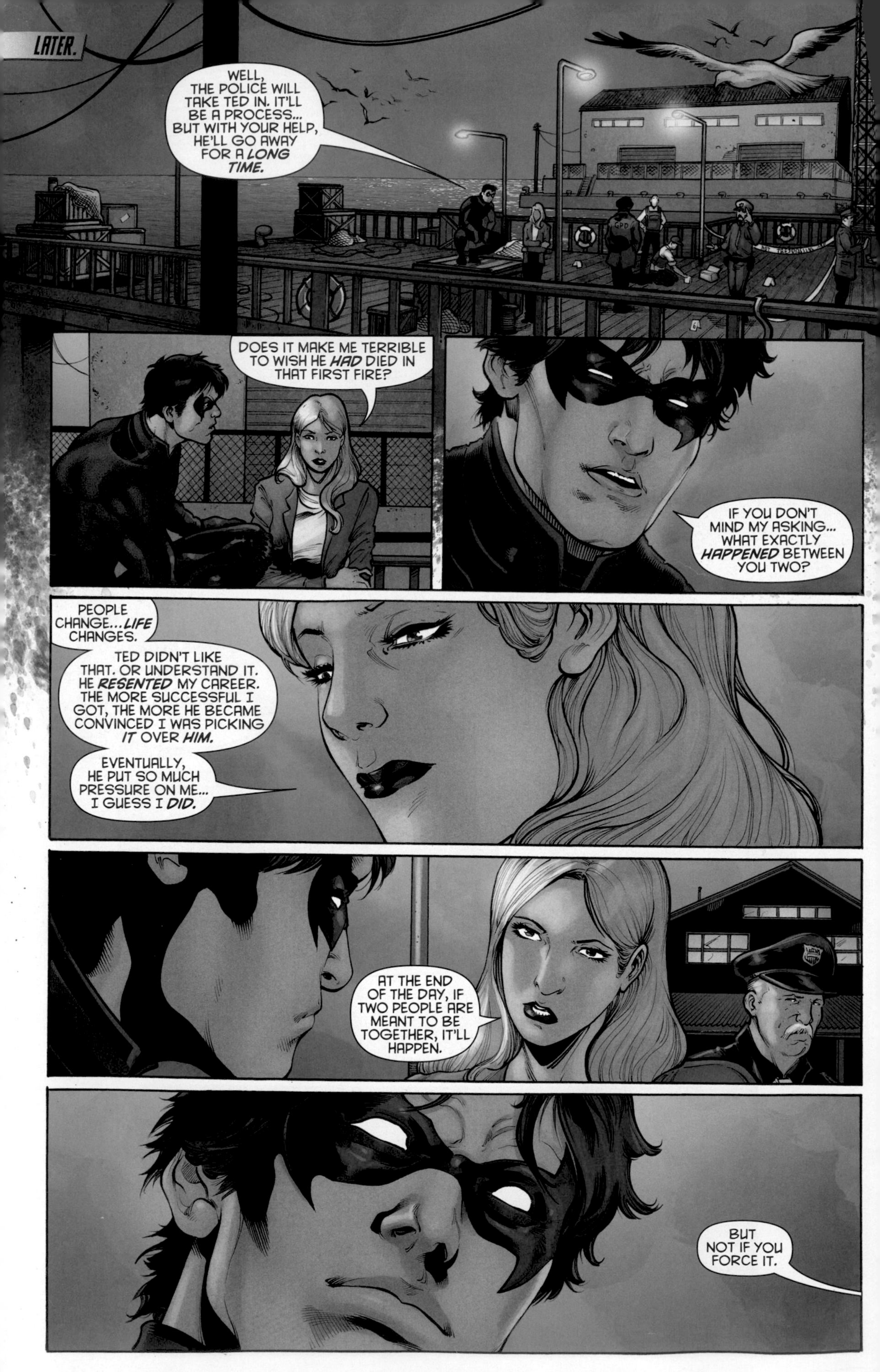
LATER.
WELL, THE POLICE WILL TAKE TED IN. IT'LL BE A PROCESS... BUT WITH YOUR HELP, HE'LL GO AWAY FOR A LONG TIME.
DOES IT MAKE ME TERRIBLE TO WISH HE HAD DIED IN THAT FIRST FIRE?
IF YOU DON'T MIND MY ASKING... WHAT EXACTLY HAPPENED BETWEEN YOU TWO?
PEOPLE CHANGE...LIFE CHANGES.
TED DIDN'T LIKE THAT. OR UNDERSTAND IT. HE RESENTED MY CAREER. THE MORE SUCCESSFUL I GOT, THE MORE HE BECAME CONVINCED I WAS PICKING IT OVER HIM.
EVENTUALLY, HE PUT SO MUCH PRESSURE ON ME... I GUESS I DID.
AT THE END OF THE DAY, IF TWO PEOPLE ARE MEANT TO BE TOGETHER, IT'LL HAPPEN.
BUT NOT IF YOU FORCE IT.

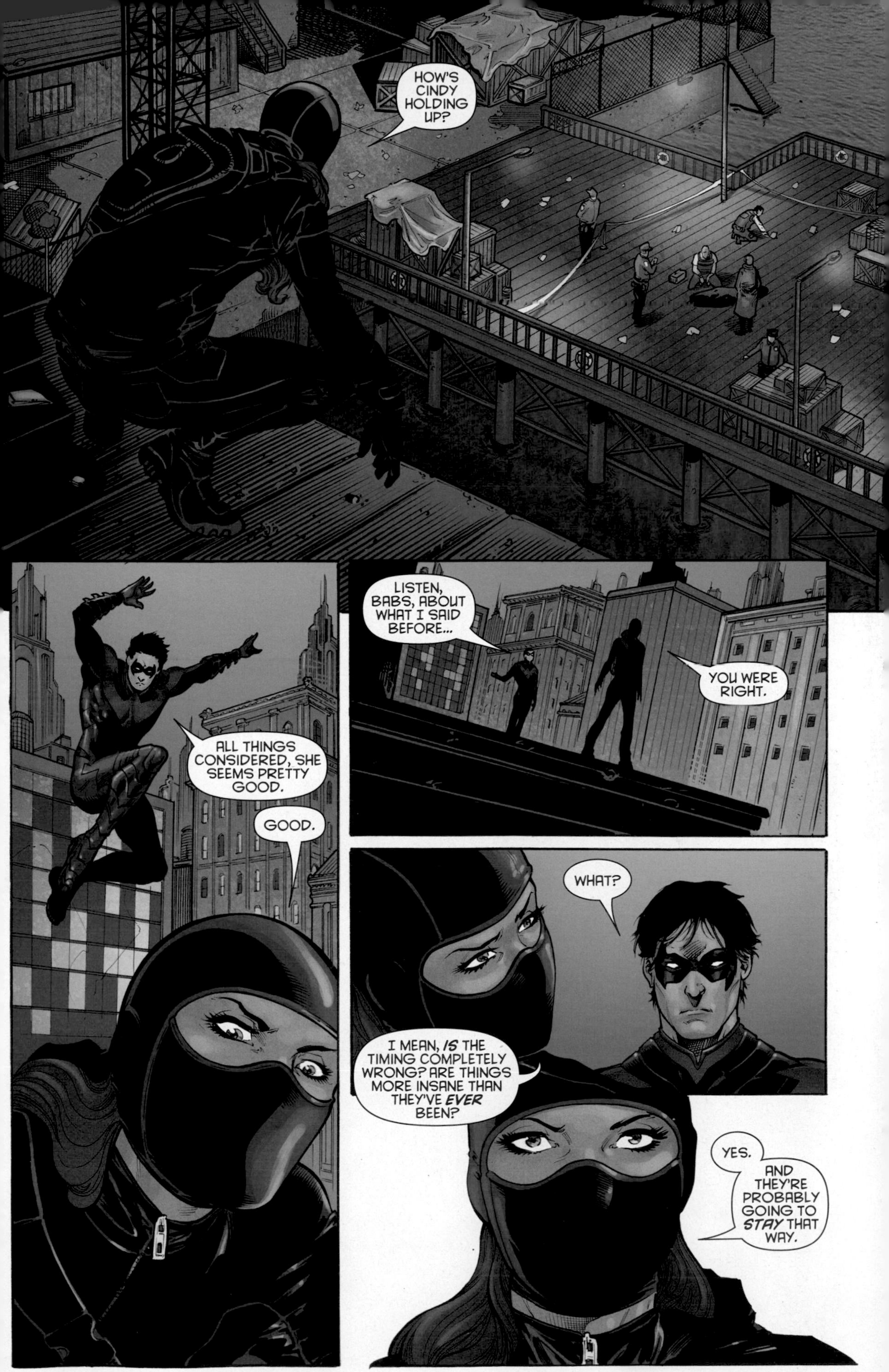
HOW'S CINDY HOLDING UP?
ALL THINGS CONSIDERED, SHE SEEMS PRETTY GOOD.
GOOD.
LISTEN, BABS, ABOUT WHAT I SAID BEFORE...
YOU WERE RIGHT.
WHAT?
I MEAN, *IS* THE TIMING COMPLETELY WRONG? ARE THINGS MORE INSANE THAN THEY'VE *EVER* BEEN?
YES.
AND THEY'RE PROBABLY GOING TO *STAY* THAT WAY.

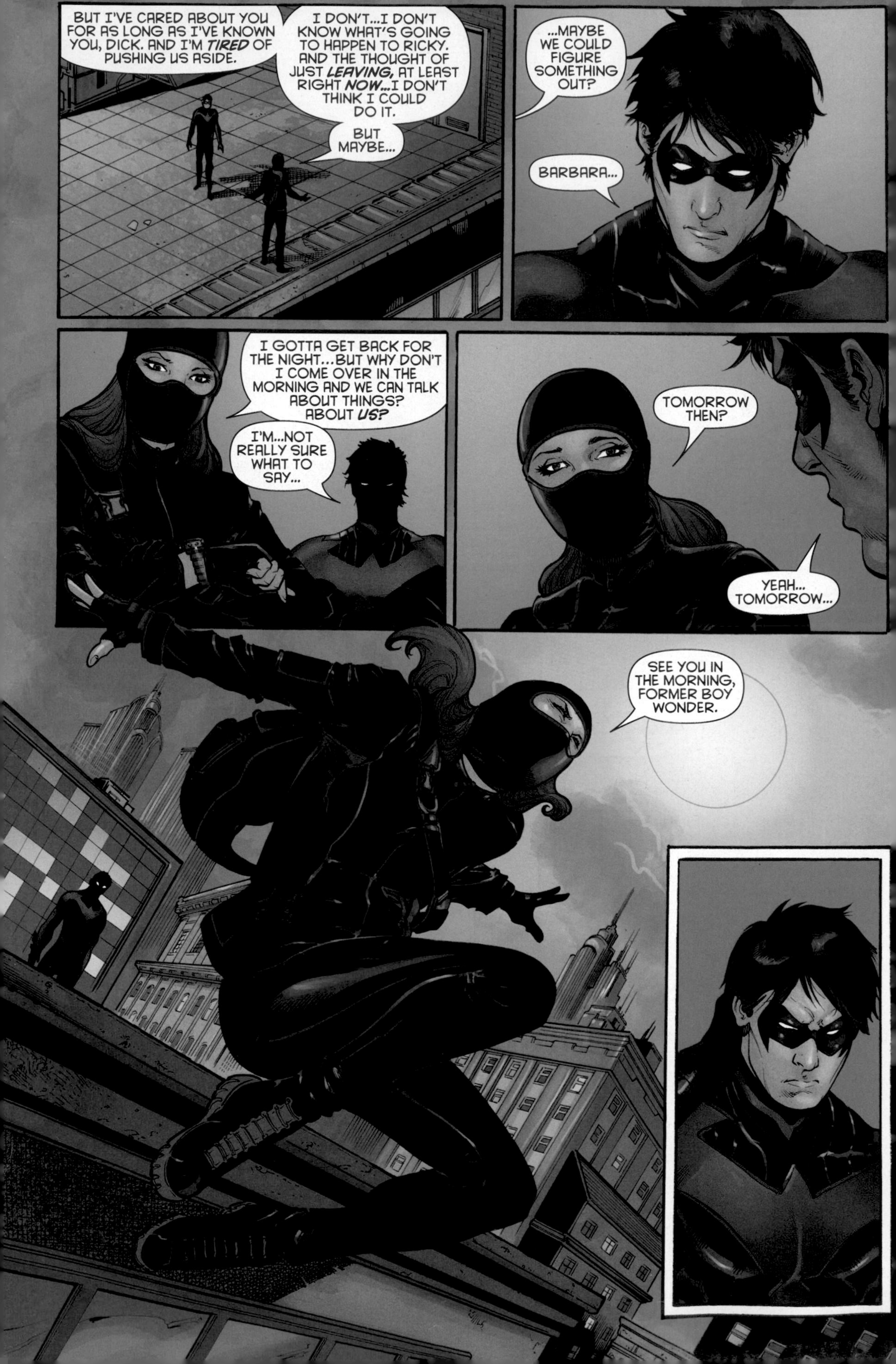
BUT I'VE CARED ABOUT YOU FOR AS LONG AS I'VE KNOWN YOU, DICK. AND I'M *TIRED* OF PUSHING US ASIDE.
I DON'T...I DON'T KNOW WHAT'S GOING TO HAPPEN TO RICKY. AND THE THOUGHT OF JUST *LEAVING,* AT LEAST RIGHT *NOW...*I DON'T THINK I COULD DO IT.
BUT MAYBE...
...MAYBE WE COULD FIGURE SOMETHING OUT?
BARBARA...
I GOTTA GET BACK FOR THE NIGHT...BUT WHY DON'T I COME OVER IN THE MORNING AND WE CAN TALK ABOUT THINGS? ABOUT *US?*
I'M...NOT REALLY SURE WHAT TO SAY...
TOMORROW THEN?
YEAH... TOMORROW...
SEE YOU IN THE MORNING, FORMER BOY WONDER.

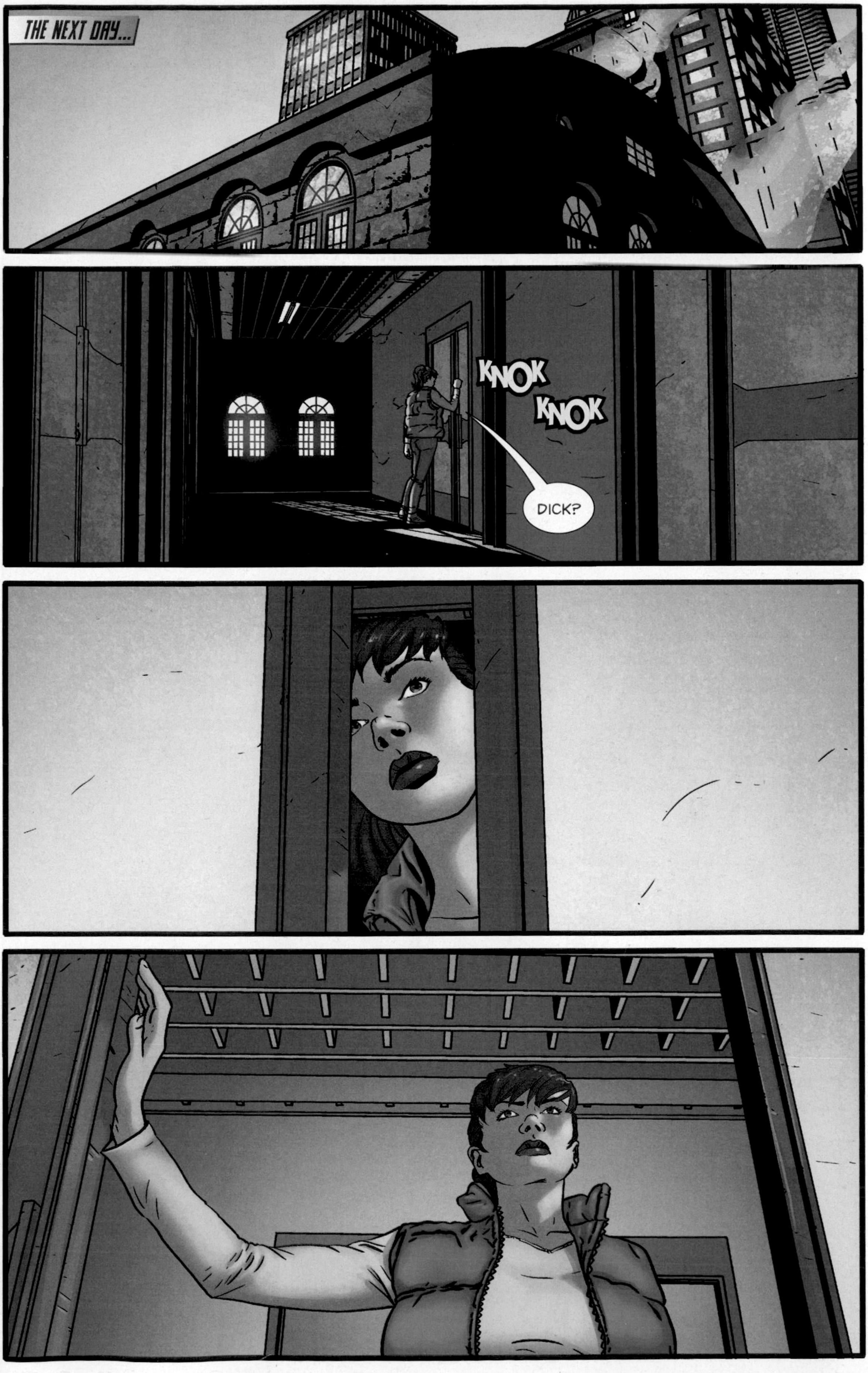
THE NEXT DAY...
KNOK
KNOK
DICK?

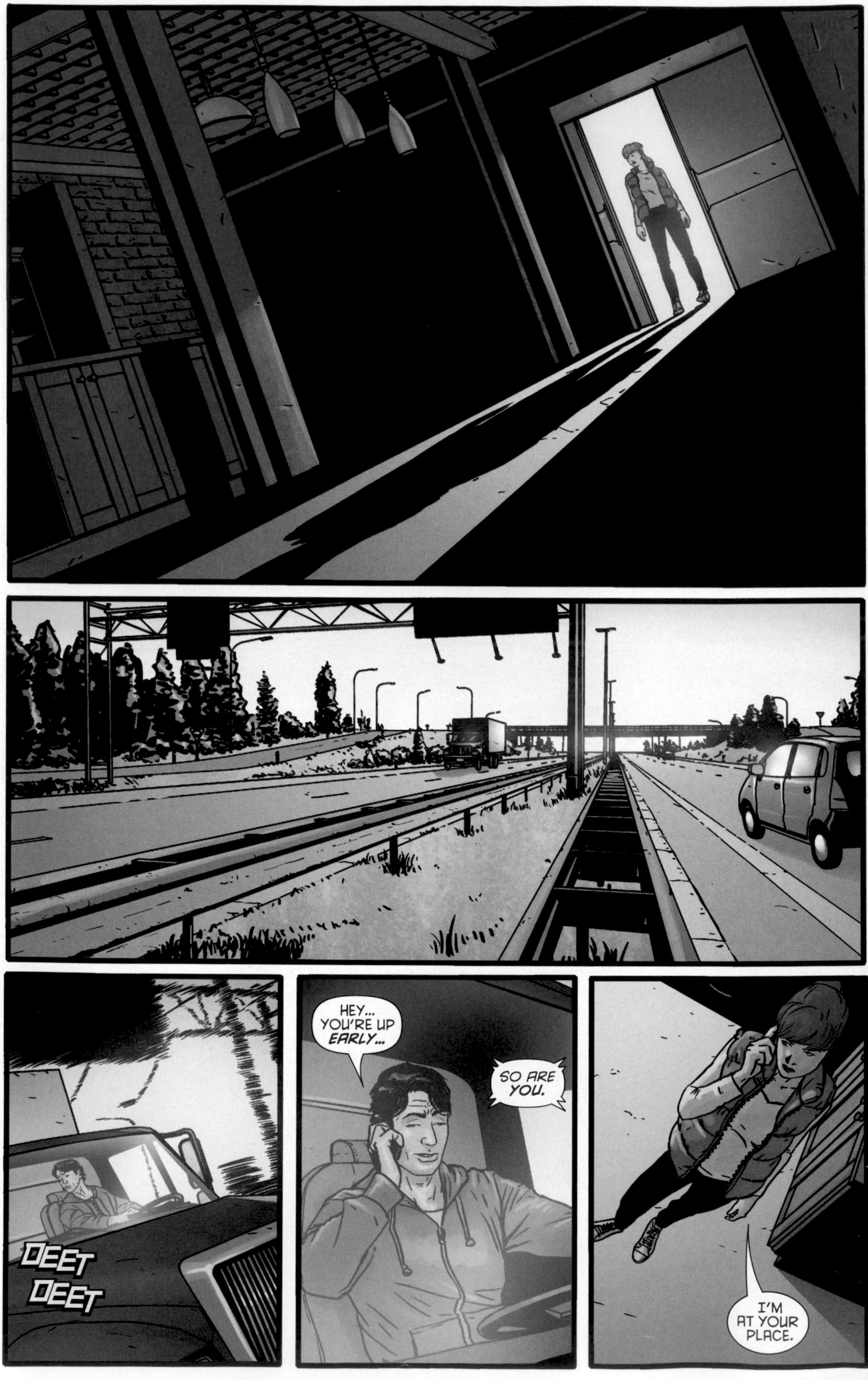
DEET
DEET
HEY... YOU'RE UP EARLY...
SO ARE YOU.
I'M AT YOUR PLACE.

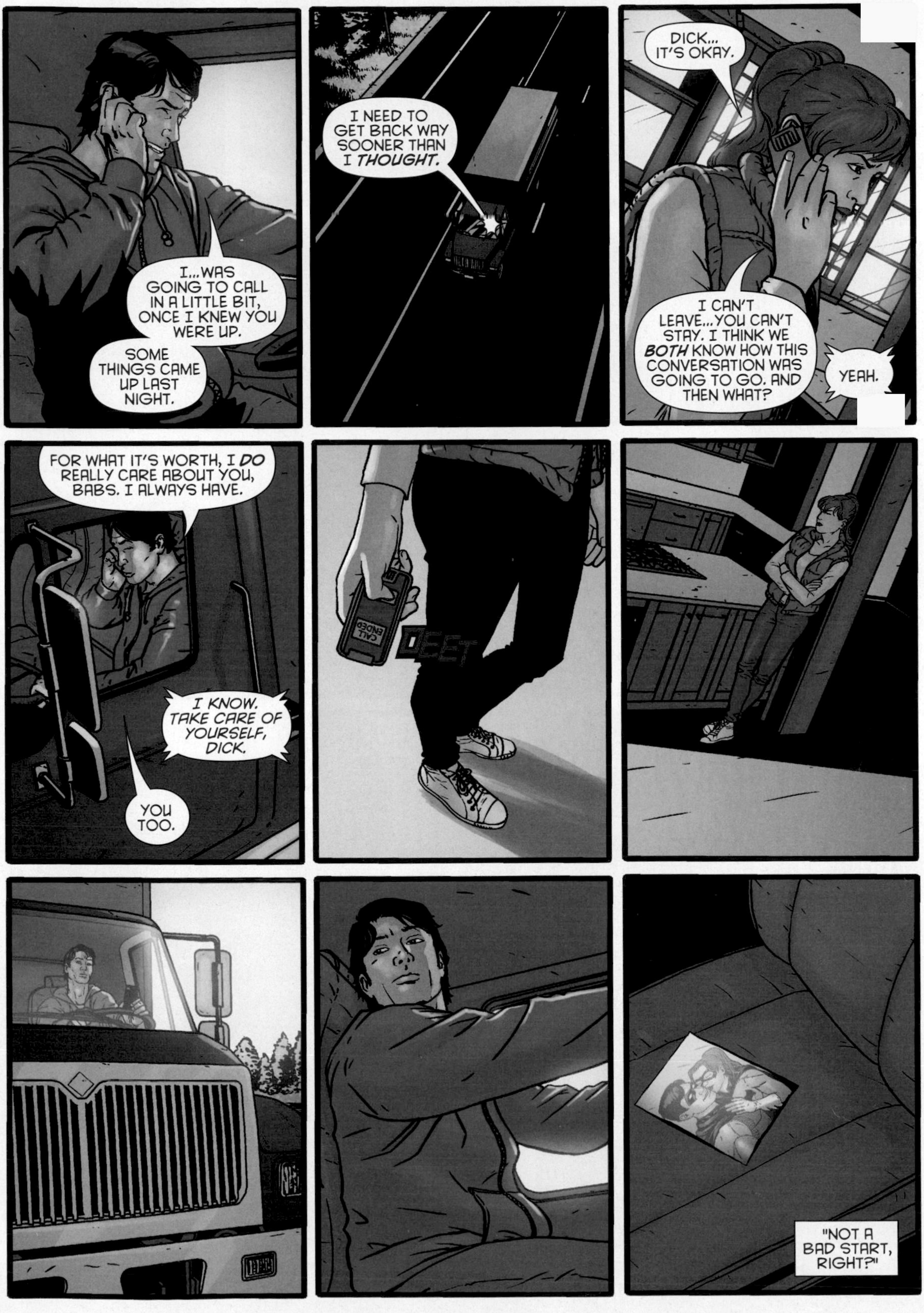
I...WAS GOING TO CALL IN A LITTLE BIT, ONCE I KNEW YOU WERE UP.
SOME THINGS CAME UP LAST NIGHT.
I NEED TO GET BACK WAY SOONER THAN I THOUGHT.
DICK... IT'S OKAY.
I CAN'T LEAVE...YOU CAN'T STAY. I THINK WE BOTH KNOW HOW THIS CONVERSATION WAS GOING TO GO. AND THEN WHAT?
YEAH.
FOR WHAT IT'S WORTH, I DO REALLY CARE ABOUT YOU, BABS. I ALWAYS HAVE.
I KNOW. TAKE CARE OF YOURSELF, DICK.
YOU TOO.
CALL ENDED
DEET
"NOT A BAD START, RIGHT?"

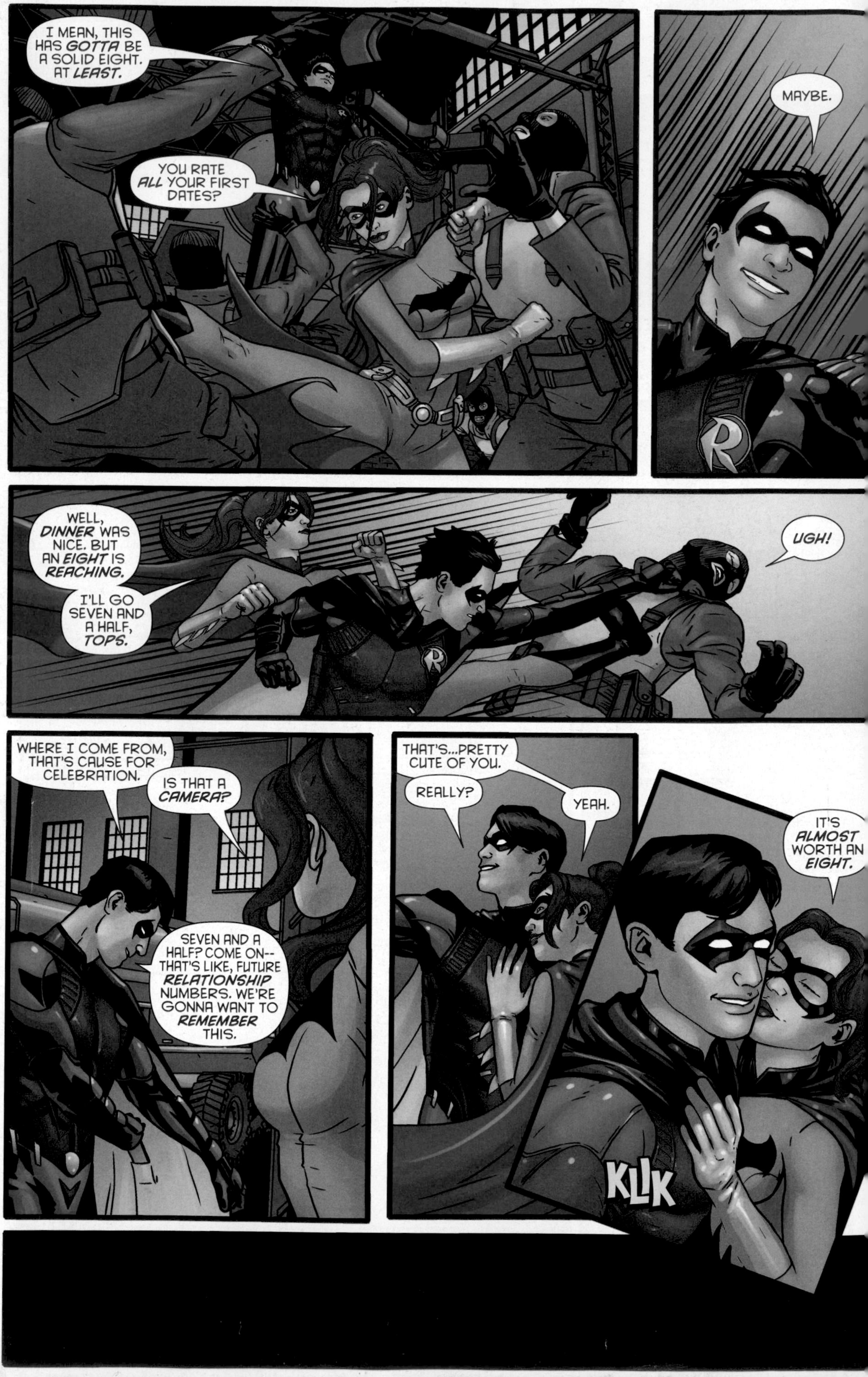
I MEAN, THIS HAS GOTTA BE A SOLID EIGHT. AT LEAST.
YOU RATE ALL YOUR FIRST DATES?
MAYBE.
WELL, DINNER WAS NICE. BUT AN EIGHT IS REACHING.
I'LL GO SEVEN AND A HALF, TOPS.
UGH!
WHERE I COME FROM, THAT'S CAUSE FOR CELEBRATION.
IS THAT A CAMERA?
SEVEN AND A HALF? COME ON-- THAT'S LIKE, FUTURE RELATIONSHIP NUMBERS. WE'RE GONNA WANT TO REMEMBER THIS.
THAT'S...PRETTY CUTE OF YOU.
REALLY?
YEAH.
IT'S ALMOST WORTH AN EIGHT.
KLIK

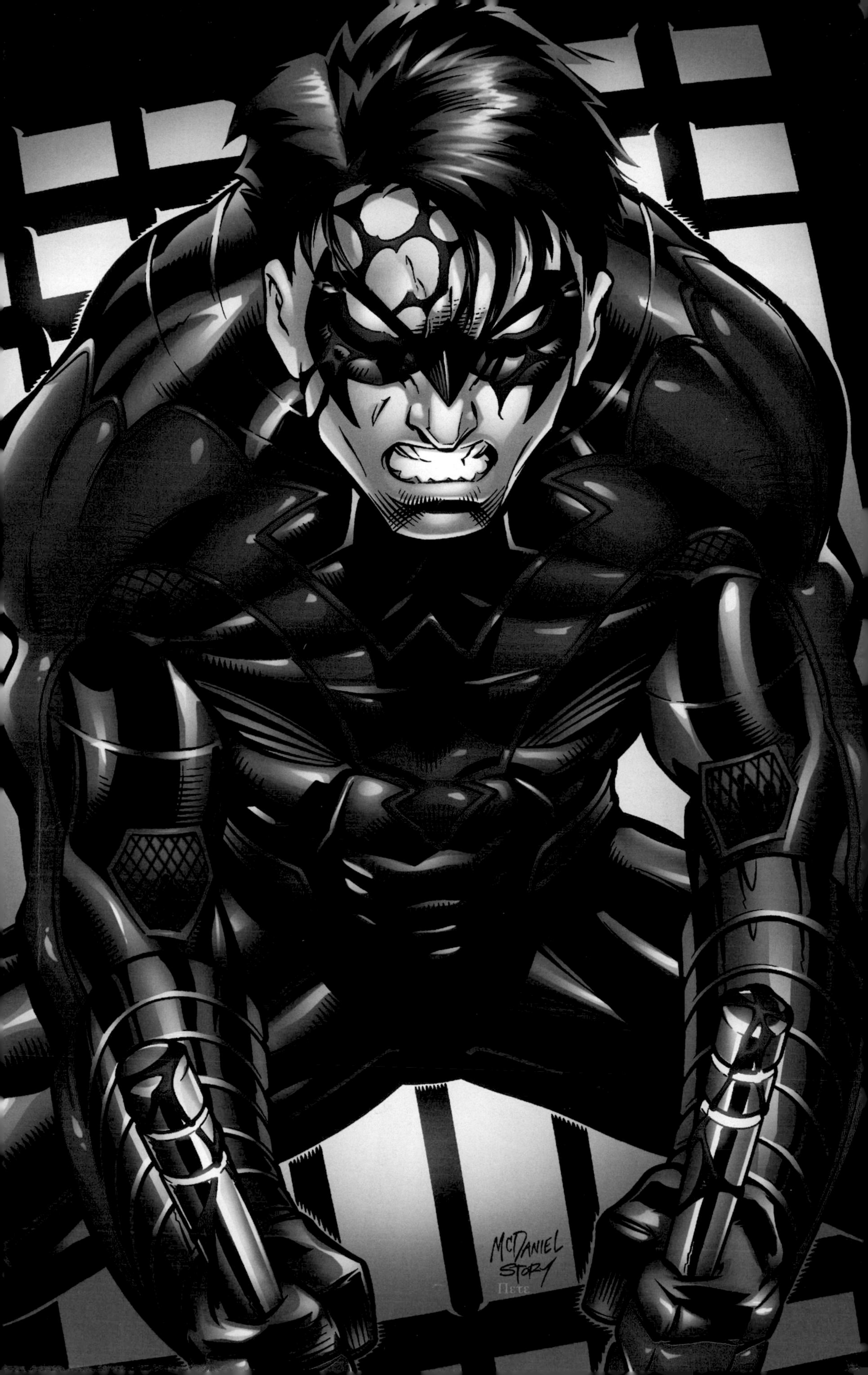
McDANIEL
STORY

SOME STRINGS ATTACHED

KYLE HIGGINS writer WILL CONRAD with CLIFF RICHARDS artists PETE PANTAZIS colorist
DEZI SIENTY letterer cover art by SCOTT MCDANIEL, KARL STORY and PETE PANTAZIS

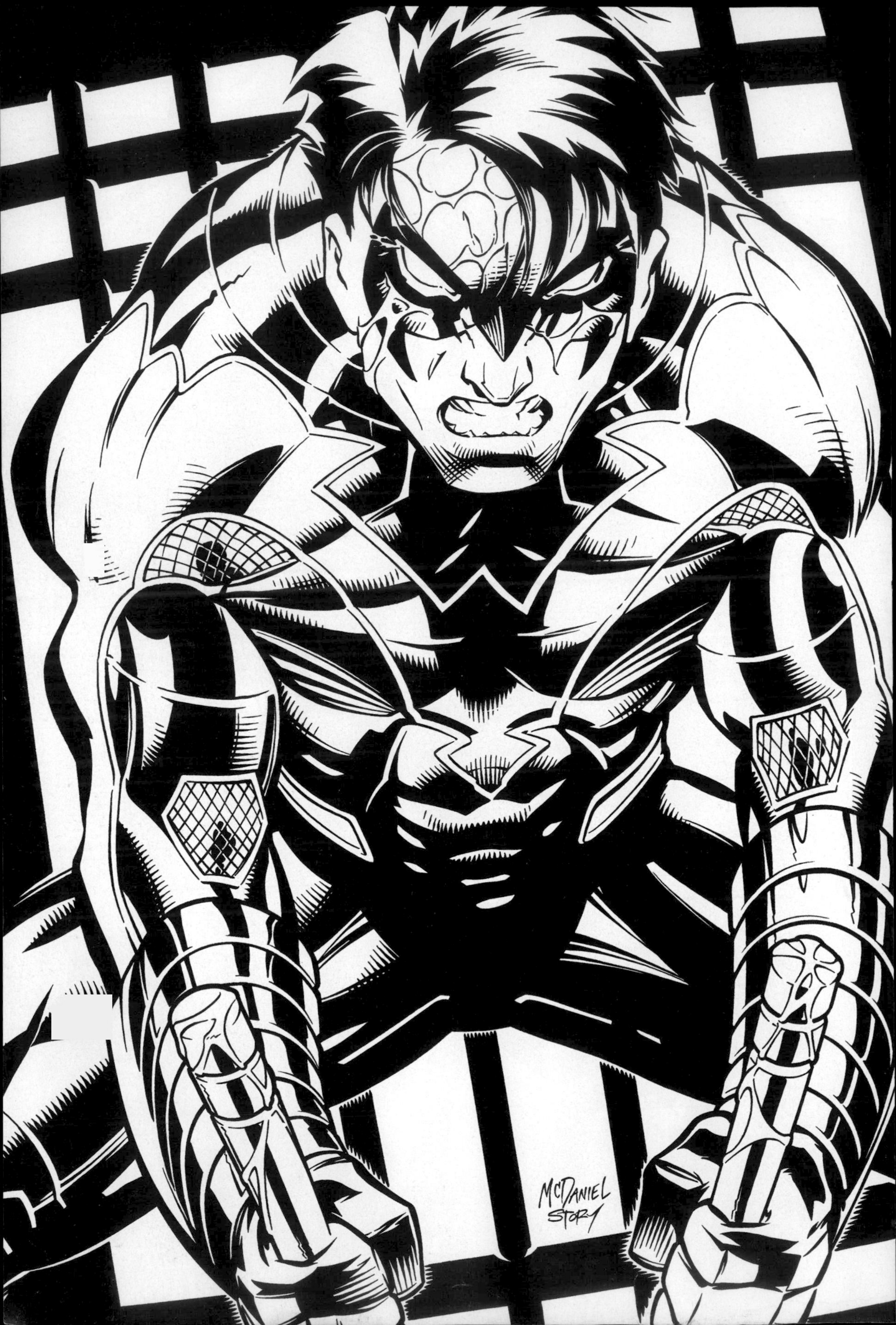
McDANIEL
STORY

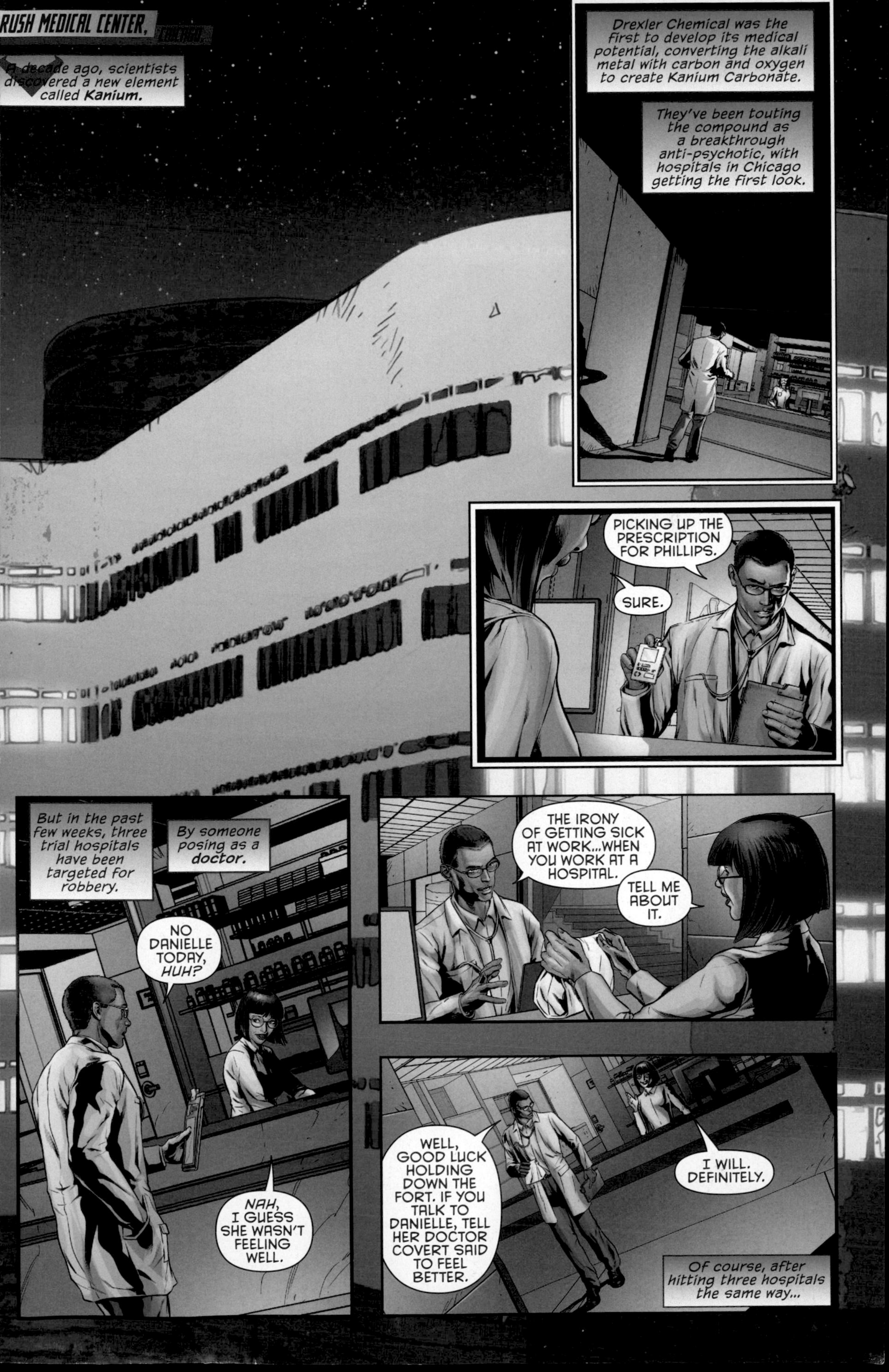
RUSH MEDICAL CENTER,
A decade ago, scientists discovered a new element called **Kanium.**
Drexler Chemical was the first to develop its medical potential, converting the alkali metal with carbon and oxygen to create Kanium Carbonate.
They've been touting the compound as a breakthrough anti-psychotic, with hospitals in Chicago getting the first look.
PICKING UP THE PRESCRIPTION FOR PHILLIPS.
SURE.
But in the past few weeks, three trial hospitals have been targeted for robbery.
By someone posing as a **doctor.**
NO DANIELLE TODAY, *HUH?*
NAH, I GUESS SHE WASN'T FEELING WELL.
THE IRONY OF GETTING SICK AT WORK...WHEN YOU WORK AT A HOSPITAL.
TELL ME ABOUT IT.
WELL, GOOD LUCK HOLDING DOWN THE FORT. IF YOU TALK TO DANIELLE, TELL HER DOCTOR COVERT SAID TO FEEL BETTER.
I WILL. DEFINITELY.
Of course, after hitting three hospitals the same way...

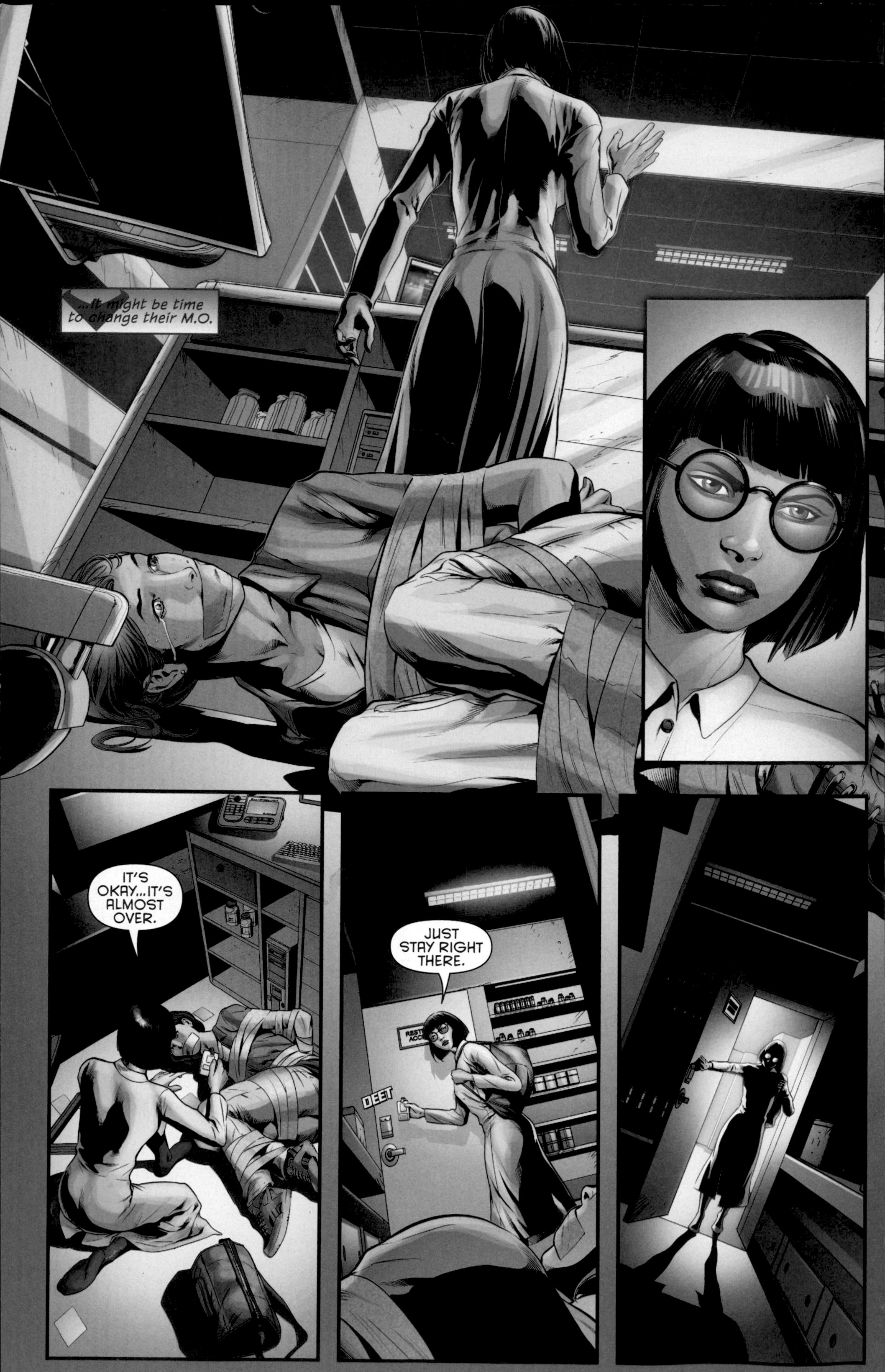
...It might be time to change their M.O.
IT'S OKAY...IT'S ALMOST OVER.
JUST STAY RIGHT THERE.
DEET

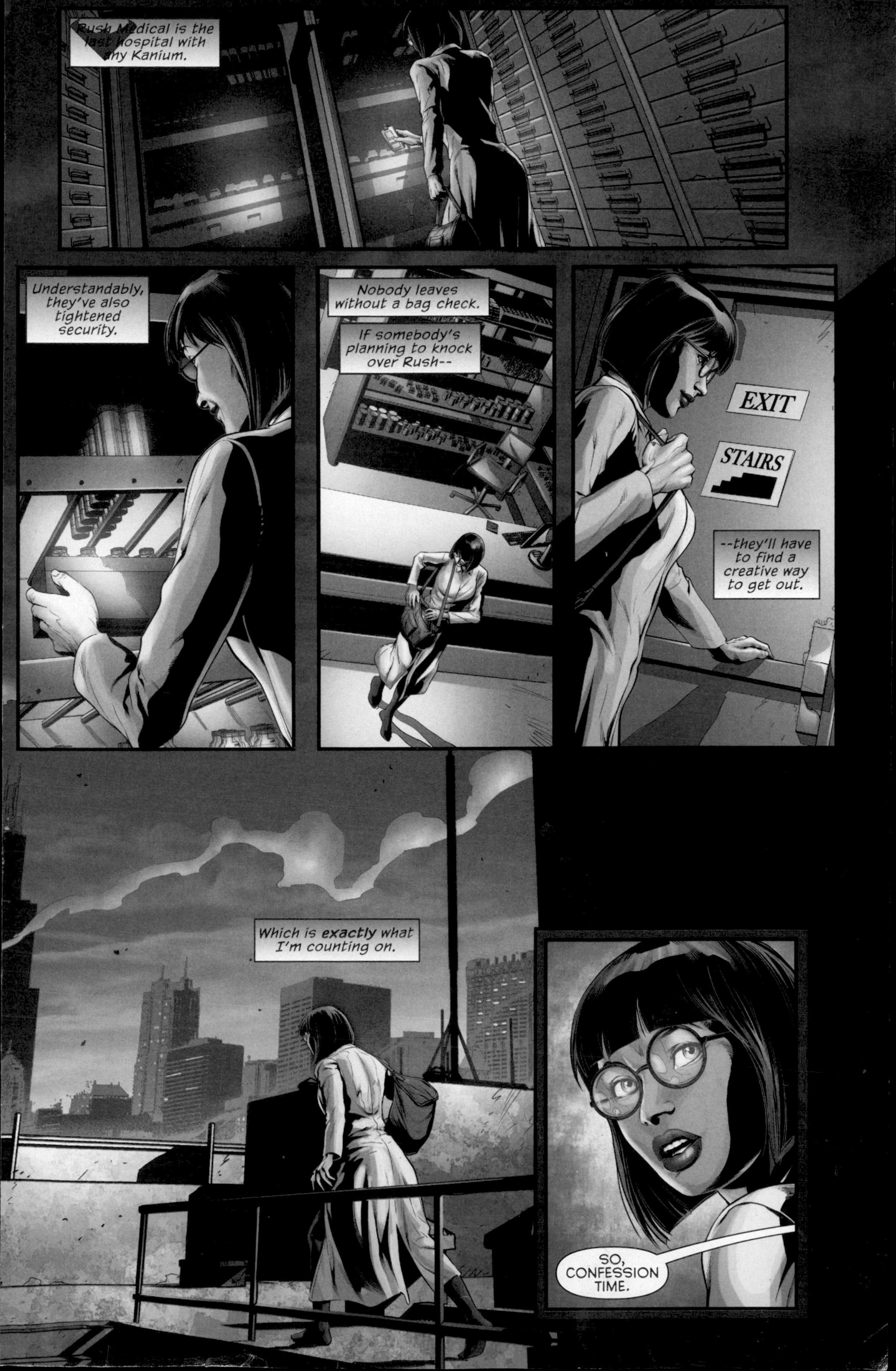
Rush Medical is the last hospital with any Kanium.
Understandably, they've also tightened security.
Nobody leaves without a bag check.
If somebody's planning to knock over Rush--
EXIT
STAIRS
--they'll have to find a creative way to get out.
Which is exactly what I'm counting on.
SO, CONFESSION TIME.

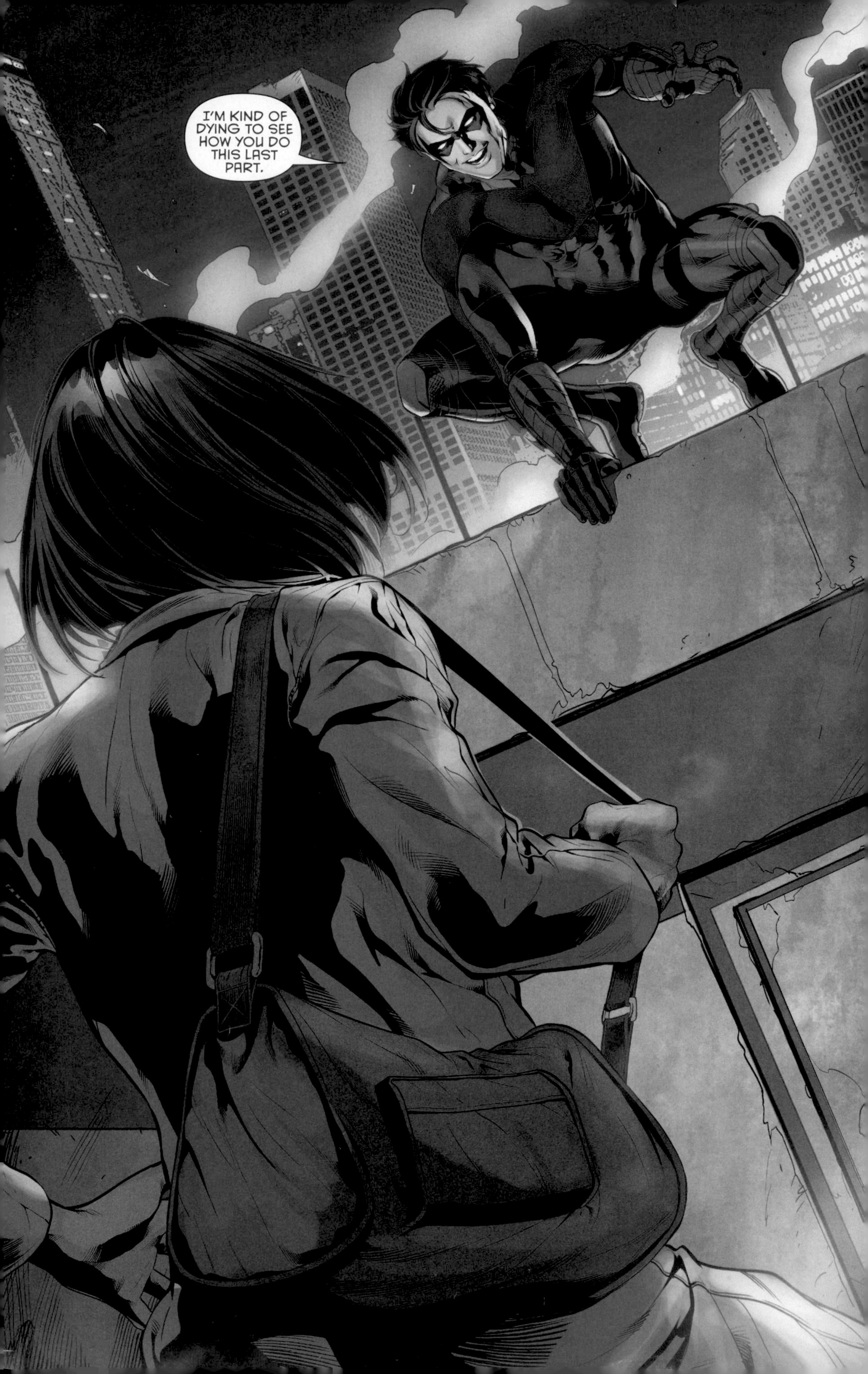
I'M KIND OF DYING TO SEE HOW YOU DO THIS LAST PART.

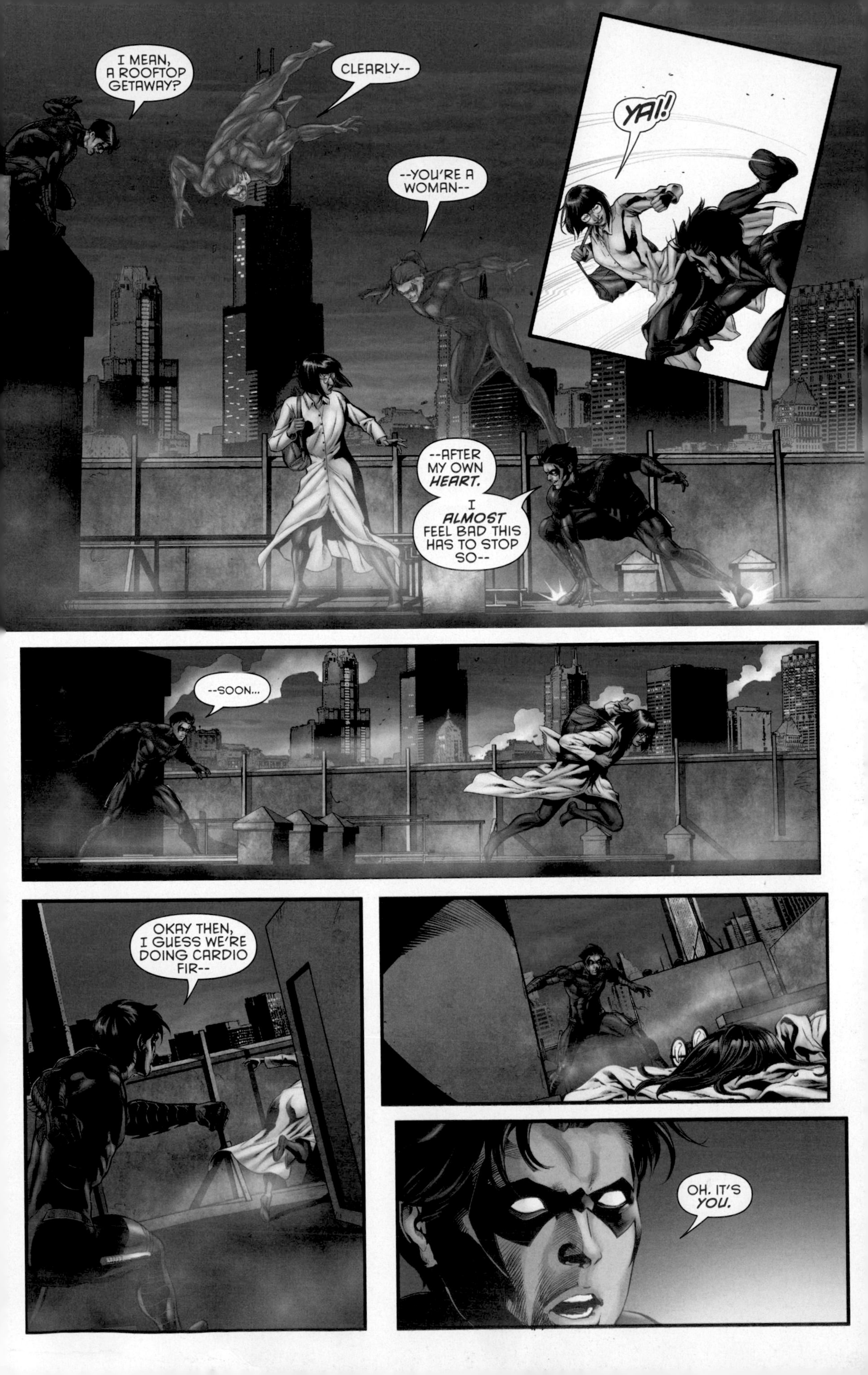
I MEAN, A ROOFTOP GETAWAY?
CLEARLY--
--YOU'RE A WOMAN--
YAI!
--AFTER MY OWN HEART.
I ALMOST FEEL BAD THIS HAS TO STOP SO--
--SOON...
OKAY THEN, I GUESS WE'RE DOING CARDIO FIR--
OH. IT'S YOU.

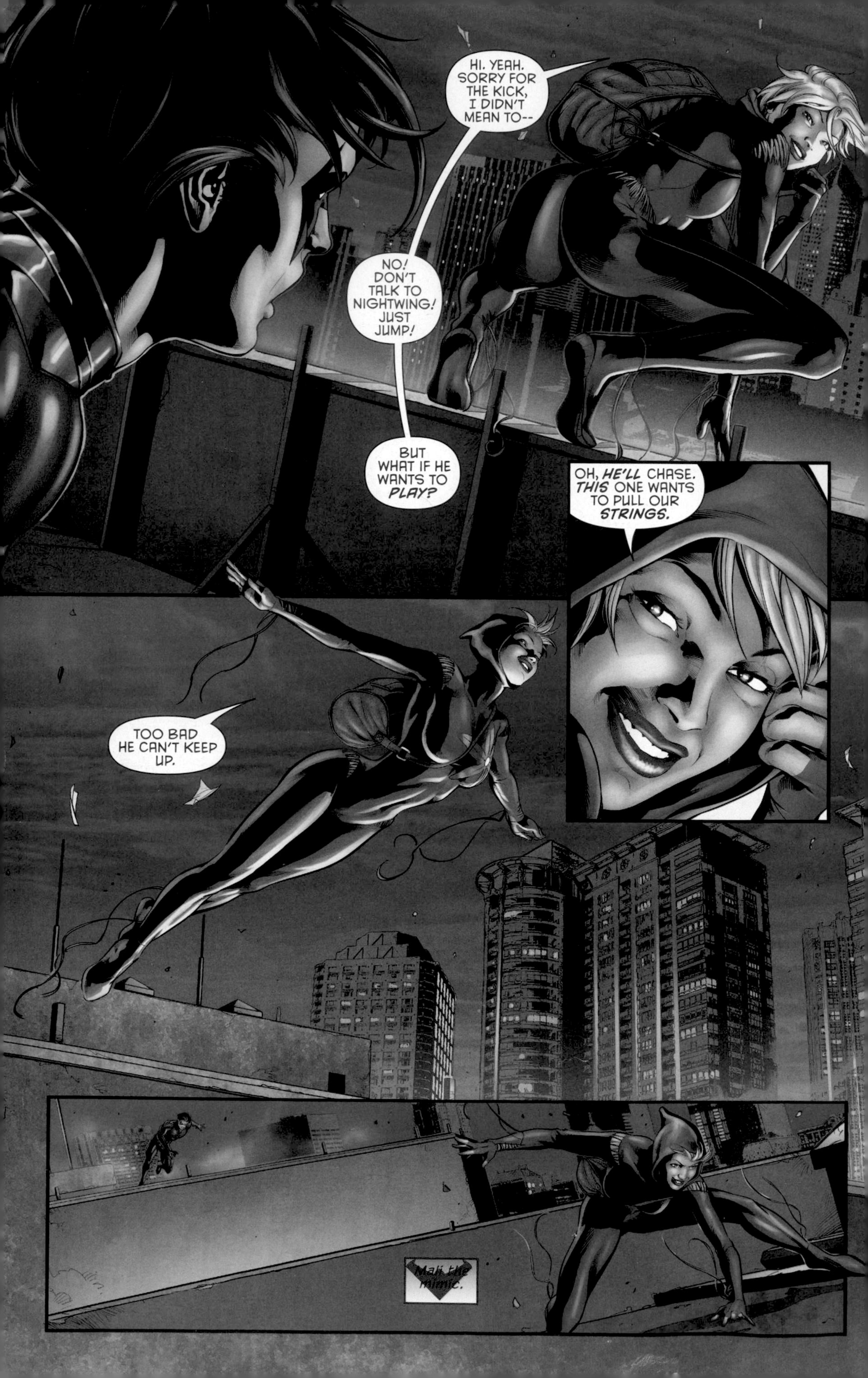
HI. YEAH. SORRY FOR THE KICK, I DIDN'T MEAN TO--
NO! DON'T TALK TO NIGHTWING! JUST JUMP!
BUT WHAT IF HE WANTS TO *PLAY?*
OH, ***HE'LL*** CHASE. ***THIS*** ONE WANTS TO PULL OUR ***STRINGS.***
TOO BAD HE CAN'T KEEP UP.
Mali the mimic.

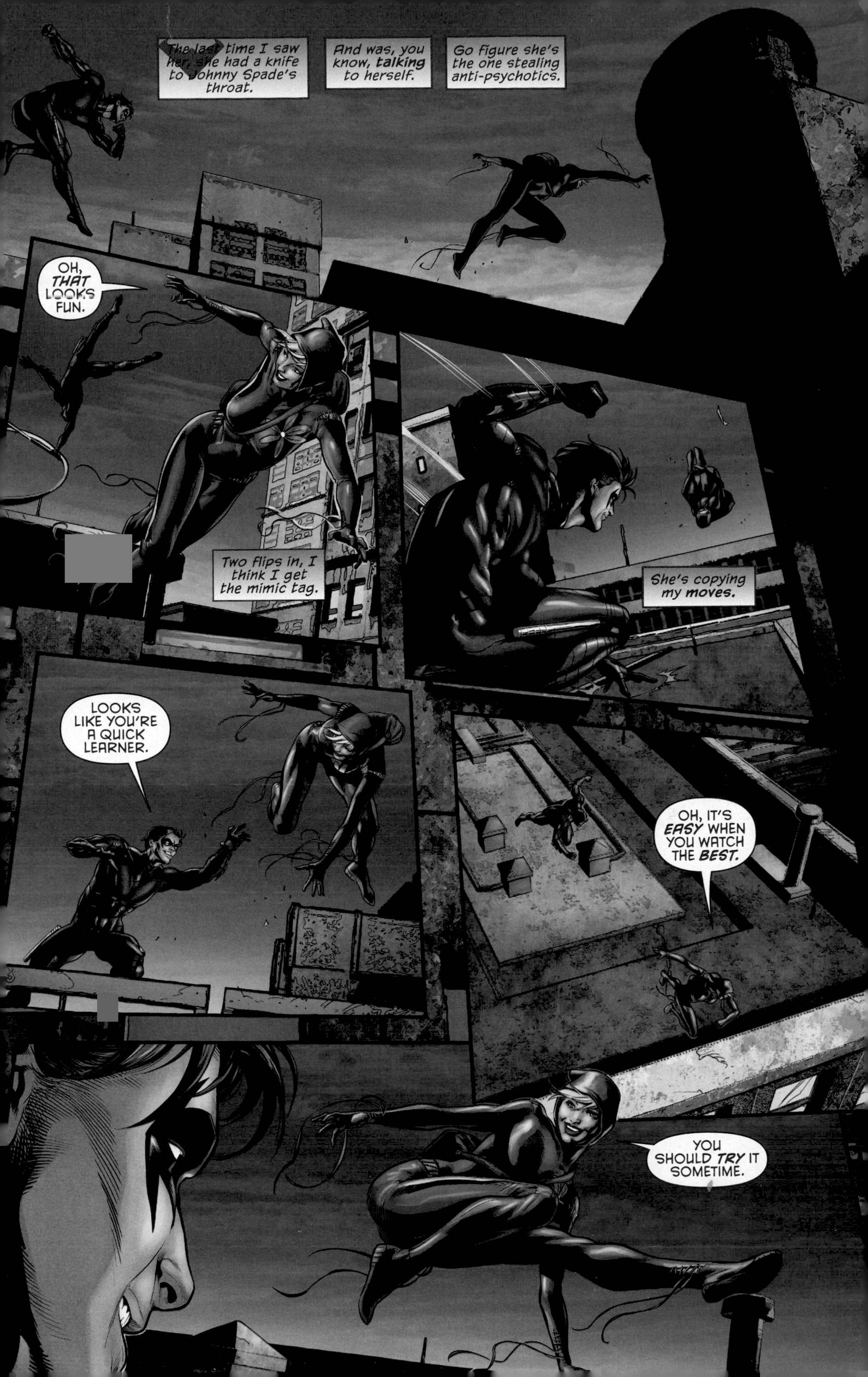
The last time I saw her, she had a knife to Johnny Spade's throat.
And was, you know, talking to herself.
Go figure she's the one stealing anti-psychotics.
OH, THAT LOOKS FUN.
Two flips in, I think I get the mimic tag.
She's copying my moves.
LOOKS LIKE YOU'RE A QUICK LEARNER.
OH, IT'S EASY WHEN YOU WATCH THE BEST.
YOU SHOULD TRY IT SOMETIME.

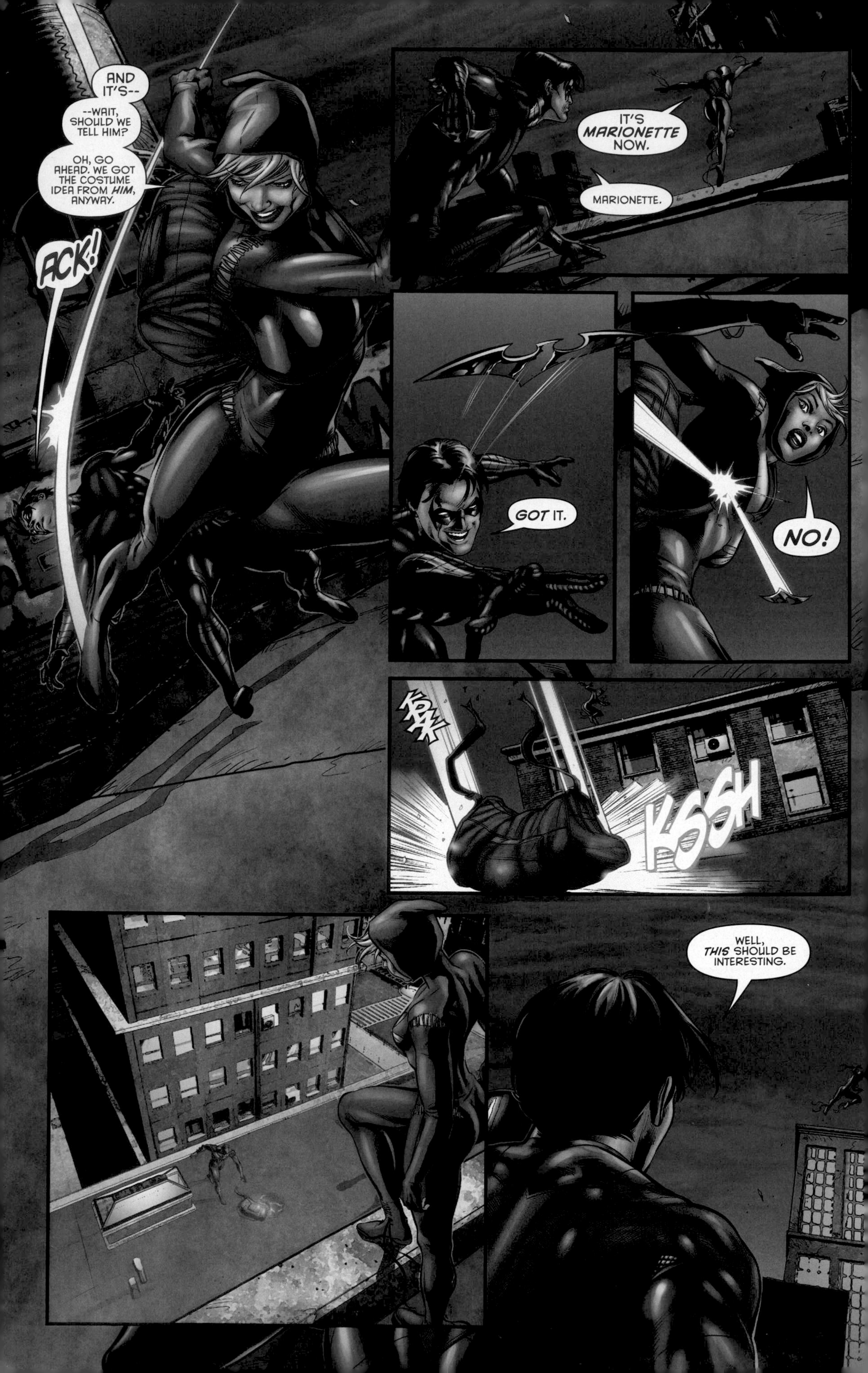
AND IT'S--
--WAIT, SHOULD WE TELL HIM?
OH, GO AHEAD. WE GOT THE COSTUME IDEA FROM HIM, ANYWAY.
ACK!
IT'S MARIONETTE NOW.
MARIONETTE.
GOT IT.
NO!
KRAK
KSSH
WELL, THIS SHOULD BE INTERESTING.

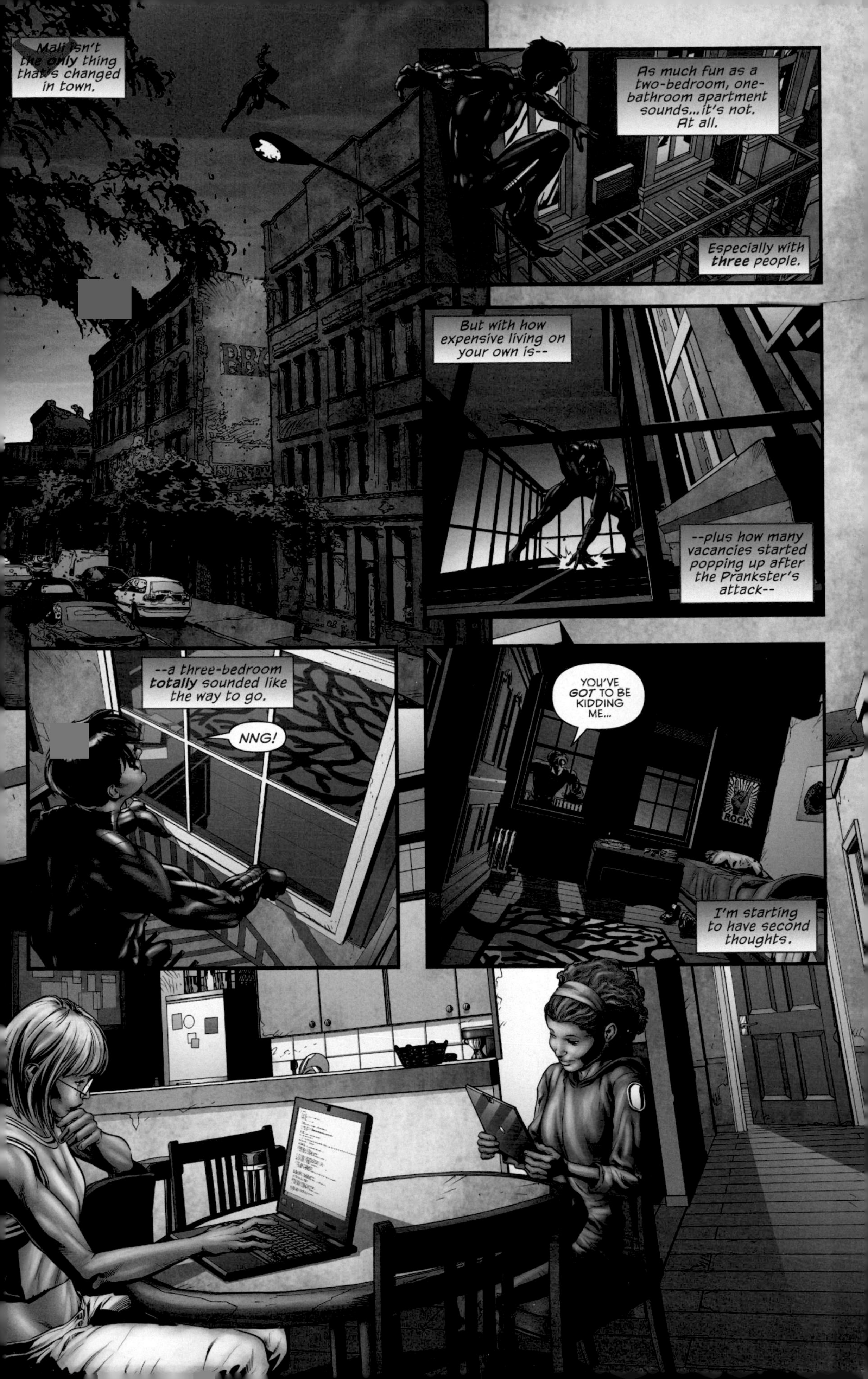

Mali isn't the only thing that's changed in town.
As much fun as a two-bedroom, one-bathroom apartment sounds...it's not. At all.
Especially with three people.
But with how expensive living on your own is--
--plus how many vacancies started popping up after the Prankster's attack--
--a three-bedroom totally sounded like the way to go.
NNG!
YOU'VE GOT TO BE KIDDING ME...
ROCK
I'm starting to have second thoughts.

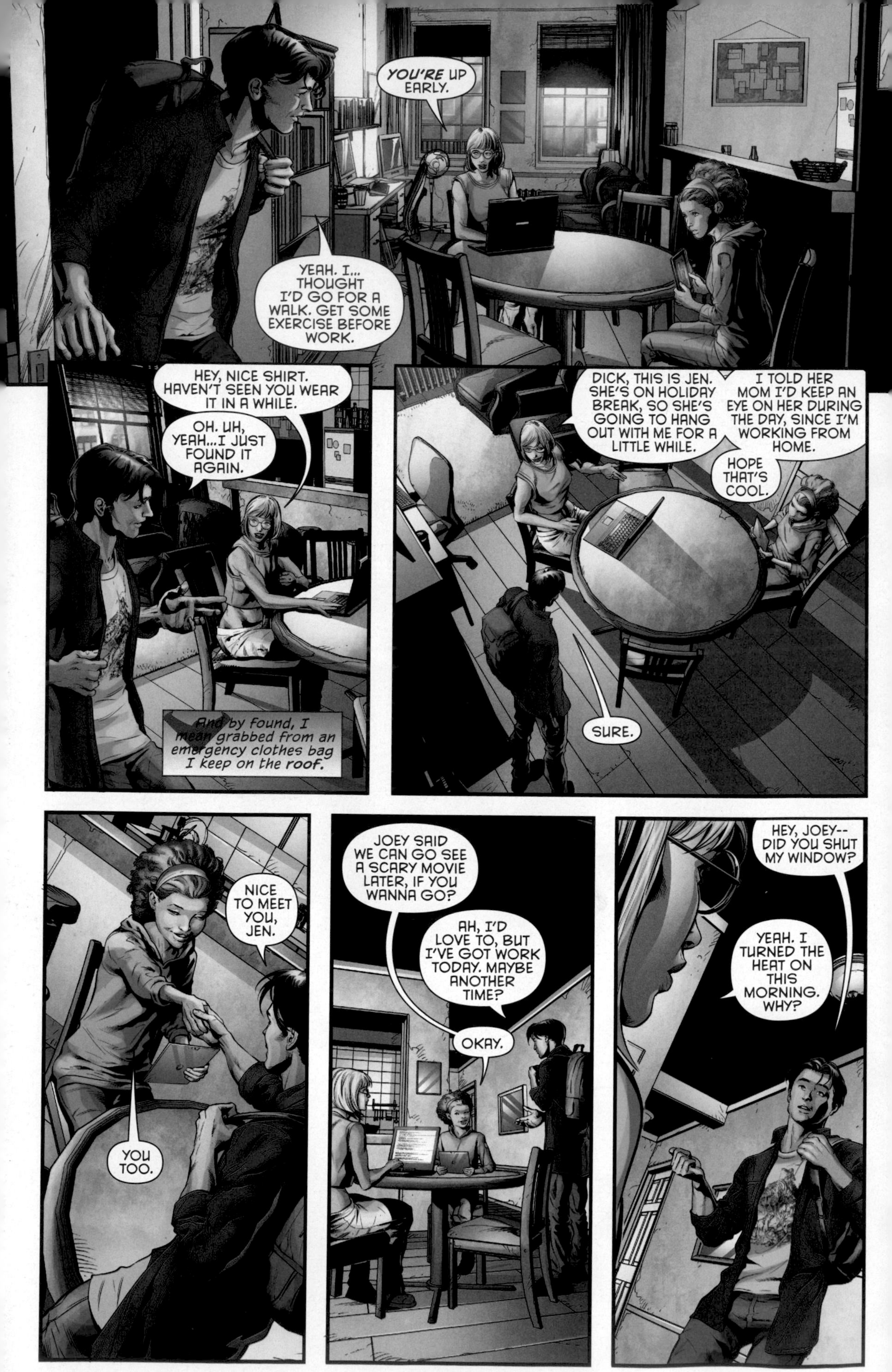
YOU'RE UP EARLY.
YEAH. I... THOUGHT I'D GO FOR A WALK. GET SOME EXERCISE BEFORE WORK.
HEY, NICE SHIRT. HAVEN'T SEEN YOU WEAR IT IN A WHILE.
OH. UH, YEAH...I JUST FOUND IT AGAIN.
And by found, I mean grabbed from an emergency clothes bag I keep on the roof.
DICK, THIS IS JEN. SHE'S ON HOLIDAY BREAK, SO SHE'S GOING TO HANG OUT WITH ME FOR A LITTLE WHILE.
I TOLD HER MOM I'D KEEP AN EYE ON HER DURING THE DAY, SINCE I'M WORKING FROM HOME.
HOPE THAT'S COOL.
SURE.
NICE TO MEET YOU, JEN.
YOU TOO.
JOEY SAID WE CAN GO SEE A SCARY MOVIE LATER, IF YOU WANNA GO?
AH, I'D LOVE TO, BUT I'VE GOT WORK TODAY. MAYBE ANOTHER TIME?
OKAY.
HEY, JOEY-- DID YOU SHUT MY WINDOW?
YEAH. I TURNED THE HEAT ON THIS MORNING. WHY?

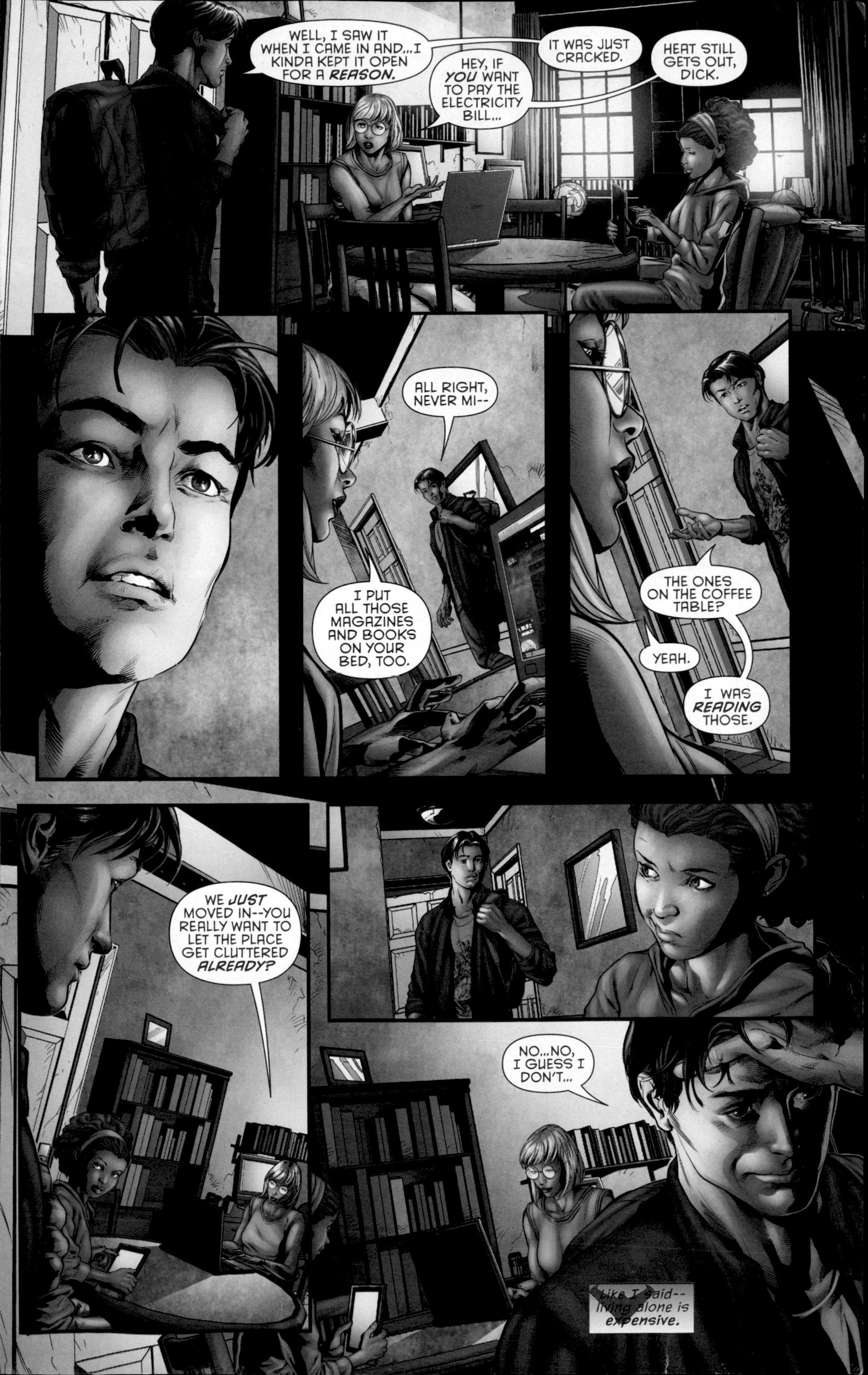
WELL, I SAW IT WHEN I CAME IN AND...I KINDA KEPT IT OPEN FOR A *REASON.*
IT WAS JUST CRACKED.
HEY, IF *YOU* WANT TO PAY THE ELECTRICITY BILL...
HEAT STILL GETS OUT, DICK.
ALL RIGHT, NEVER MI--
I PUT ALL THOSE MAGAZINES AND BOOKS ON YOUR BED, TOO.
THE ONES ON THE COFFEE TABLE?
YEAH.
I WAS *READING* THOSE.
WE *JUST* MOVED IN--YOU REALLY WANT TO LET THE PLACE GET CLUTTERED *ALREADY?*
NO...NO, I GUESS I DON'T...
Like I said-- living alone is expensive.

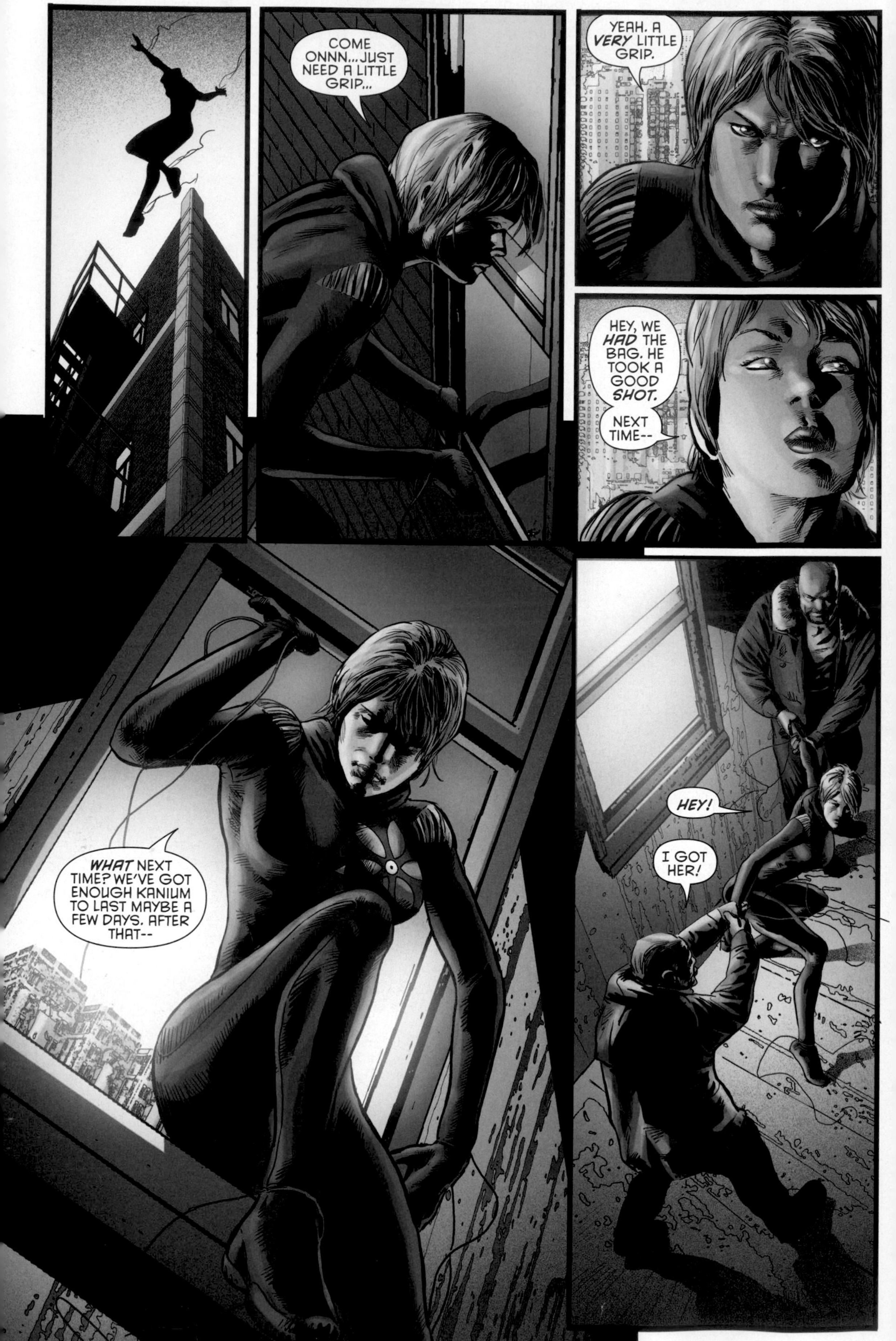
COME ONNN...JUST NEED A LITTLE GRIP...
YEAH. A VERY LITTLE GRIP.
HEY, WE HAD THE BAG. HE TOOK A GOOD SHOT.
NEXT TIME--
WHAT NEXT TIME? WE'VE GOT ENOUGH KANIUM TO LAST MAYBE A FEW DAYS. AFTER THAT--
HEY!
I GOT HER!

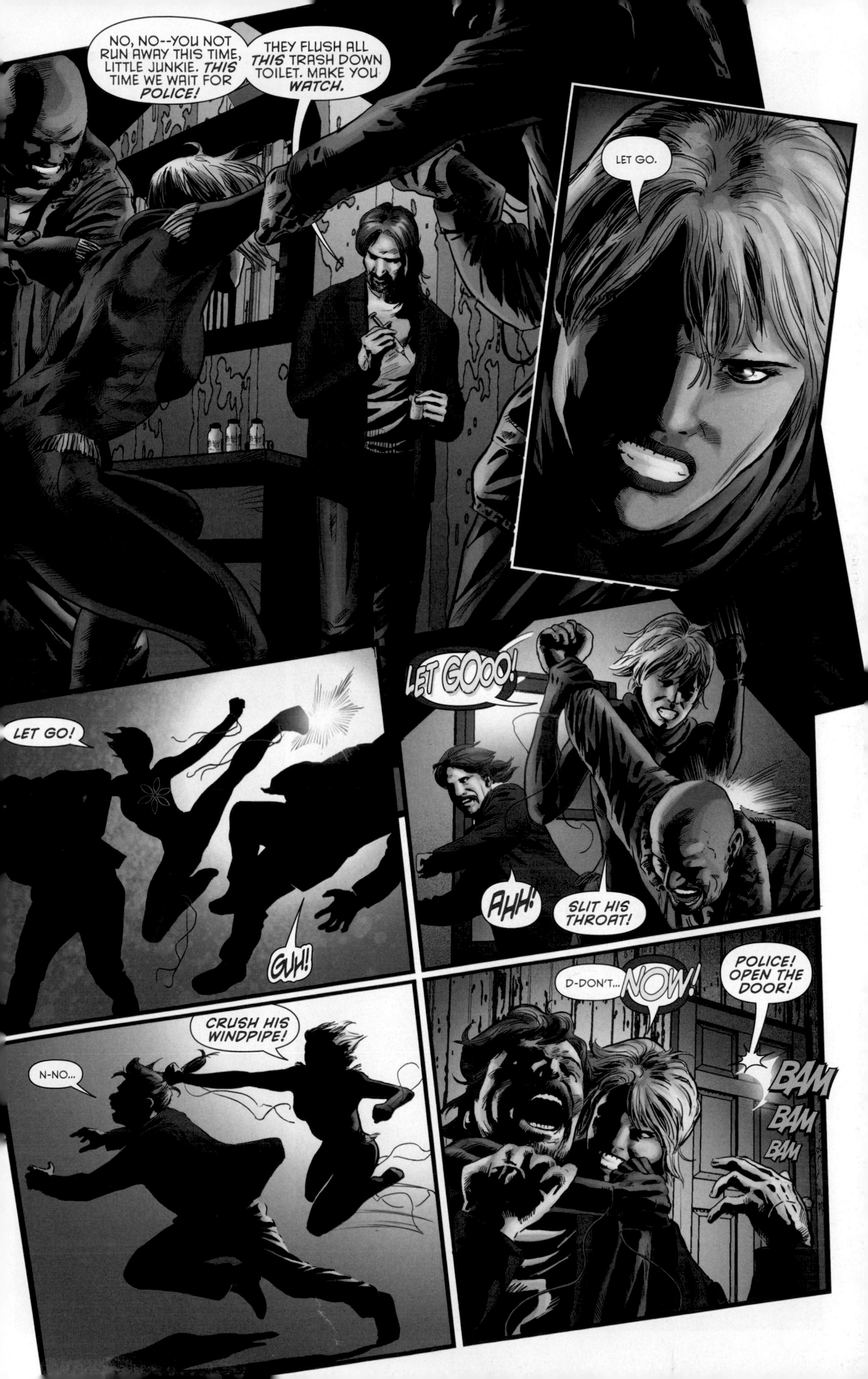
NO, NO--YOU NOT RUN AWAY THIS TIME, LITTLE JUNKIE. *THIS* TIME WE WAIT FOR *POLICE!*
THEY FLUSH ALL *THIS* TRASH DOWN TOILET. MAKE YOU *WATCH.*
LET GO.
LET GO!
GUH!
LET GOOO!
AHH!
SLIT HIS THROAT!
N-NO...
CRUSH HIS WINDPIPE!
D-DON'T...
NOW!
POLICE! OPEN THE DOOR!
BAM
BAM
BAM

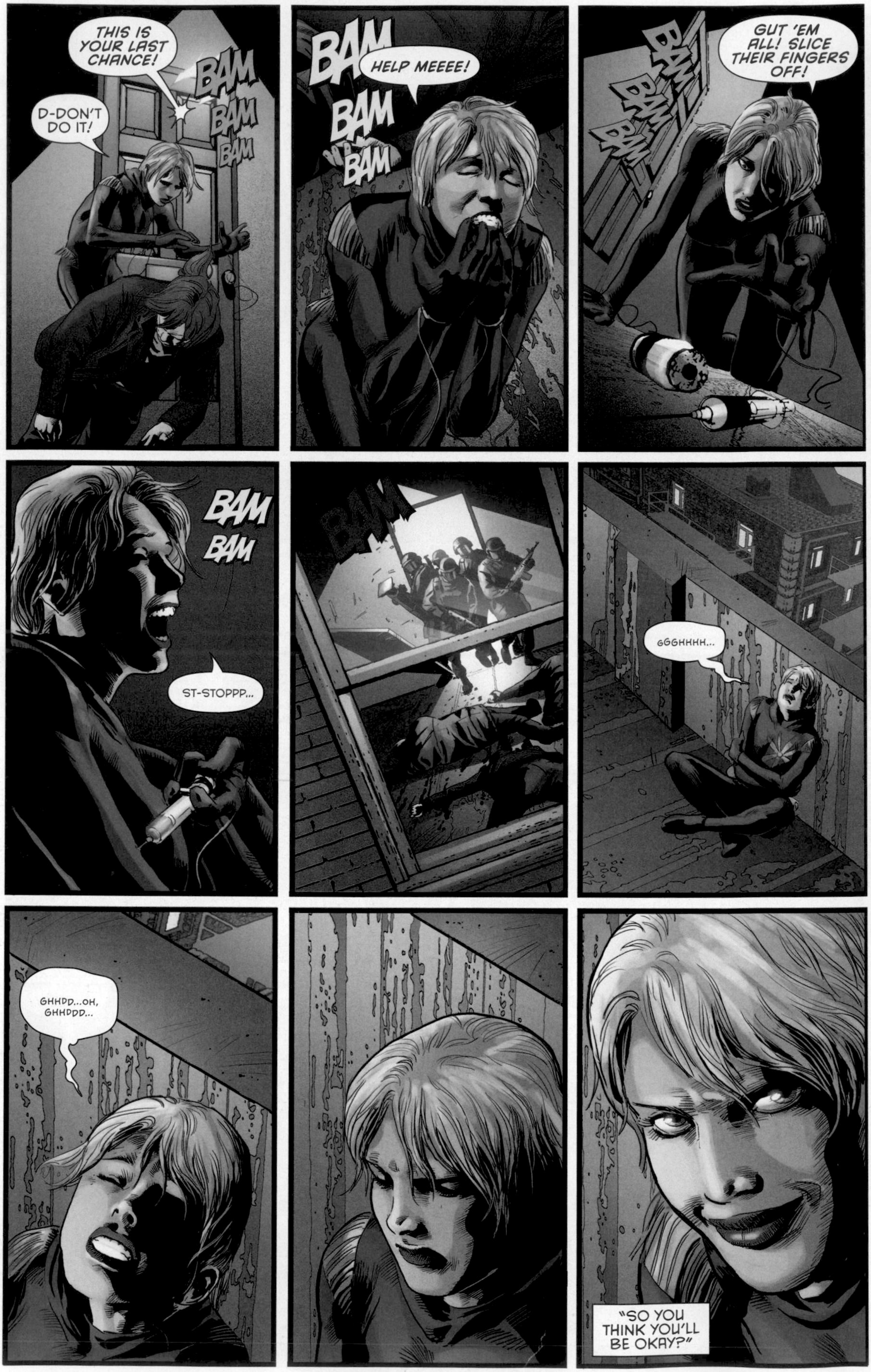
THIS IS YOUR LAST CHANCE!
BAM BAM BAM
D-DON'T DO IT!
BAM
HELP MEEEE!
BAM
BAM
GUT 'EM ALL! SLICE THEIR FINGERS OFF!
BAM BAM BAM
BAM BAM
ST-STOPPP...
BAM
GGGHHHH...
GHHDD...OH, GHHDDD...
"SO YOU THINK YOU'LL BE OKAY?"

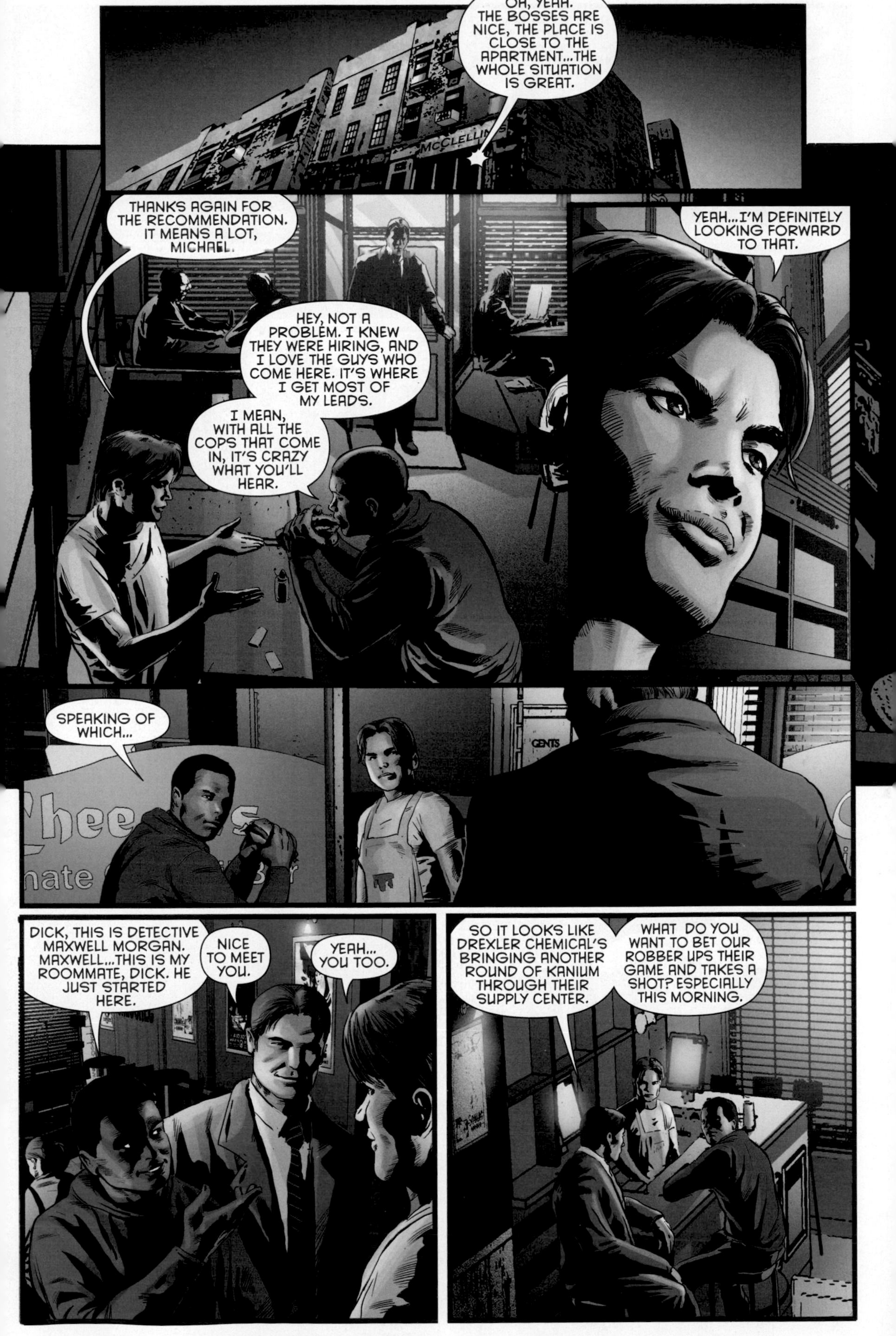
OH, YEAH. THE BOSSES ARE NICE, THE PLACE IS CLOSE TO THE APARTMENT...THE WHOLE SITUATION IS GREAT.
McCLELLIN
THANKS AGAIN FOR THE RECOMMENDATION. IT MEANS A LOT, MICHAEL.
HEY, NOT A PROBLEM. I KNEW THEY WERE HIRING, AND I LOVE THE GUYS WHO COME HERE. IT'S WHERE I GET MOST OF MY LEADS.
I MEAN, WITH ALL THE COPS THAT COME IN, IT'S CRAZY WHAT YOU'LL HEAR.
YEAH...I'M DEFINITELY LOOKING FORWARD TO THAT.
SPEAKING OF WHICH...
GENTS
DICK, THIS IS DETECTIVE MAXWELL MORGAN. MAXWELL...THIS IS MY ROOMMATE, DICK. HE JUST STARTED HERE.
NICE TO MEET YOU.
YEAH... YOU TOO.
SO IT LOOKS LIKE DREXLER CHEMICAL'S BRINGING ANOTHER ROUND OF KANIUM THROUGH THEIR SUPPLY CENTER.
WHAT DO YOU WANT TO BET OUR ROBBER UPS THEIR GAME AND TAKES A SHOT? ESPECIALLY THIS MORNING.

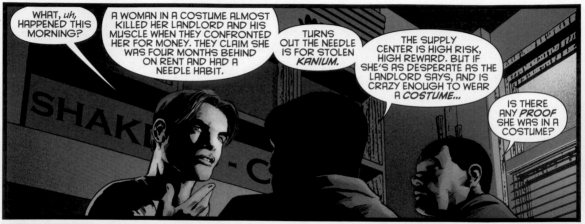

WHAT, *uh*, HAPPENED THIS MORNING?

A WOMAN IN A COSTUME ALMOST KILLED HER LANDLORD AND HIS MUSCLE WHEN THEY CONFRONTED HER FOR MONEY. THEY CLAIM SHE WAS FOUR MONTHS BEHIND ON RENT AND HAD A NEEDLE HABIT.

TURNS OUT THE NEEDLE IS FOR STOLEN *KANIUM*.

THE SUPPLY CENTER IS HIGH RISK, HIGH REWARD. BUT IF SHE'S AS DESPERATE AS THE LANDLORD SAYS, AND IS CRAZY ENOUGH TO WEAR A *COSTUME*...

IS THERE ANY *PROOF* SHE WAS IN A COSTUME?

MEET ME AT SIX IF YOU'RE INTERESTED IN SITTING ON DREXLER.

WHO *KNOWS* WHAT KIND OF PROOF WE MIGHT FIND.

WHAT WAS *THAT*?

WHAT WAS WHAT?

THAT LOOK HE GAVE YOU.

THINGS ARE... *COMPLICATED* WITH MAXWELL.

MEANING?

HE...HAS THIS VENDETTA AGAINST MASKS. MORE THAN ANYONE I'VE EVER MET.

AND AFTER THE PRANKSTER FOOTAGE, I'VE KIND OF BECOME THE "MASKS GUY" AT THE PAPER. WHICH IS *GREAT* FOR MY CAREER.

BUT YOU NEED MAXWELL TO GIVE YOU ACCESS.

AND AS LONG AS I PUT A SPIN ON THINGS THE WAY HE LIKES...HE *DOES*.

THAT... DOESN'T SEEM RIGHT, MICHAEL.

YEAH, WELL...I'M NOT REALLY SURE *WHAT* TO DO. I'M *TRAPPED* FOR NOW.

ANYWAY, SOUNDS LIKE I'LL BE OUT PRETTY LATE. I'LL SEE YOU LATER THOUGH.

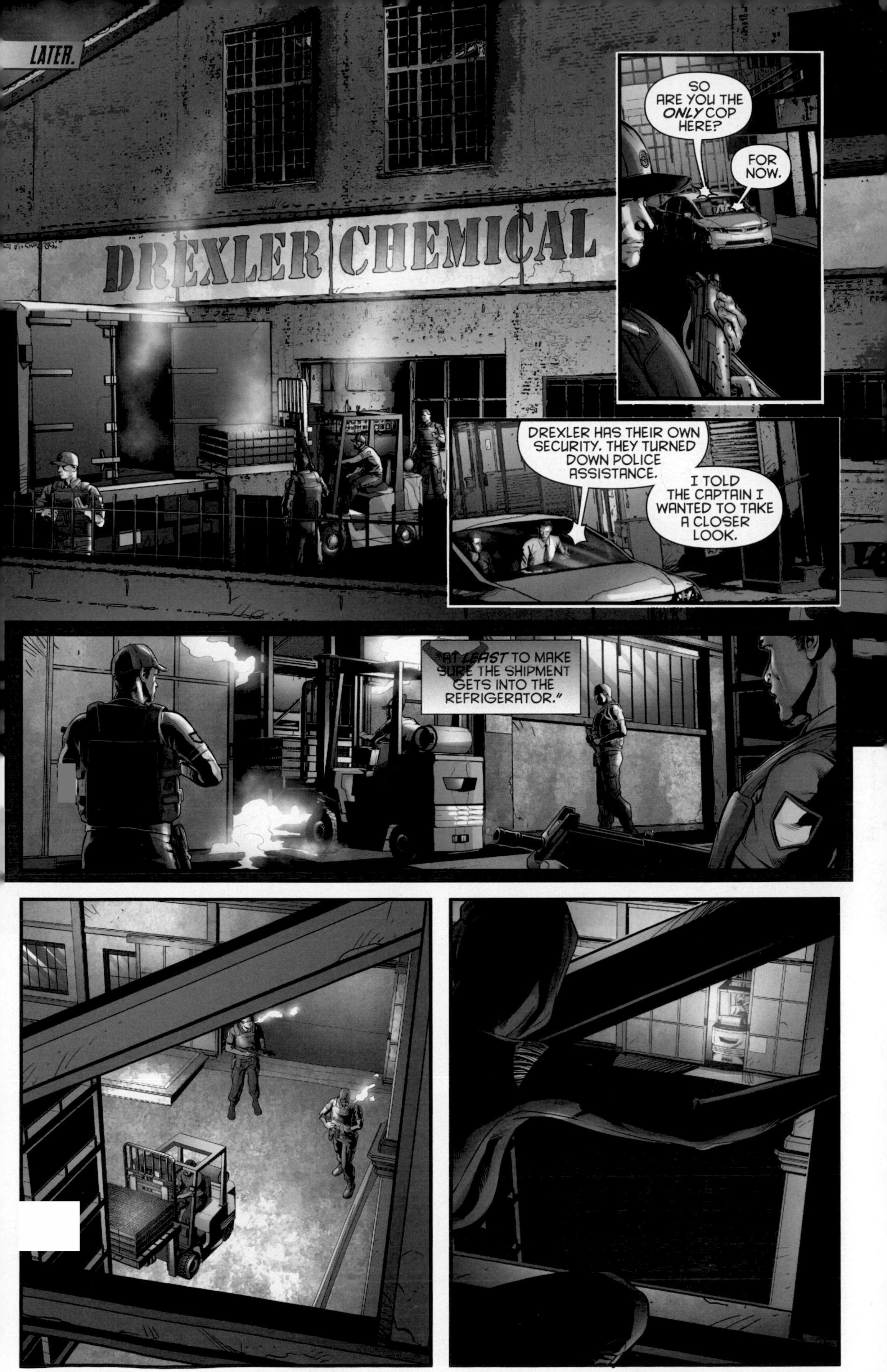
LATER.
DREXLER CHEMICAL
SO ARE YOU THE ONLY COP HERE?
FOR NOW.
DREXLER HAS THEIR OWN SECURITY. THEY TURNED DOWN POLICE ASSISTANCE.
I TOLD THE CAPTAIN I WANTED TO TAKE A CLOSER LOOK.
"AT LEAST TO MAKE SURE THE SHIPMENT GETS INTO THE REFRIGERATOR."

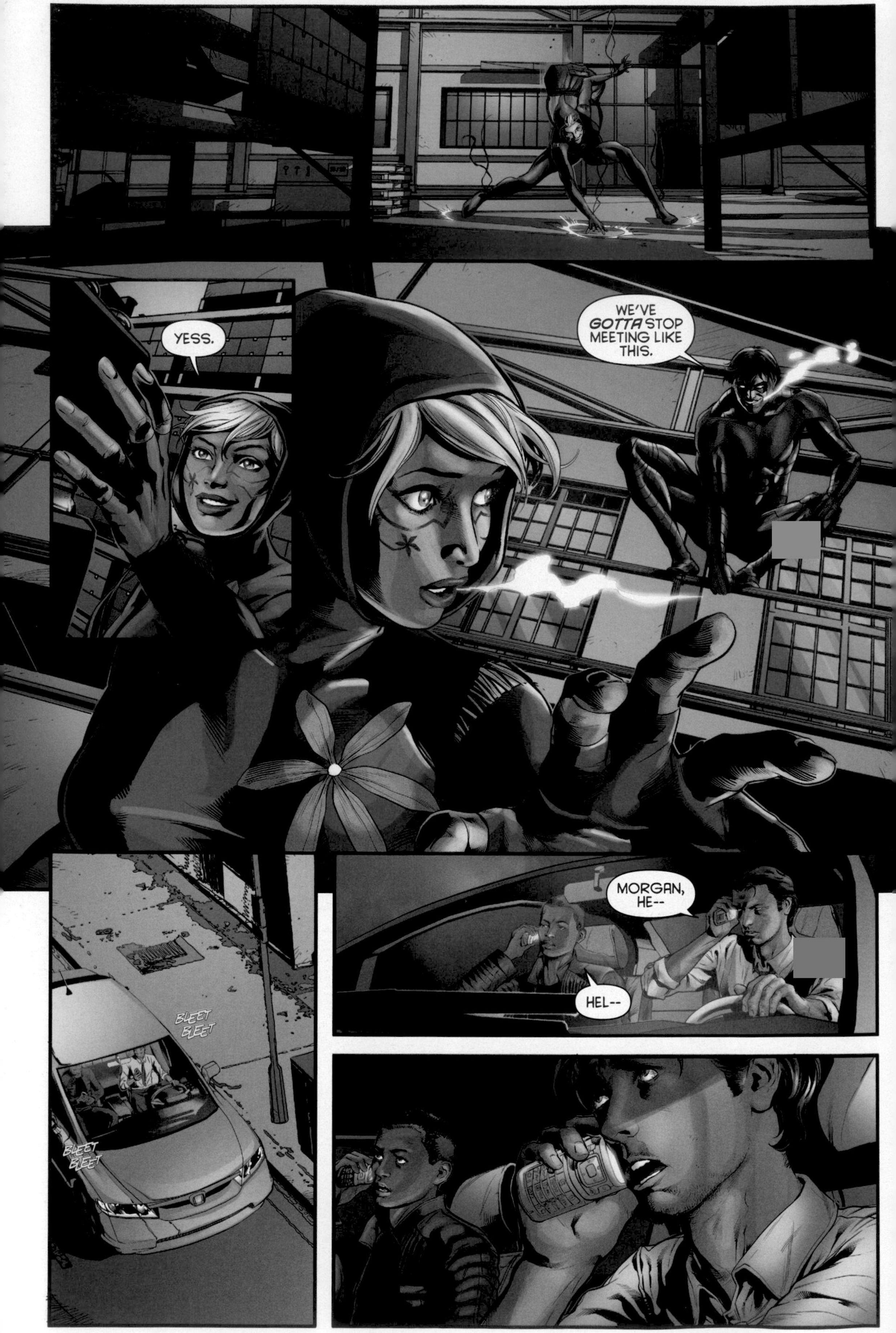
YESS.
WE'VE *GOTTA* STOP MEETING LIKE THIS.
BLEET BLEET
BLEET BLEET
MORGAN, HE--
HEL--

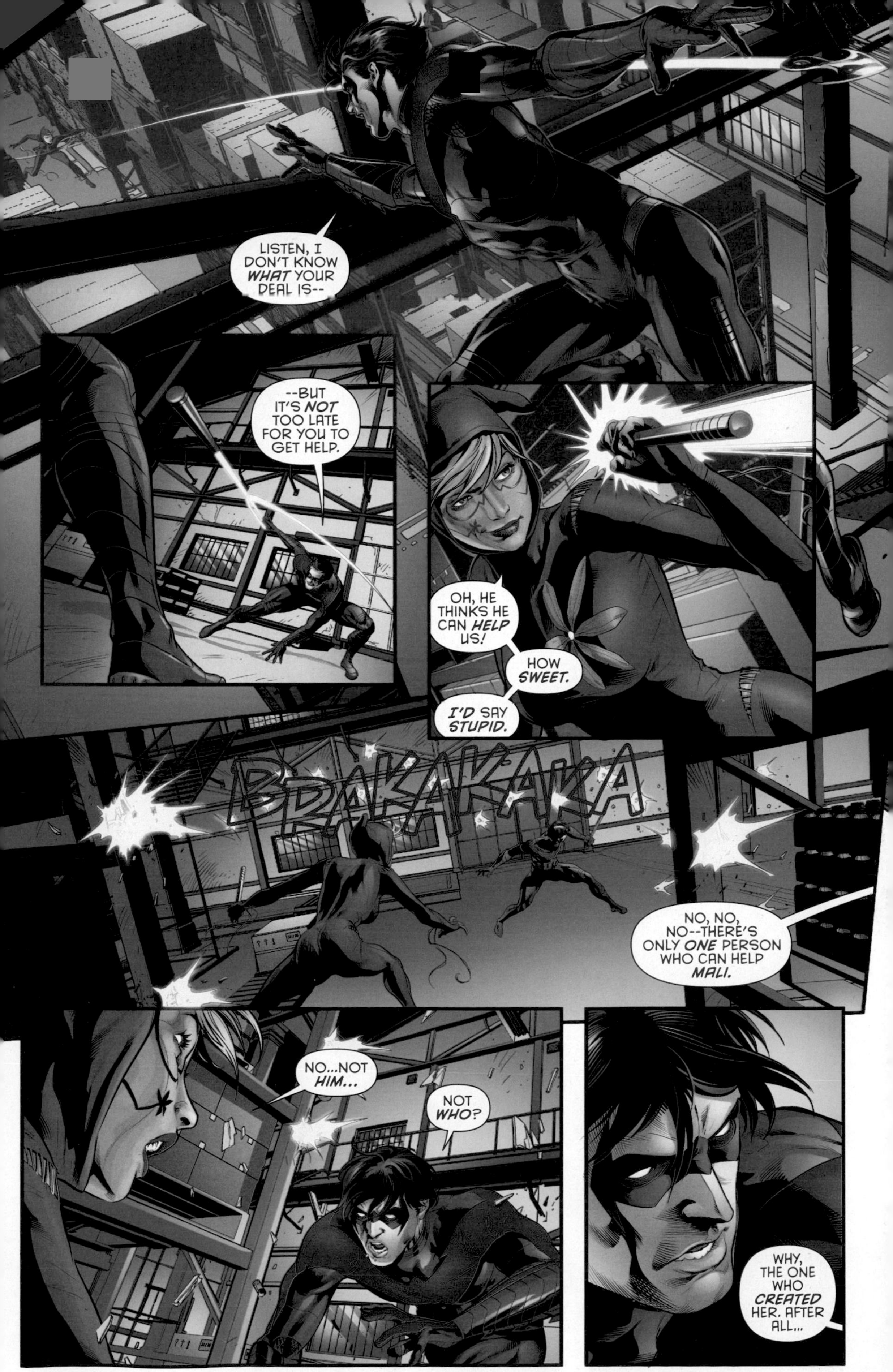
LISTEN, I DON'T KNOW *WHAT* YOUR DEAL IS--
--BUT IT'S *NOT* TOO LATE FOR YOU TO GET HELP.
OH, HE THINKS HE CAN *HELP* US!
HOW *SWEET.*
I'D SAY *STUPID.*
BRAKAKAKA
NO, NO, NO--THERE'S ONLY *ONE* PERSON WHO CAN HELP *MALI.*
NO...NOT *HIM...*
NOT *WHO?*
WHY, THE ONE WHO *CREATED* HER. AFTER ALL...

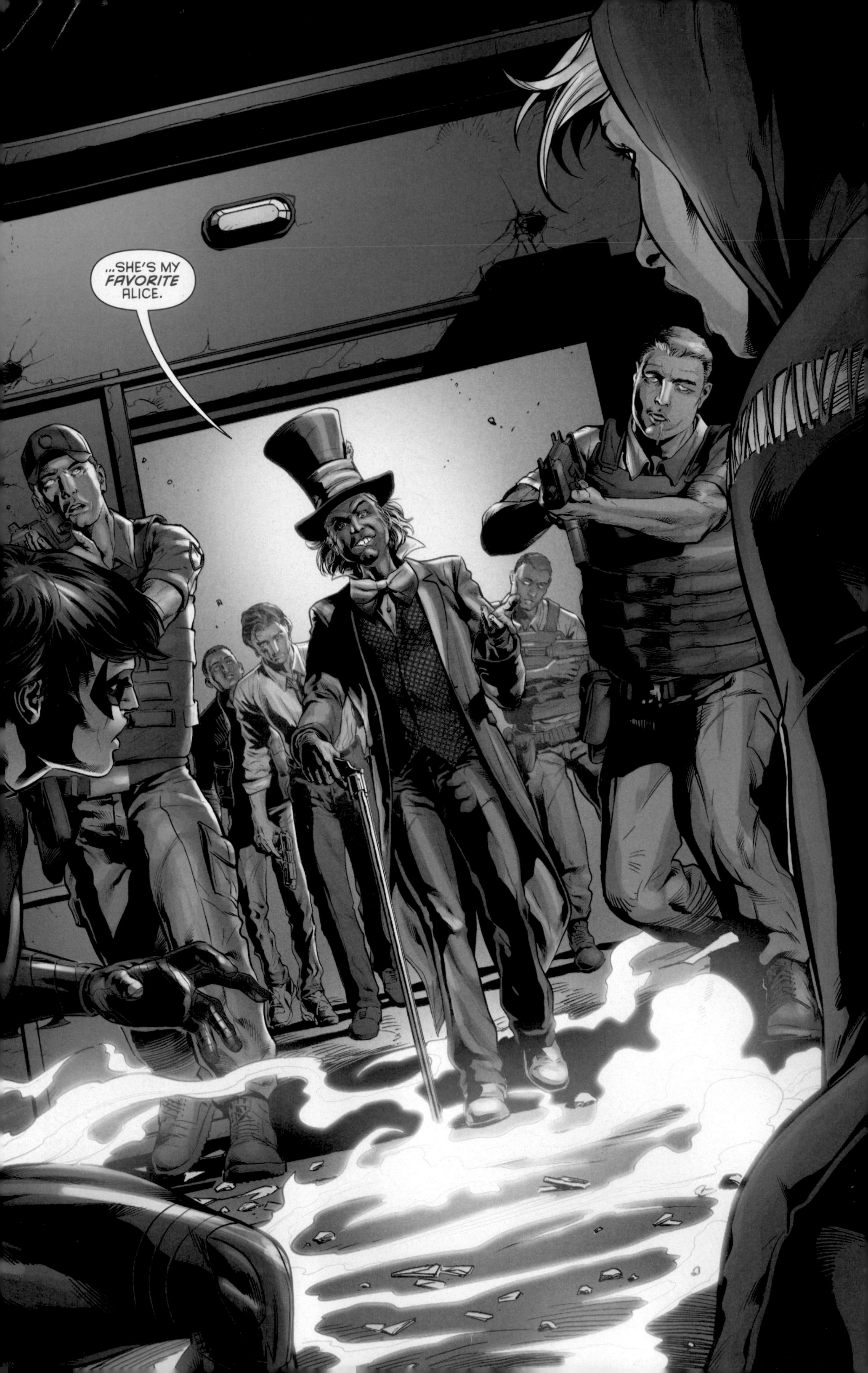
...SHE'S MY *FAVORITE* ALICE.

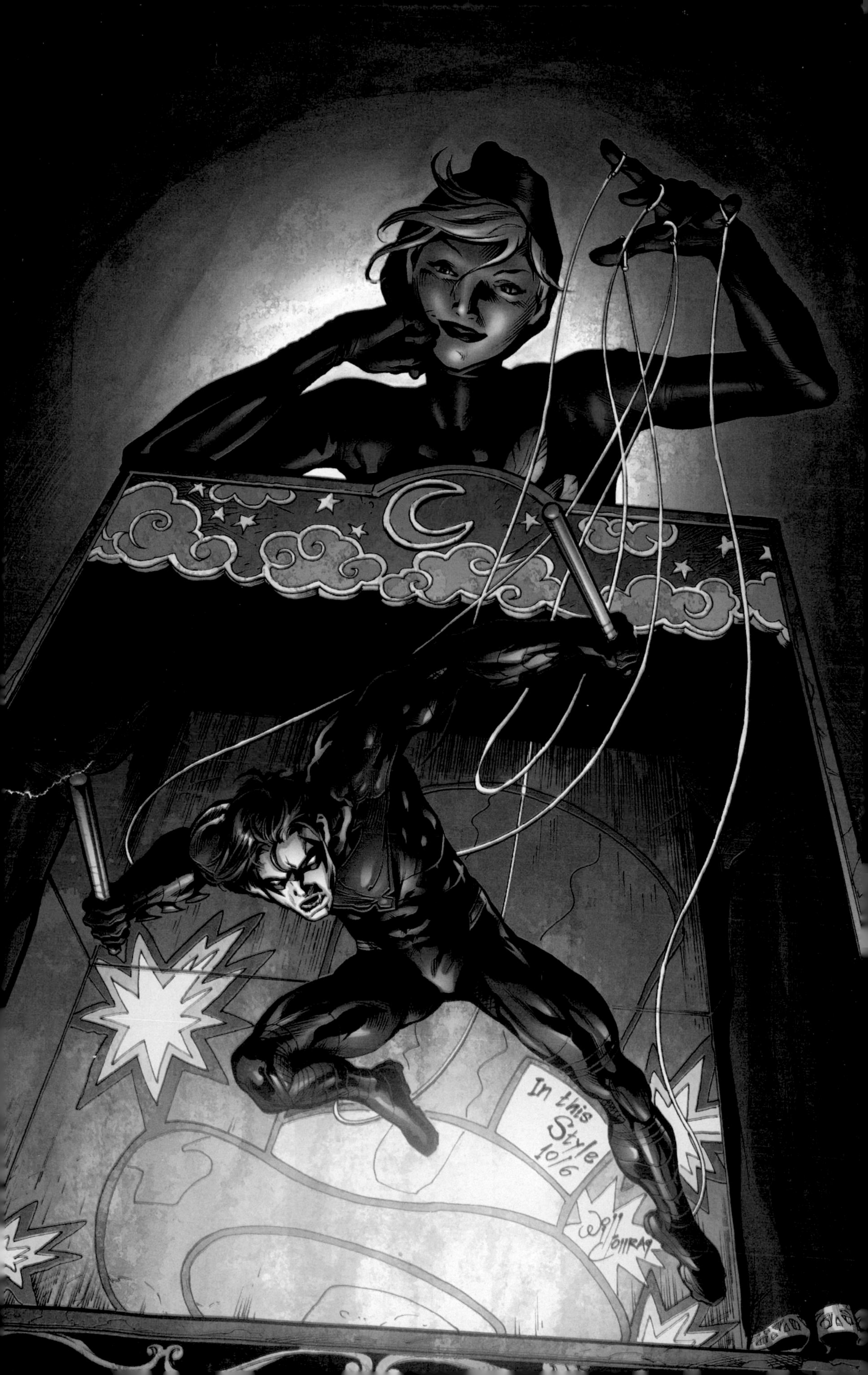
In this Style 10/6

CURIOUSER AND CURIOUSER

KYLE HIGGINS writer **WILL CONRAD** with **CLIFF RICHARDS** artists **PETE PANTAZIS** colorist
CARLOS M. MANGUAL letterer cover art by **WILL CONRAD** and **PETE PANTAZIS**

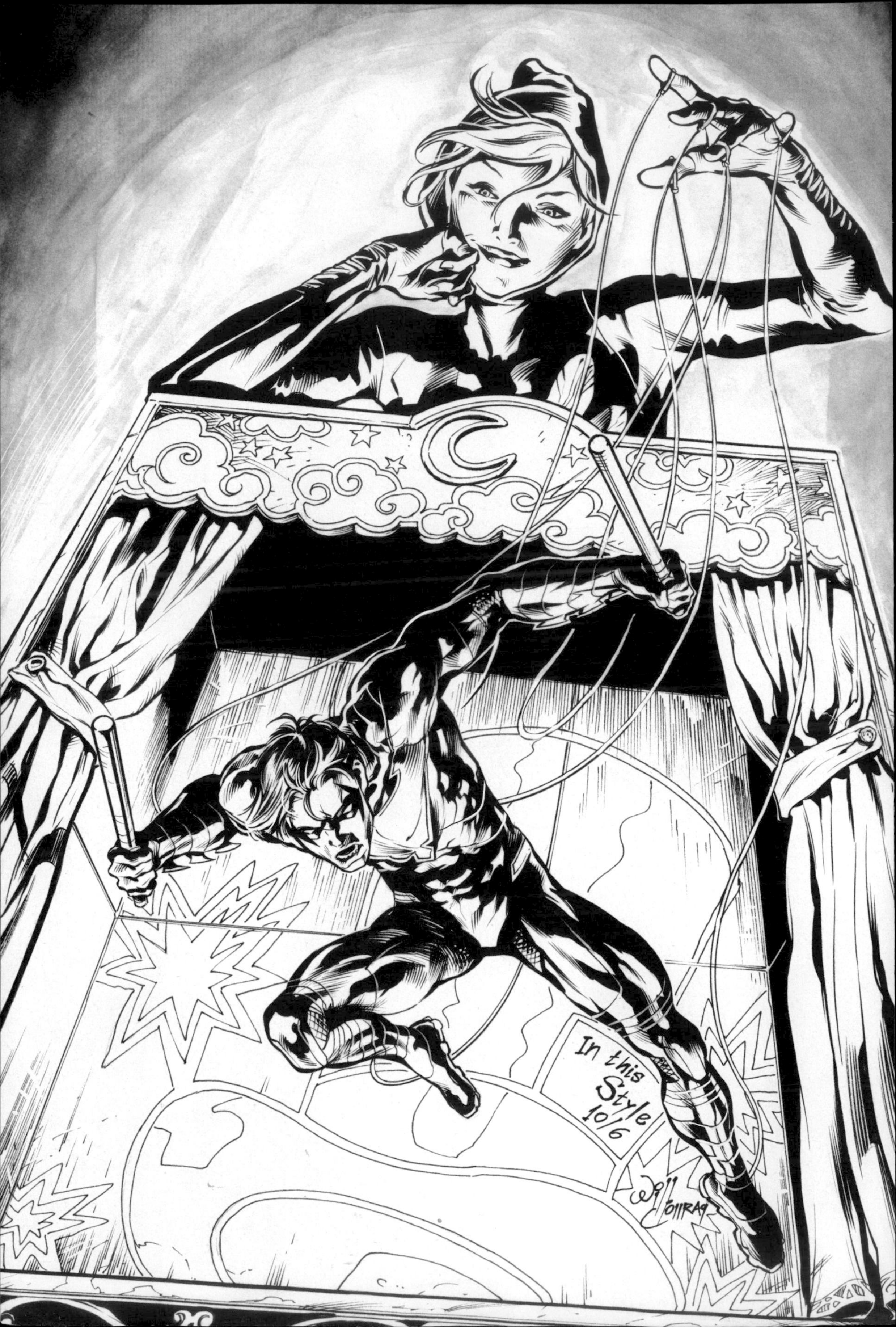
In this Style 10/6

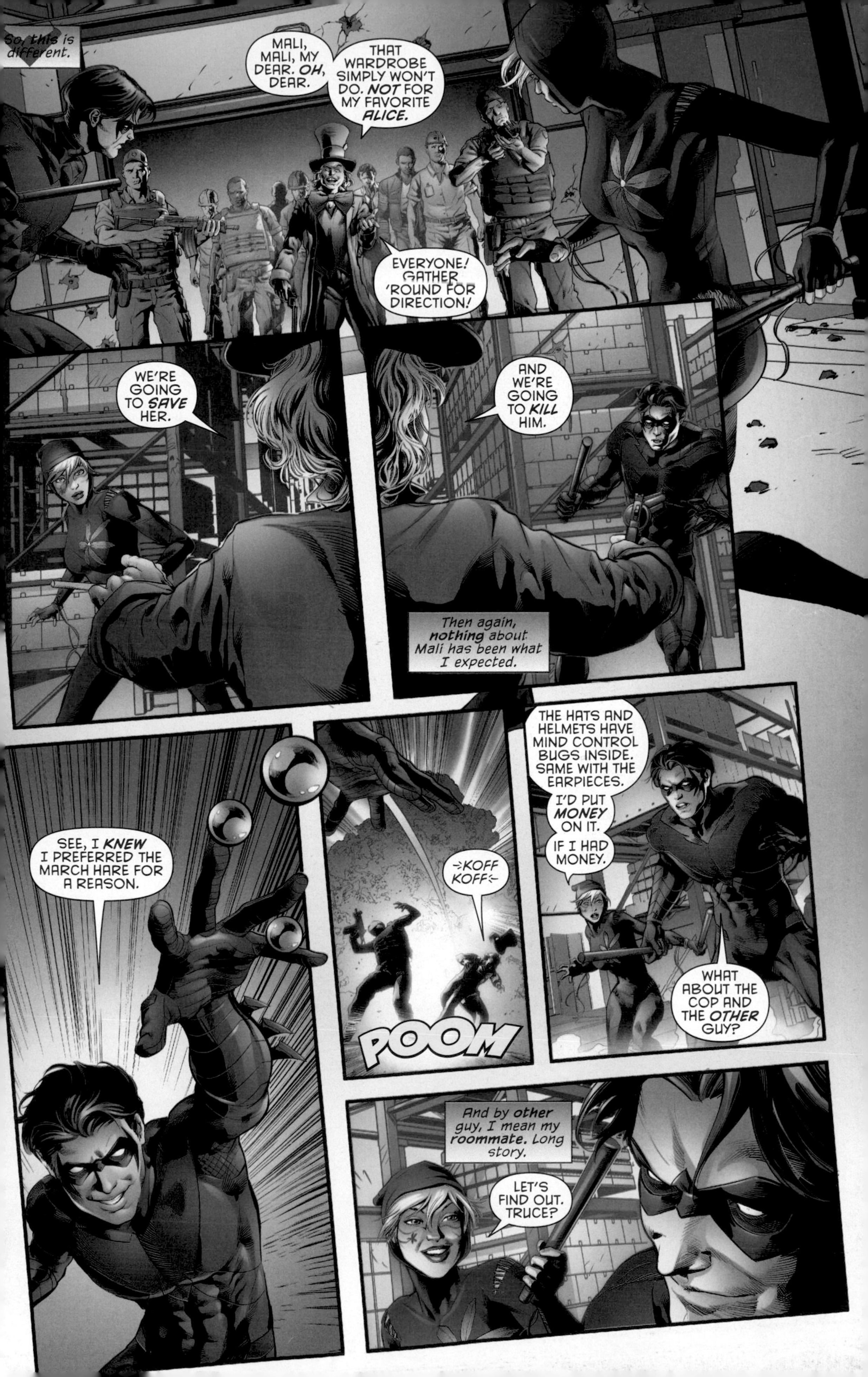
So, this is different.
MALI, MALI, MY DEAR. OH, DEAR.
THAT WARDROBE SIMPLY WON'T DO. NOT FOR MY FAVORITE ALICE.
EVERYONE! GATHER 'ROUND FOR DIRECTION!
WE'RE GOING TO SAVE HER.
AND WE'RE GOING TO KILL HIM.
Then again, nothing about Mali has been what I expected.
SEE, I KNEW I PREFERRED THE MARCH HARE FOR A REASON.
KOFF KOFF
POOM
THE HATS AND HELMETS HAVE MIND CONTROL BUGS INSIDE. SAME WITH THE EARPIECES.
I'D PUT MONEY ON IT.
IF I HAD MONEY.
WHAT ABOUT THE COP AND THE OTHER GUY?
And by other guy, I mean my roommate. Long story.
LET'S FIND OUT. TRUCE?

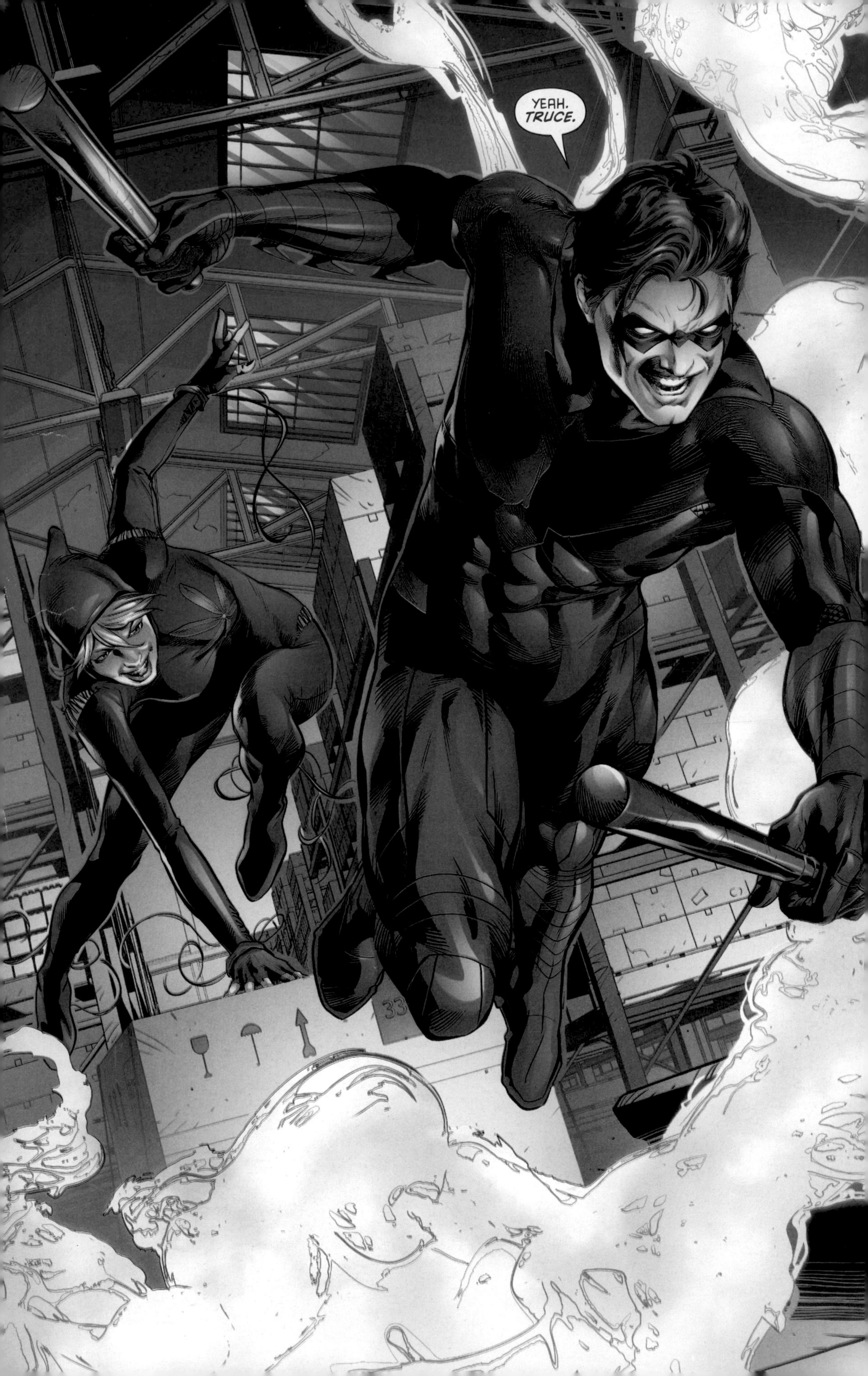
YEAH. TRUCE.

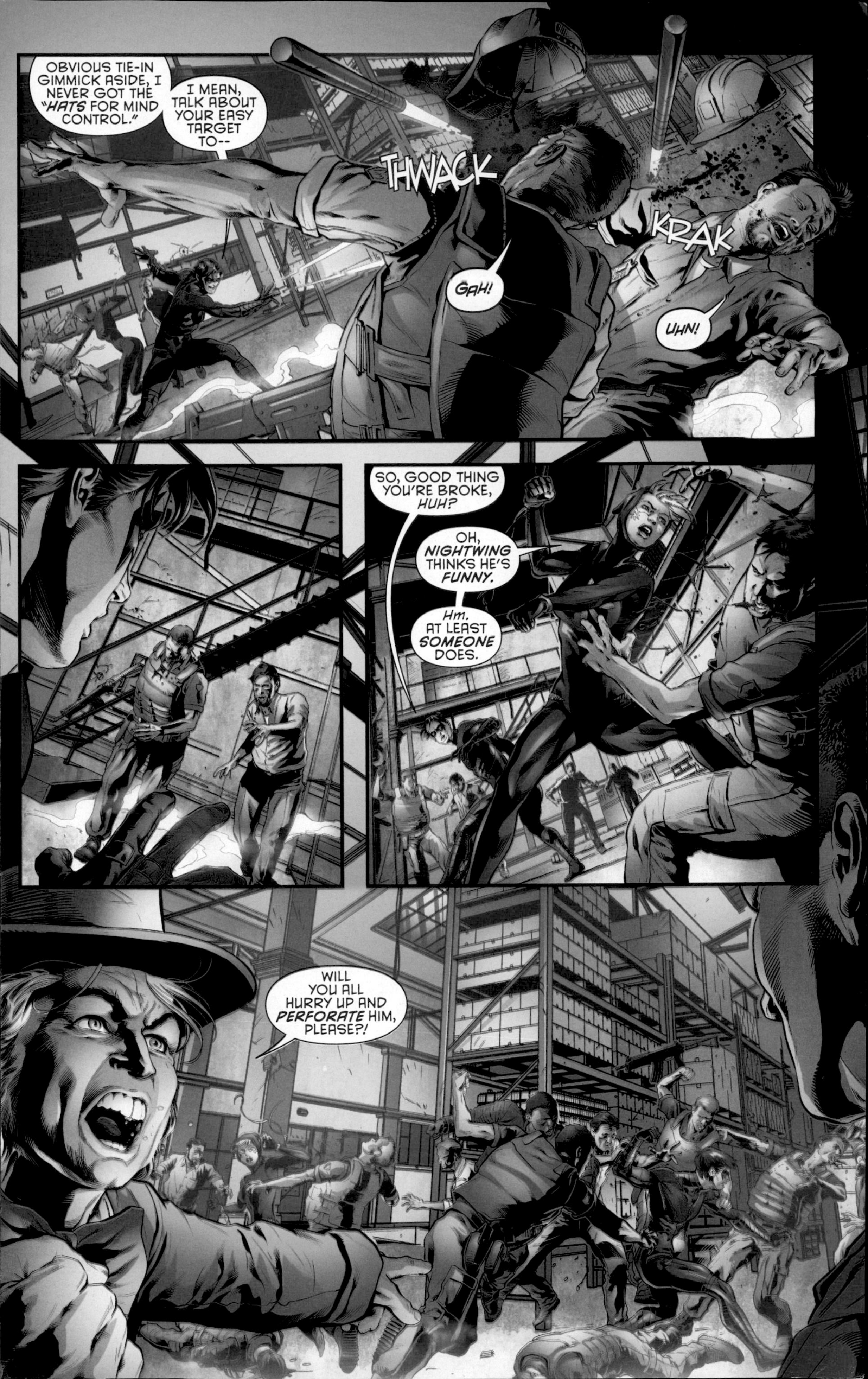

OBVIOUS TIE-IN GIMMICK ASIDE, I NEVER GOT THE "HATS FOR MIND CONTROL."
I MEAN, TALK ABOUT YOUR EASY TARGET TO--
THWACK
KRAK
GAH!
UHN!
SO, GOOD THING YOU'RE BROKE, HUH?
OH, NIGHTWING THINKS HE'S FUNNY.
Hm. AT LEAST SOMEONE DOES.
WILL YOU ALL HURRY UP AND PERFORATE HIM, PLEASE?!

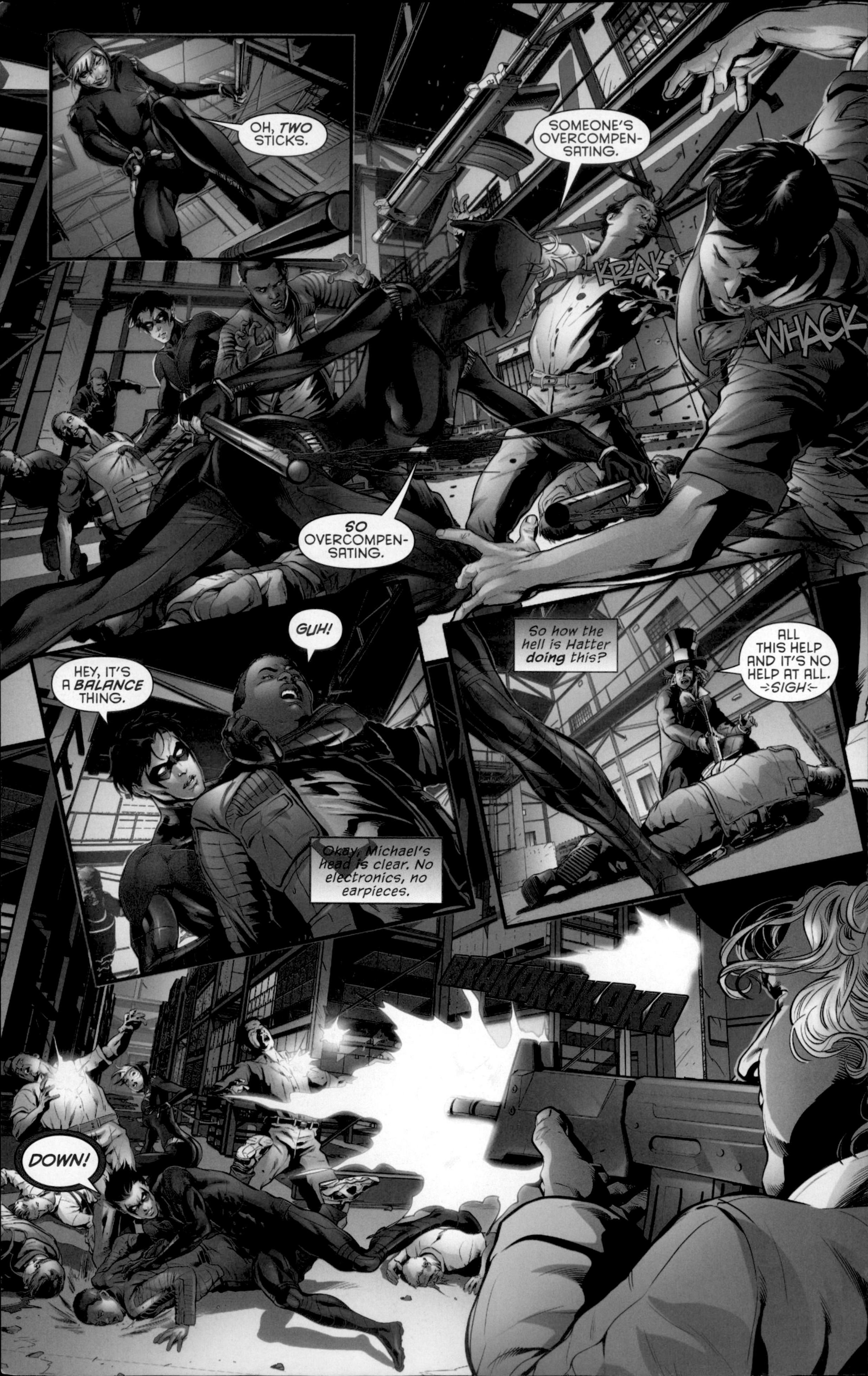
OH, *TWO* STICKS.
SOMEONE'S OVERCOMPEN-SATING.
KRAK
WHACK
SO OVERCOMPEN-SATING.
HEY, IT'S A *BALANCE* THING.
GUH!
Okay, Michael's head is clear. No electronics, no earpieces.
So how the hell is Hatter **doing** this?
ALL THIS HELP AND IT'S NO HELP AT ALL. *-SIGH-*
DOWN!

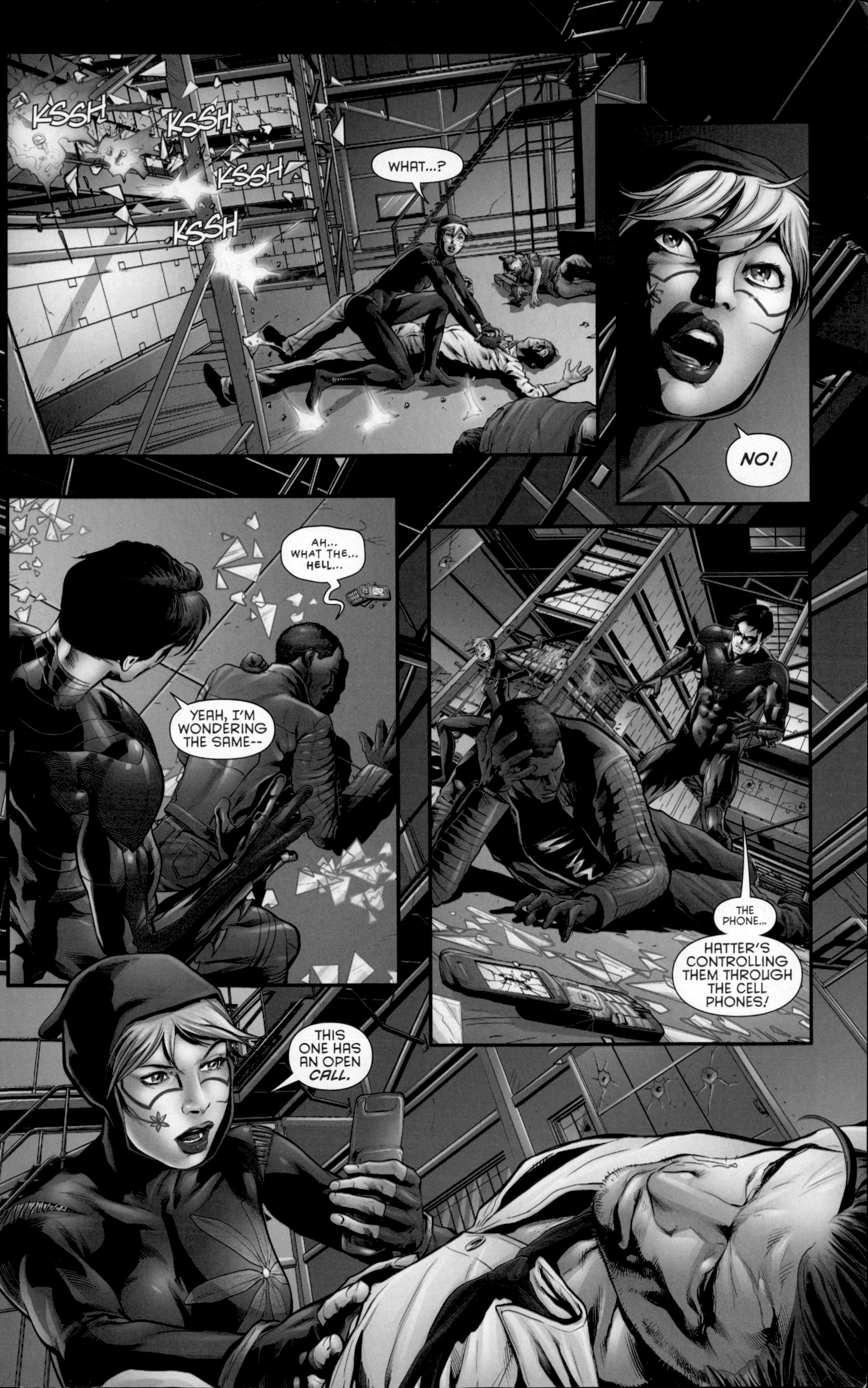
KSSH
KSSH
KSSH
KSSH
WHAT...?
NO!
AH... WHAT THE... HELL...
YEAH, I'M WONDERING THE SAME--
THE PHONE...
HATTER'S CONTROLLING THEM THROUGH THE CELL PHONES!
THIS ONE HAS AN OPEN CALL.

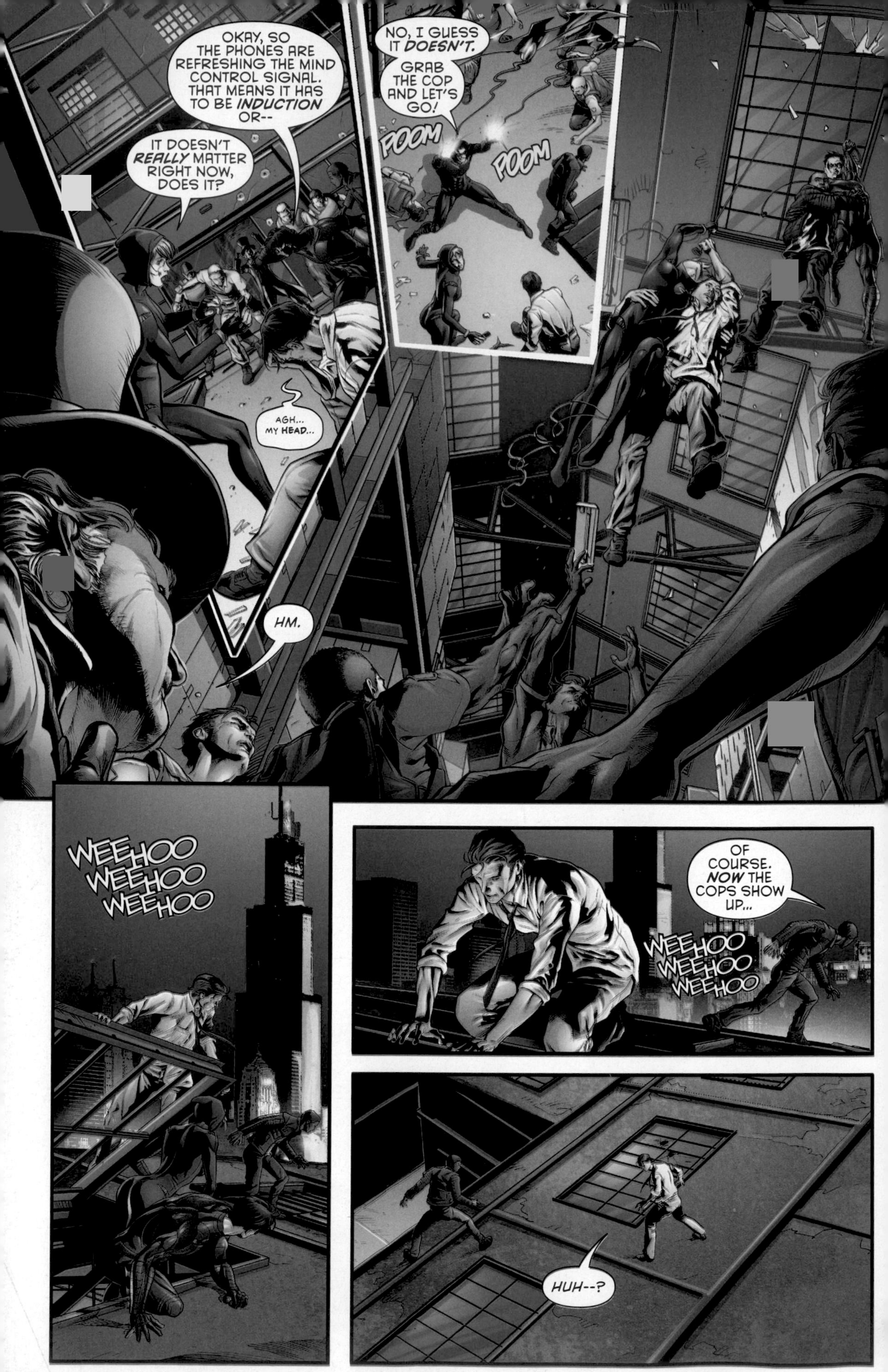
OKAY, SO THE PHONES ARE REFRESHING THE MIND CONTROL SIGNAL. THAT MEANS IT HAS TO BE INDUCTION OR--
IT DOESN'T REALLY MATTER RIGHT NOW, DOES IT?
NO, I GUESS IT DOESN'T.
GRAB THE COP AND LET'S GO!
POOM
POOM
AGH... MY HEAD...
HM.
WEEHOO WEEHOO WEEHOO
OF COURSE. NOW THE COPS SHOW UP...
WEEHOO WEEHOO WEEHOO
HUH--?

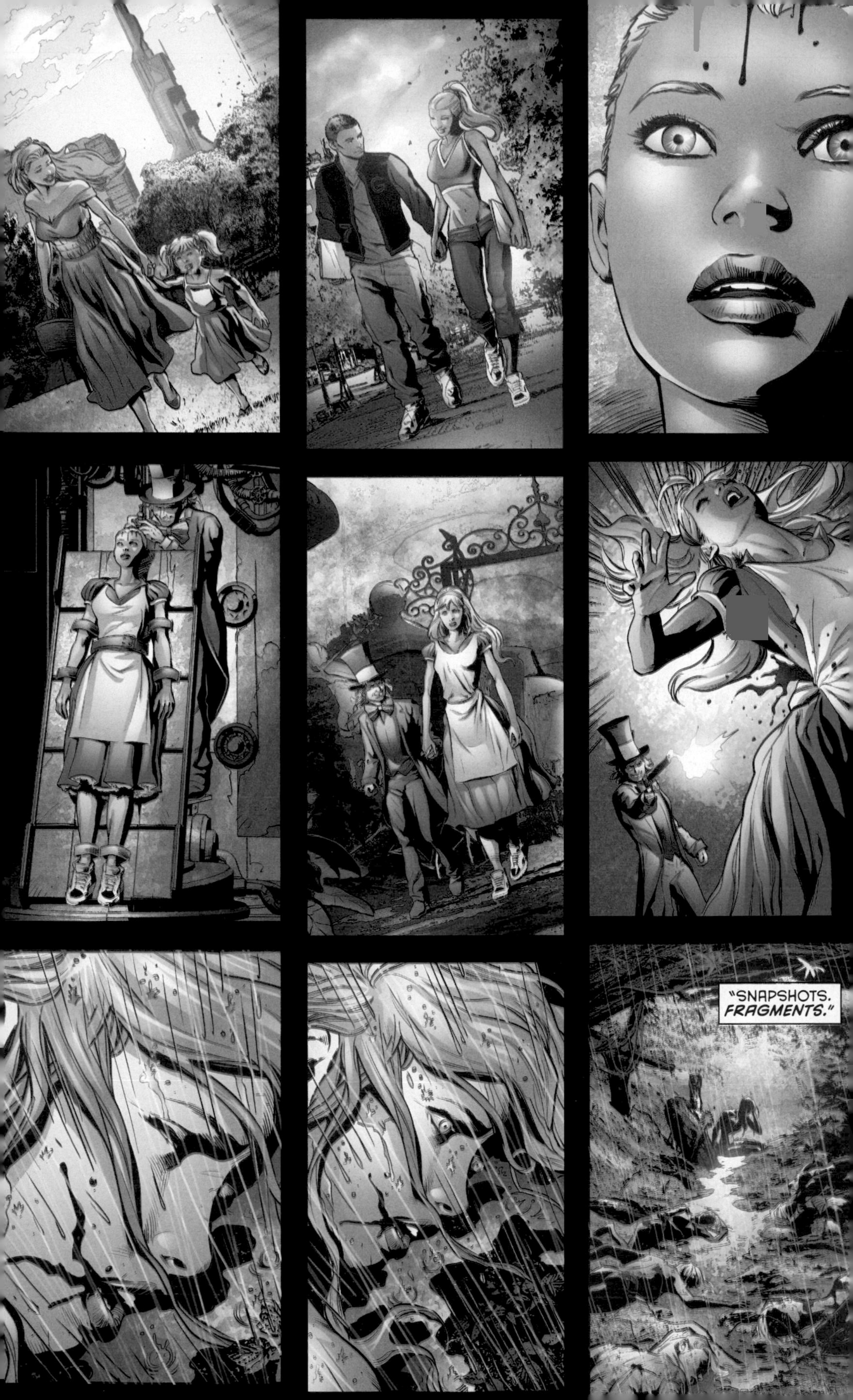
"SNAPSHOTS.
FRAGMENTS."

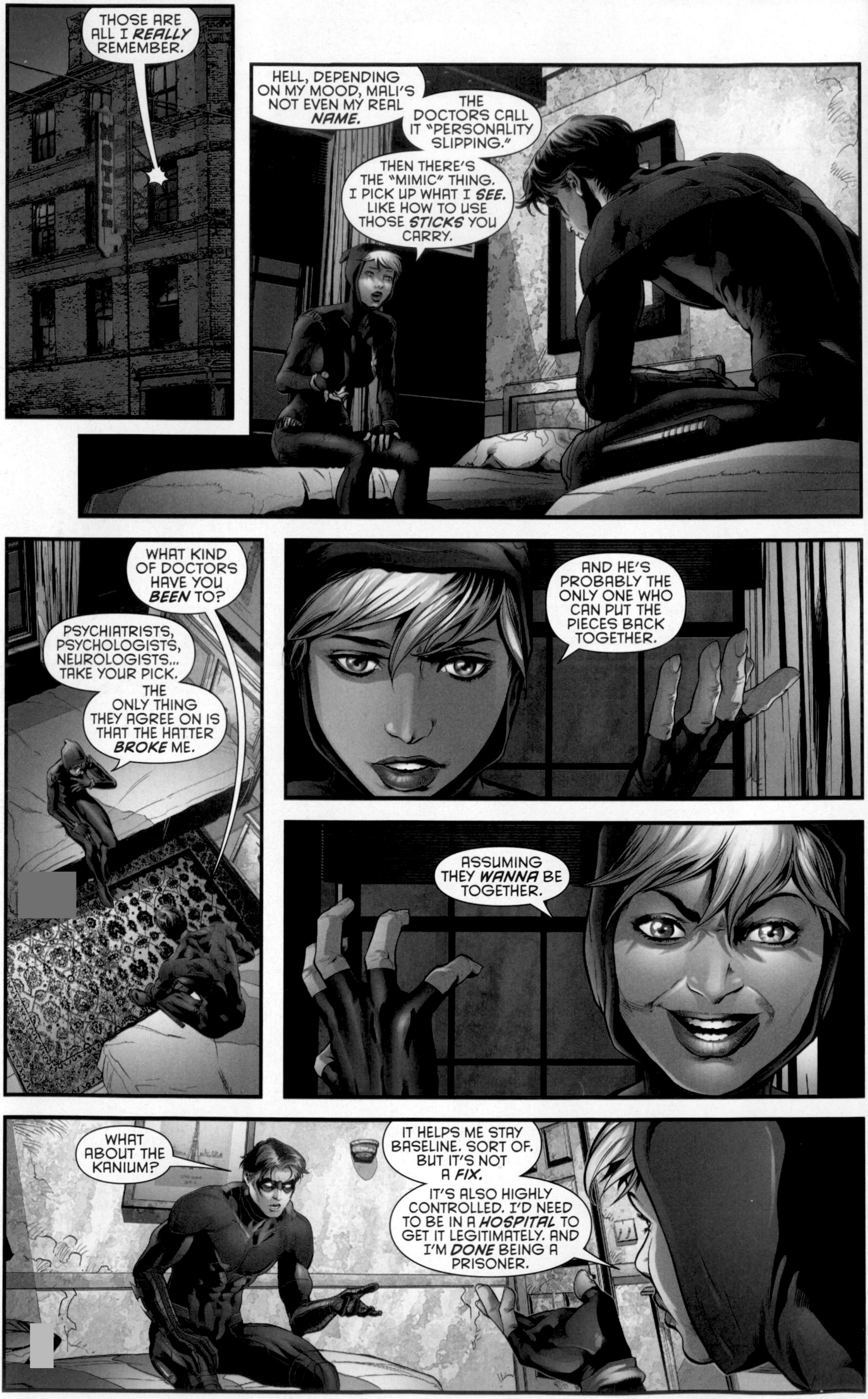
THOSE ARE ALL I REALLY REMEMBER.
HELL, DEPENDING ON MY MOOD, MALI'S NOT EVEN MY REAL NAME.
THE DOCTORS CALL IT "PERSONALITY SLIPPING."
THEN THERE'S THE "MIMIC" THING. I PICK UP WHAT I SEE. LIKE HOW TO USE THOSE STICKS YOU CARRY.
WHAT KIND OF DOCTORS HAVE YOU BEEN TO?
PSYCHIATRISTS, PSYCHOLOGISTS, NEUROLOGISTS... TAKE YOUR PICK.
THE ONLY THING THEY AGREE ON IS THAT THE HATTER BROKE ME.
AND HE'S PROBABLY THE ONLY ONE WHO CAN PUT THE PIECES BACK TOGETHER.
ASSUMING THEY WANNA BE TOGETHER.
WHAT ABOUT THE KANIUM?
IT HELPS ME STAY BASELINE. SORT OF. BUT IT'S NOT A FIX.
IT'S ALSO HIGHLY CONTROLLED. I'D NEED TO BE IN A HOSPITAL TO GET IT LEGITIMATELY. AND I'M DONE BEING A PRISONER.

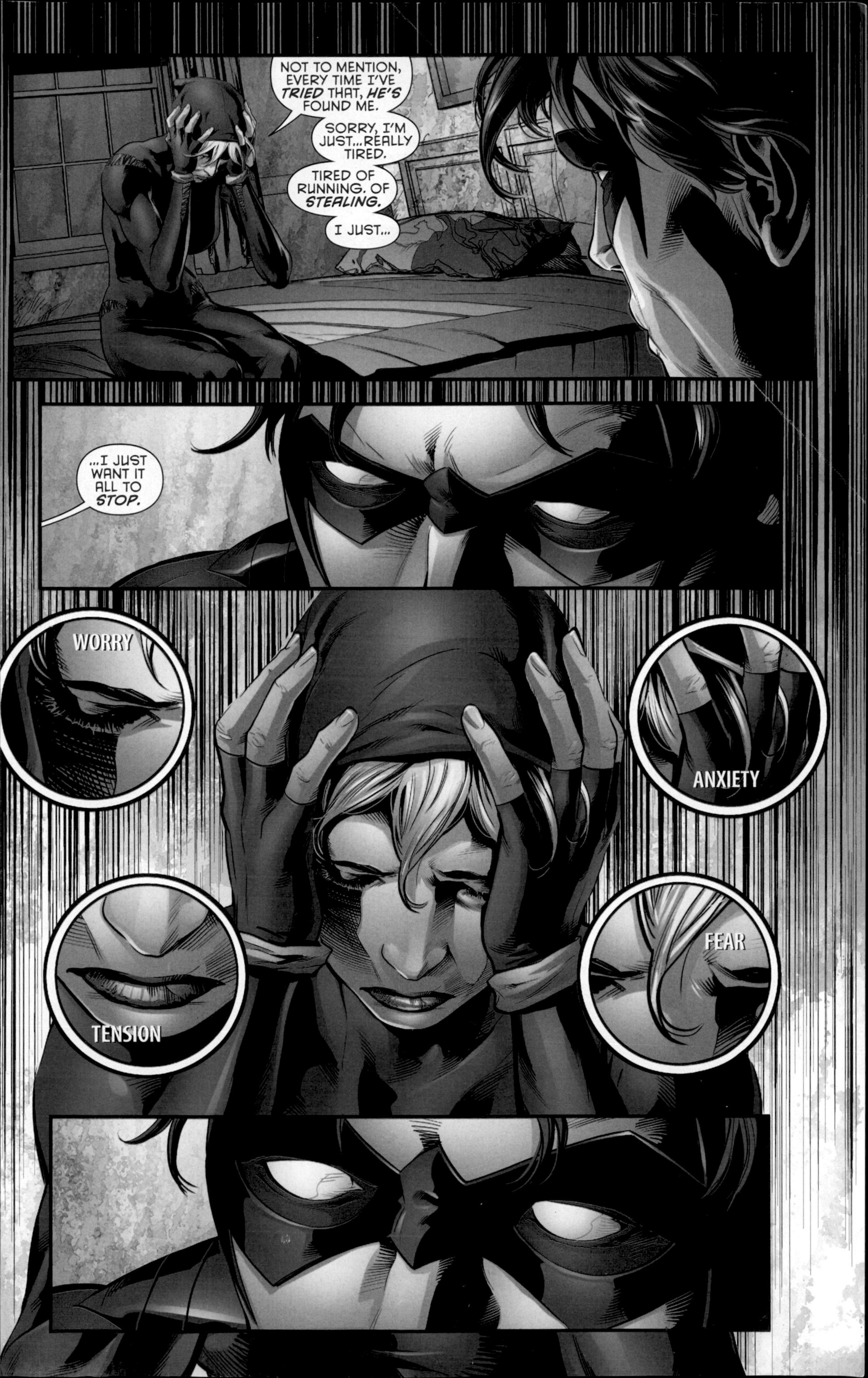
NOT TO MENTION, EVERY TIME I'VE TRIED THAT, HE'S FOUND ME.
SORRY, I'M JUST...REALLY TIRED.
TIRED OF RUNNING. OF STEALING.
I JUST...
...I JUST WANT IT ALL TO STOP.
WORRY
ANXIETY
FEAR
TENSION

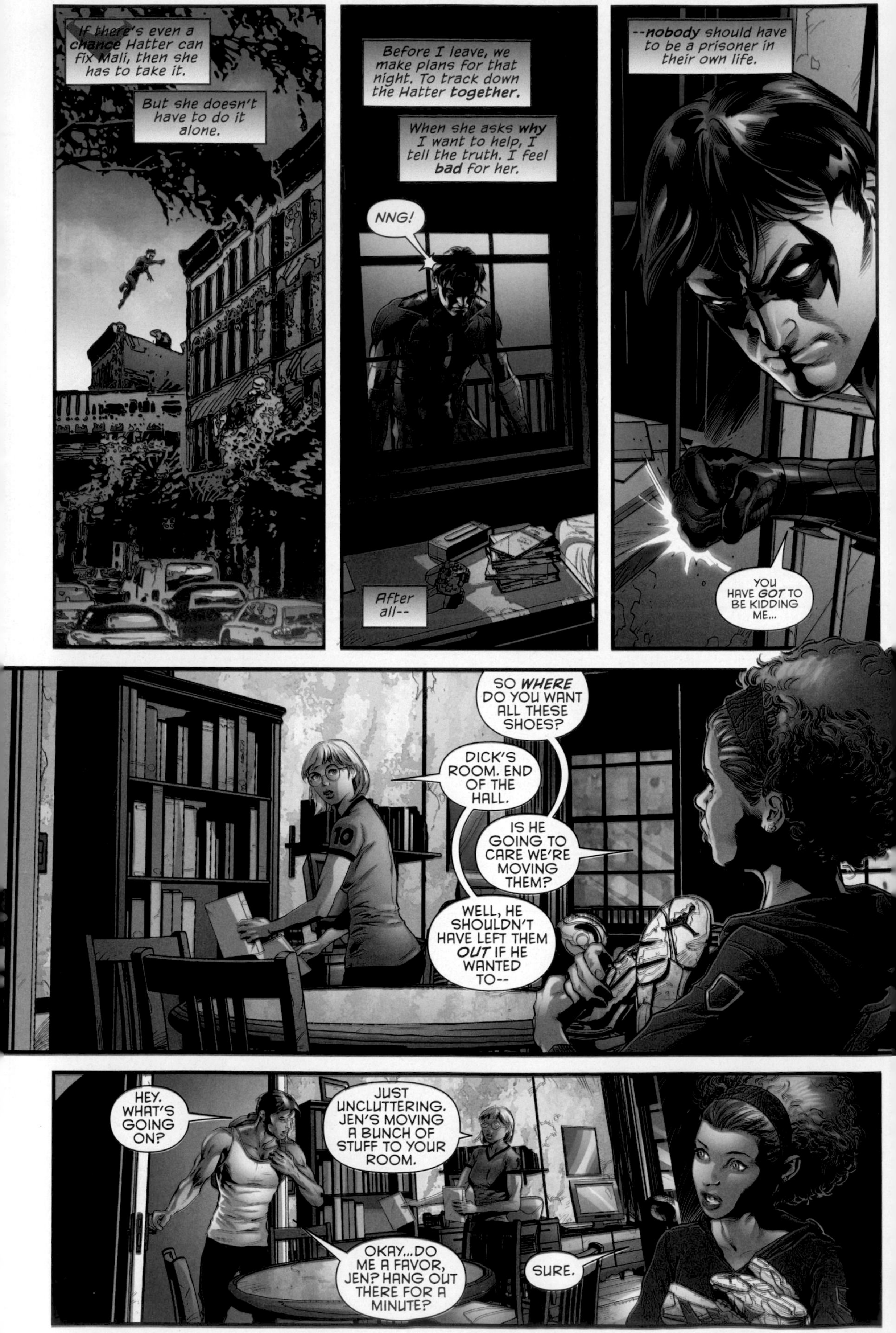
If there's even a chance Hatter can fix Mali, then she has to take it.
But she doesn't have to do it alone.
Before I leave, we make plans for that night. To track down the Hatter together.
When she asks why I want to help, I tell the truth. I feel bad for her.
NNG!
After all--
--nobody should have to be a prisoner in their own life.
YOU HAVE GOT TO BE KIDDING ME...
SO WHERE DO YOU WANT ALL THESE SHOES?
DICK'S ROOM. END OF THE HALL.
IS HE GOING TO CARE WE'RE MOVING THEM?
WELL, HE SHOULDN'T HAVE LEFT THEM OUT IF HE WANTED TO--
HEY. WHAT'S GOING ON?
JUST UNCLUTTERING. JEN'S MOVING A BUNCH OF STUFF TO YOUR ROOM.
OKAY...DO ME A FAVOR, JEN? HANG OUT THERE FOR A MINUTE?
SURE.

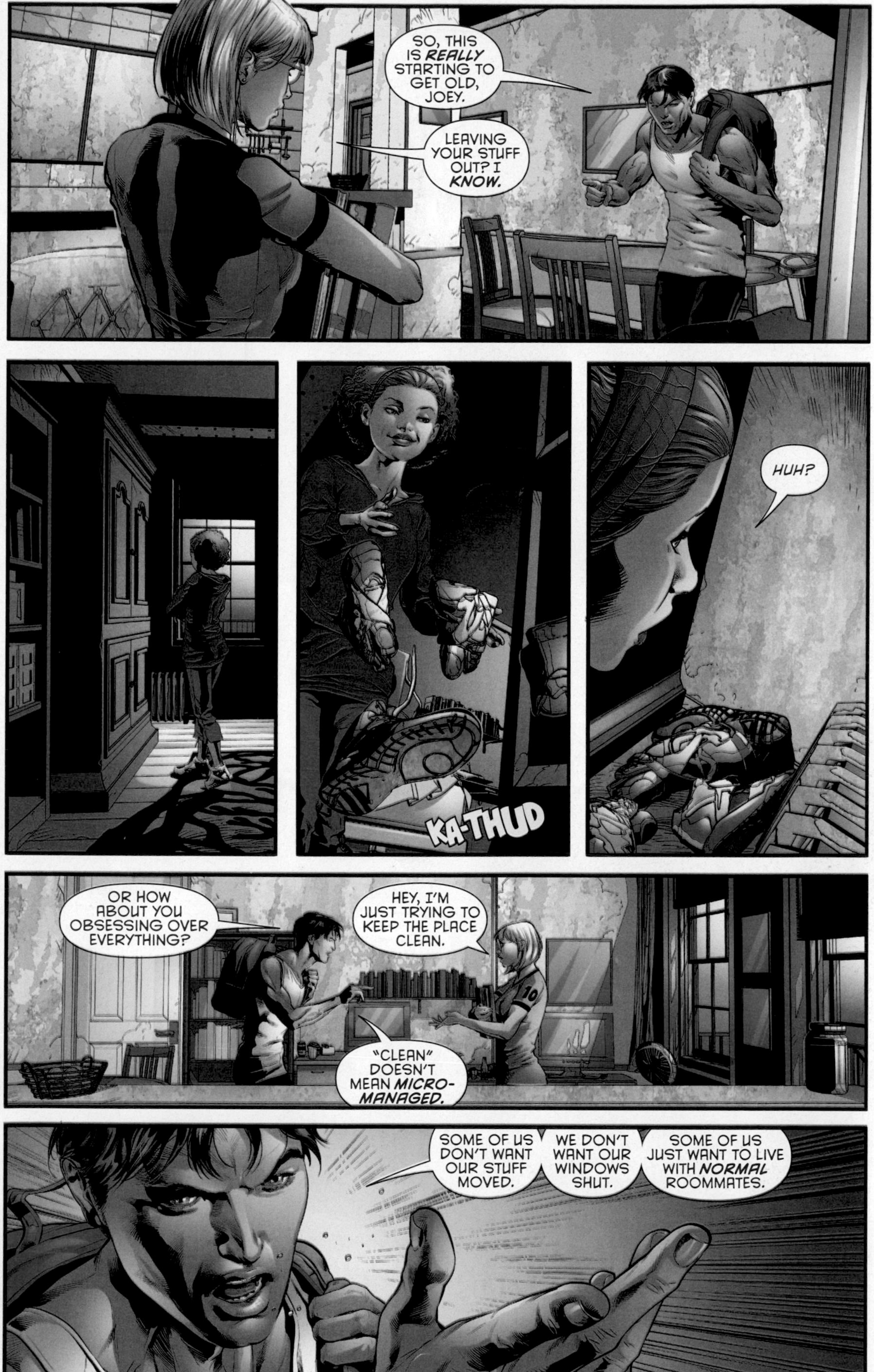
SO, THIS IS *REALLY* STARTING TO GET OLD, JOEY.
LEAVING YOUR STUFF OUT? I *KNOW*.
KA-THUD
HUH?
OR HOW ABOUT YOU OBSESSING OVER EVERYTHING?
HEY, I'M JUST TRYING TO KEEP THE PLACE CLEAN.
"CLEAN" DOESN'T MEAN *MICRO-MANAGED*.
SOME OF US DON'T WANT OUR STUFF MOVED.
WE DON'T WANT OUR WINDOWS SHUT.
SOME OF US JUST WANT TO LIVE WITH *NORMAL* ROOMMATES.

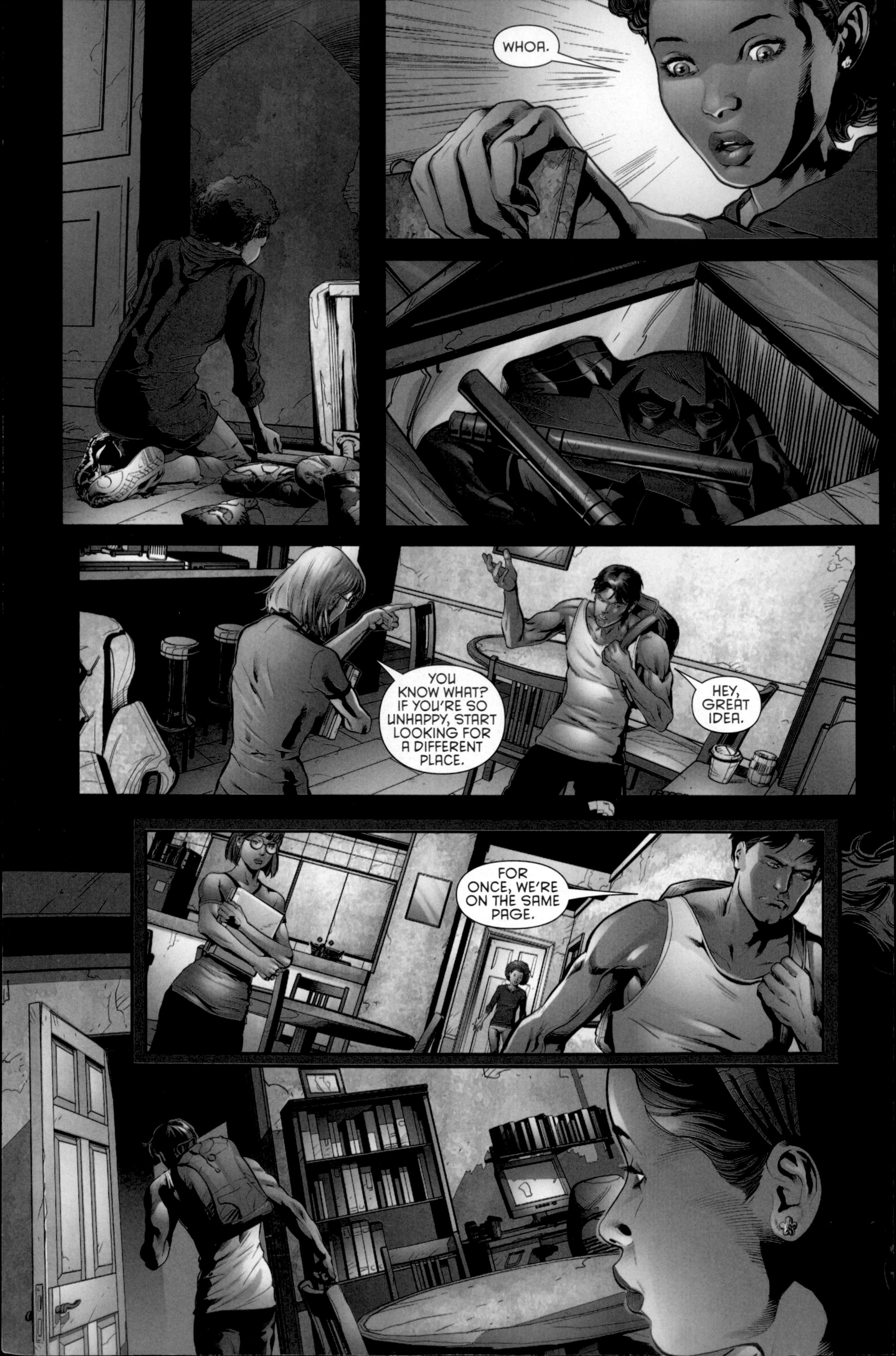
WHOA.
YOU KNOW WHAT? IF YOU'RE SO UNHAPPY, START LOOKING FOR A DIFFERENT PLACE.
HEY, GREAT IDEA.
FOR ONCE, WE'RE ON THE SAME PAGE.

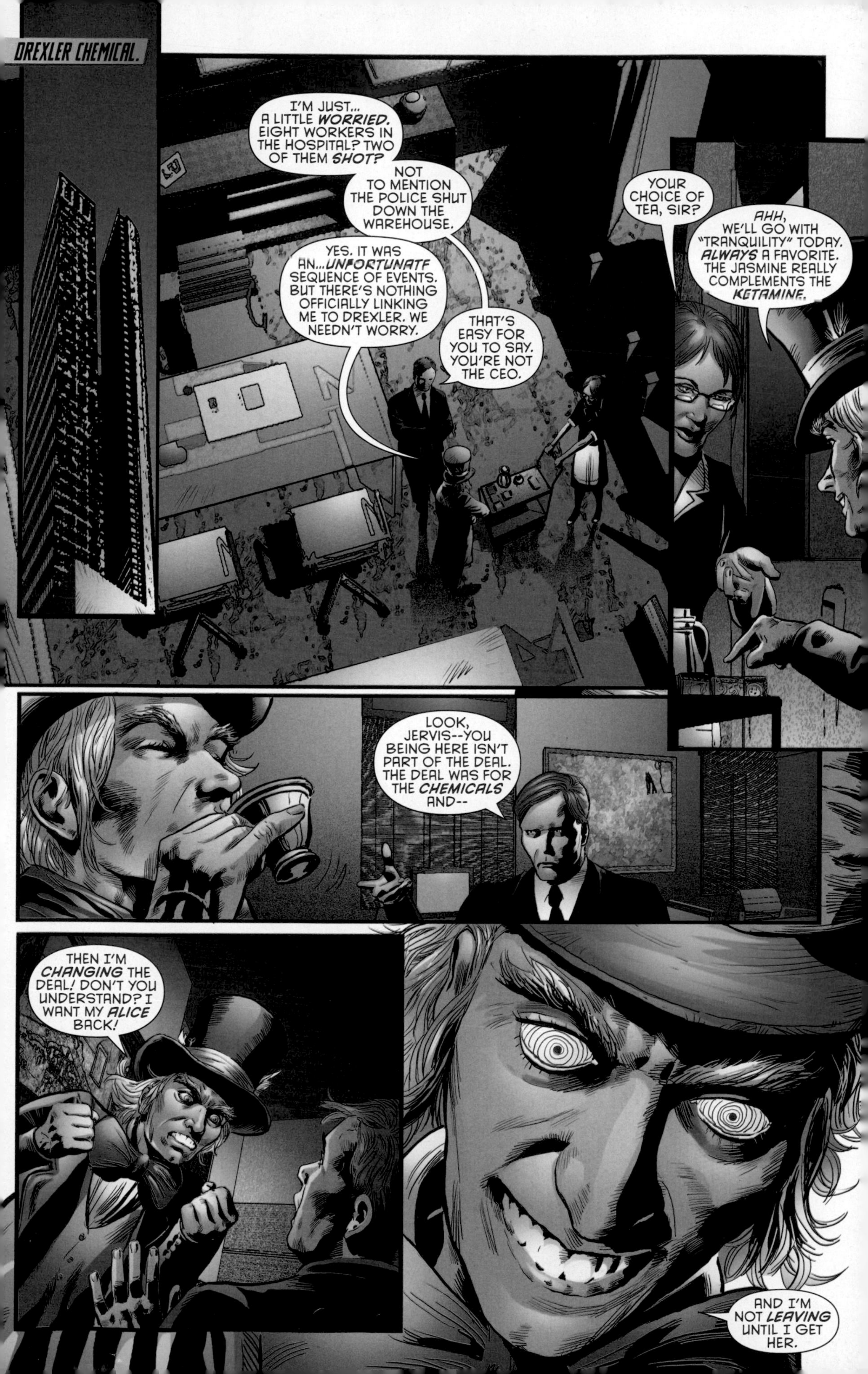
DREXLER CHEMICAL.
I'M JUST... A LITTLE WORRIED. EIGHT WORKERS IN THE HOSPITAL? TWO OF THEM SHOT?
NOT TO MENTION THE POLICE SHUT DOWN THE WAREHOUSE.
YES. IT WAS AN...UNFORTUNATE SEQUENCE OF EVENTS. BUT THERE'S NOTHING OFFICIALLY LINKING ME TO DREXLER. WE NEEDN'T WORRY.
THAT'S EASY FOR YOU TO SAY. YOU'RE NOT THE CEO.
YOUR CHOICE OF TEA, SIR?
AHH, WE'LL GO WITH "TRANQUILITY" TODAY. ALWAYS A FAVORITE. THE JASMINE REALLY COMPLEMENTS THE KETAMINE.
LOOK, JERVIS--YOU BEING HERE ISN'T PART OF THE DEAL. THE DEAL WAS FOR THE CHEMICALS AND--
THEN I'M CHANGING THE DEAL! DON'T YOU UNDERSTAND? I WANT MY ALICE BACK!
AND I'M NOT LEAVING UNTIL I GET HER.

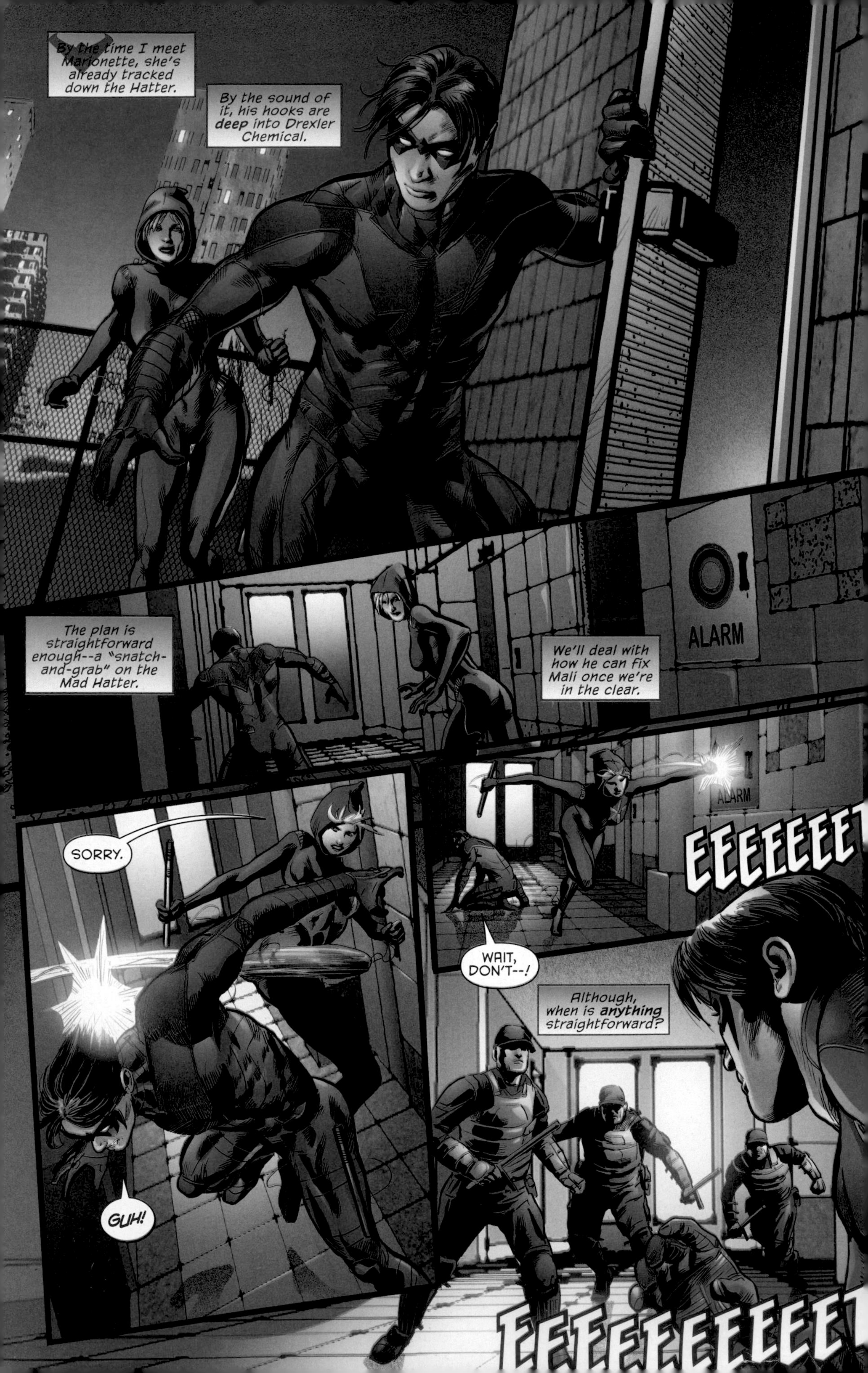
By the time I meet Marionette, she's already tracked down the Hatter.
By the sound of it, his hooks are deep into Drexler Chemical.
The plan is straightforward enough--a "snatch-and-grab" on the Mad Hatter.
We'll deal with how he can fix Mali once we're in the clear.
ALARM
SORRY.
GUH!
ALARM
WAIT, DON'T--!
EEEEEEET
Although, when is anything straightforward?
EEEEEEEEEET

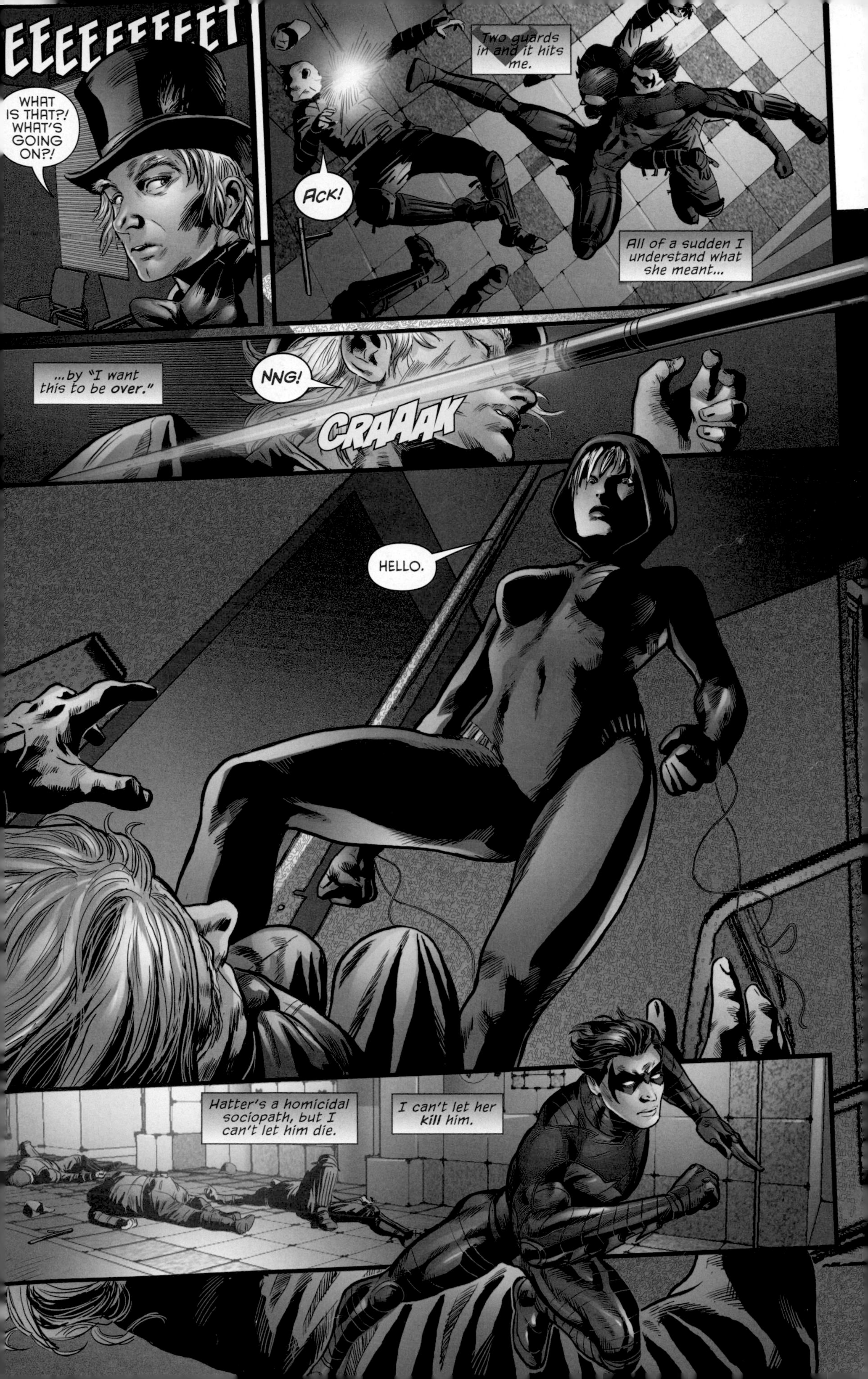
EEEEFFFFFEET
WHAT IS THAT?! WHAT'S GOING ON?!
Two guards in and it hits me.
ACK!
All of a sudden I understand what she meant...
...by "I want this to be over."
NNG!
CRAAAK
HELLO.
Hatter's a homicidal sociopath, but I can't let him die.
I can't let her kill him.

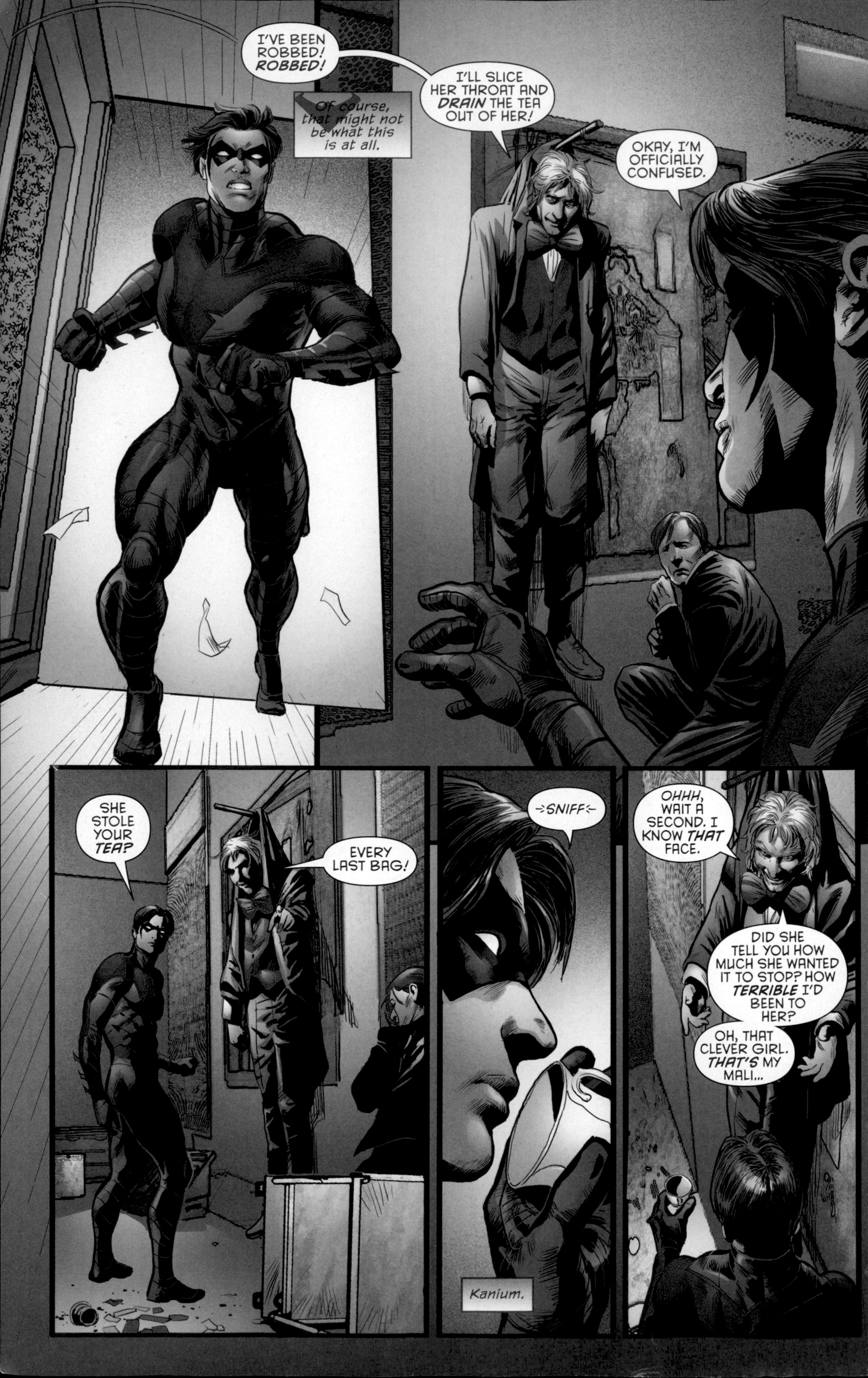
I'VE BEEN ROBBED! ROBBED!
Of course, that might not be what this is at all.
I'LL SLICE HER THROAT AND DRAIN THE TEA OUT OF HER!
OKAY, I'M OFFICIALLY CONFUSED.
SHE STOLE YOUR TEA?
EVERY LAST BAG!
-SNIFF-
Kanium.
OHHH, WAIT A SECOND. I KNOW THAT FACE.
DID SHE TELL YOU HOW MUCH SHE WANTED IT TO STOP? HOW TERRIBLE I'D BEEN TO HER?
OH, THAT CLEVER GIRL. THAT'S MY MALI...

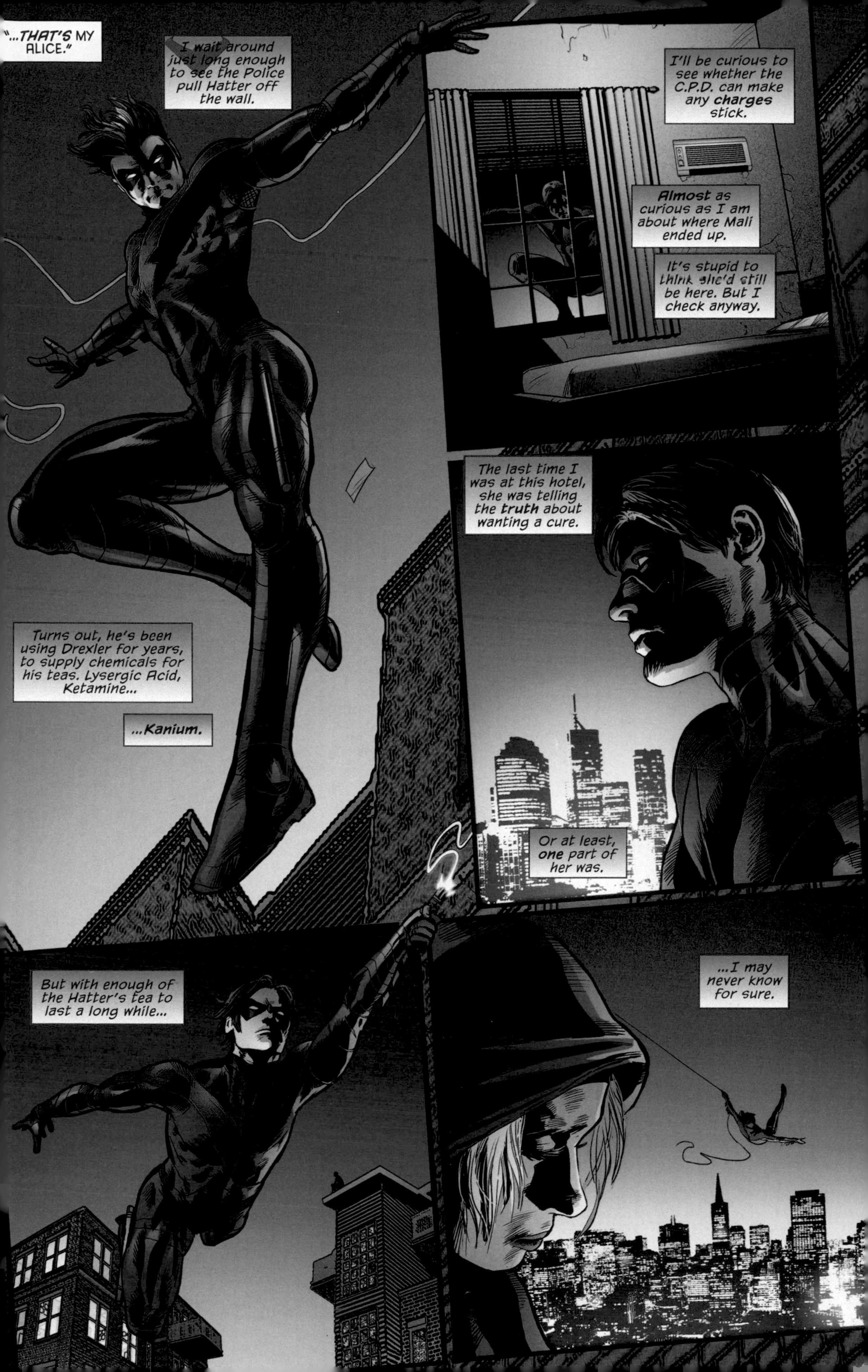
"...THAT'S MY ALICE."
I wait around just long enough to see the Police pull Hatter off the wall.
I'll be curious to see whether the C.P.D. can make any charges stick.
Almost as curious as I am about where Mali ended up.
It's stupid to think she'd still be here. But I check anyway.
Turns out, he's been using Drexler for years, to supply chemicals for his teas. Lysergic Acid, Ketamine...
...Kanium.
The last time I was at this hotel, she was telling the truth about wanting a cure.
Or at least, one part of her was.
But with enough of the Hatter's tea to last a long while...
...I may never know for sure.

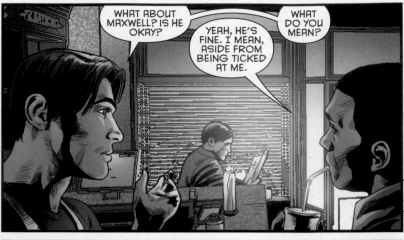

WHAT ABOUT MAXWELL? IS HE OKAY?

YEAH, HE'S FINE. I MEAN, ASIDE FROM BEING TICKED AT ME.

WHAT DO YOU MEAN?

--SO AFTER THE M.R.I. AND THE BRAIN SCAN, THEY LET US GO HOME. I FEEL OKAY NOW, BUT MAN...WHAT A WEIRD COUPLE OF DAYS.

I MEAN, WHO EVER THINKS THEY'RE GOING TO BE POSSESSED BY THE MAD HATTER?

GEEZ. THAT SOUNDS TERRIBLE, MICHAEL.

THE WHOLE HATTER SITUATION...

...FEELING SO HELPLESS...SO POWERLESS...IT WAS ONE OF THE SCARIEST THINGS I'VE EVER BEEN THROUGH.

IT MADE ME REALIZE HOW MUCH I RESENTED BEING MAXWELL'S PAWN. I TOLD HIM I WAS DONE HELPING HIM, AND IF THAT TANKED MY CAREER... SO BE IT.

GOOD FOR YOU.

YOU KNOW, A LOT OF TIMES PEOPLE GET MANIPULATIVE LIKE THAT BECAUSE SOMETHING BIG BLOWS UP IN THEIR LIFE.

THEY CLING EXTRA HARD TO WHATEVER LAST SHREDS THEY CAN, TO WHATEVER THEY DO HAVE CONTROL OVER.

I GUESS WHAT I'M SAYING IS THAT IT WAS PROBABLY NOTHING PERSONAL AGAINST YOU OR--

UH, YOU STILL THERE?

YEAH... YEAH. SORRY, I WAS JUST THINKING ABOUT SOMEONE ELSE...

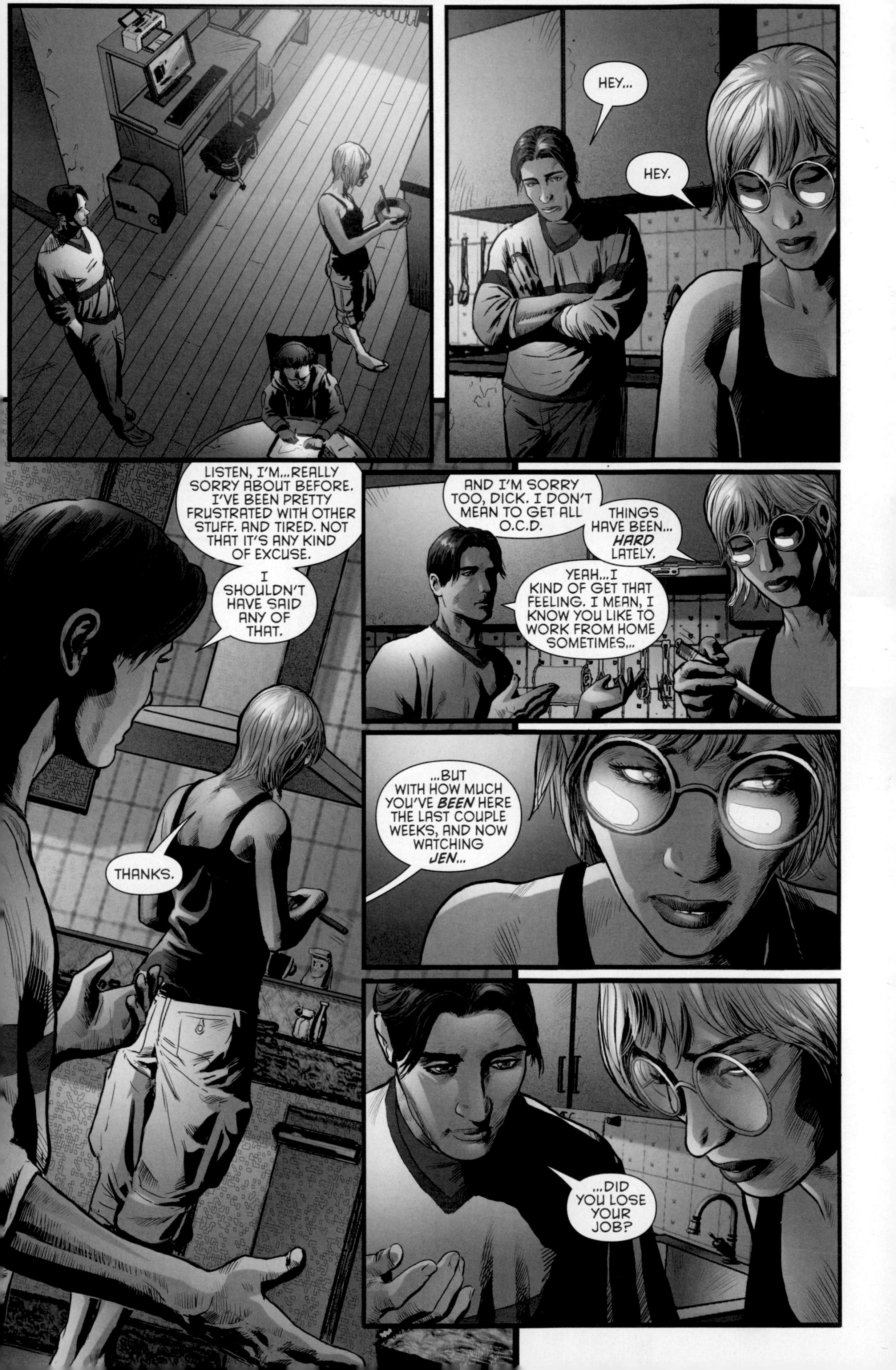
HEY...
HEY.
LISTEN, I'M...REALLY SORRY ABOUT BEFORE. I'VE BEEN PRETTY FRUSTRATED WITH OTHER STUFF. AND TIRED. NOT THAT IT'S ANY KIND OF EXCUSE.
I SHOULDN'T HAVE SAID ANY OF THAT.
THANKS.
AND I'M SORRY TOO, DICK. I DON'T MEAN TO GET ALL O.C.D.
THINGS HAVE BEEN... *HARD* LATELY.
YEAH...I KIND OF GET THAT FEELING. I MEAN, I KNOW YOU LIKE TO WORK FROM HOME SOMETIMES...
...BUT WITH HOW MUCH YOU'VE *BEEN* HERE THE LAST COUPLE WEEKS, AND NOW WATCHING *JEN*...
...DID YOU LOSE YOUR JOB?

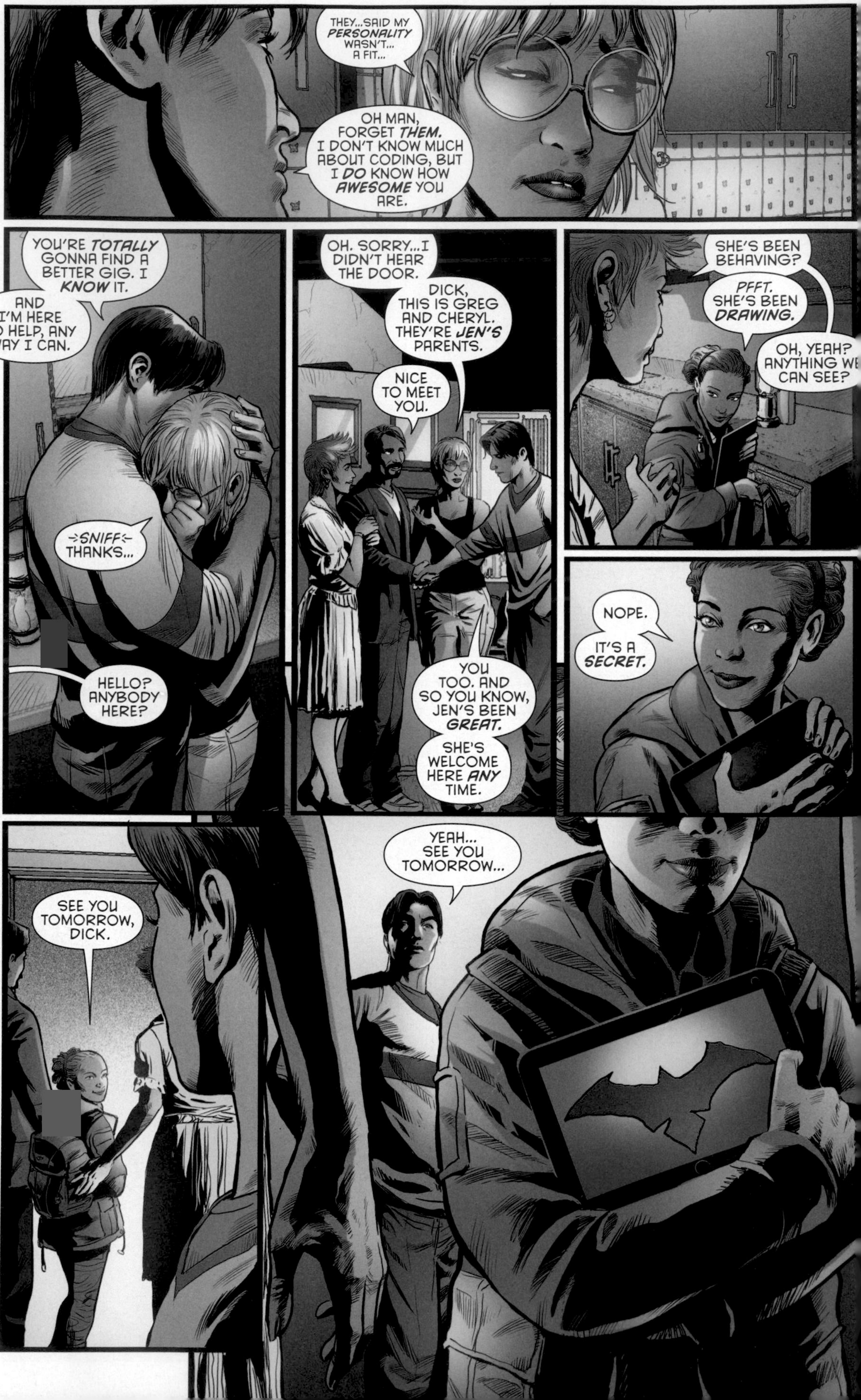
THEY...SAID MY PERSONALITY WASN'T... A FIT...
OH MAN, FORGET THEM. I DON'T KNOW MUCH ABOUT CODING, BUT I DO KNOW HOW AWESOME YOU ARE.
YOU'RE TOTALLY GONNA FIND A BETTER GIG. I KNOW IT.
AND I'M HERE TO HELP, ANY WAY I CAN.
SNIFF THANKS...
HELLO? ANYBODY HERE?
OH. SORRY...I DIDN'T HEAR THE DOOR.
DICK, THIS IS GREG AND CHERYL. THEY'RE JEN'S PARENTS.
NICE TO MEET YOU.
YOU TOO. AND SO YOU KNOW, JEN'S BEEN GREAT.
SHE'S WELCOME HERE ANY TIME.
SHE'S BEEN BEHAVING?
PFFT. SHE'S BEEN DRAWING.
OH, YEAH? ANYTHING WE CAN SEE?
NOPE.
IT'S A SECRET.
SEE YOU TOMORROW, DICK.
YEAH... SEE YOU TOMORROW...

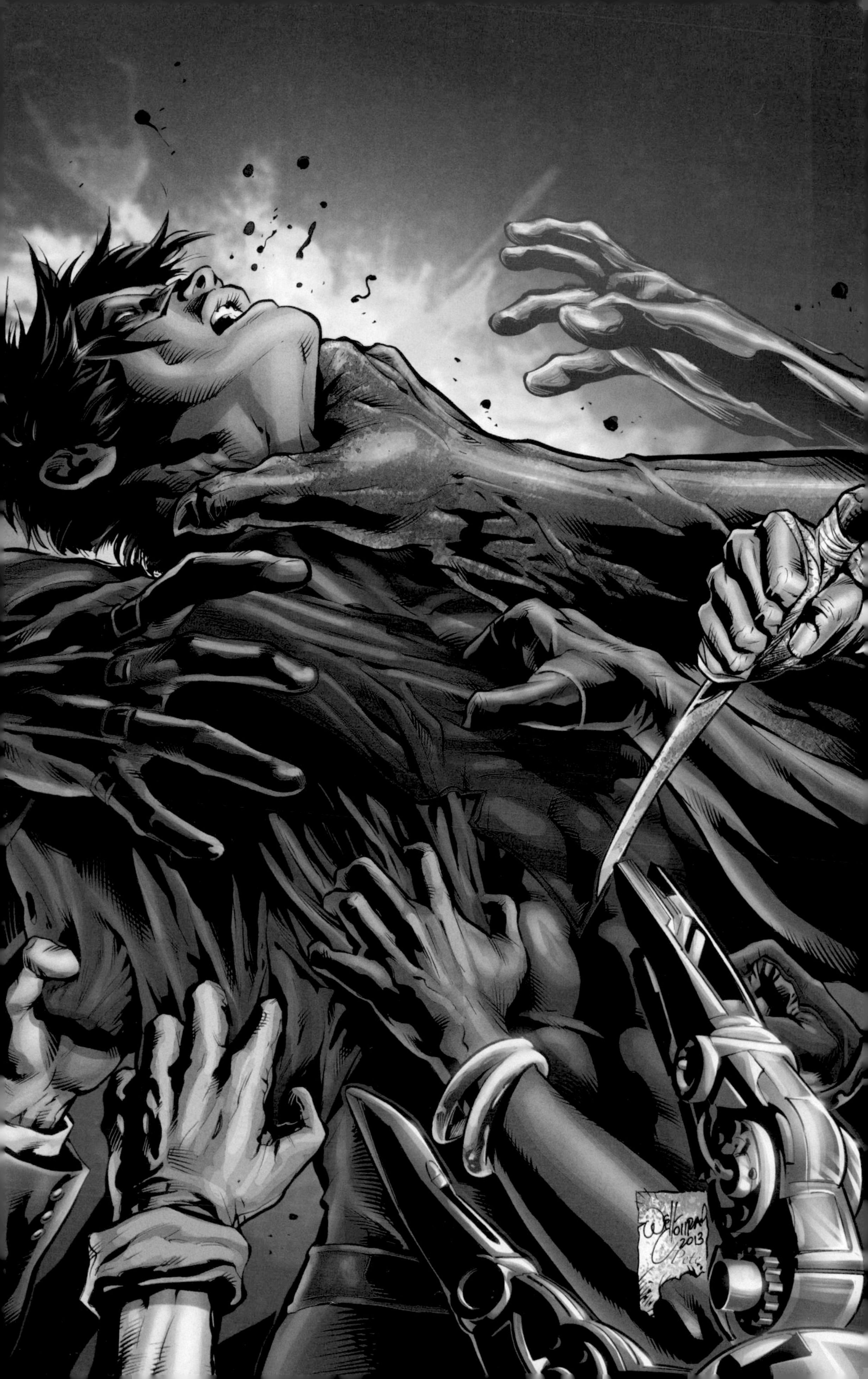

KYLE HIGGINS writer **RUSSELL DAUTERMAN** artist **PETE PANTAZIS** colorist
CARLOS M. MANGUAL letterer cover art by **WILL CONRAD** and **PETE PANTAZIS**

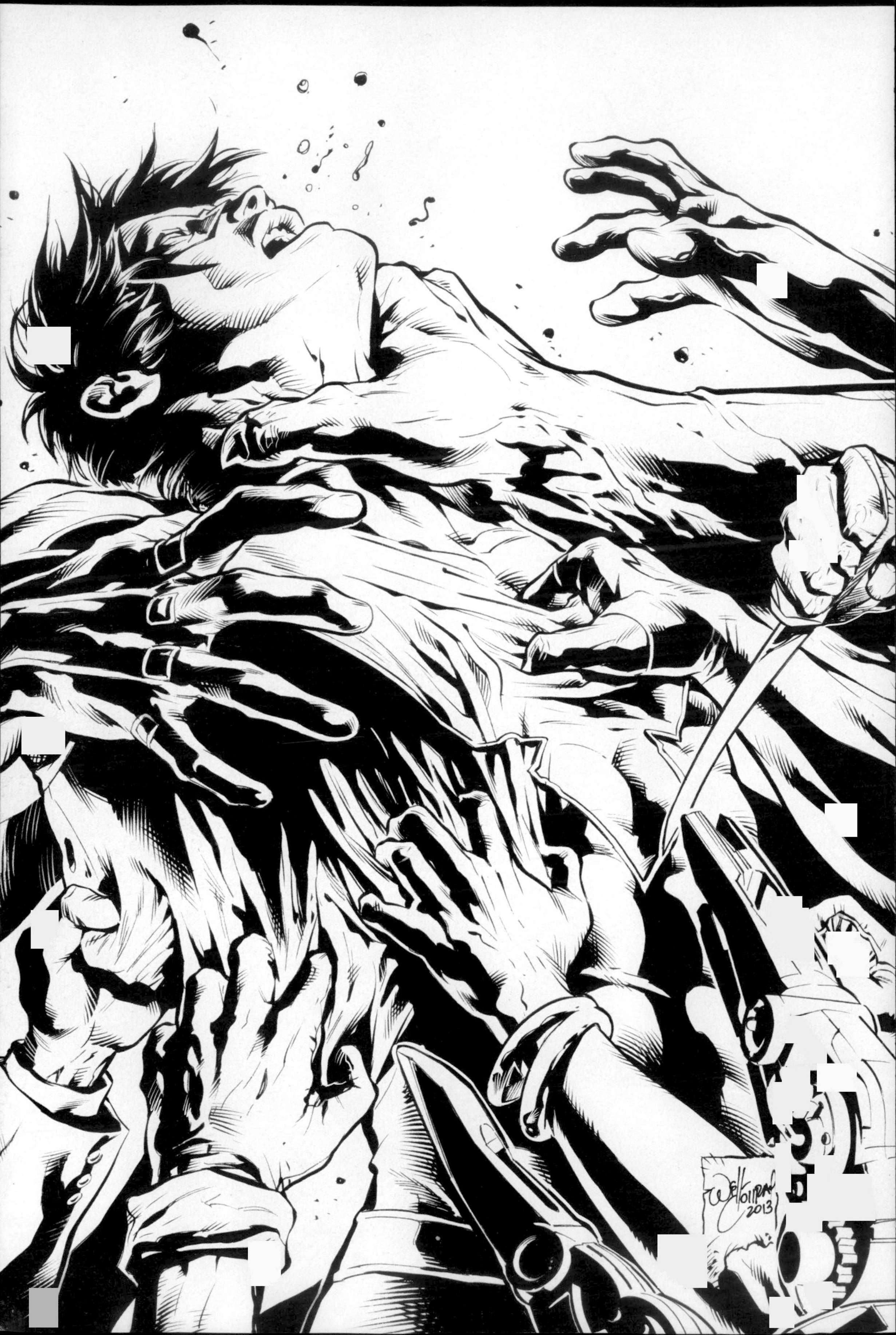

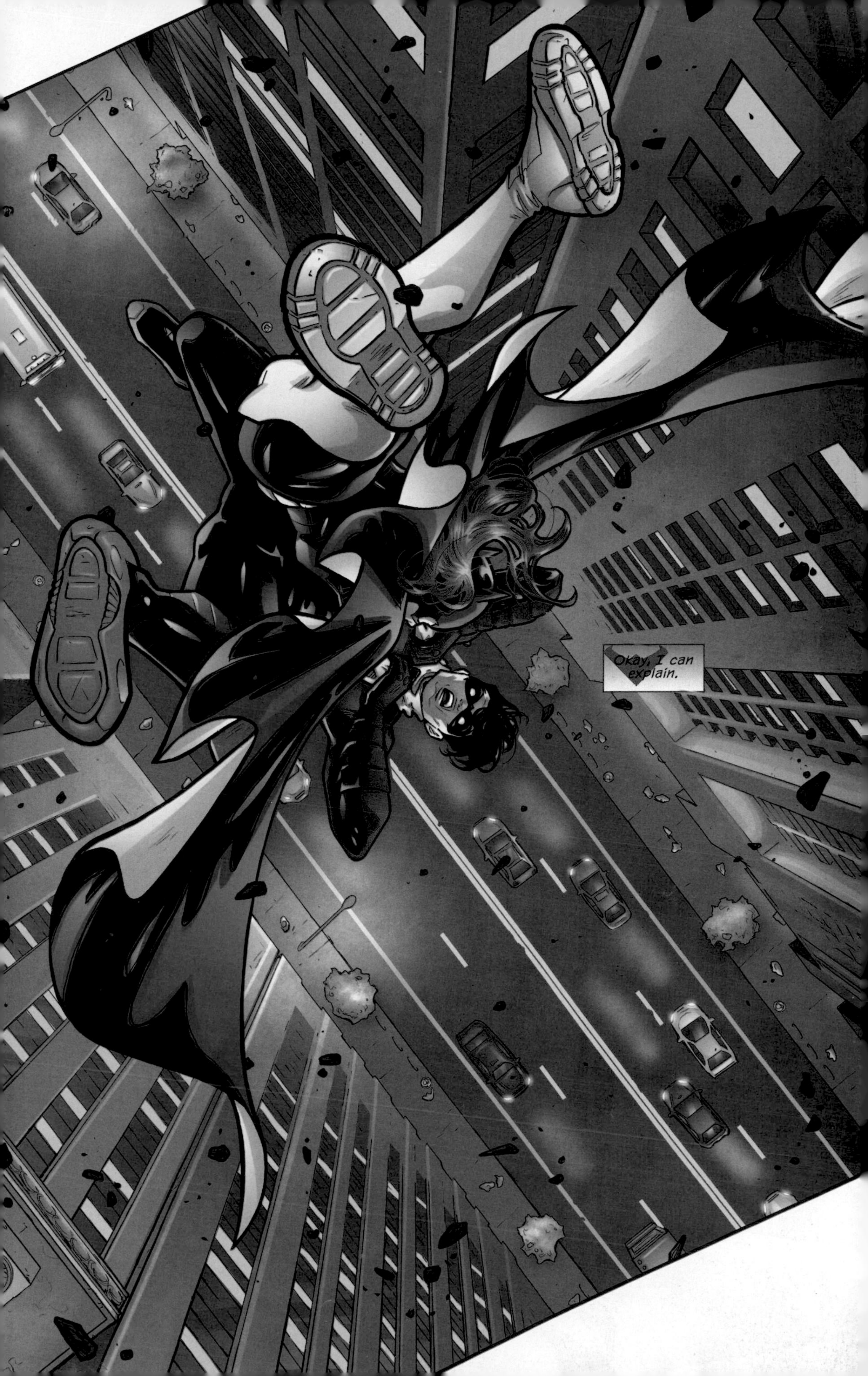
Okay, I can explain.

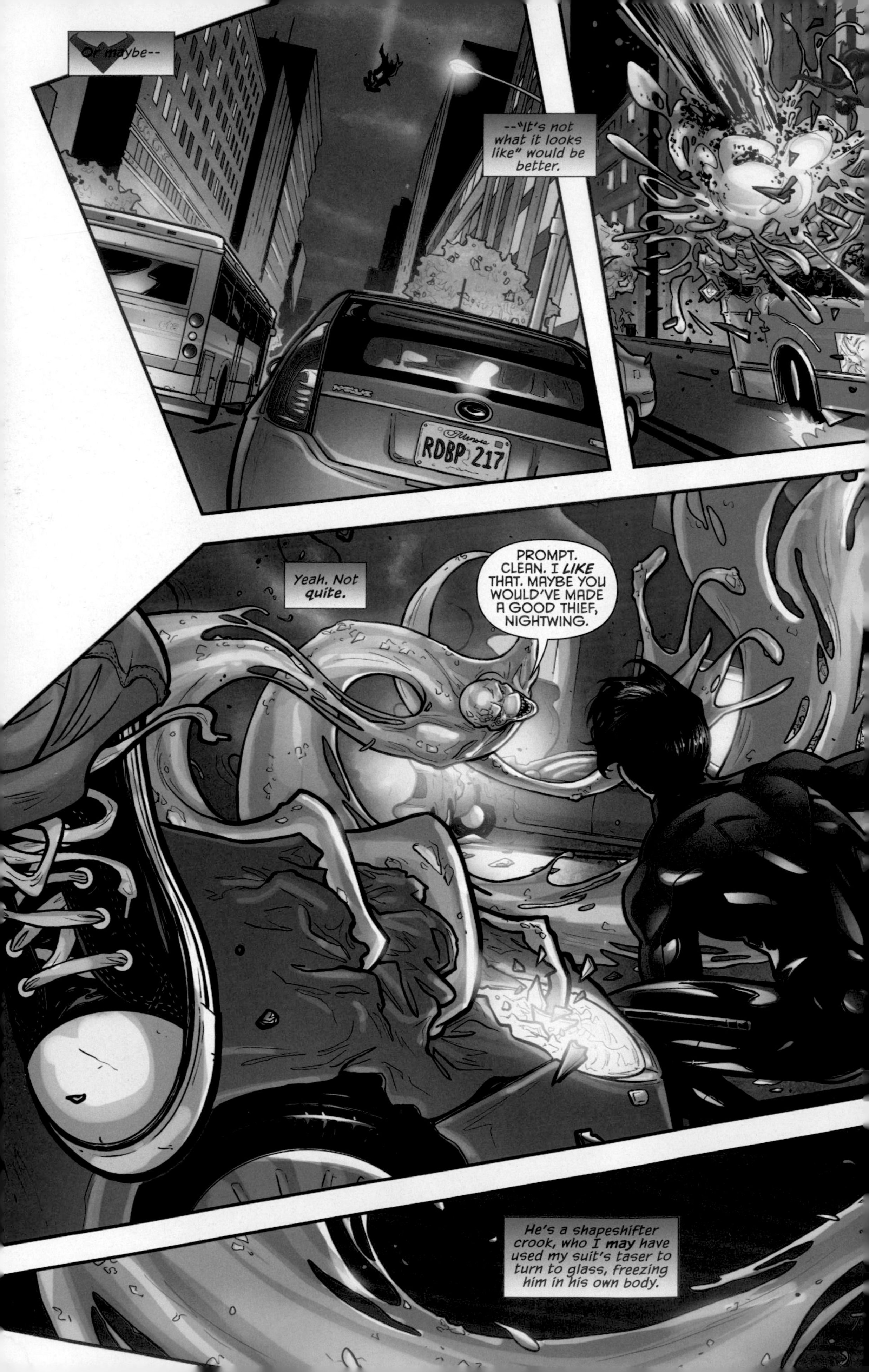

Or maybe--
--"It's not what it looks like" would be better.
RDBP 217
Yeah. Not quite.
PROMPT. CLEAN. I LIKE THAT. MAYBE YOU WOULD'VE MADE A GOOD THIEF, NIGHTWING.
He's a shapeshifter crook, who I may have used my suit's taser to turn to glass, freezing him in his own body.

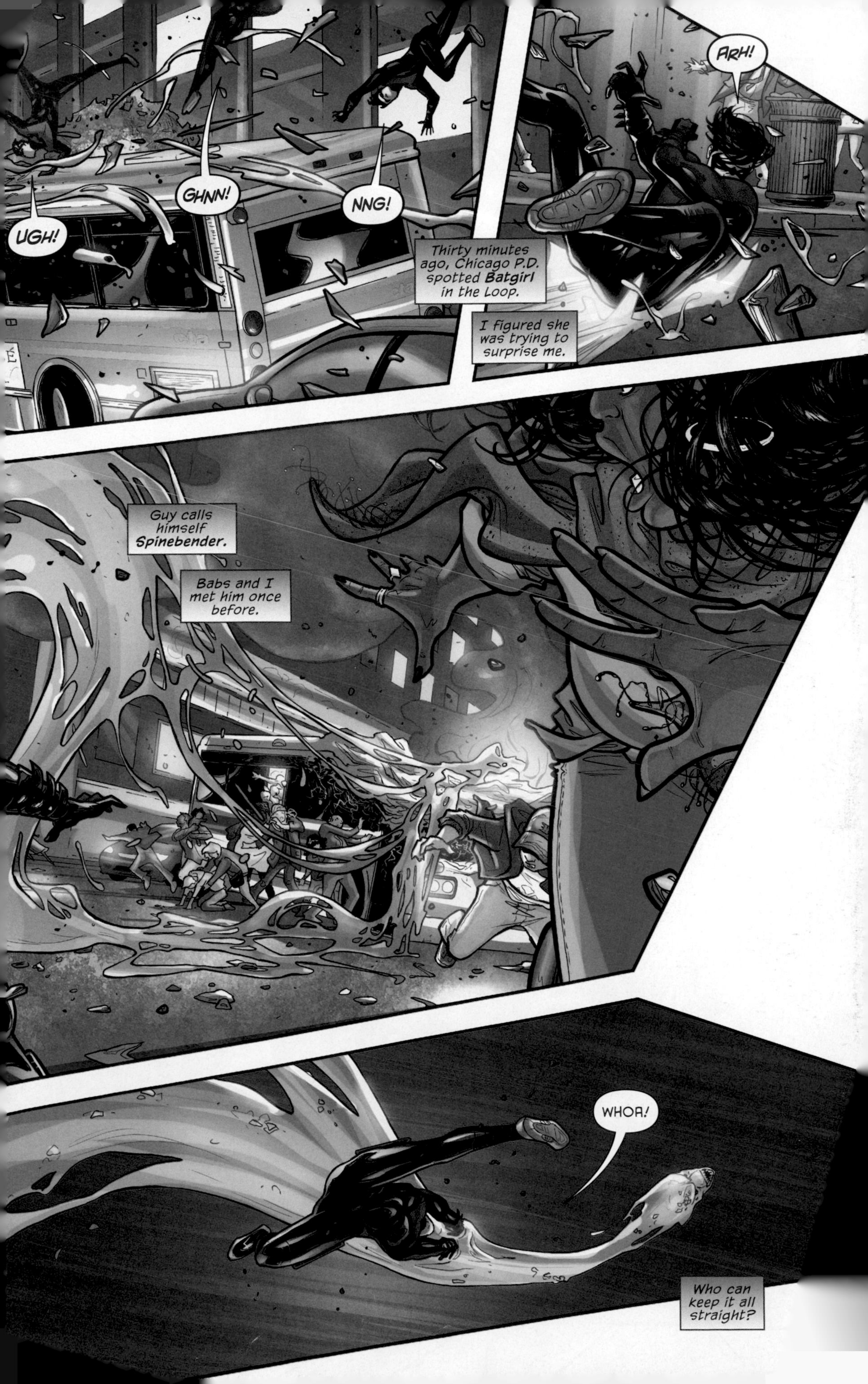
UGH!
GHNN!
NNG!
ARH!
Thirty minutes ago, Chicago P.D. spotted Batgirl in the Loop.
I figured she was trying to surprise me.
Guy calls himself Spinebender.
Babs and I met him once before.
WHOA!
Who can keep it all straight?

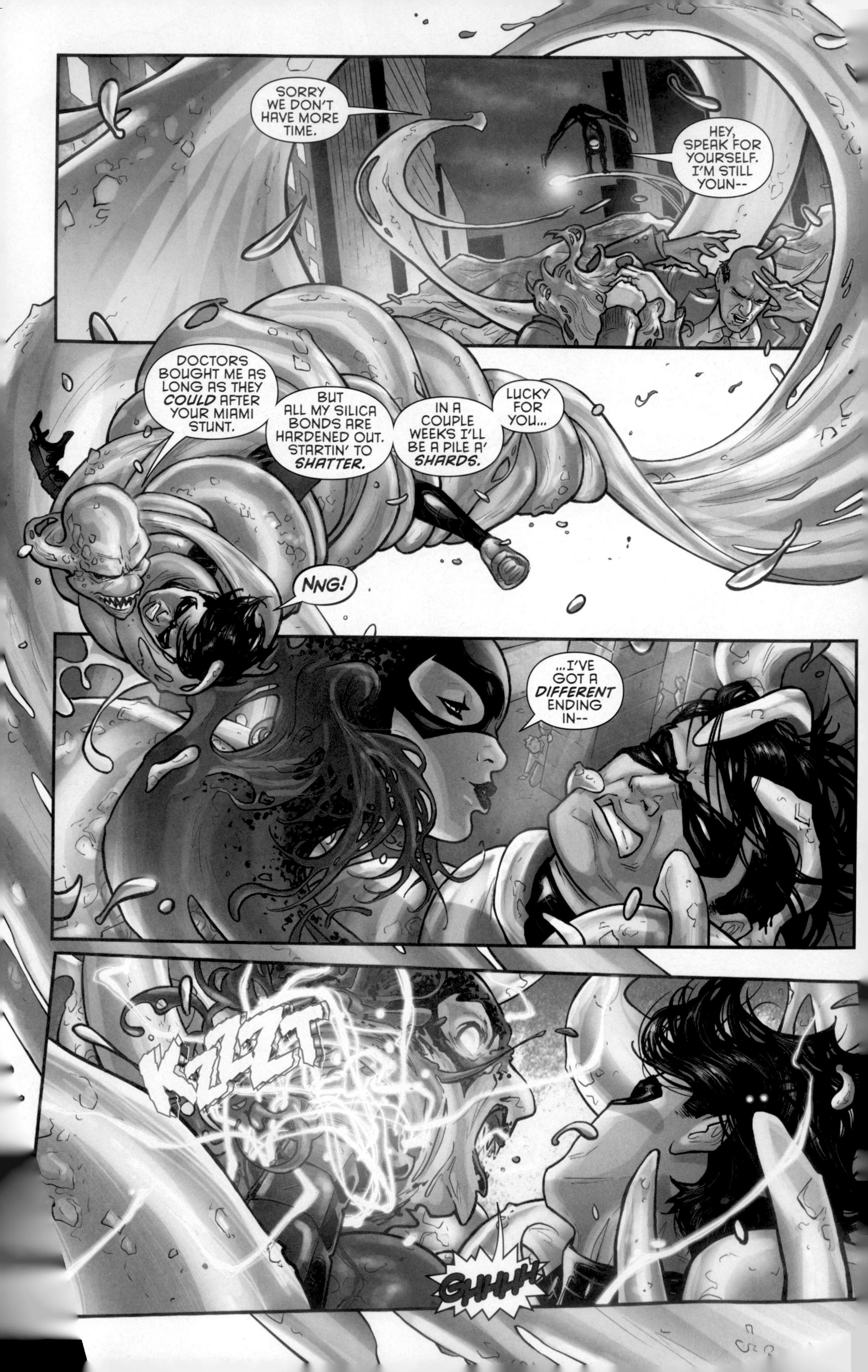
SORRY WE DON'T HAVE MORE TIME.
HEY, SPEAK FOR YOURSELF. I'M STILL YOUN--
DOCTORS BOUGHT ME AS LONG AS THEY *COULD* AFTER YOUR MIAMI STUNT.
BUT ALL MY SILICA BONDS ARE HARDENED OUT. STARTIN' TO *SHATTER.*
IN A COUPLE WEEKS I'LL BE A PILE A' *SHARDS.*
LUCKY FOR YOU...
NNG!
...I'VE GOT A *DIFFERENT* ENDING IN--
KZZZT
GHHHH

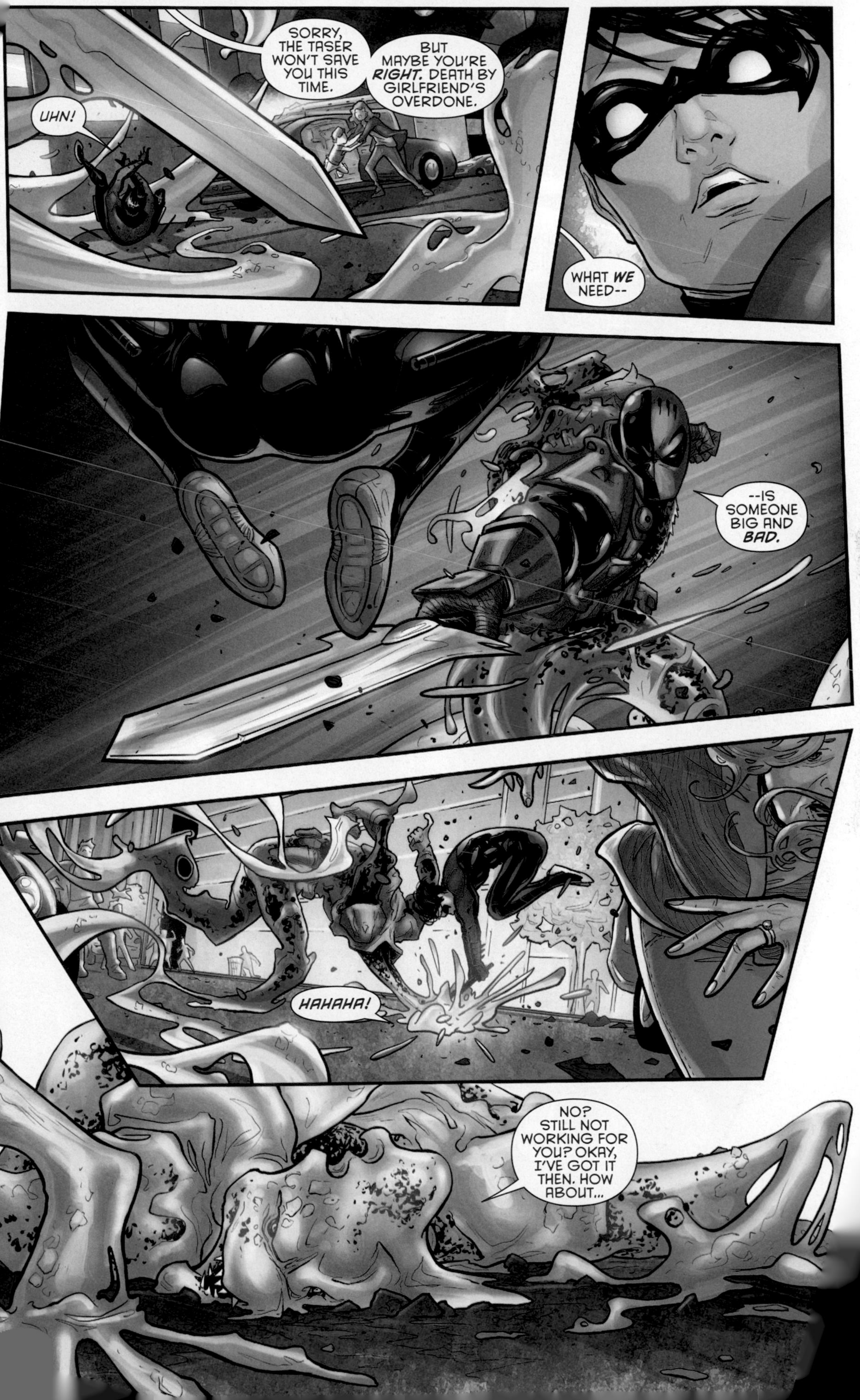
UHN!
SORRY, THE TASER WON'T SAVE YOU THIS TIME.
BUT MAYBE YOU'RE RIGHT. DEATH BY GIRLFRIEND'S OVERDONE.
WHAT WE NEED--
--IS SOMEONE BIG AND BAD.
HAHAHA!
NO? STILL NOT WORKING FOR YOU? OKAY, I'VE GOT IT THEN. HOW ABOUT...

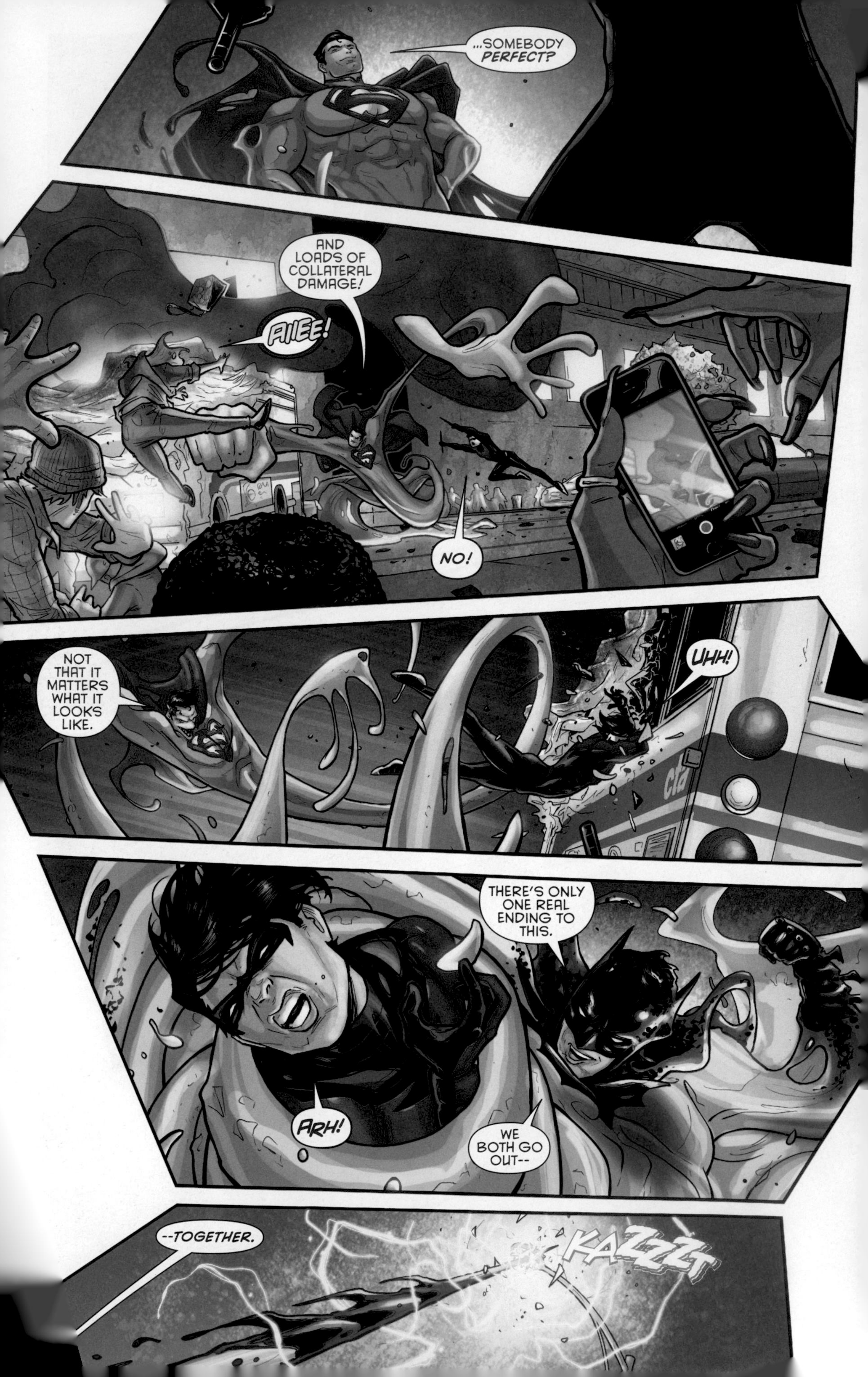

...SOMEBODY PERFECT?
AND LOADS OF COLLATERAL DAMAGE!
AIIEE!
NO!
NOT THAT IT MATTERS WHAT IT LOOKS LIKE.
UHH!
THERE'S ONLY ONE REAL ENDING TO THIS.
ARH!
WE BOTH GO OUT--
--TOGETHER.
KAZZZT

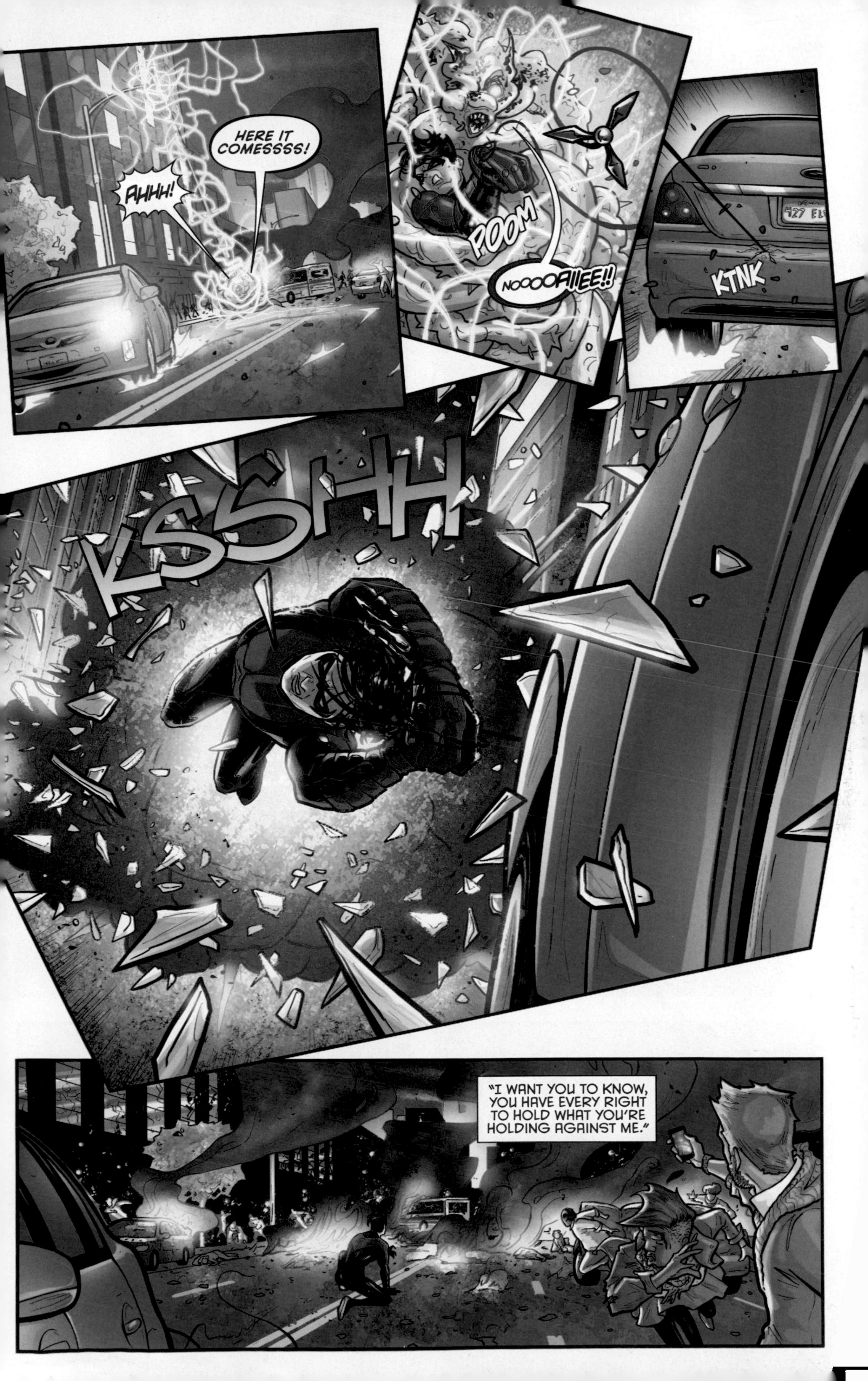

AHHH!
HERE IT COMESSSS!
POOM
NOOOOAIIEE!!
KTNK
KSSHH
"I WANT YOU TO KNOW, YOU HAVE EVERY RIGHT TO HOLD WHAT YOU'RE HOLDING AGAINST ME."

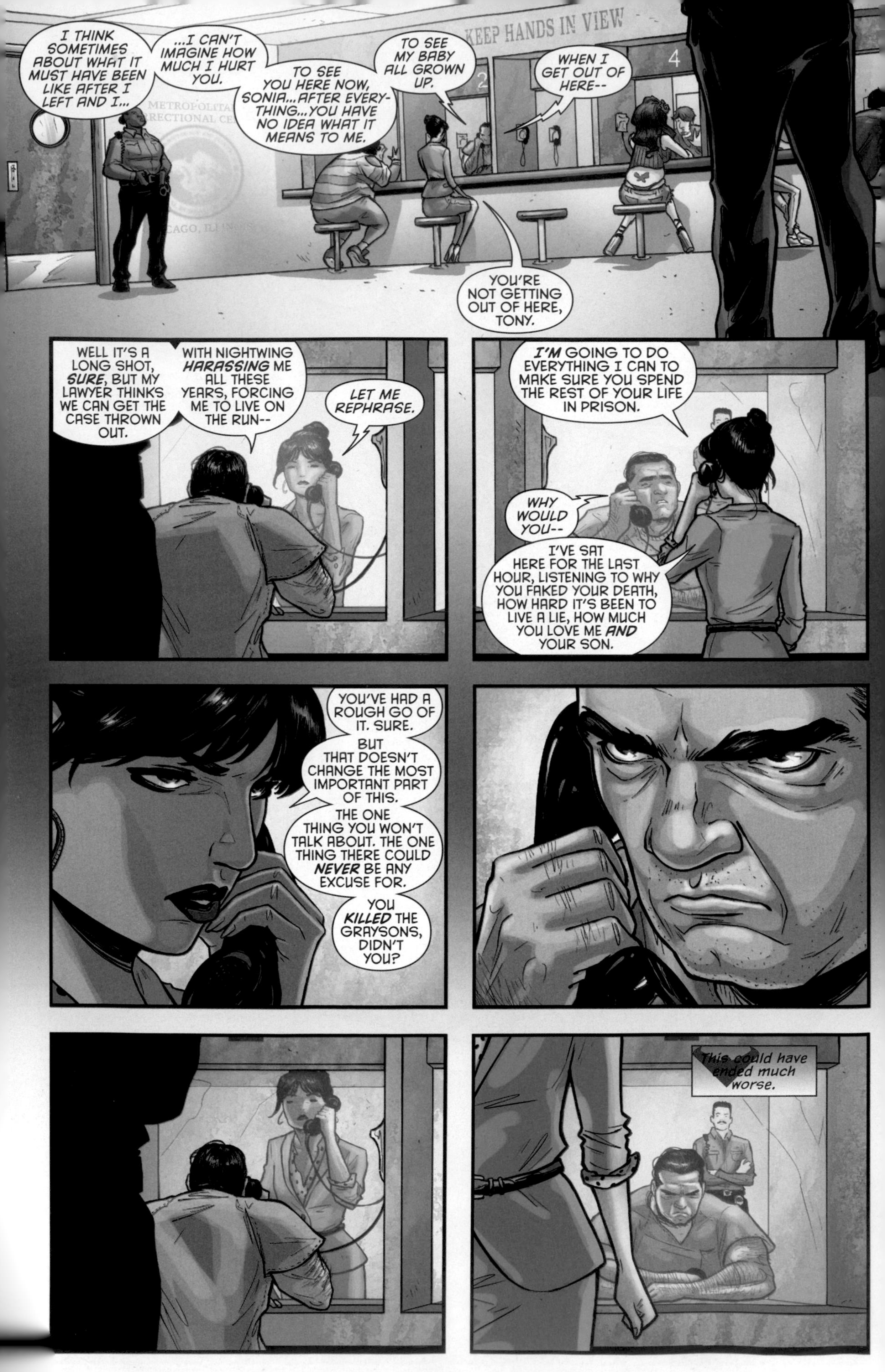
KEEP HANDS IN VIEW
I THINK SOMETIMES ABOUT WHAT IT MUST HAVE BEEN LIKE AFTER I LEFT AND I...
...I CAN'T IMAGINE HOW MUCH I HURT YOU.
TO SEE YOU HERE NOW, SONIA...AFTER EVERYTHING...YOU HAVE NO IDEA WHAT IT MEANS TO ME.
TO SEE MY BABY ALL GROWN UP.
WHEN I GET OUT OF HERE--
YOU'RE NOT GETTING OUT OF HERE, TONY.
WELL IT'S A LONG SHOT, SURE, BUT MY LAWYER THINKS WE CAN GET THE CASE THROWN OUT.
WITH NIGHTWING HARASSING ME ALL THESE YEARS, FORCING ME TO LIVE ON THE RUN--
LET ME REPHRASE.
I'M GOING TO DO EVERYTHING I CAN TO MAKE SURE YOU SPEND THE REST OF YOUR LIFE IN PRISON.
WHY WOULD YOU--
I'VE SAT HERE FOR THE LAST HOUR, LISTENING TO WHY YOU FAKED YOUR DEATH, HOW HARD IT'S BEEN TO LIVE A LIE, HOW MUCH YOU LOVE ME AND YOUR SON.
YOU'VE HAD A ROUGH GO OF IT. SURE.
BUT THAT DOESN'T CHANGE THE MOST IMPORTANT PART OF THIS.
THE ONE THING YOU WON'T TALK ABOUT. THE ONE THING THERE COULD NEVER BE ANY EXCUSE FOR.
YOU KILLED THE GRAYSONS, DIDN'T YOU?
This could have ended much worse.

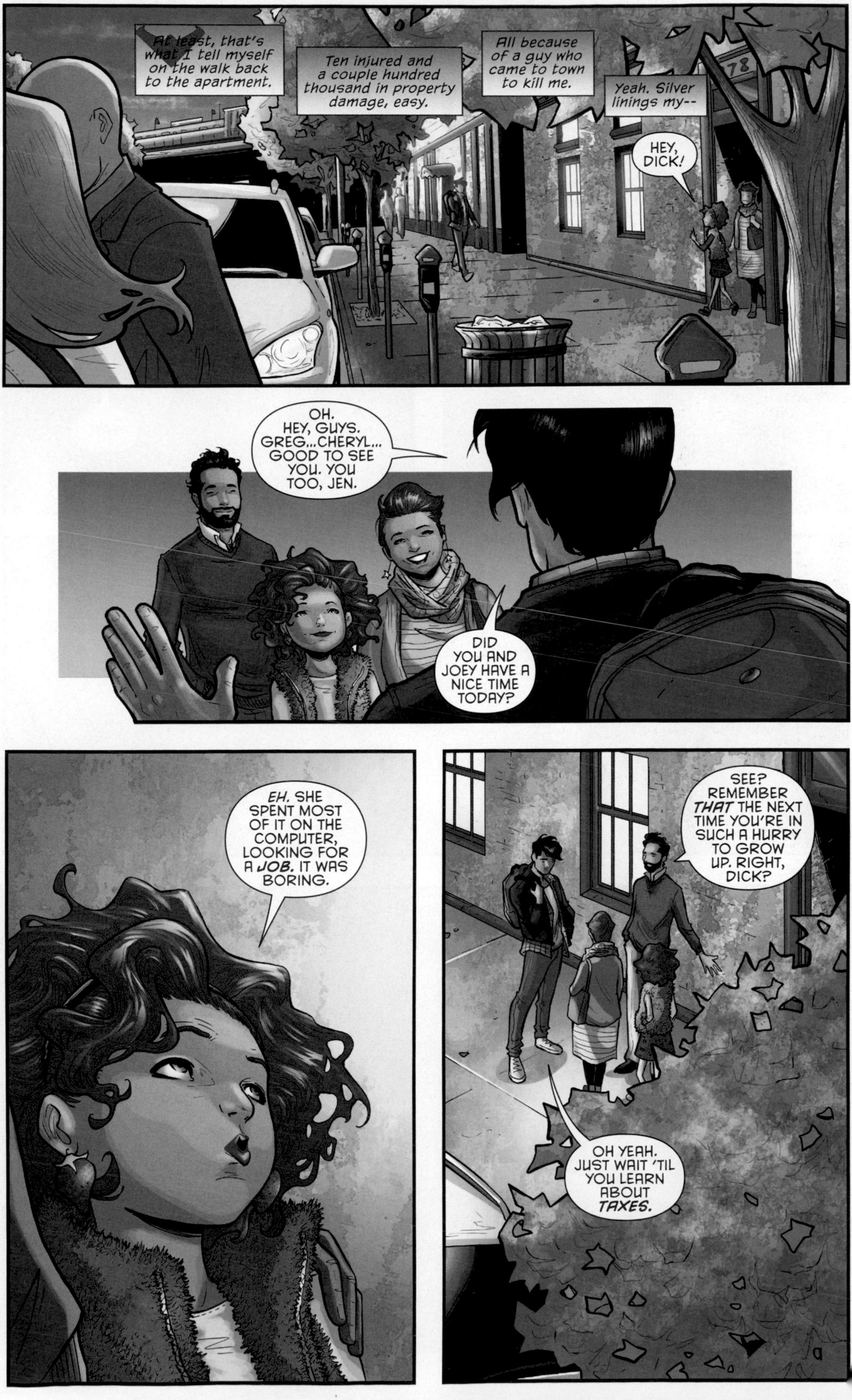
At least, that's what I tell myself on the walk back to the apartment.
Ten injured and a couple hundred thousand in property damage, easy.
All because of a guy who came to town to kill me.
Yeah. Silver linings my--
HEY, DICK!
OH. HEY, GUYS. GREG...CHERYL... GOOD TO SEE YOU. YOU TOO, JEN.
DID YOU AND JOEY HAVE A NICE TIME TODAY?
EH. SHE SPENT MOST OF IT ON THE COMPUTER, LOOKING FOR A JOB. IT WAS BORING.
SEE? REMEMBER THAT THE NEXT TIME YOU'RE IN SUCH A HURRY TO GROW UP. RIGHT, DICK?
OH YEAH. JUST WAIT 'TIL YOU LEARN ABOUT TAXES.

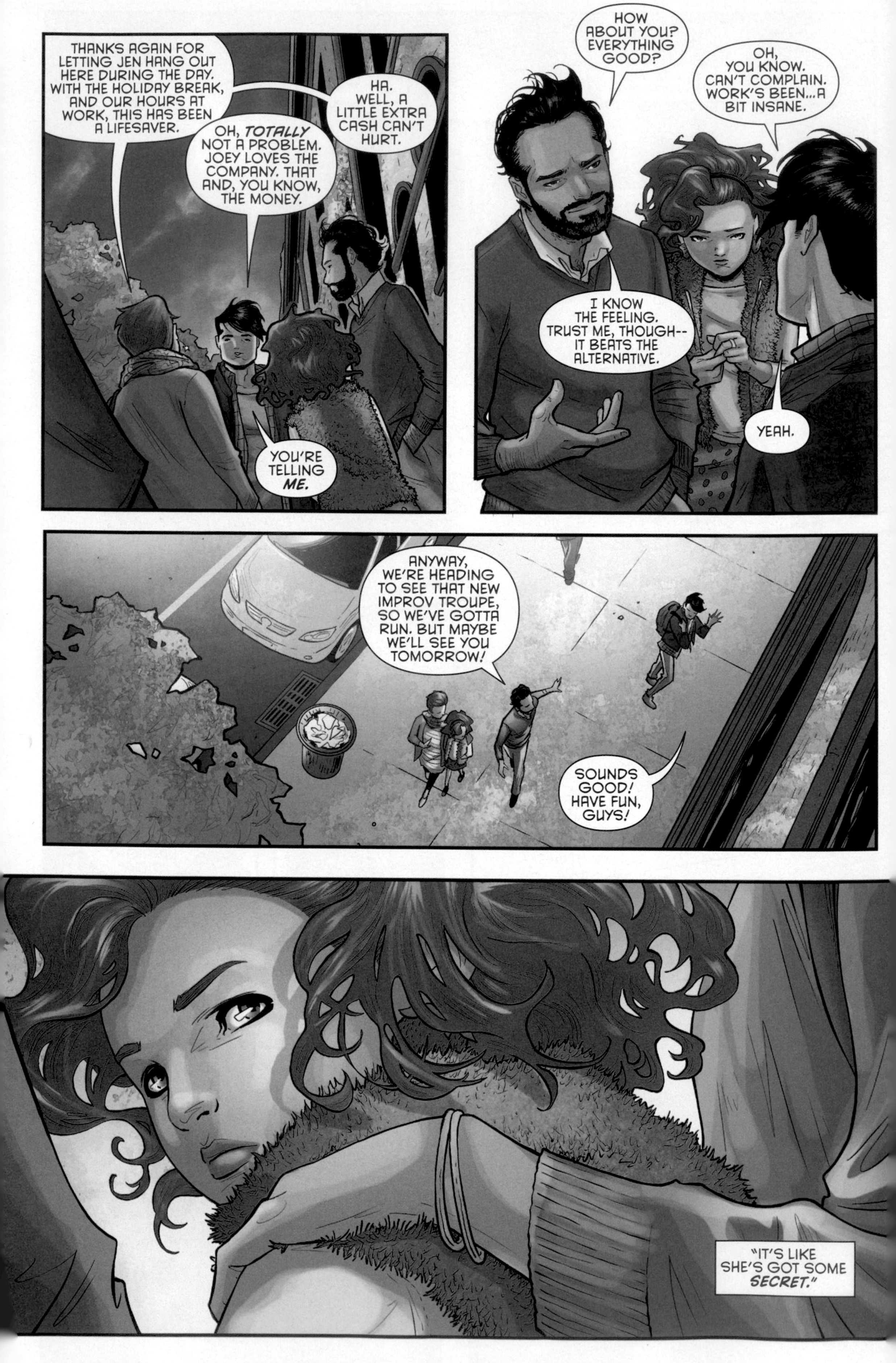
THANKS AGAIN FOR LETTING JEN HANG OUT HERE DURING THE DAY. WITH THE HOLIDAY BREAK, AND OUR HOURS AT WORK, THIS HAS BEEN A LIFESAVER.
OH, *TOTALLY* NOT A PROBLEM. JOEY LOVES THE COMPANY. THAT AND, YOU KNOW, THE MONEY.
HA. WELL, A LITTLE EXTRA CASH CAN'T HURT.
YOU'RE TELLING ***ME.***
HOW ABOUT YOU? EVERYTHING GOOD?
OH, YOU KNOW. CAN'T COMPLAIN. WORK'S BEEN...A BIT INSANE.
I KNOW THE FEELING. TRUST ME, THOUGH-- IT BEATS THE ALTERNATIVE.
YEAH.
ANYWAY, WE'RE HEADING TO SEE THAT NEW IMPROV TROUPE, SO WE'VE GOTTA RUN. BUT MAYBE WE'LL SEE YOU TOMORROW!
SOUNDS GOOD! HAVE FUN, GUYS!
"IT'S LIKE SHE'S GOT SOME ***SECRET.***"

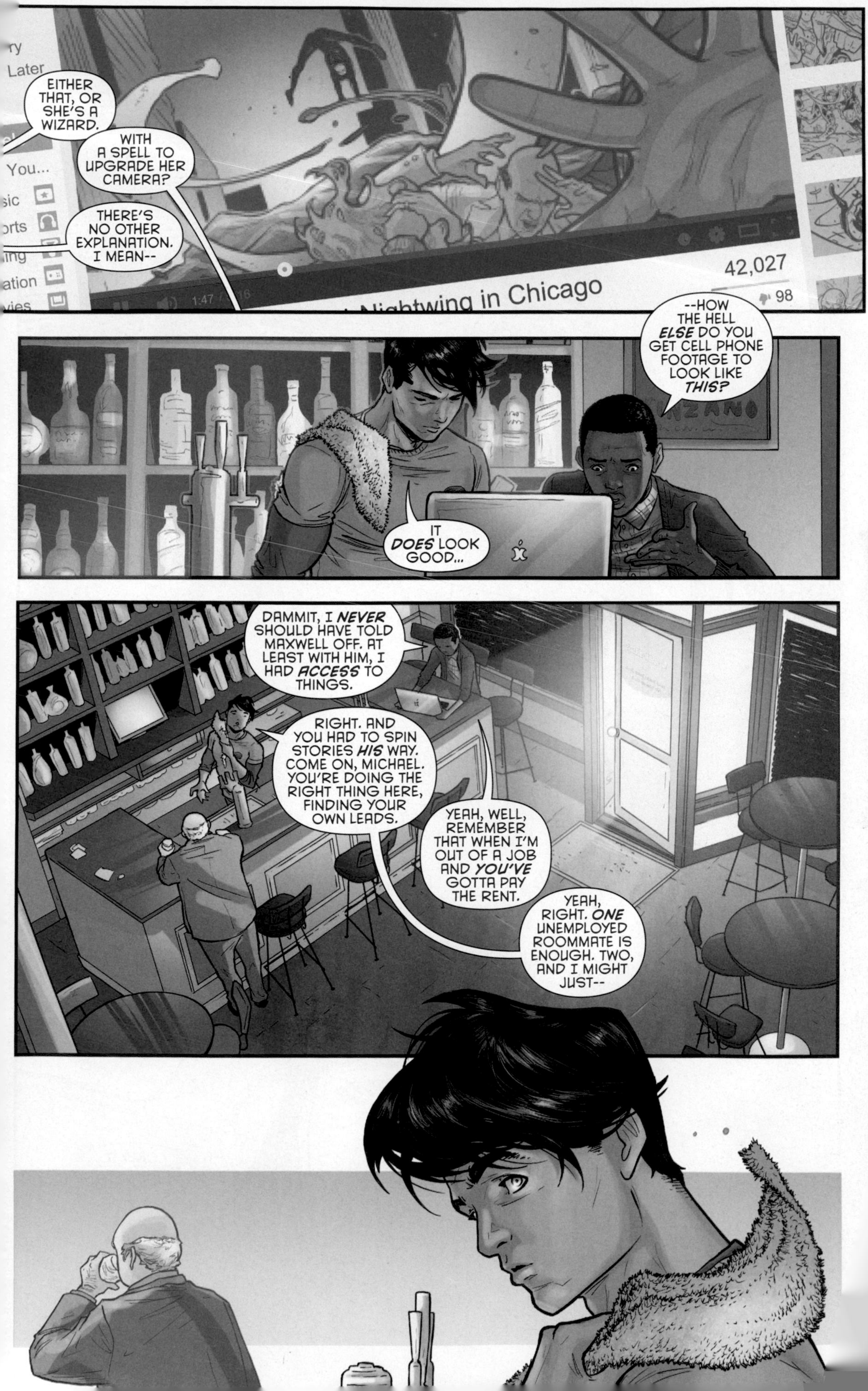

ry
Later
You...
sic
orts
ation
EITHER THAT, OR SHE'S A WIZARD.
WITH A SPELL TO UPGRADE HER CAMERA?
THERE'S NO OTHER EXPLANATION. I MEAN--
42,027
Nightwing in Chicago
98
--HOW THE HELL ELSE DO YOU GET CELL PHONE FOOTAGE TO LOOK LIKE THIS?
IT DOES LOOK GOOD...
DAMMIT, I NEVER SHOULD HAVE TOLD MAXWELL OFF. AT LEAST WITH HIM, I HAD ACCESS TO THINGS.
RIGHT. AND YOU HAD TO SPIN STORIES HIS WAY. COME ON, MICHAEL. YOU'RE DOING THE RIGHT THING HERE, FINDING YOUR OWN LEADS.
YEAH, WELL, REMEMBER THAT WHEN I'M OUT OF A JOB AND YOU'VE GOTTA PAY THE RENT.
YEAH, RIGHT. ONE UNEMPLOYED ROOMMATE IS ENOUGH. TWO, AND I MIGHT JUST--

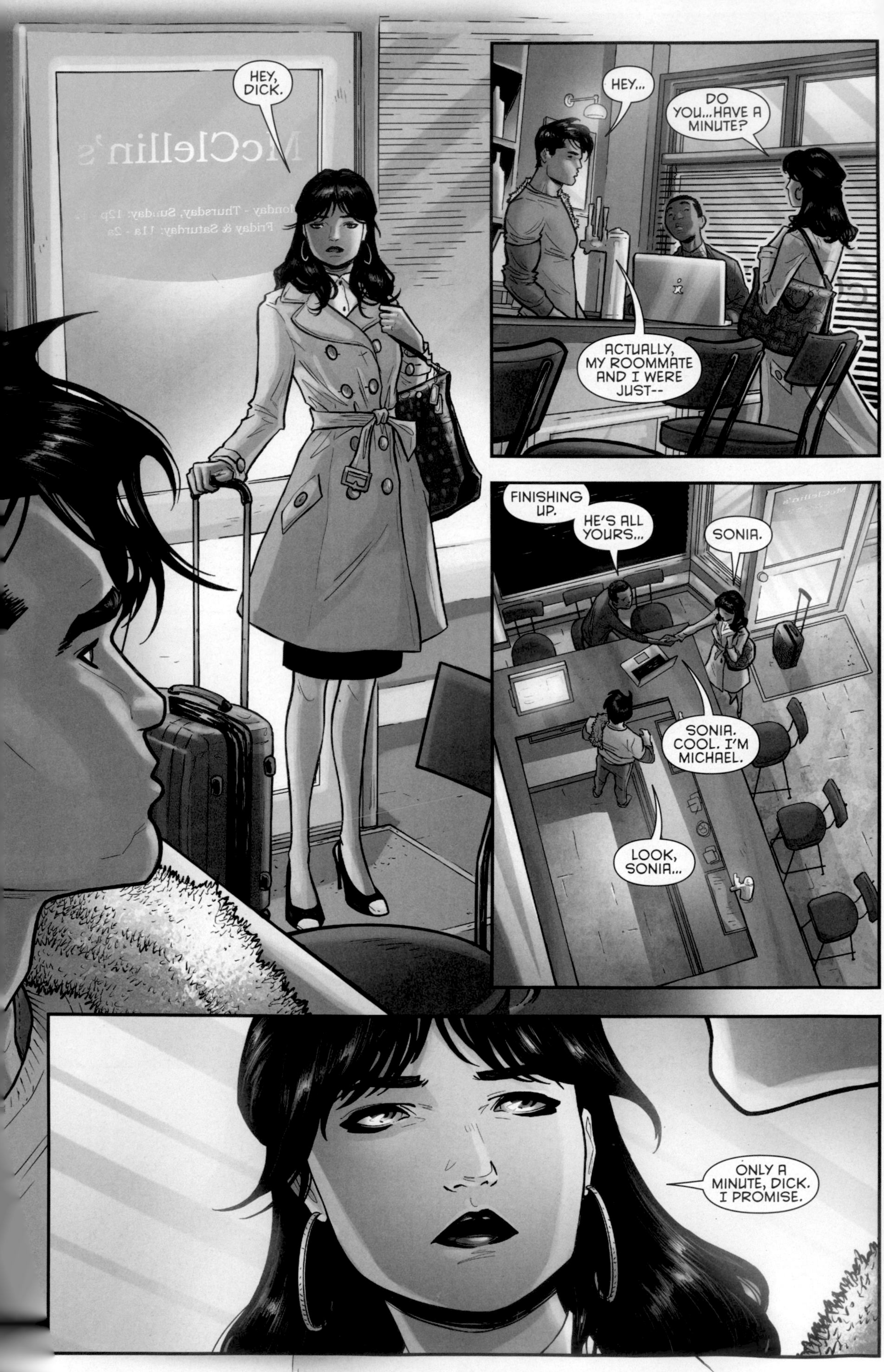
HEY, DICK.
McClellin's
Monday - Thursday, Sunday: 12p -
Friday & Saturday: 11a - 2a
HEY...
DO YOU...HAVE A MINUTE?
ACTUALLY, MY ROOMMATE AND I WERE JUST--
FINISHING UP.
HE'S ALL YOURS...
SONIA.
SONIA. COOL. I'M MICHAEL.
LOOK, SONIA...
ONLY A MINUTE, DICK. I PROMISE.

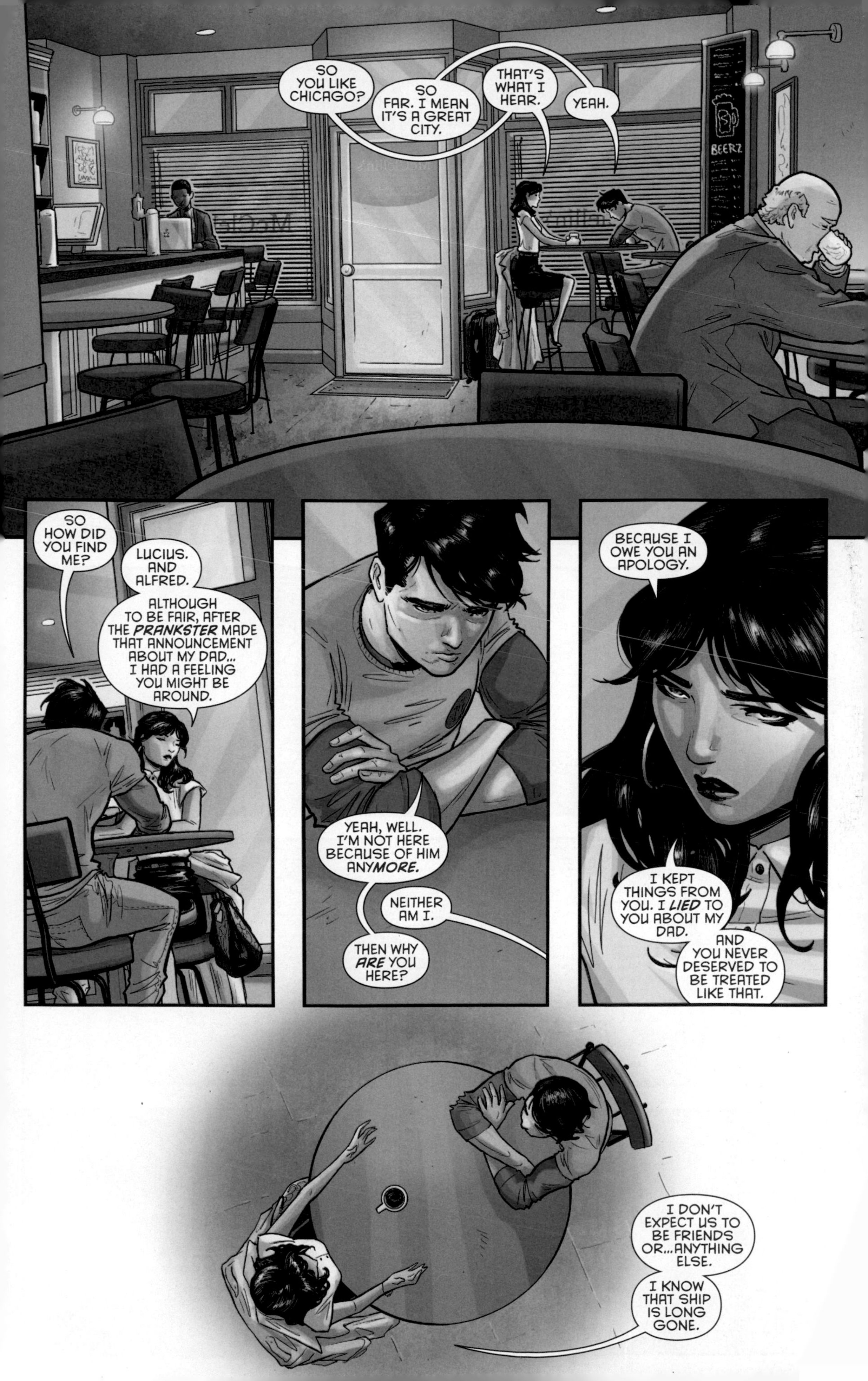
SO YOU LIKE CHICAGO?
SO FAR. I MEAN IT'S A GREAT CITY.
THAT'S WHAT I HEAR.
YEAH.
BEERZ
SO HOW DID YOU FIND ME?
LUCIUS. AND ALFRED.
ALTHOUGH TO BE FAIR, AFTER THE ***PRANKSTER*** MADE THAT ANNOUNCEMENT ABOUT MY DAD... I HAD A FEELING YOU MIGHT BE AROUND.
YEAH, WELL. I'M NOT HERE BECAUSE OF HIM ANY***MORE.***
NEITHER AM I.
THEN WHY ***ARE*** YOU HERE?
BECAUSE I OWE YOU AN APOLOGY.
I KEPT THINGS FROM YOU. I ***LIED*** TO YOU ABOUT MY DAD.
AND YOU NEVER DESERVED TO BE TREATED LIKE THAT.
I DON'T EXPECT US TO BE FRIENDS OR...ANYTHING ELSE.
I KNOW THAT SHIP IS LONG GONE.

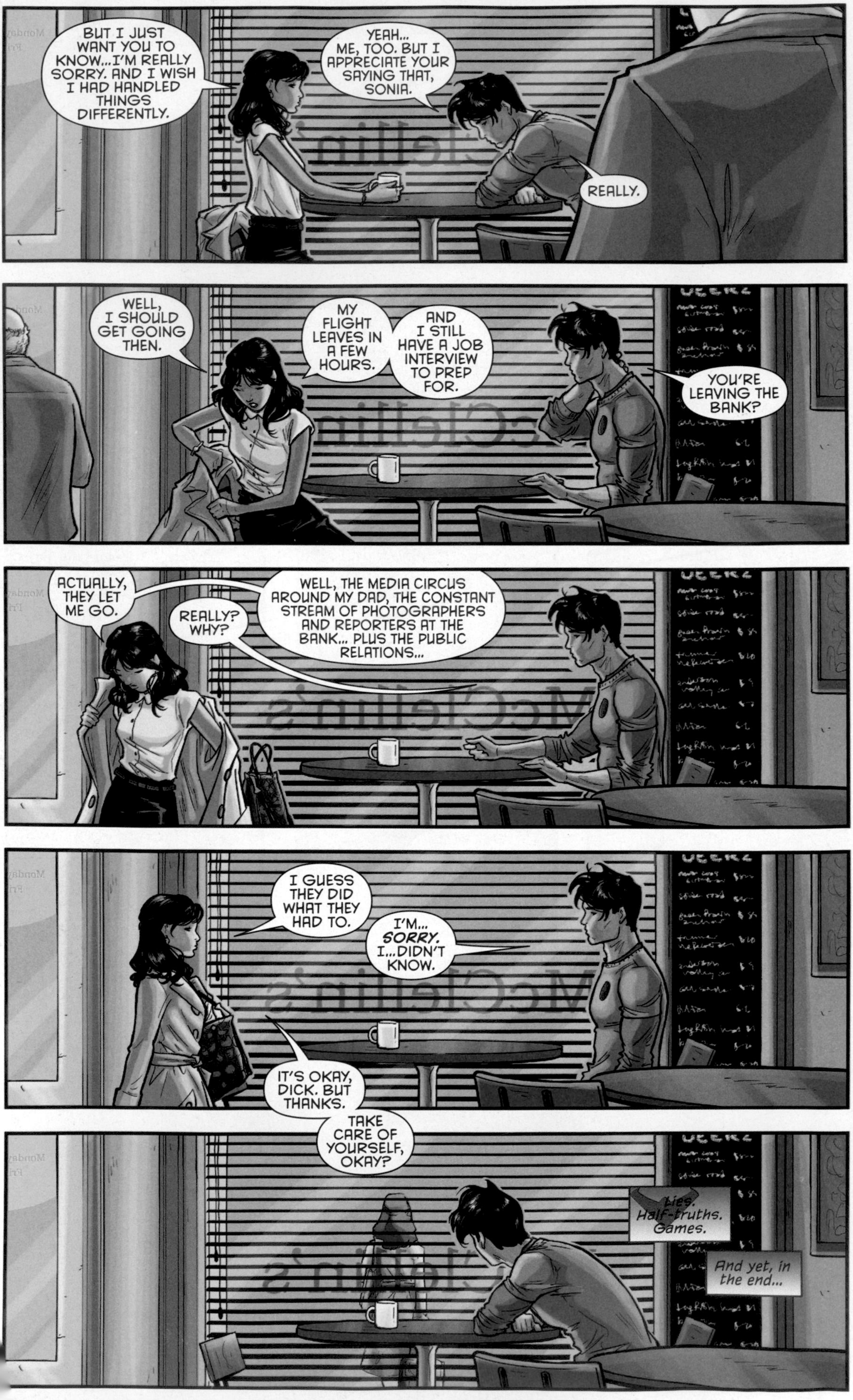
BUT I JUST WANT YOU TO KNOW...I'M REALLY SORRY. AND I WISH I HAD HANDLED THINGS DIFFERENTLY.
YEAH... ME, TOO. BUT I APPRECIATE YOUR SAYING THAT, SONIA.
REALLY.
WELL, I SHOULD GET GOING THEN.
MY FLIGHT LEAVES IN A FEW HOURS.
AND I STILL HAVE A JOB INTERVIEW TO PREP FOR.
YOU'RE LEAVING THE BANK?
ACTUALLY, THEY LET ME GO.
REALLY? WHY?
WELL, THE MEDIA CIRCUS AROUND MY DAD, THE CONSTANT STREAM OF PHOTOGRAPHERS AND REPORTERS AT THE BANK... PLUS THE PUBLIC RELATIONS...
I GUESS THEY DID WHAT THEY HAD TO.
I'M... *SORRY.* I...DIDN'T KNOW.
IT'S OKAY, DICK. BUT THANKS.
TAKE CARE OF YOURSELF, OKAY?
Lies. Half-truths. Games.
And yet, in the end...

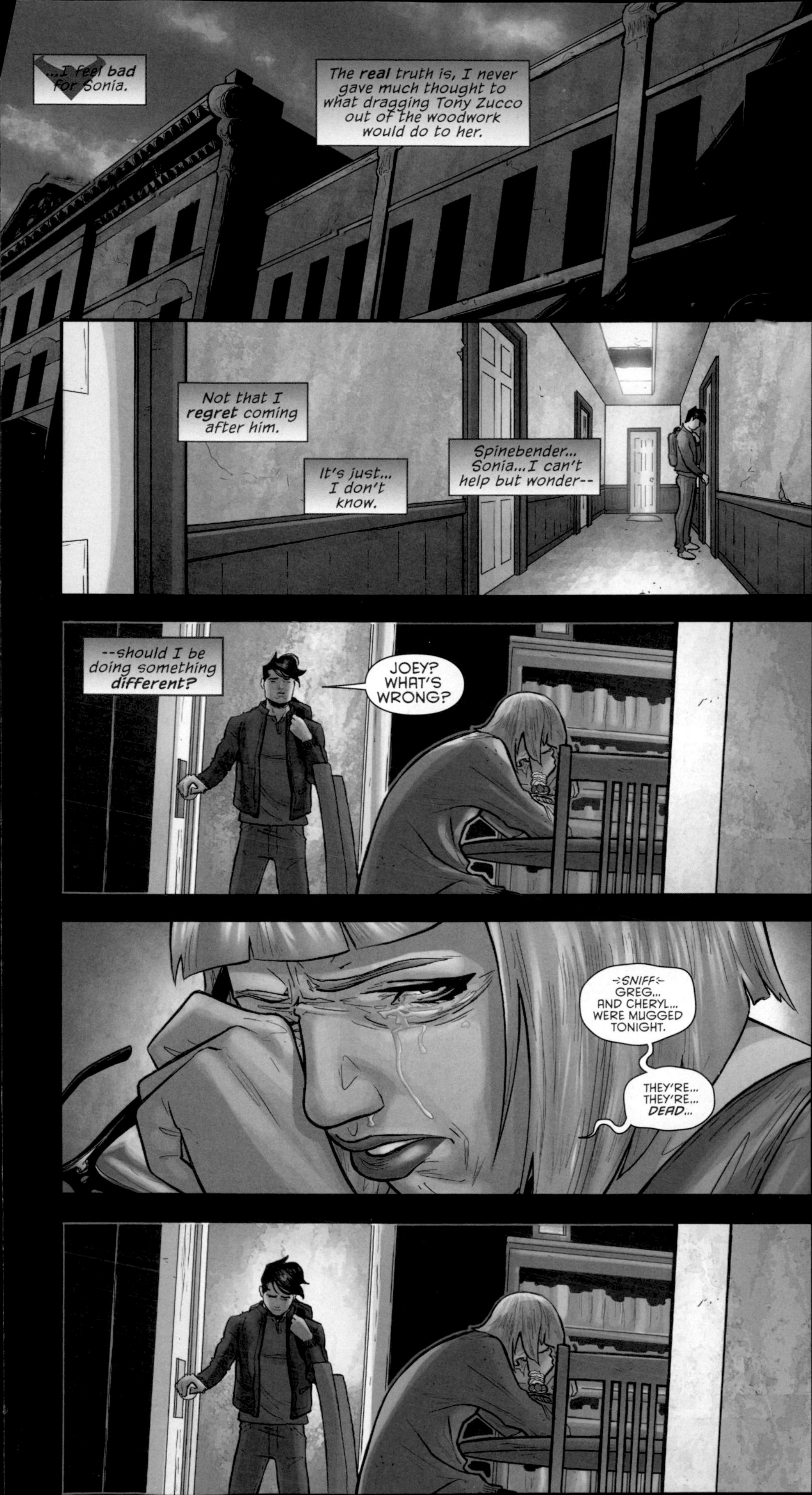
...I feel bad for Sonia.
The real truth is, I never gave much thought to what dragging Tony Zucco out of the woodwork would do to her.
Not that I regret coming after him.
It's just... I don't know.
Spinebender... Sonia...I can't help but wonder--
--should I be doing something different?
JOEY? WHAT'S WRONG?
-SNIFF- GREG... AND CHERYL... WERE MUGGED TONIGHT.
THEY'RE... THEY'RE... DEAD...

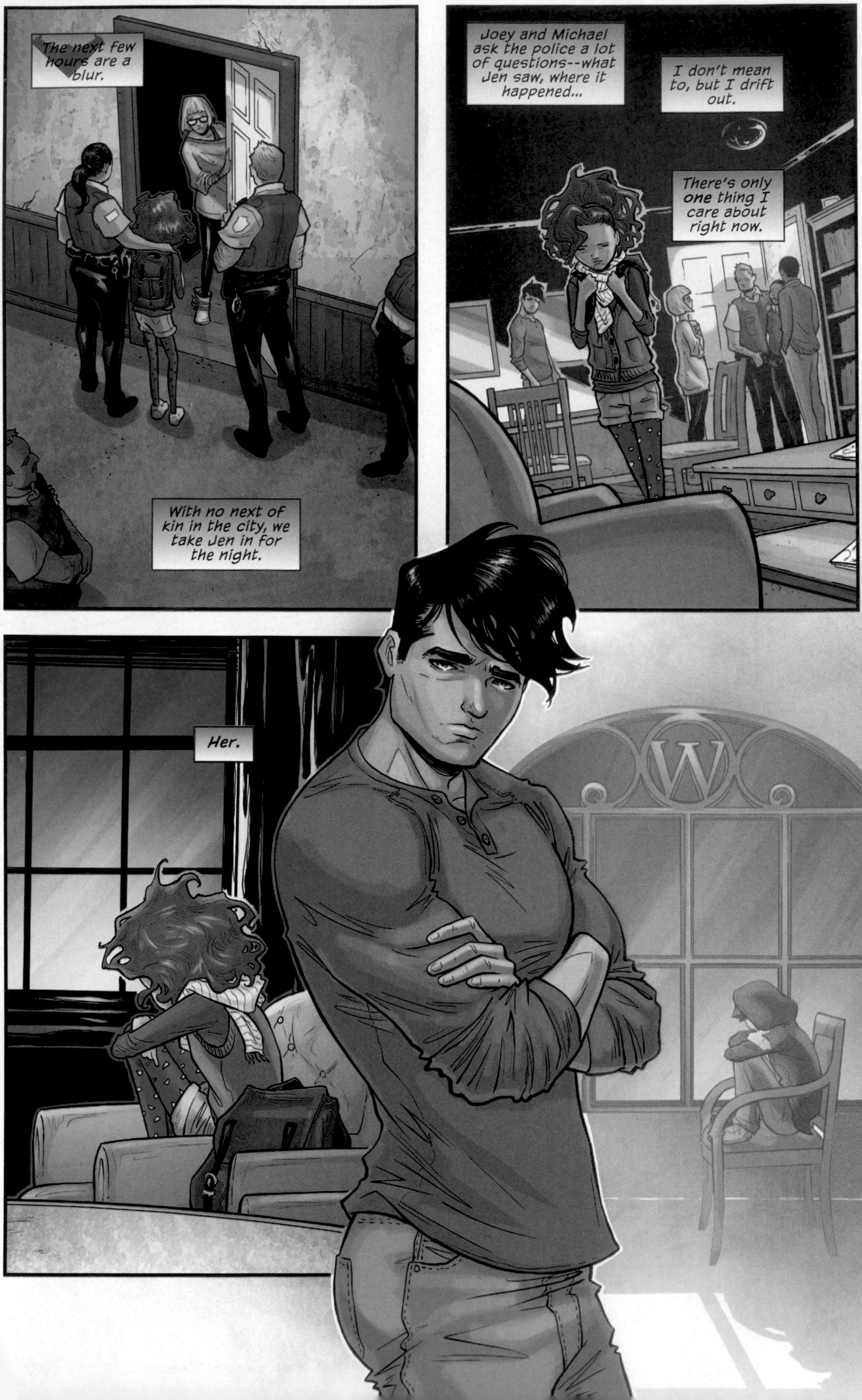
The next few hours are a blur.
With no next of kin in the city, we take Jen in for the night.
Joey and Michael ask the police a lot of questions--what Jen saw, where it happened...
I don't mean to, but I drift out.
There's only one thing I care about right now.
Her.

HEY, JEN...MIND IF I--

I KNOW WHO YOU *ARE*.

I...DIDN'T MEAN TO, BUT I *FOUND* ALL YOUR STUFF IN THE FLOOR. THE COSTUME AND THE STICKS.

AND...I KNOW WHAT HAPPENED TO *YOUR* MOM AND DAD.

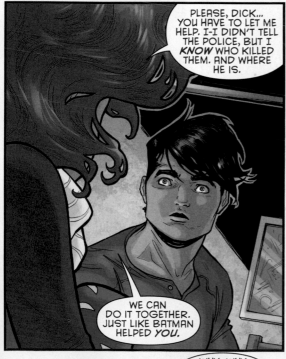

PLEASE, DICK... YOU HAVE TO LET ME HELP. I-I DIDN'T TELL THE POLICE, BUT I *KNOW* WHO KILLED THEM. AND WHERE HE IS.

WE CAN DO IT TOGETHER. JUST LIKE BATMAN HELPED *YOU*.

I DON'T... I MEAN...

WHY...WHY DON'T I GET US SOME WATER AND WE CAN... *TALK* ABOUT WHAT YOU THINK YOU SAW...?

YEAH, THAT'S WHAT I *FIGURED* YOU'D SAY.

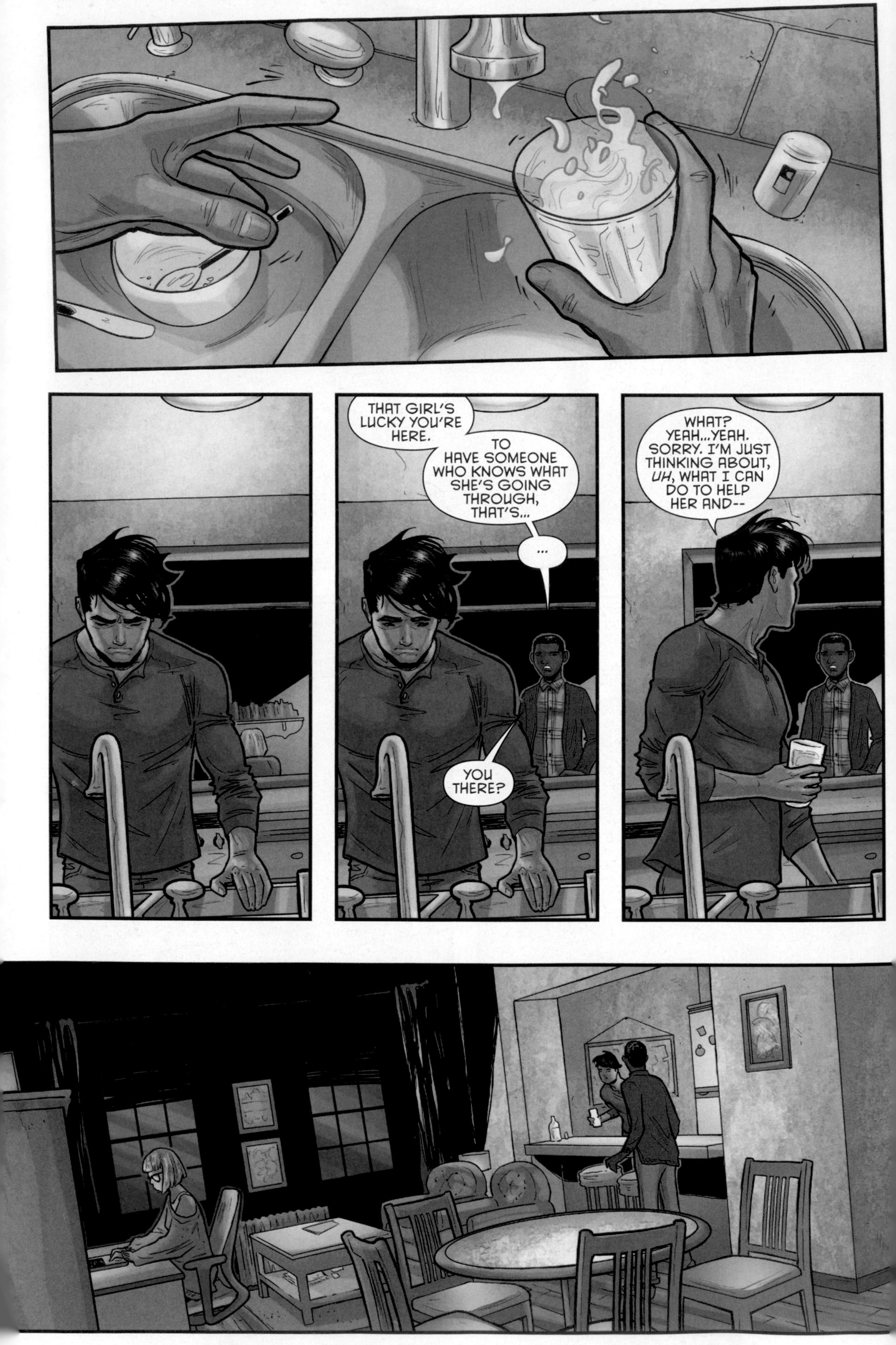
THAT GIRL'S LUCKY YOU'RE HERE.
TO HAVE SOMEONE WHO KNOWS WHAT SHE'S GOING THROUGH, THAT'S...
...
YOU THERE?
WHAT? YEAH...YEAH. SORRY. I'M JUST THINKING ABOUT, *UH*, WHAT I CAN DO TO HELP HER AND--

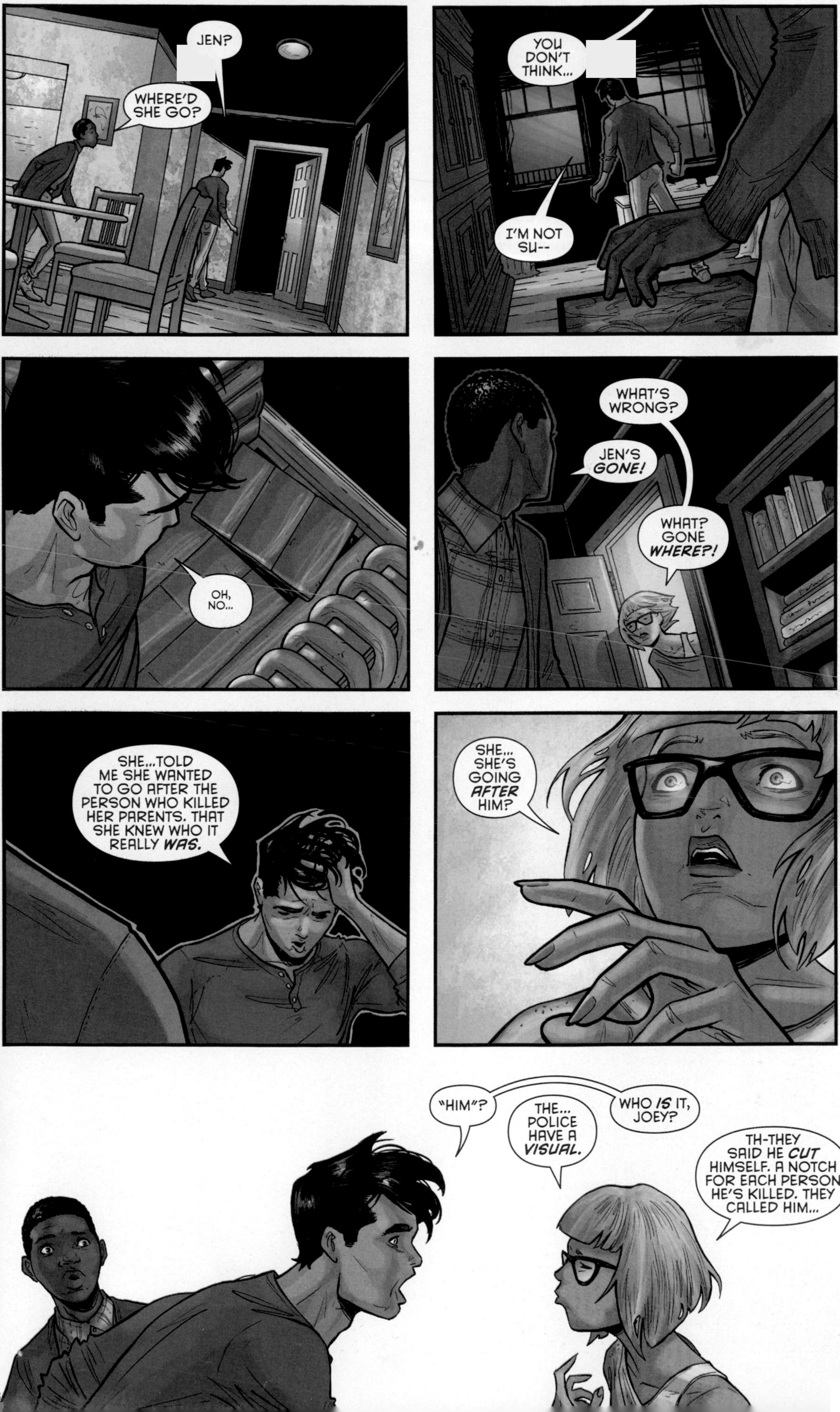
JEN?
WHERE'D SHE GO?
YOU DON'T THINK...
I'M NOT SU--
OH, NO...
WHAT'S WRONG?
JEN'S *GONE!*
WHAT? GONE *WHERE?!*
SHE...TOLD ME SHE WANTED TO GO AFTER THE PERSON WHO KILLED HER PARENTS. THAT SHE KNEW WHO IT REALLY *WAS.*
SHE... SHE'S GOING *AFTER* HIM?
"HIM"?
WHO *IS* IT, JOEY?
THE... POLICE HAVE A *VISUAL.*
TH-THEY SAID HE *CUT* HIMSELF. A NOTCH FOR EACH PERSON HE'S KILLED. THEY CALLED HIM...

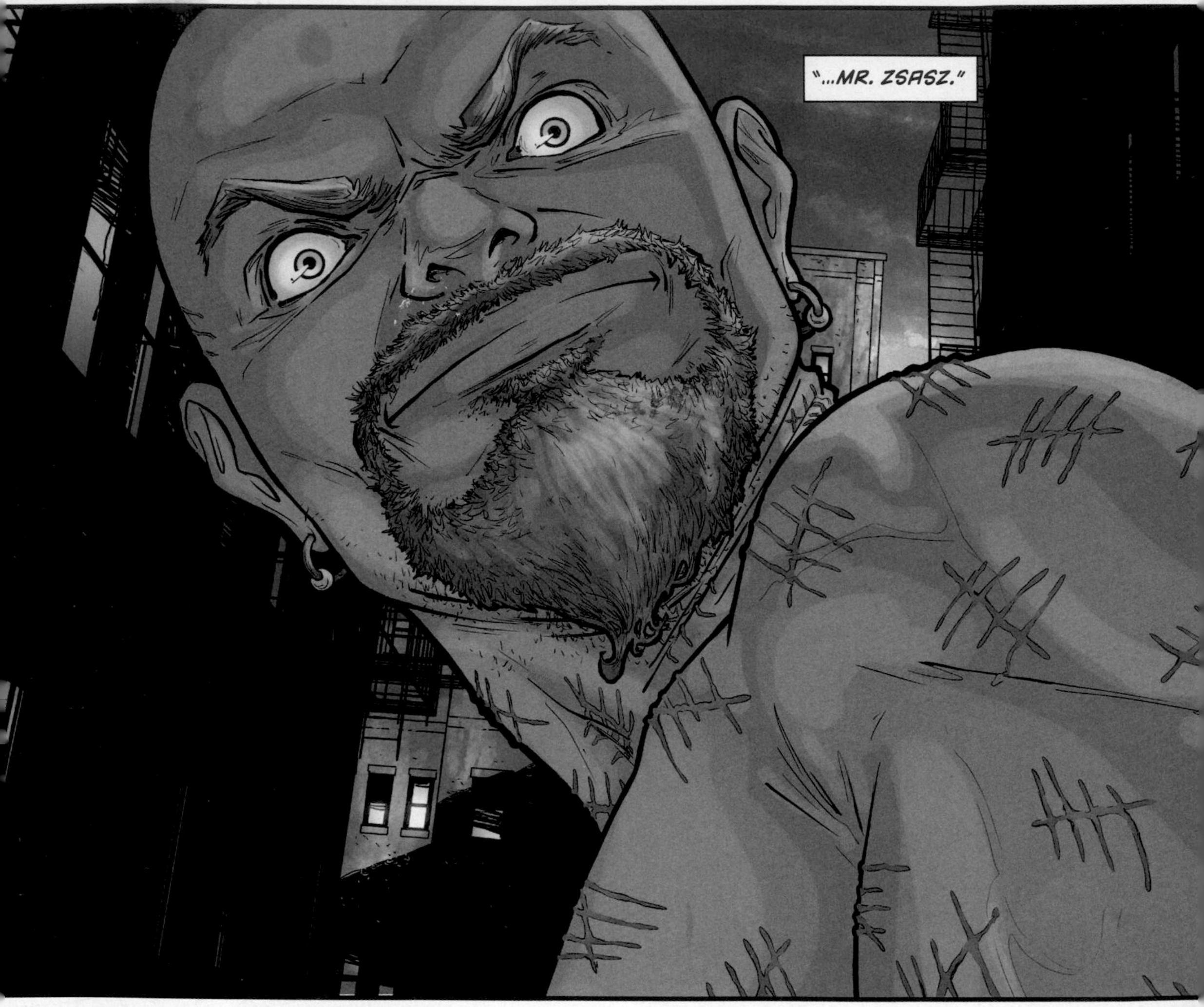
"...MR. ZSASZ."

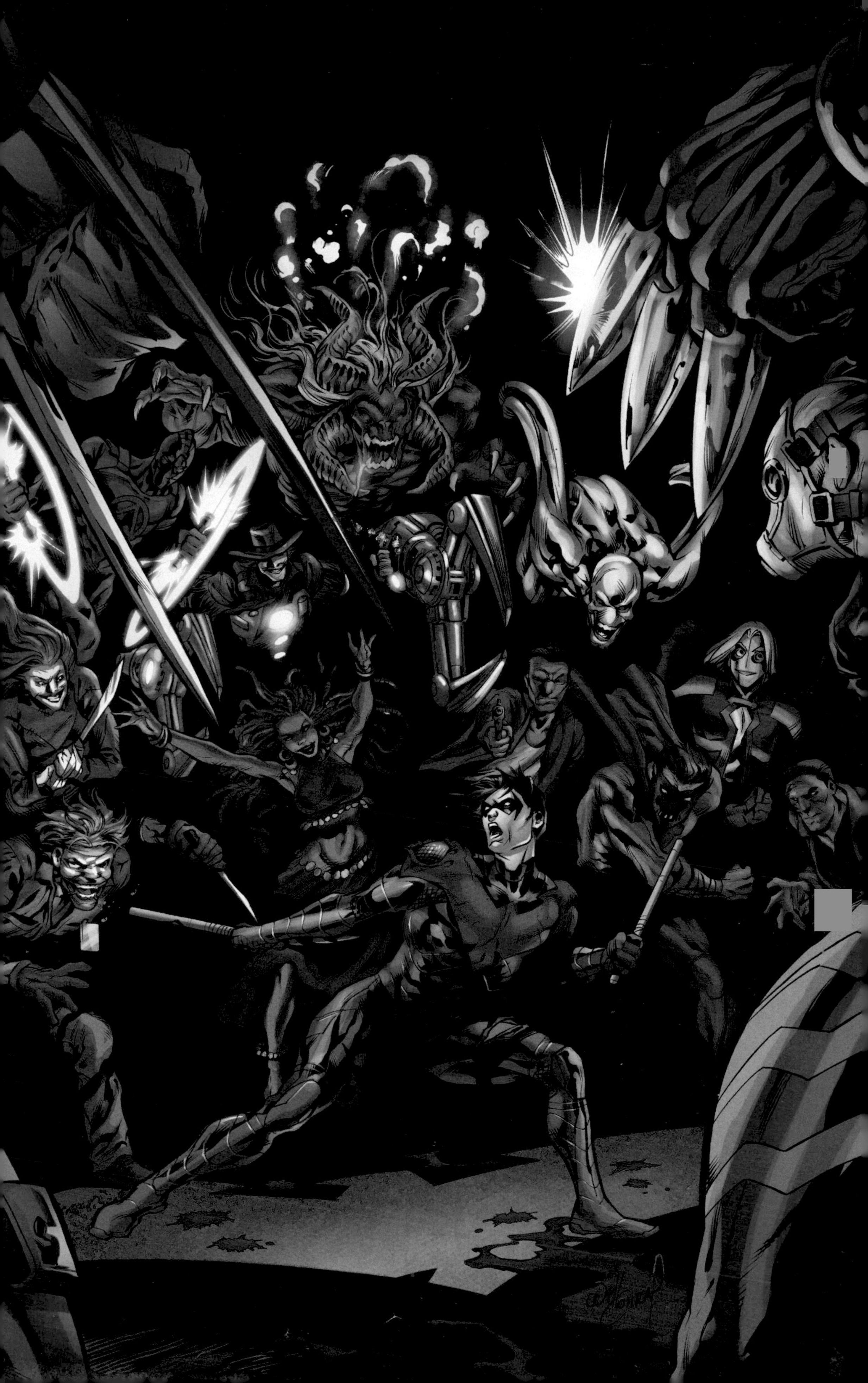

SAFETY NET

KYLE HIGGINS writer RUSSELL DAUTERMAN artist PETE PANTAZIS colorist
CARLOS M. MANGUAL letterer cover art by WILL CONRAD and PETE PANTAZIS

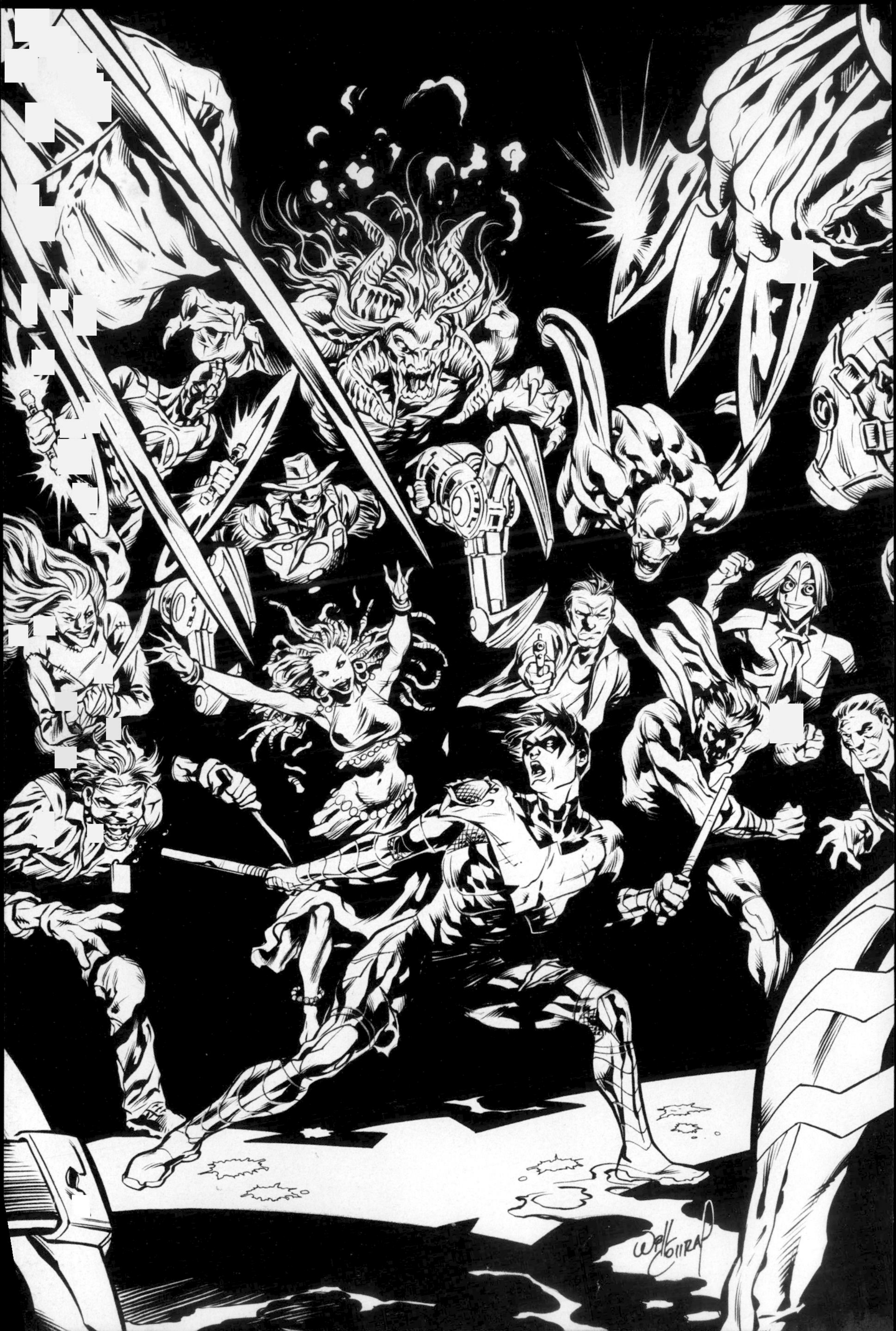

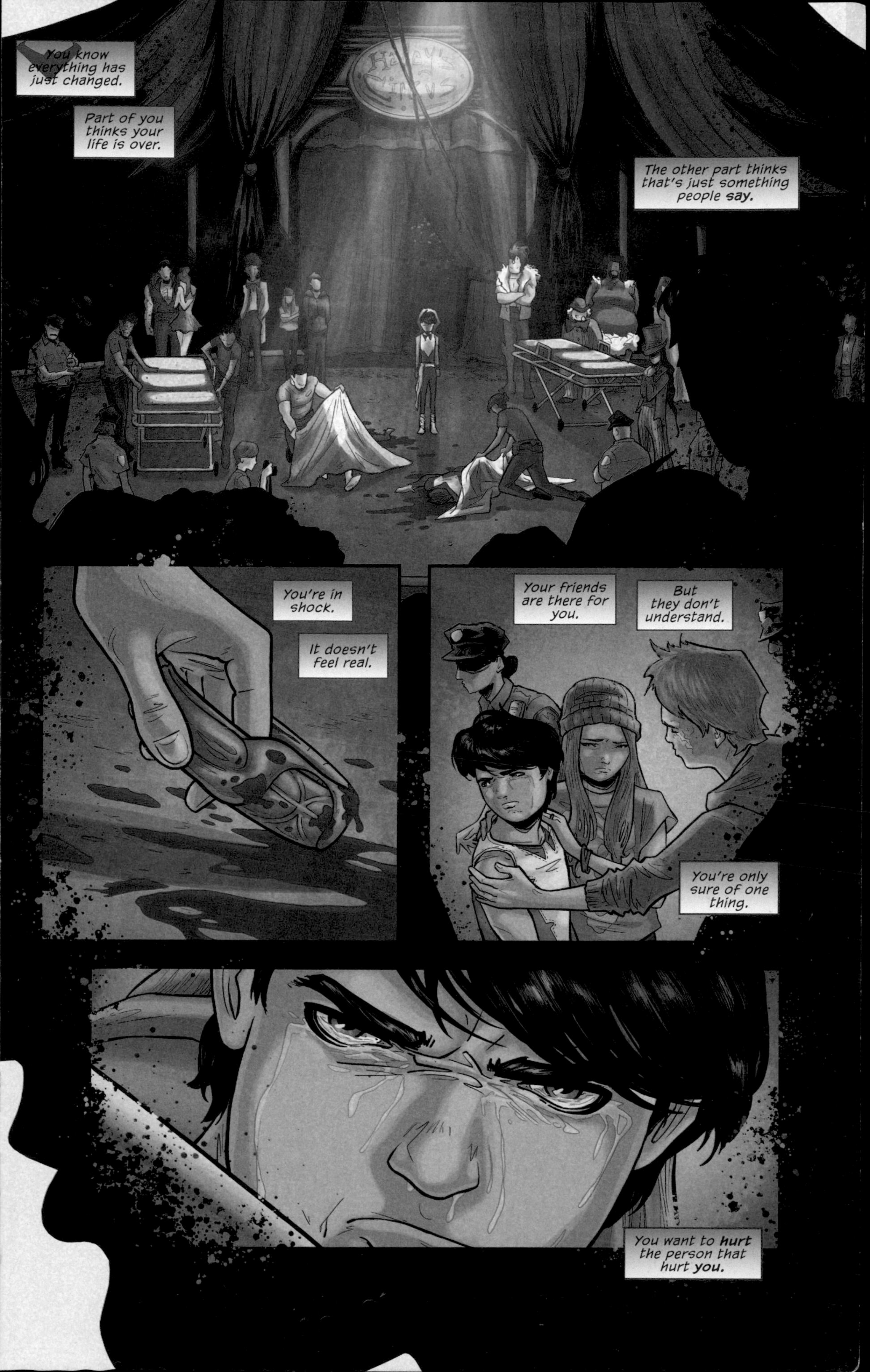
You know everything has just changed.
Part of you thinks your life is over.
The other part thinks that's just something people **say.**
You're in shock.
It doesn't feel real.
Your friends are there for you.
But they don't understand.
You're only sure of one thing.
You want to **hurt** the person that hurt **you.**

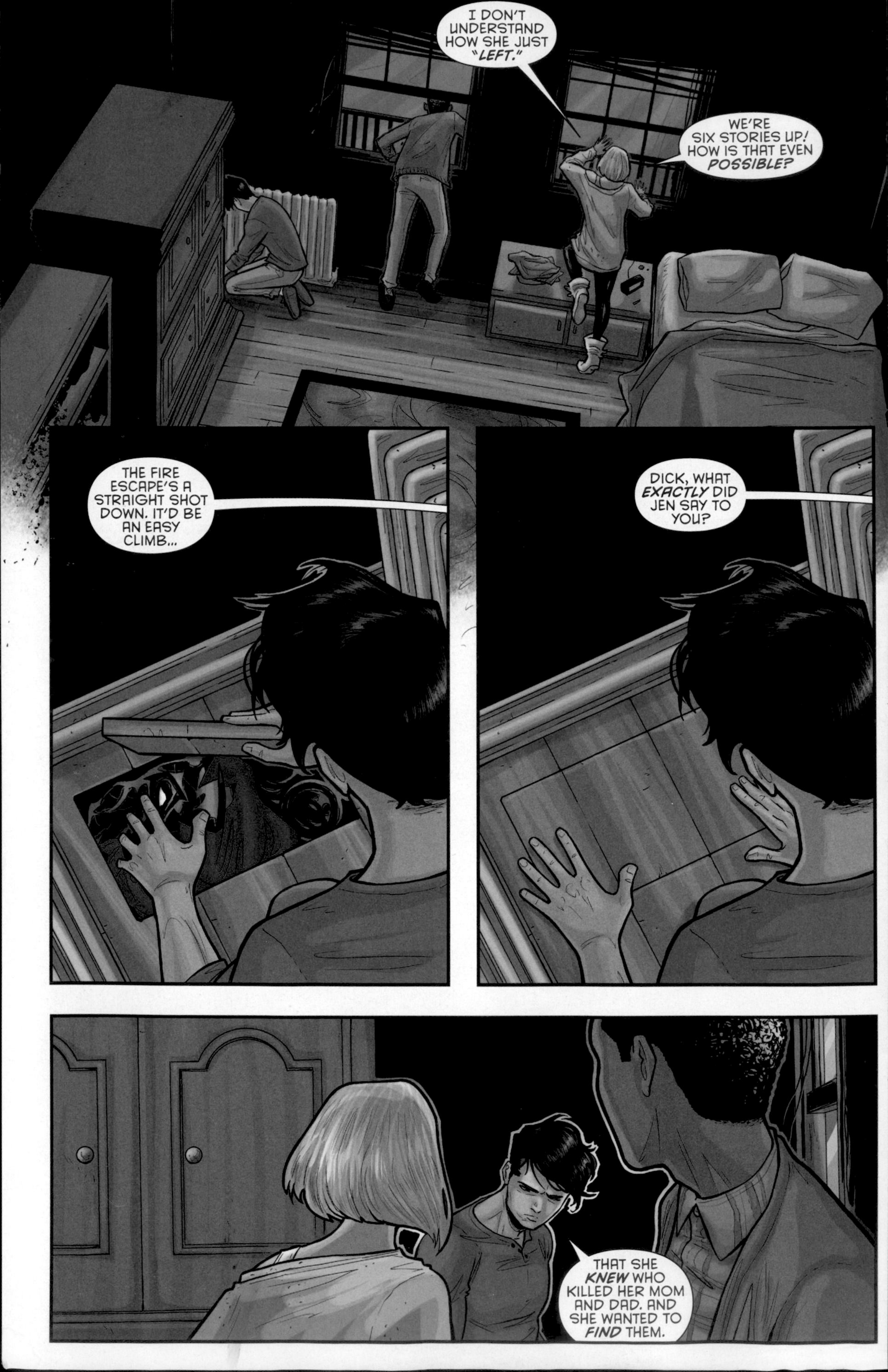

I DON'T UNDERSTAND HOW SHE JUST "LEFT."
WE'RE SIX STORIES UP! HOW IS THAT EVEN POSSIBLE?
THE FIRE ESCAPE'S A STRAIGHT SHOT DOWN. IT'D BE AN EASY CLIMB...
DICK, WHAT EXACTLY DID JEN SAY TO YOU?
THAT SHE KNEW WHO KILLED HER MOM AND DAD. AND SHE WANTED TO FIND THEM.

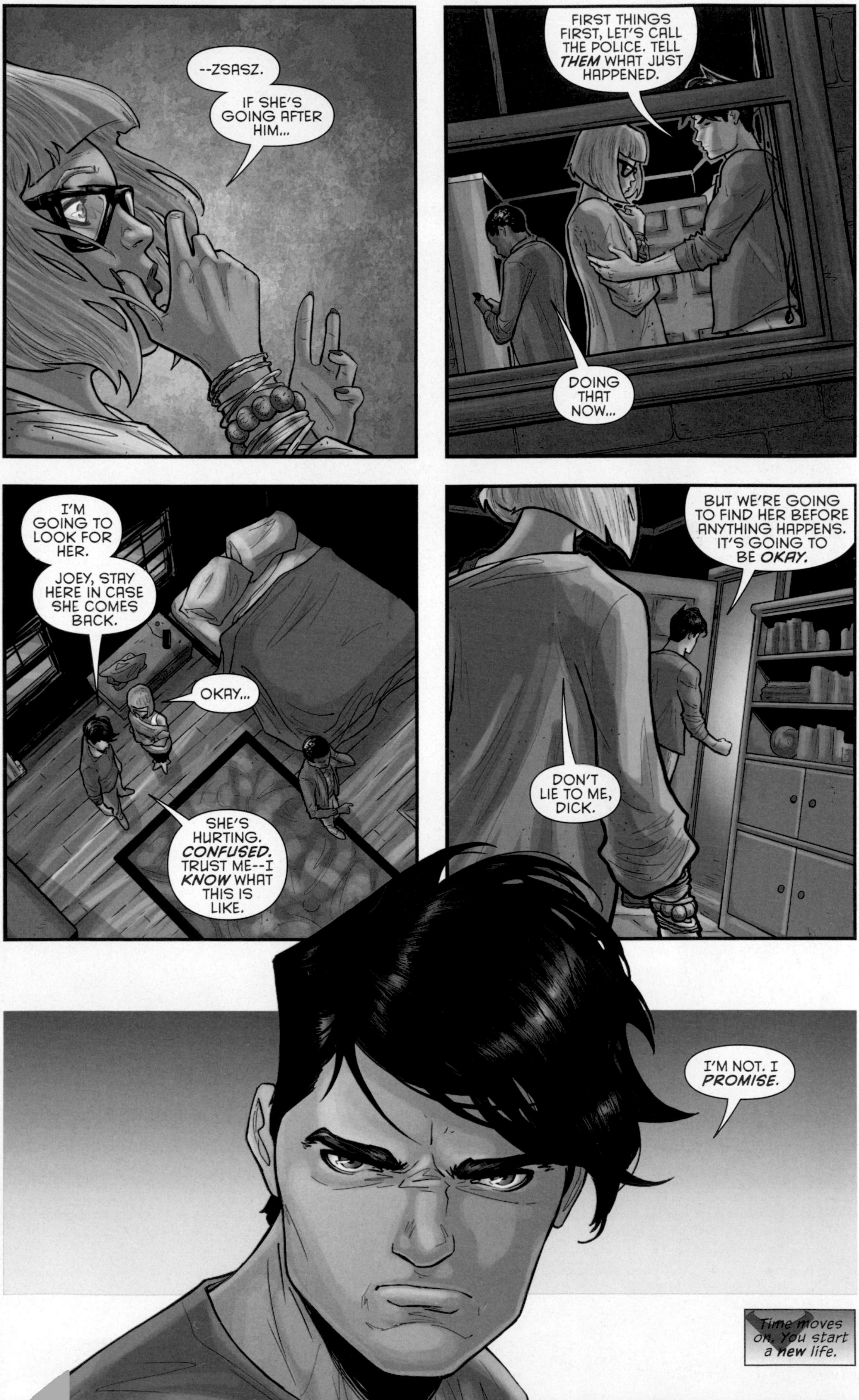
--ZSASZ.
IF SHE'S GOING AFTER HIM...
FIRST THINGS FIRST, LET'S CALL THE POLICE. TELL THEM WHAT JUST HAPPENED.
DOING THAT NOW...
I'M GOING TO LOOK FOR HER.
JOEY, STAY HERE IN CASE SHE COMES BACK.
OKAY...
SHE'S HURTING. CONFUSED. TRUST ME--I KNOW WHAT THIS IS LIKE.
BUT WE'RE GOING TO FIND HER BEFORE ANYTHING HAPPENS. IT'S GOING TO BE OKAY.
DON'T LIE TO ME, DICK.
I'M NOT. I PROMISE.
Time moves on. You start a new life.

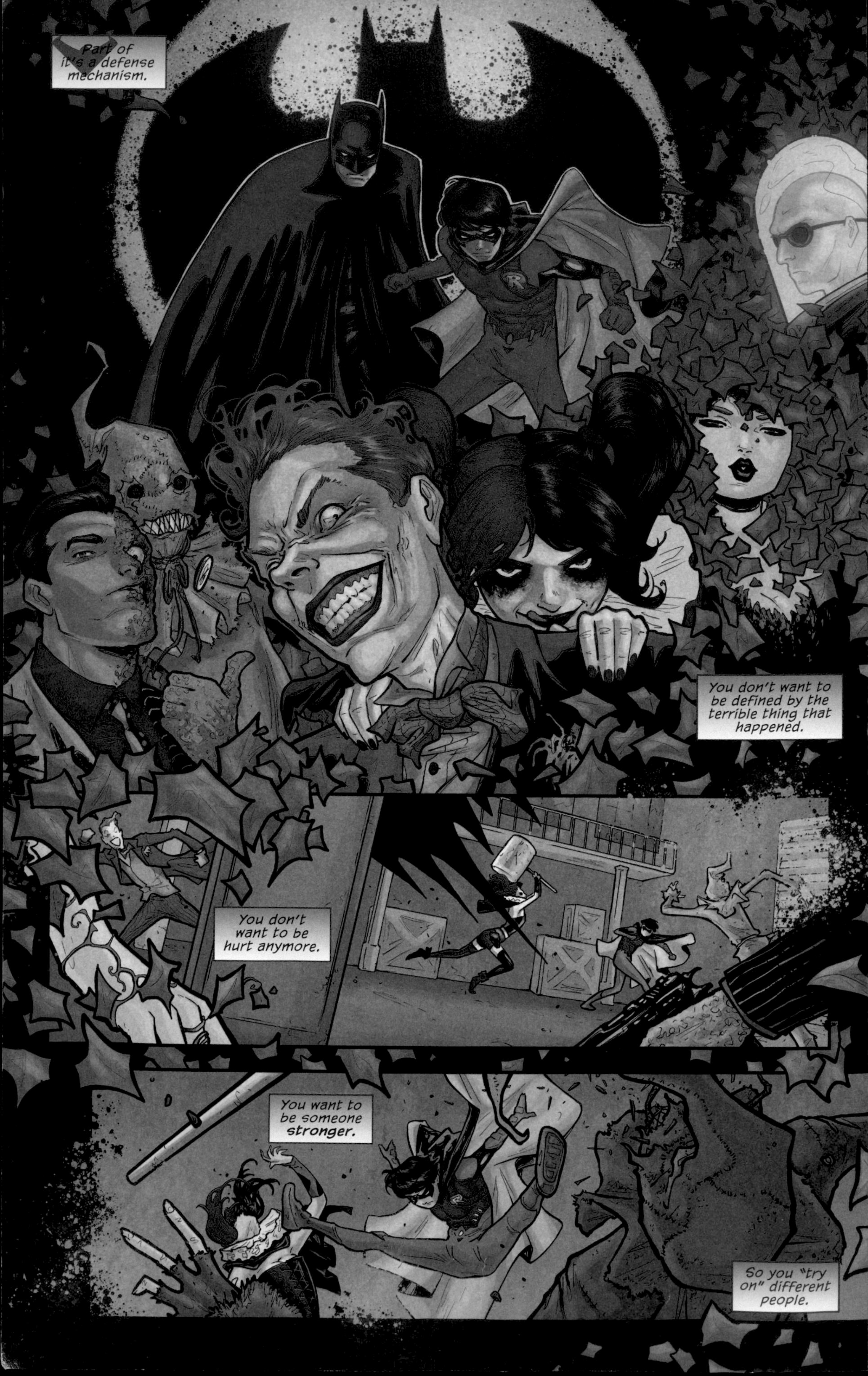
Part of it's a defense mechanism.
You don't want to be defined by the terrible thing that happened.
You don't want to be hurt anymore.
You want to be someone stronger.
So you "try on" different people.

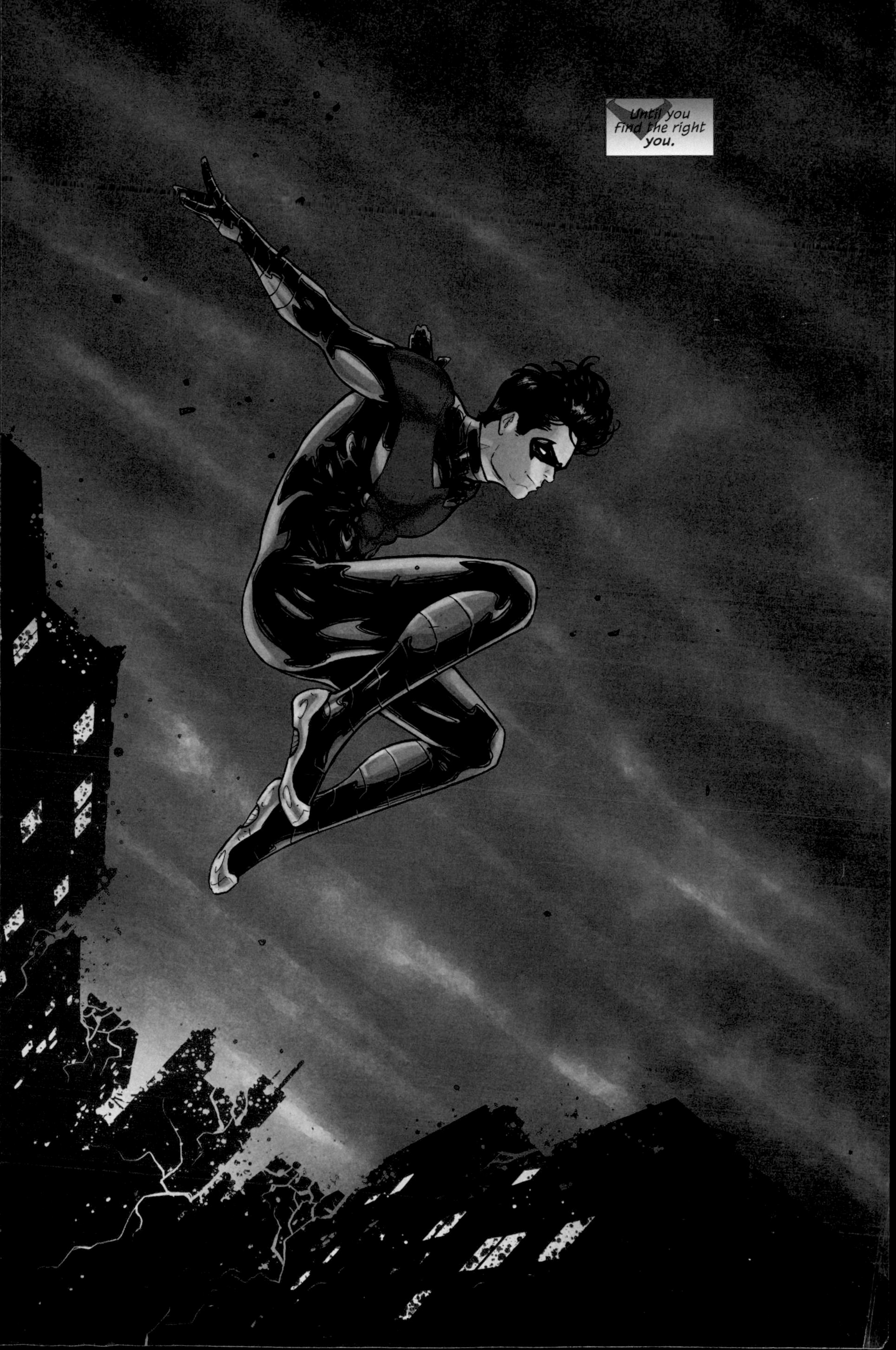
Until you find the right you.

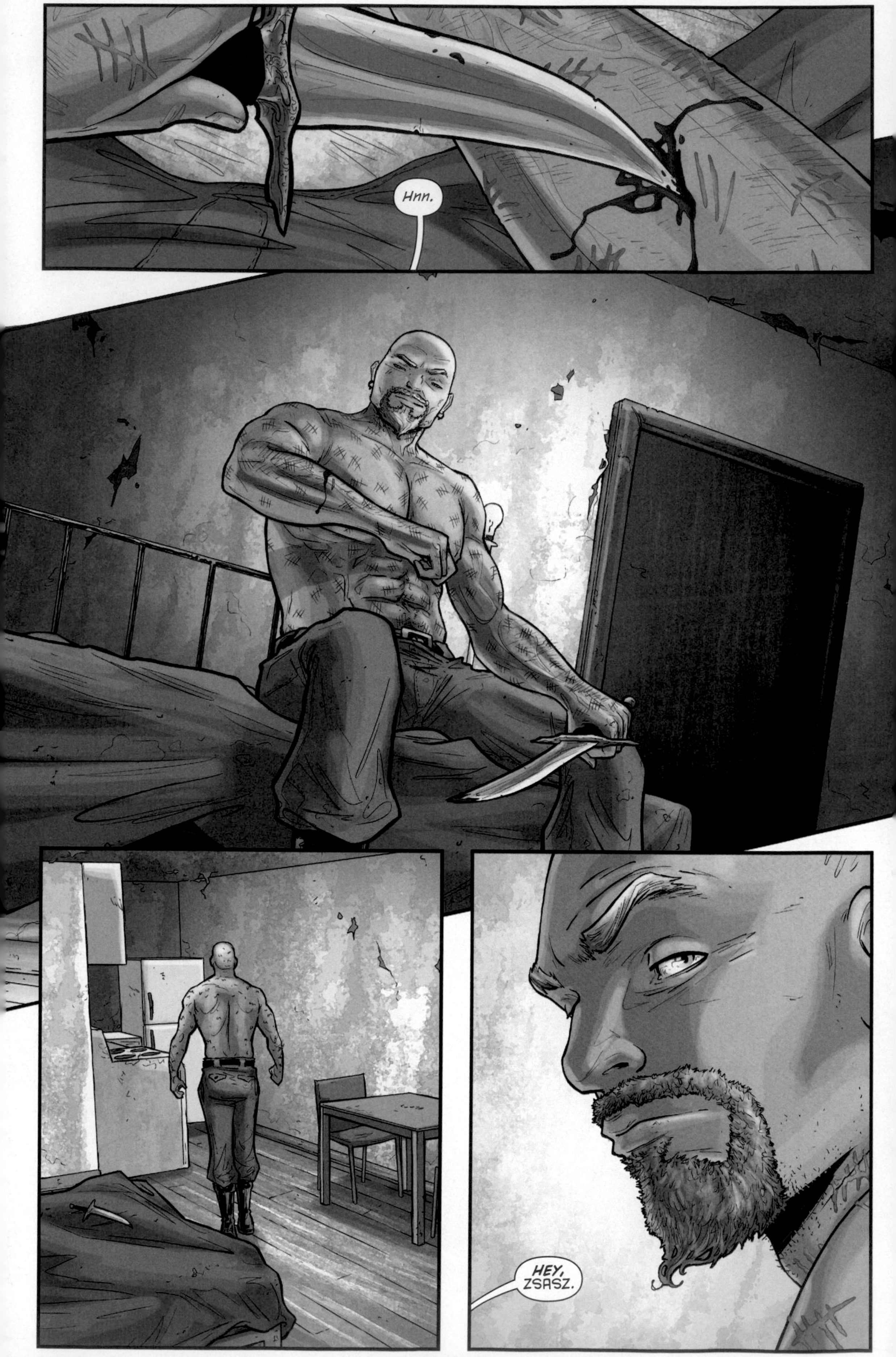
Hnn.
HEY, ZSASZ.

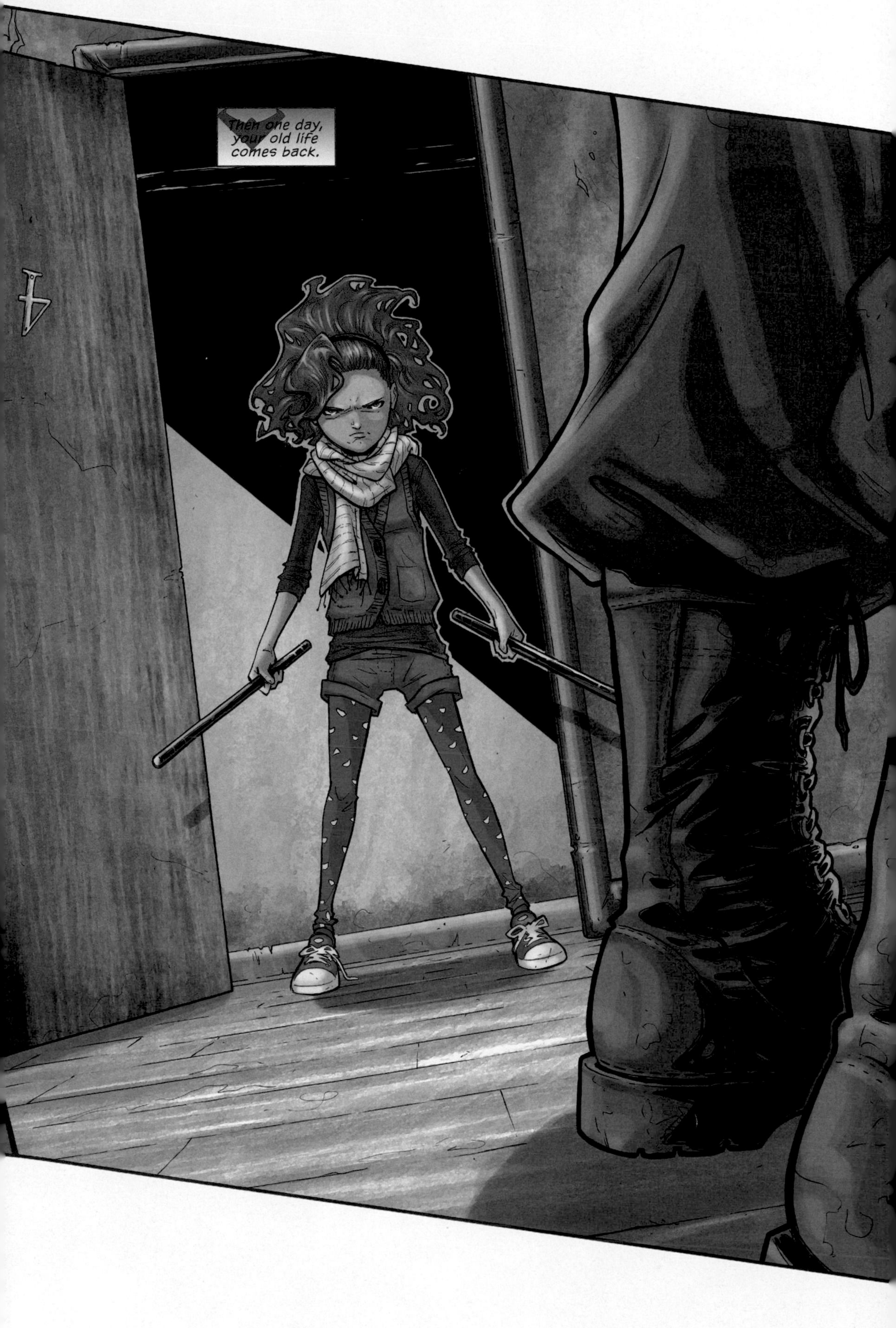
Then one day, your old life comes back.

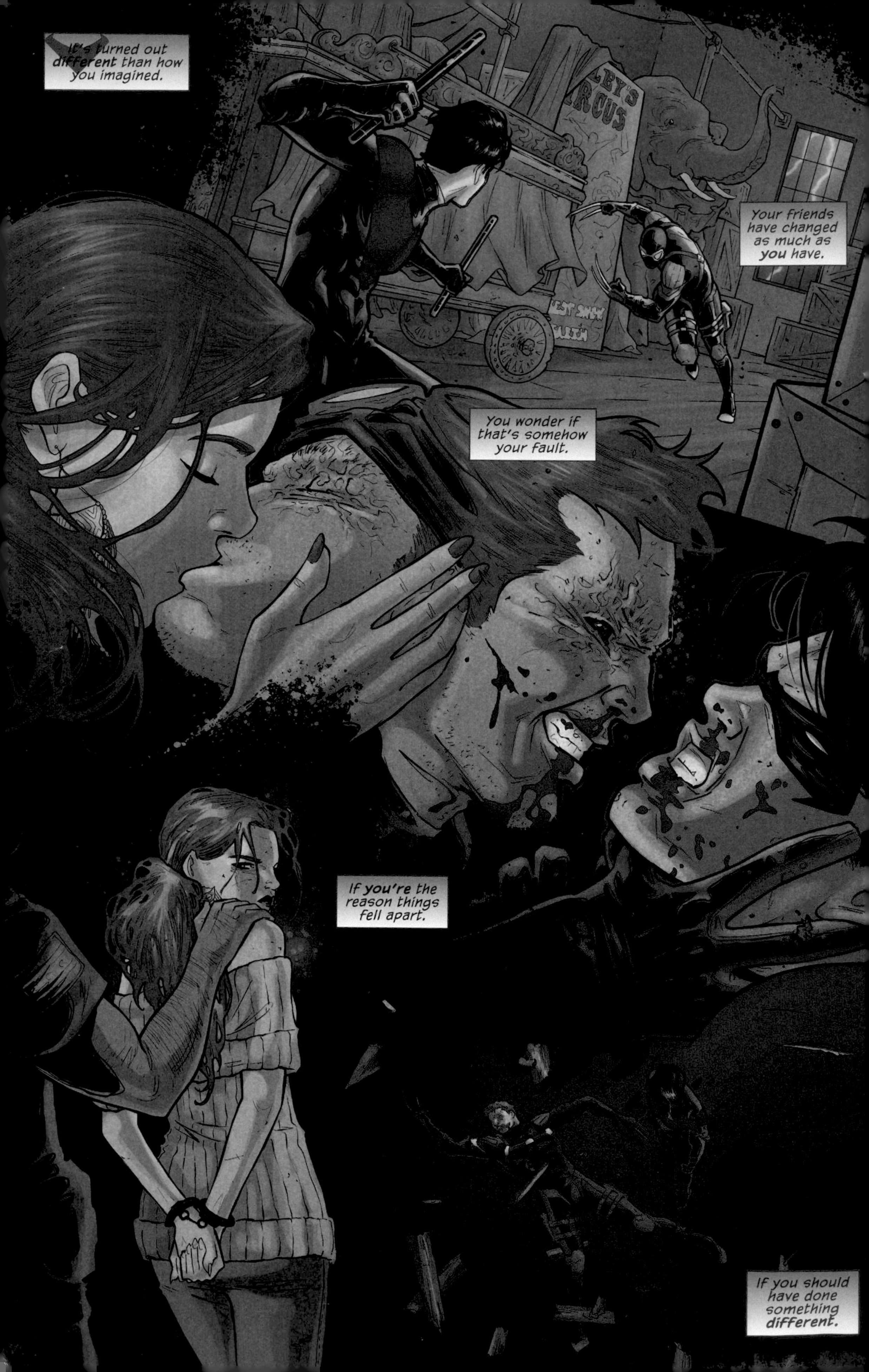
It's turned out different than how you imagined.
Your friends have changed as much as you have.
You wonder if that's somehow your fault.
If you're the reason things fell apart.
If you should have done something different.

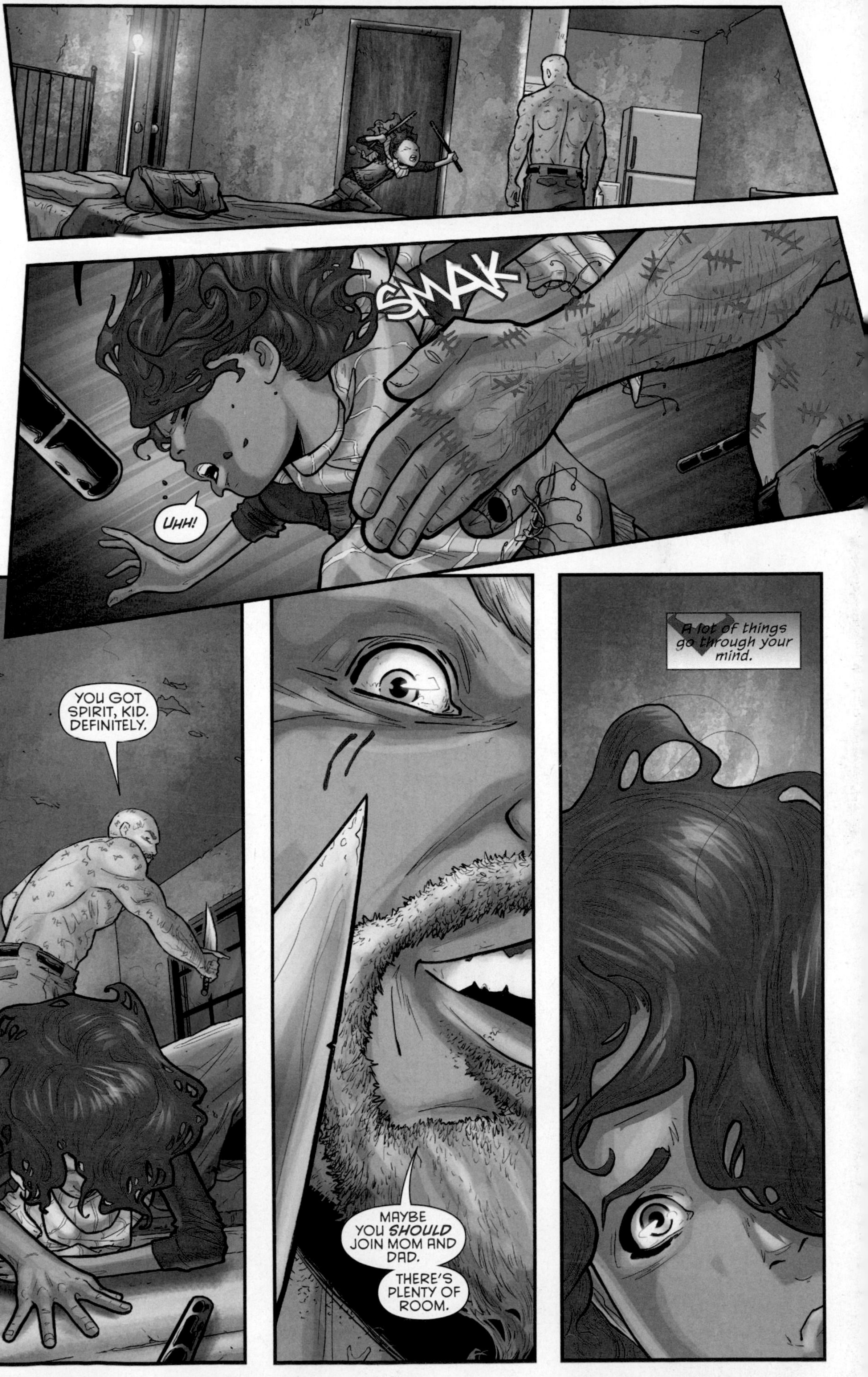
SMAK
UHH!
YOU GOT SPIRIT, KID. DEFINITELY.
MAYBE YOU SHOULD JOIN MOM AND DAD.
THERE'S PLENTY OF ROOM.
A lot of things go through your mind.

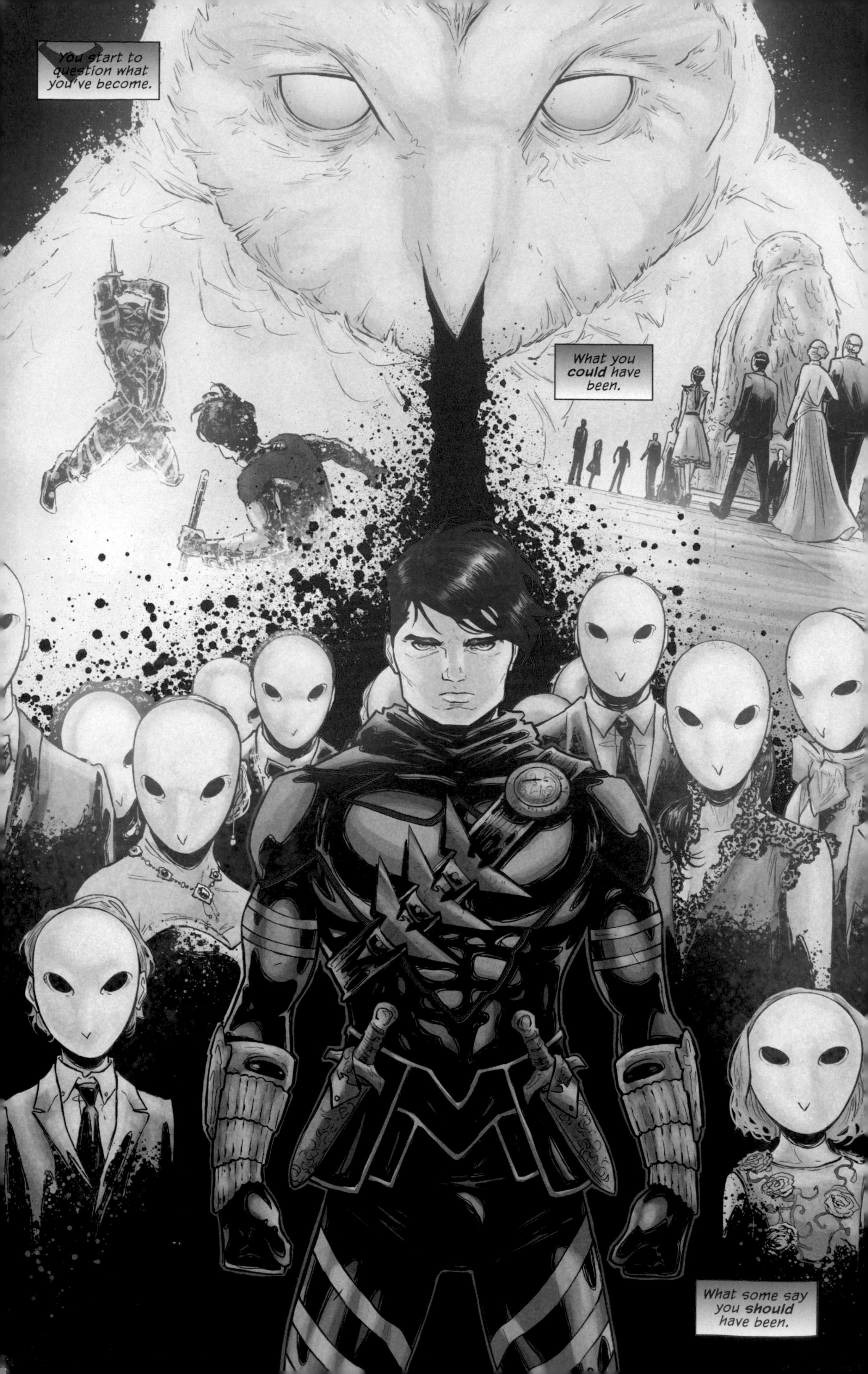
You start to question what you've become.
What you could have been.
What some say you should have been.

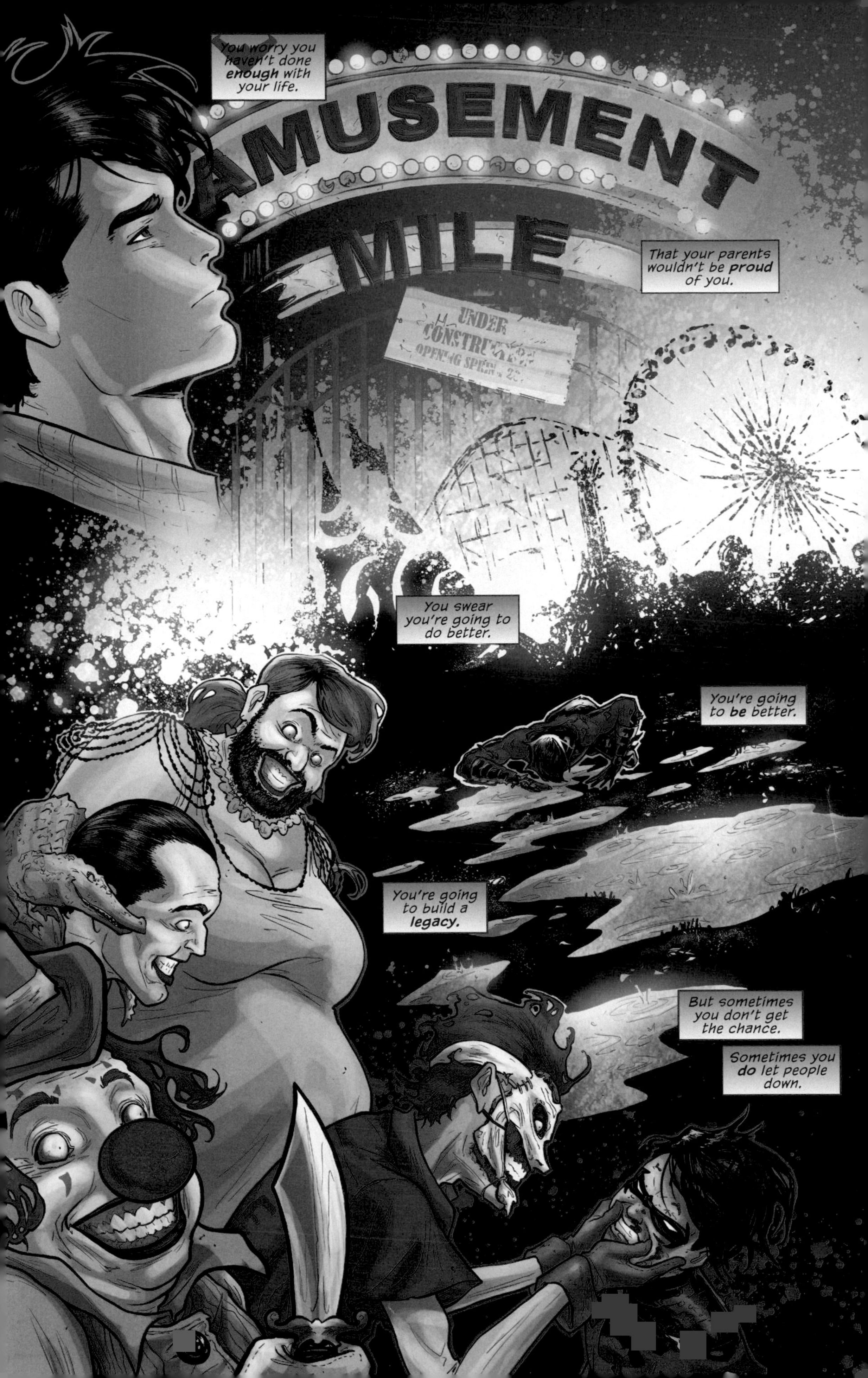
You worry you haven't done **enough** with your life.
AMUSEMENT
MILE
UNDER
That your parents wouldn't be **proud** of you.
You swear you're going to do better.
You're going to **be** better.
You're going to build a **legacy.**
But sometimes you don't get the chance.
Sometimes you **do** let people down.

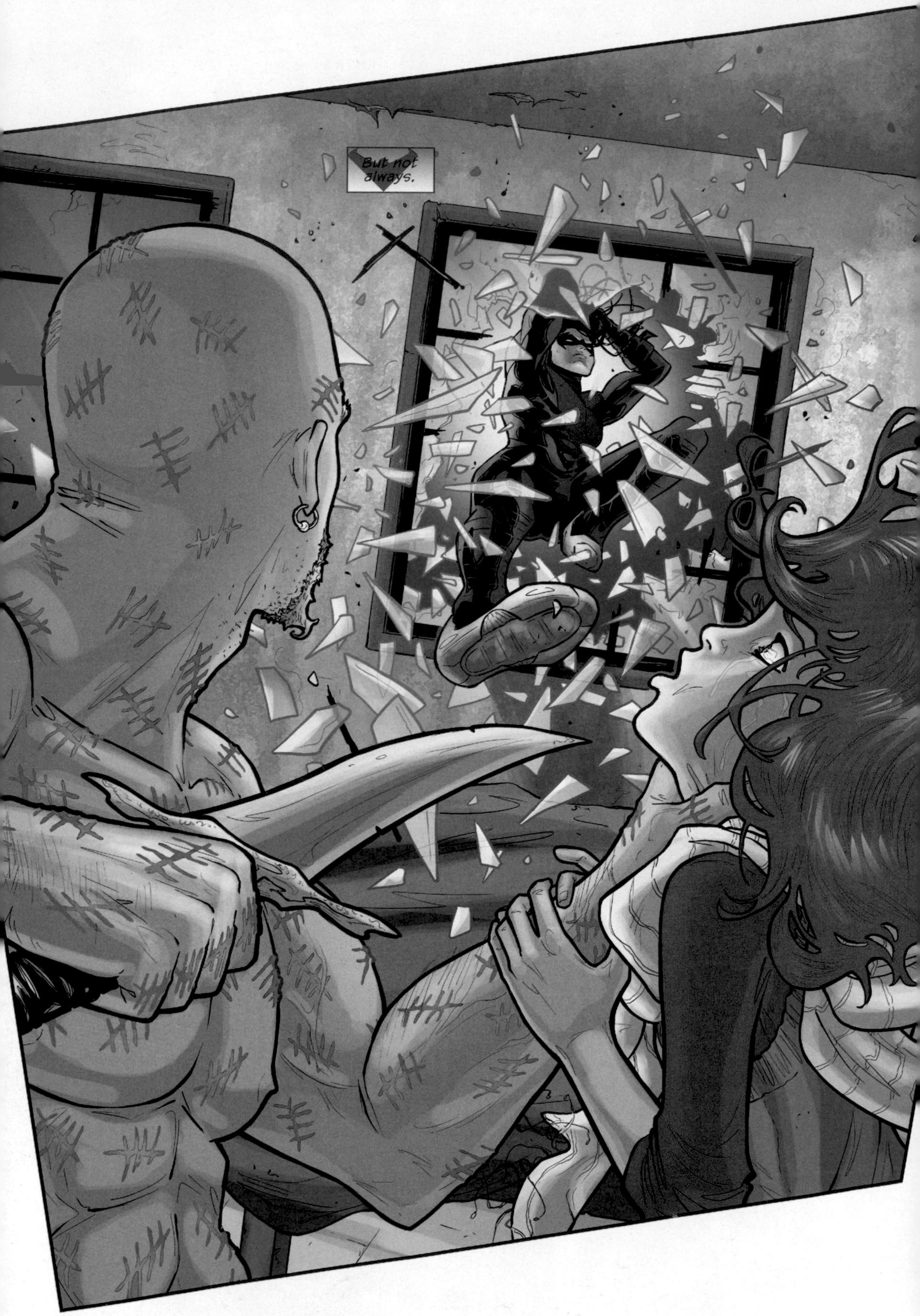
But not always.

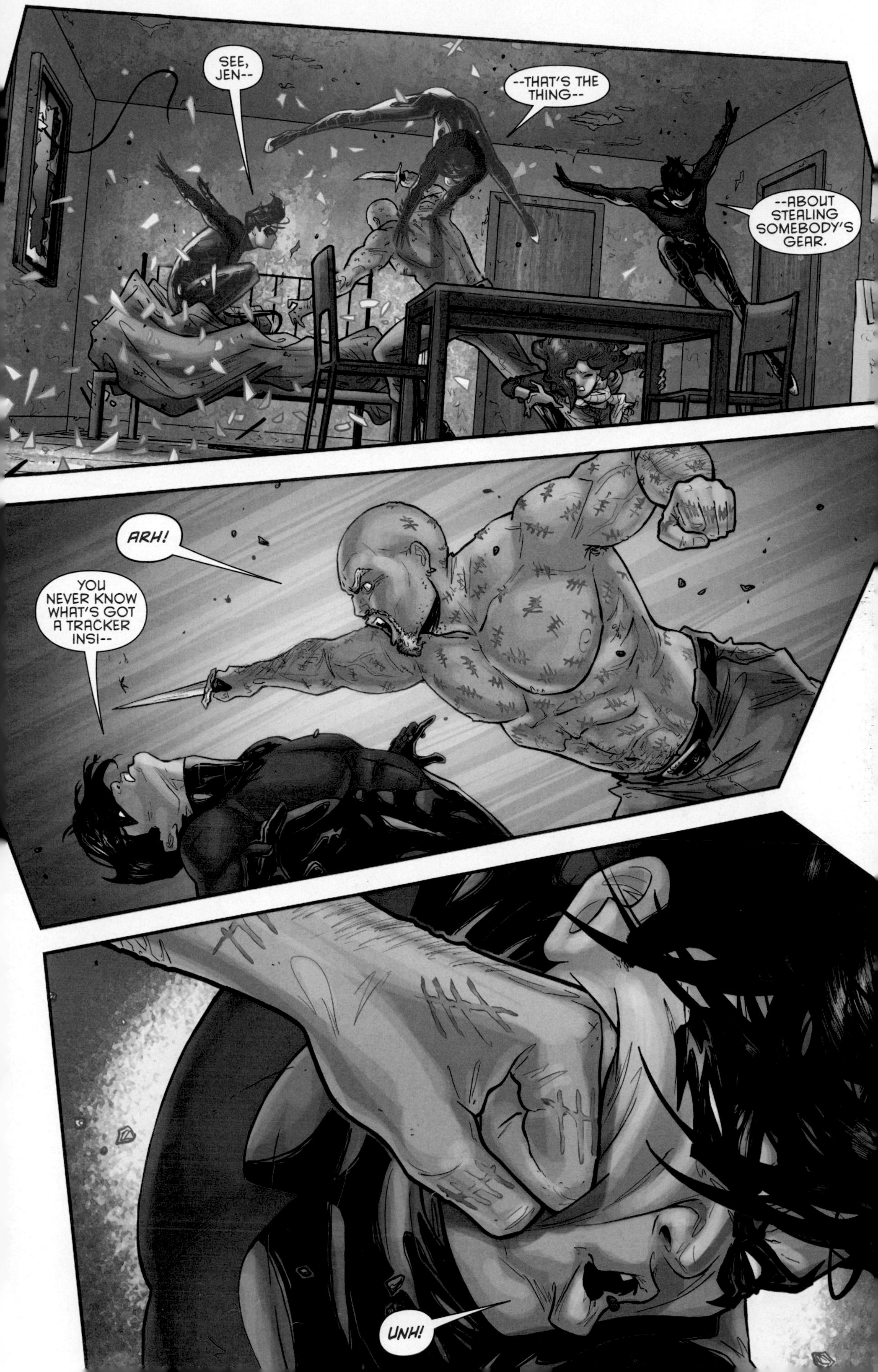
SEE, JEN--
--THAT'S THE THING--
--ABOUT STEALING SOMEBODY'S GEAR.
ARH!
YOU NEVER KNOW WHAT'S GOT A TRACKER INSI--
UNH!

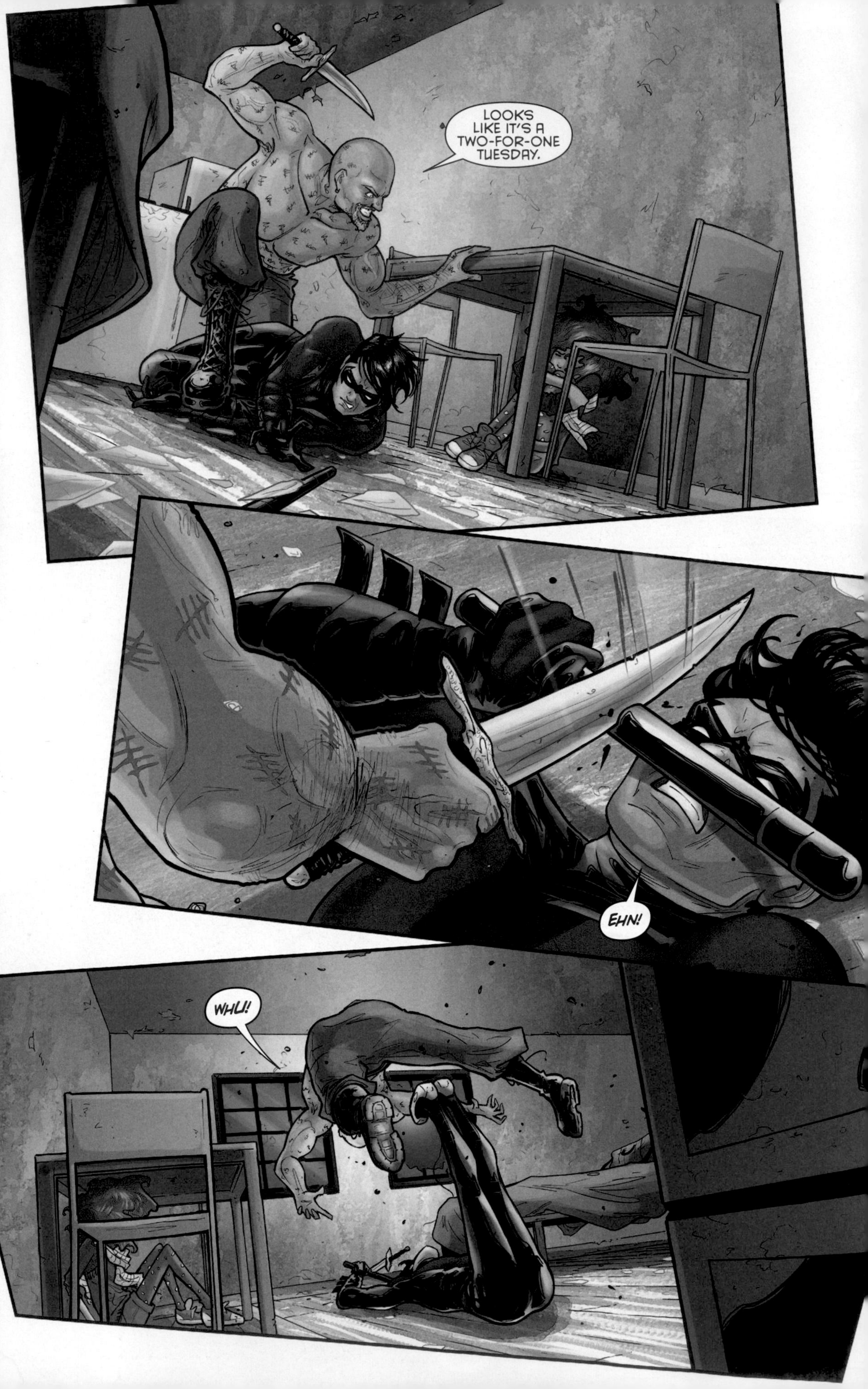

LOOKS LIKE IT'S A TWO-FOR-ONE TUESDAY.
EHN!
WHU!

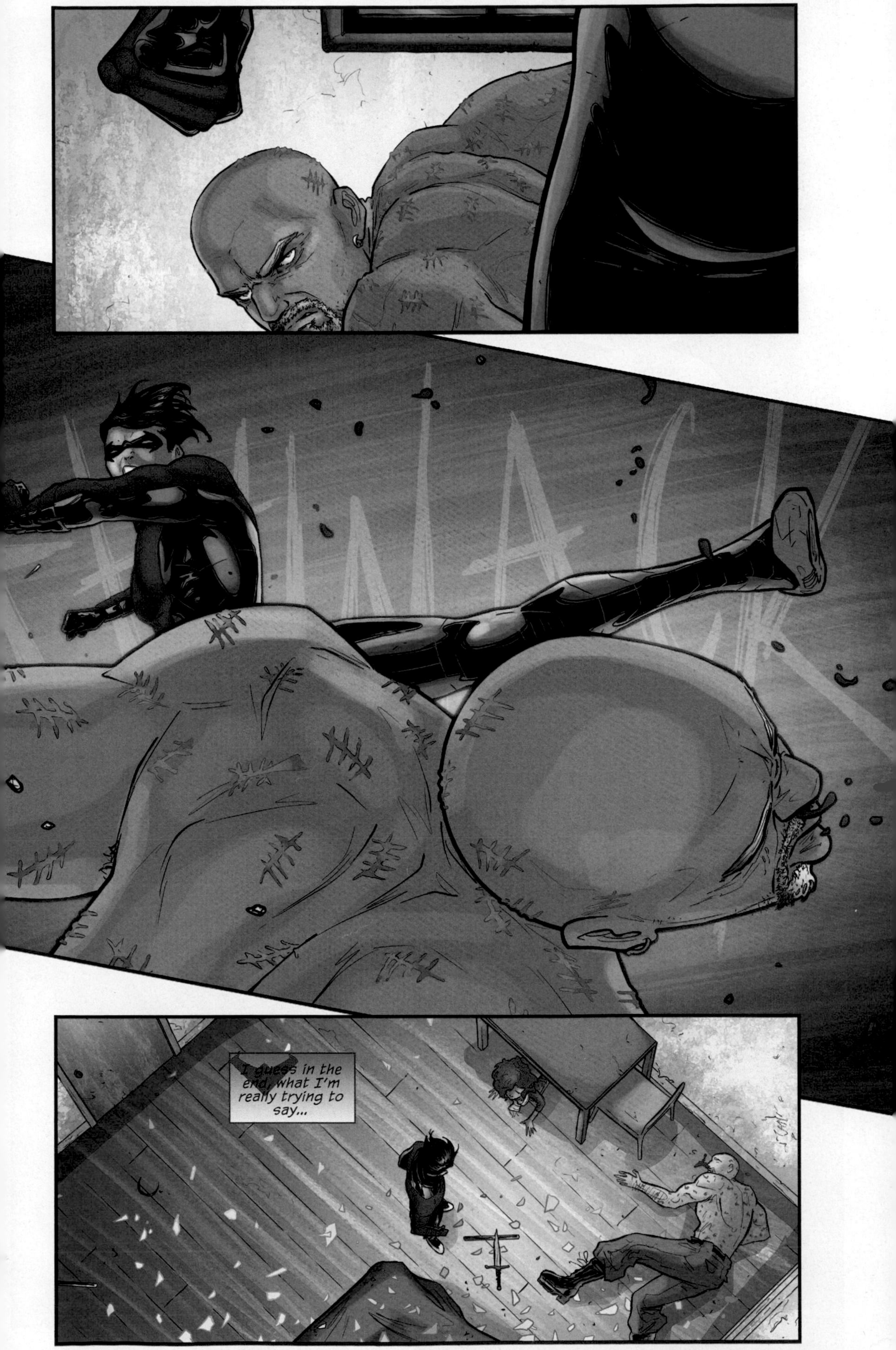
I guess in the end, what I'm really trying to say...

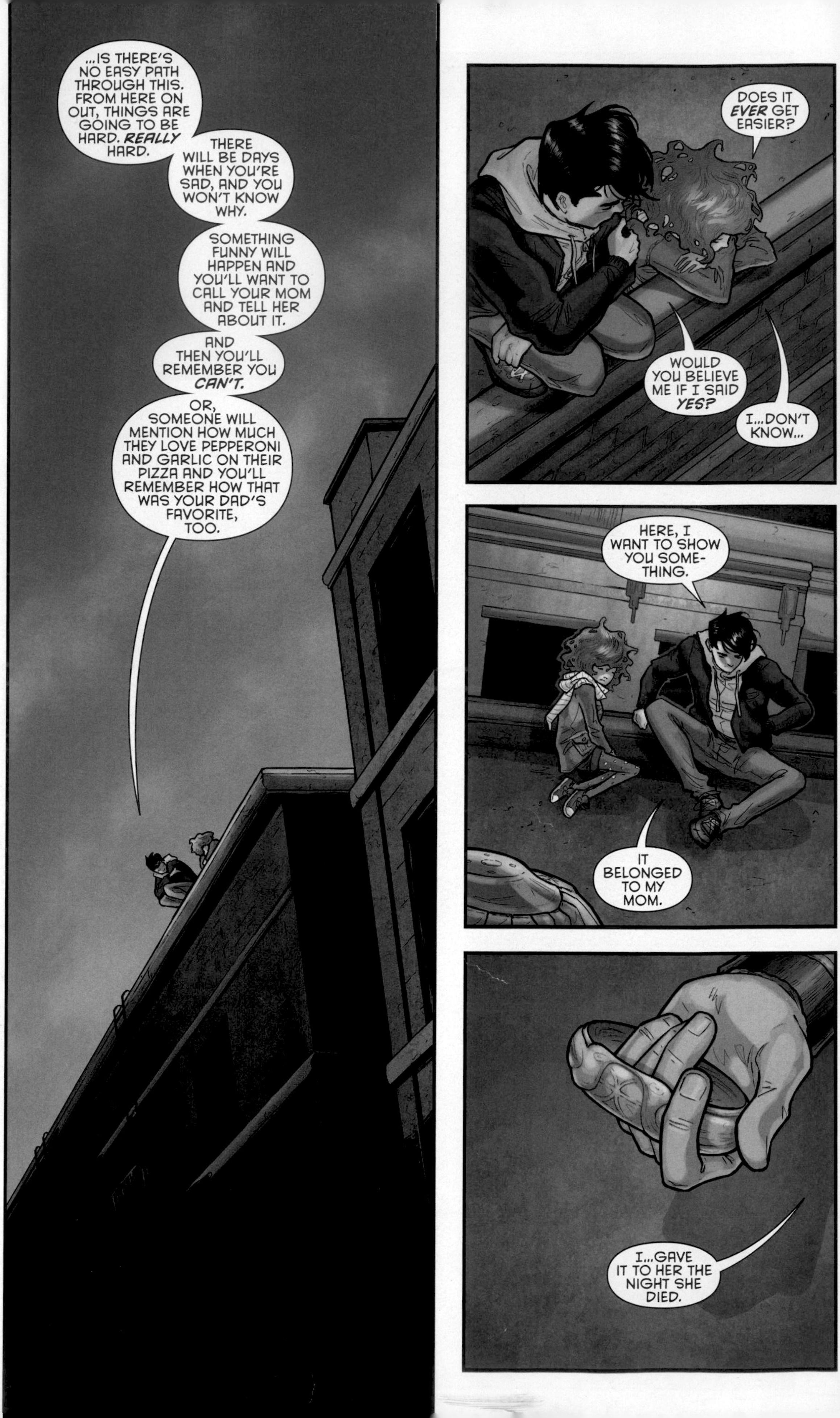
...IS THERE'S NO EASY PATH THROUGH THIS. FROM HERE ON OUT, THINGS ARE GOING TO BE HARD. *REALLY* HARD.
THERE WILL BE DAYS WHEN YOU'RE SAD, AND YOU WON'T KNOW WHY.
SOMETHING FUNNY WILL HAPPEN AND YOU'LL WANT TO CALL YOUR MOM AND TELL HER ABOUT IT.
AND THEN YOU'LL REMEMBER YOU *CAN'T.*
OR, SOMEONE WILL MENTION HOW MUCH THEY LOVE PEPPERONI AND GARLIC ON THEIR PIZZA AND YOU'LL REMEMBER HOW THAT WAS YOUR DAD'S FAVORITE, TOO.
DOES IT *EVER* GET EASIER?
WOULD YOU BELIEVE ME IF I SAID *YES?*
I...DON'T KNOW...
HERE, I WANT TO SHOW YOU SOME-THING.
IT BELONGED TO MY MOM.
I...GAVE IT TO HER THE NIGHT SHE DIED.

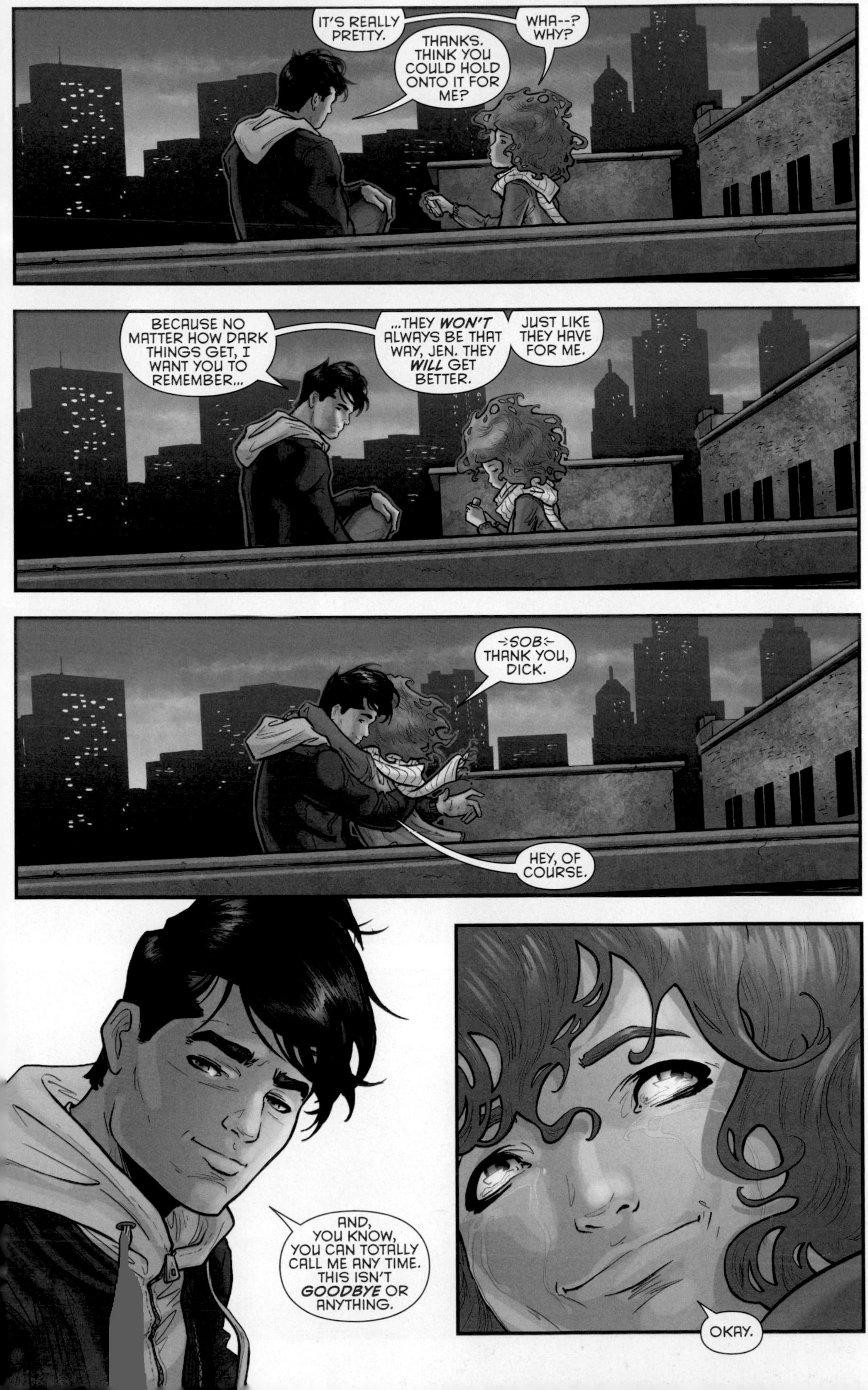
IT'S REALLY PRETTY.
WHA--? WHY?
THANKS. THINK YOU COULD HOLD ONTO IT FOR ME?
BECAUSE NO MATTER HOW DARK THINGS GET, I WANT YOU TO REMEMBER...
...THEY WON'T ALWAYS BE THAT WAY, JEN. THEY WILL GET BETTER.
JUST LIKE THEY HAVE FOR ME.
SOB THANK YOU, DICK.
HEY, OF COURSE.
AND, YOU KNOW, YOU CAN TOTALLY CALL ME ANY TIME. THIS ISN'T GOODBYE OR ANYTHING.
OKAY.

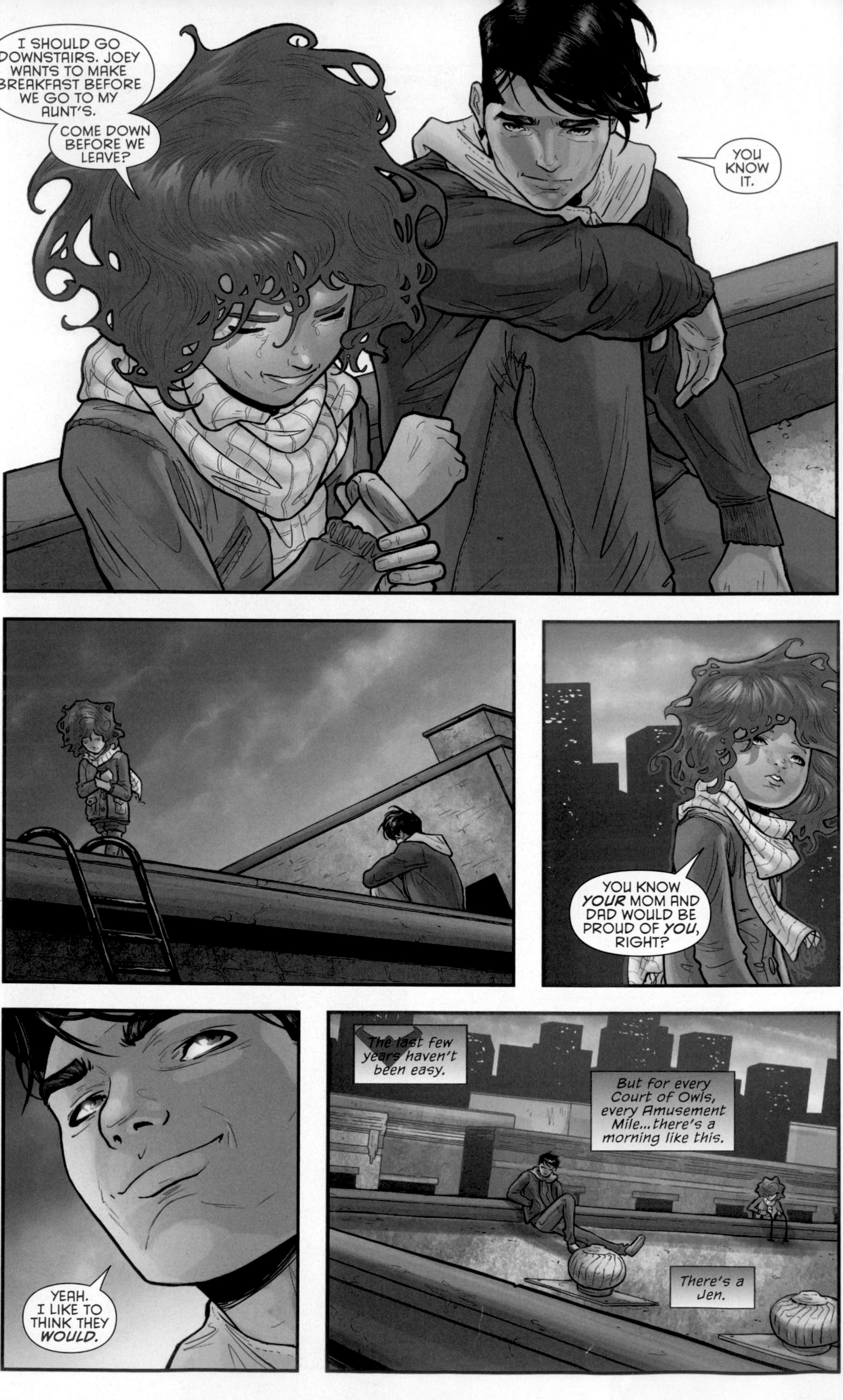
I SHOULD GO DOWNSTAIRS. JOEY WANTS TO MAKE BREAKFAST BEFORE WE GO TO MY AUNT'S.
COME DOWN BEFORE WE LEAVE?
YOU KNOW IT.
YOU KNOW YOUR MOM AND DAD WOULD BE PROUD OF YOU, RIGHT?
YEAH. I LIKE TO THINK THEY WOULD.
The last few years haven't been easy.
But for every Court of Owls, every Amusement Mile...there's a morning like this.
There's a Jen.

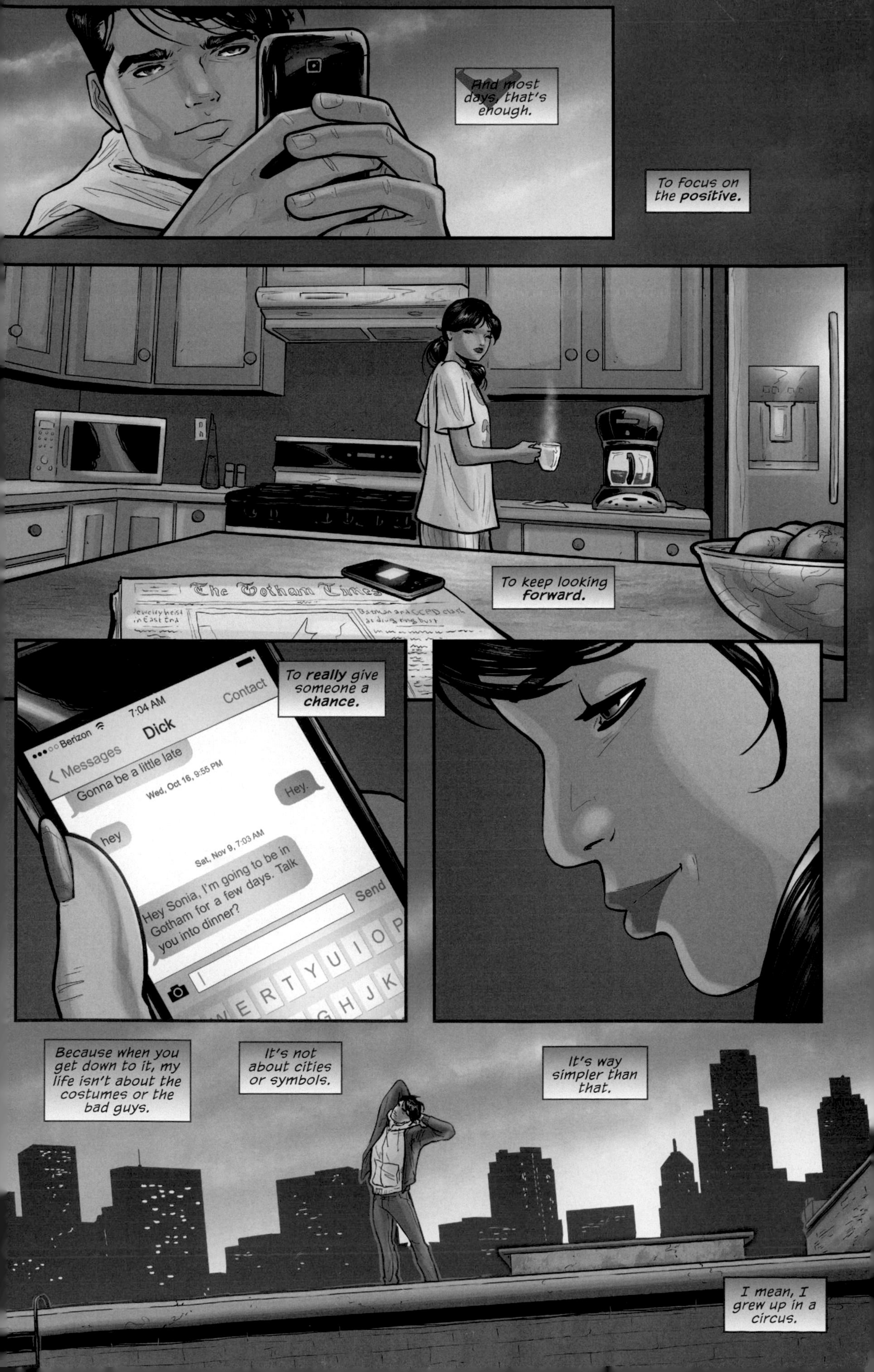
And most days, that's enough.
To focus on the positive.
The Gotham Times
Jewelry heist in East End
To keep looking forward.
To really give someone a chance.
Berizon
7:04 AM
Messages
Dick
Contact
Gonna be a little late
Wed, Oct 16, 9:55 PM
Hey.
hey
Sat, Nov 9, 7:03 AM
Hey Sonia, I'm going to be in Gotham for a few days. Talk you into dinner?
Send
Because when you get down to it, my life isn't about the costumes or the bad guys.
It's not about cities or symbols.
It's way simpler than that.
I mean, I grew up in a circus.

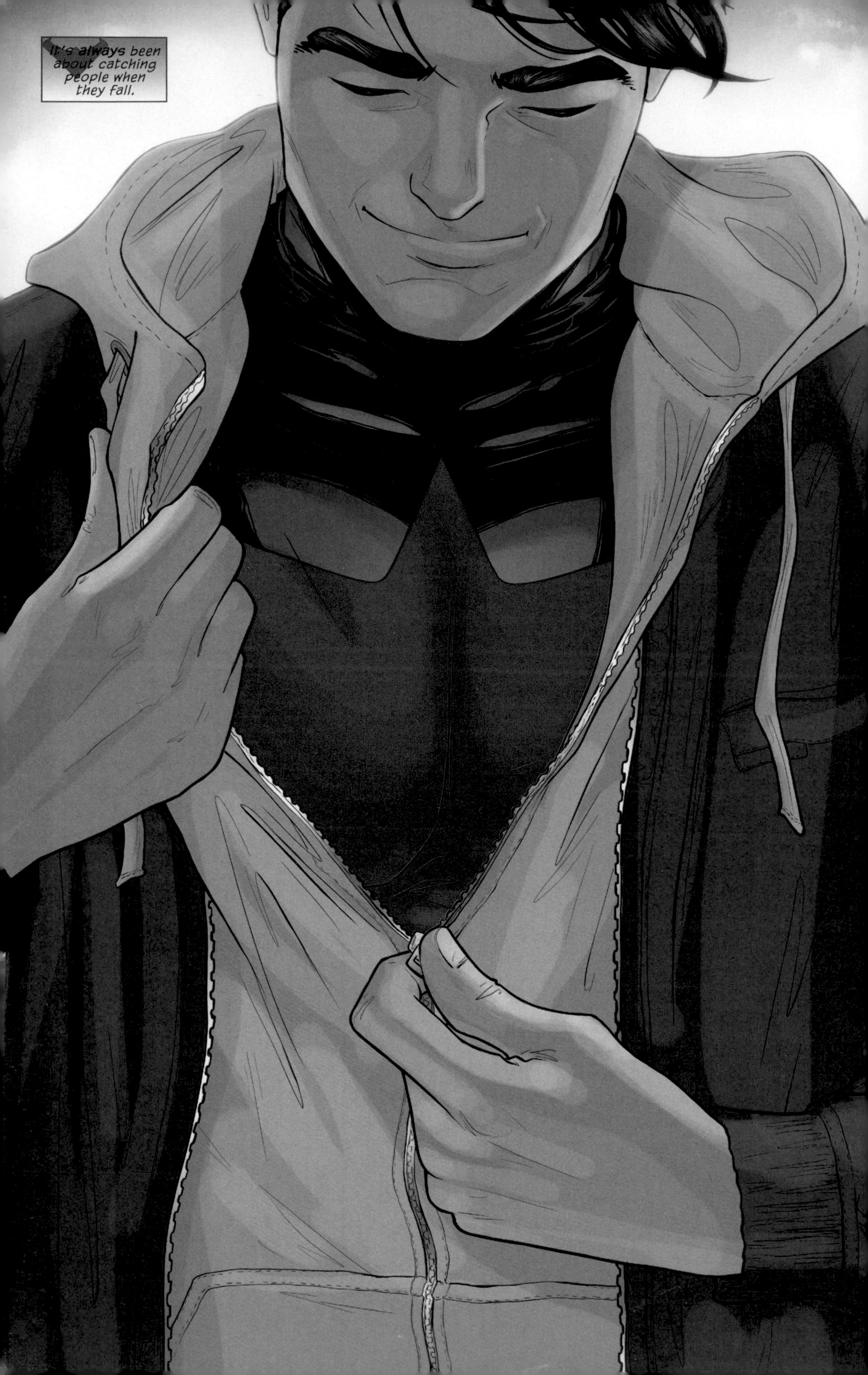
It's always been about catching people when they fall.

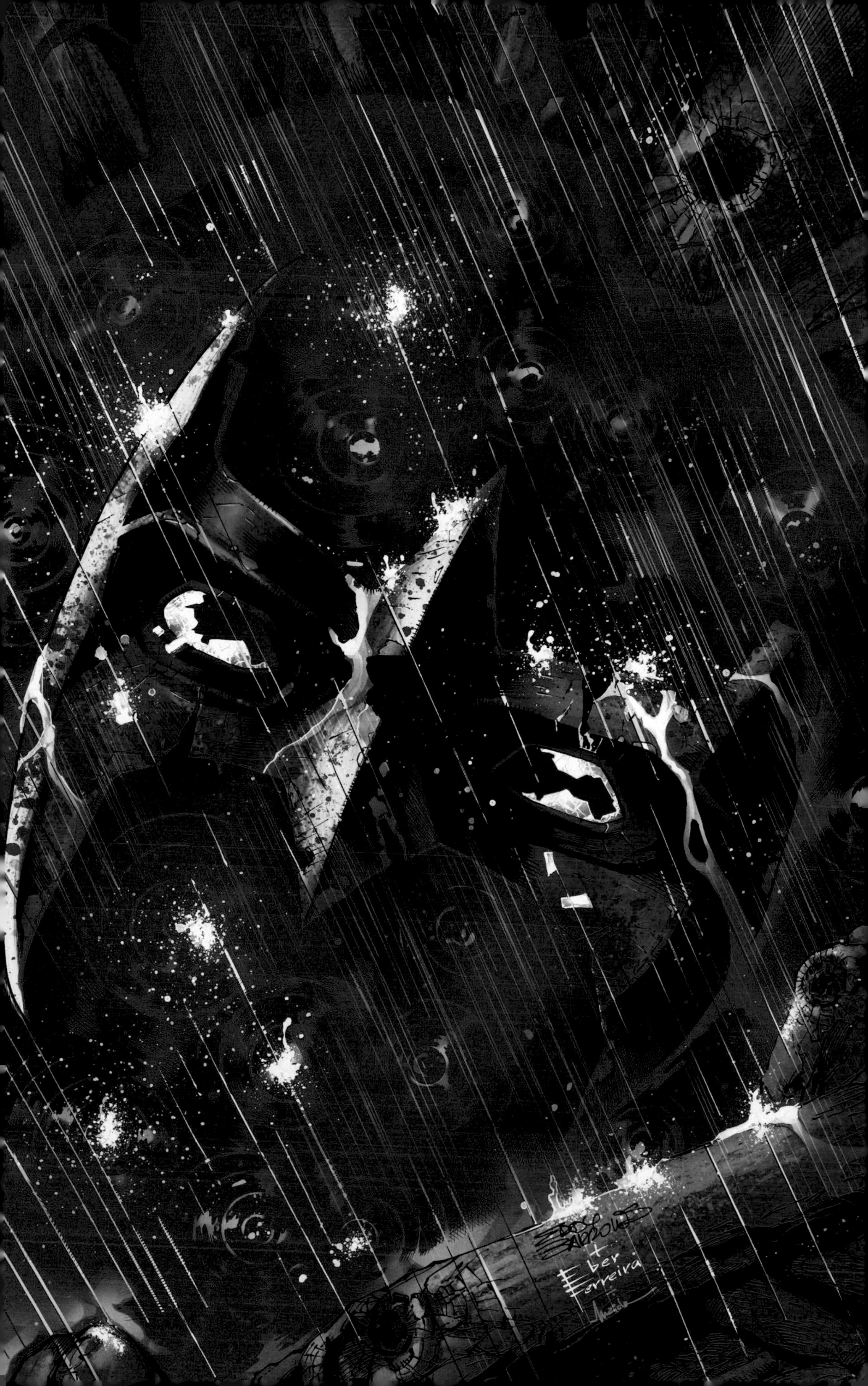

SETTING SON

TIM SEELEY and **TOM KING** writers **JAVIER GARRÓN** artist – part one **JORGE LUCAS** artist – part two **MIKEL JANIN** penciller **GUILLERMO ORTEGO** inker – part three **JEREMY COX** colorist **CARLOS M. MANGUAL** letterer

cover art by **EDDY BARROWS, EBER FERREIRA** and **MARCELO MAIOLO**

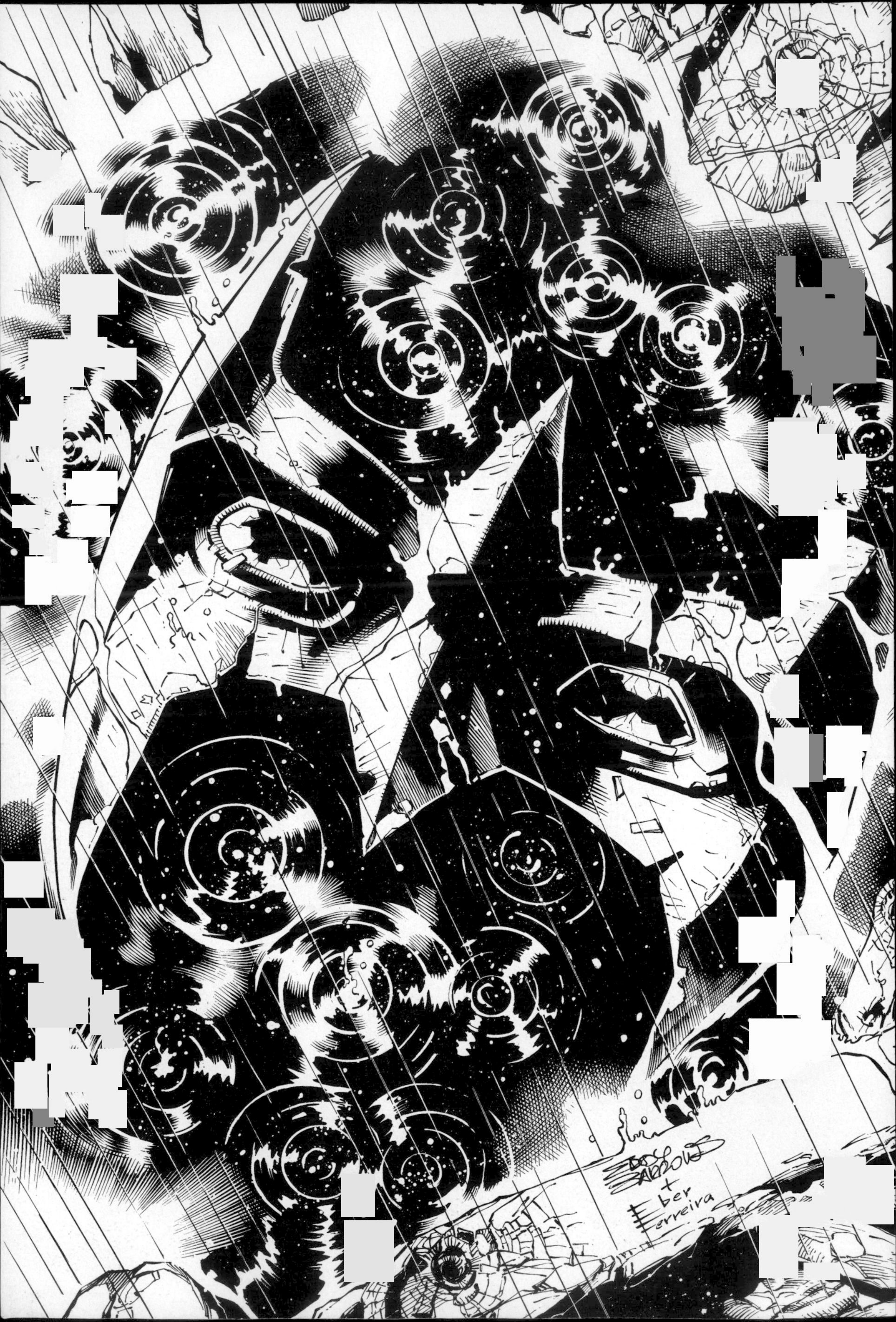
Eddy Barrows
+
Eber Ferreira

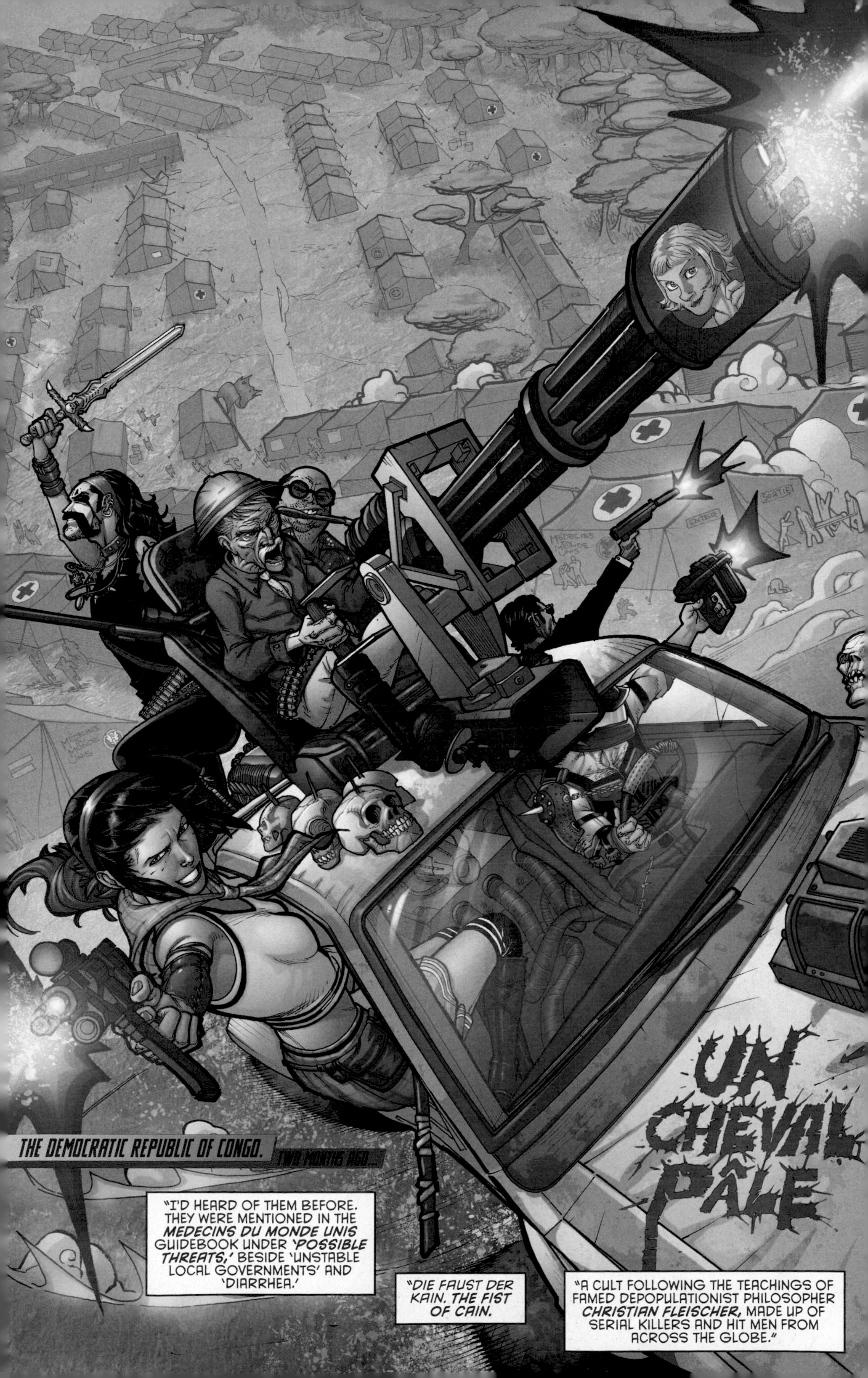

THE DEMOCRATIC REPUBLIC OF CONGO.
TWO MONTHS AGO...
"I'D HEARD OF THEM BEFORE. THEY WERE MENTIONED IN THE MEDECINS DU MONDE UNIS GUIDEBOOK UNDER 'POSSIBLE THREATS,' BESIDE 'UNSTABLE LOCAL GOVERNMENTS' AND 'DIARRHEA.'
"DIE FAUST DER KAIN. THE FIST OF CAIN.
"A CULT FOLLOWING THE TEACHINGS OF FAMED DEPOPULATIONIST PHILOSOPHER CHRISTIAN FLEISCHER, MADE UP OF SERIAL KILLERS AND HIT MEN FROM ACROSS THE GLOBE."
UN CHEVAL PÂLE

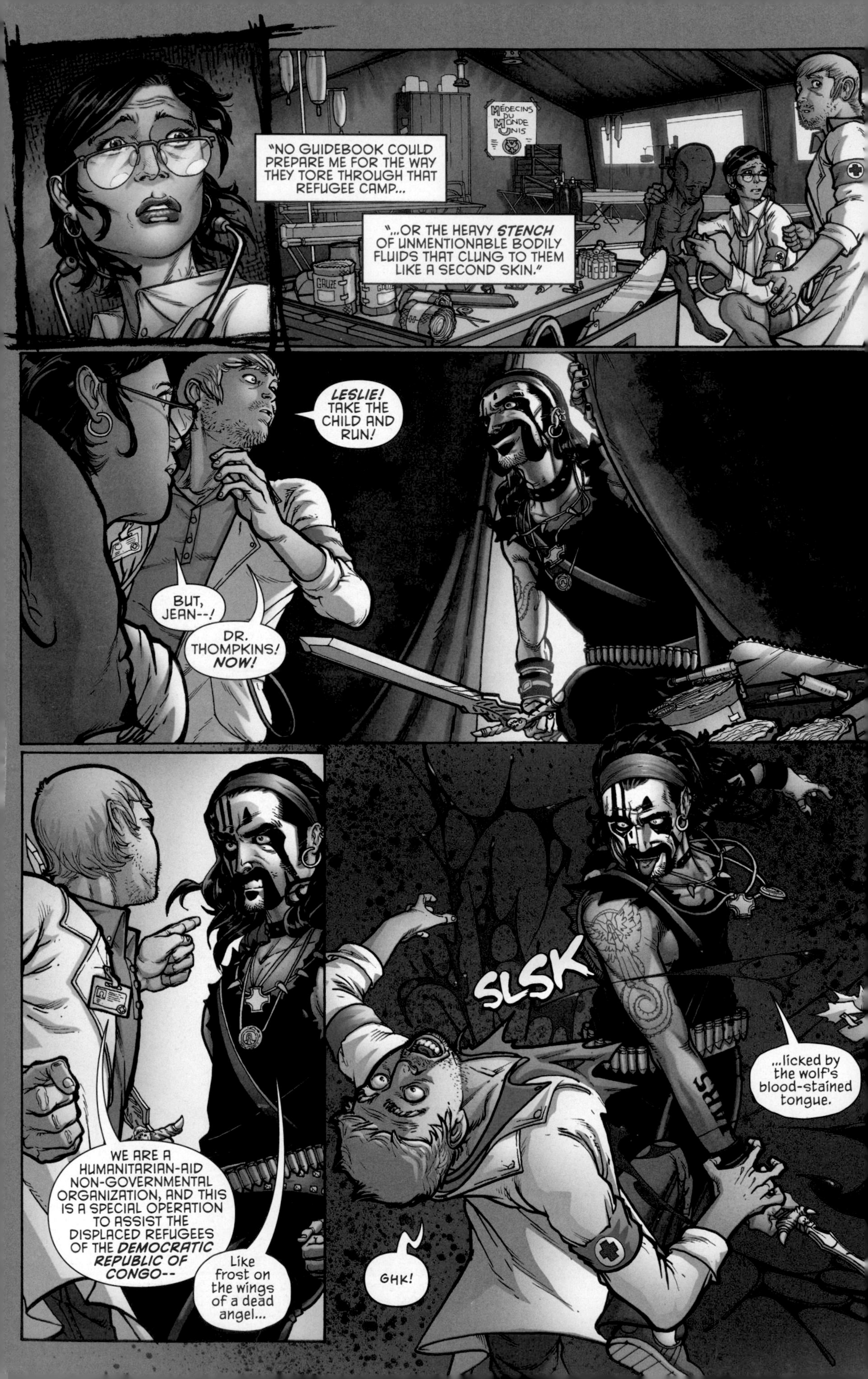

"NO GUIDEBOOK COULD PREPARE ME FOR THE WAY THEY TORE THROUGH THAT REFUGEE CAMP...
"...OR THE HEAVY STENCH OF UNMENTIONABLE BODILY FLUIDS THAT CLUNG TO THEM LIKE A SECOND SKIN."
MÉDECINS DU MONDE UNIS
GAUZE
LESLIE! TAKE THE CHILD AND RUN!
BUT, JEAN--!
DR. THOMPKINS! NOW!
WE ARE A HUMANITARIAN-AID NON-GOVERNMENTAL ORGANIZATION, AND THIS IS A SPECIAL OPERATION TO ASSIST THE DISPLACED REFUGEES OF THE DEMOCRATIC REPUBLIC OF CONGO--
Like frost on the wings of a dead angel...
SLSK
...licked by the wolf's blood-stained tongue.
GHK!

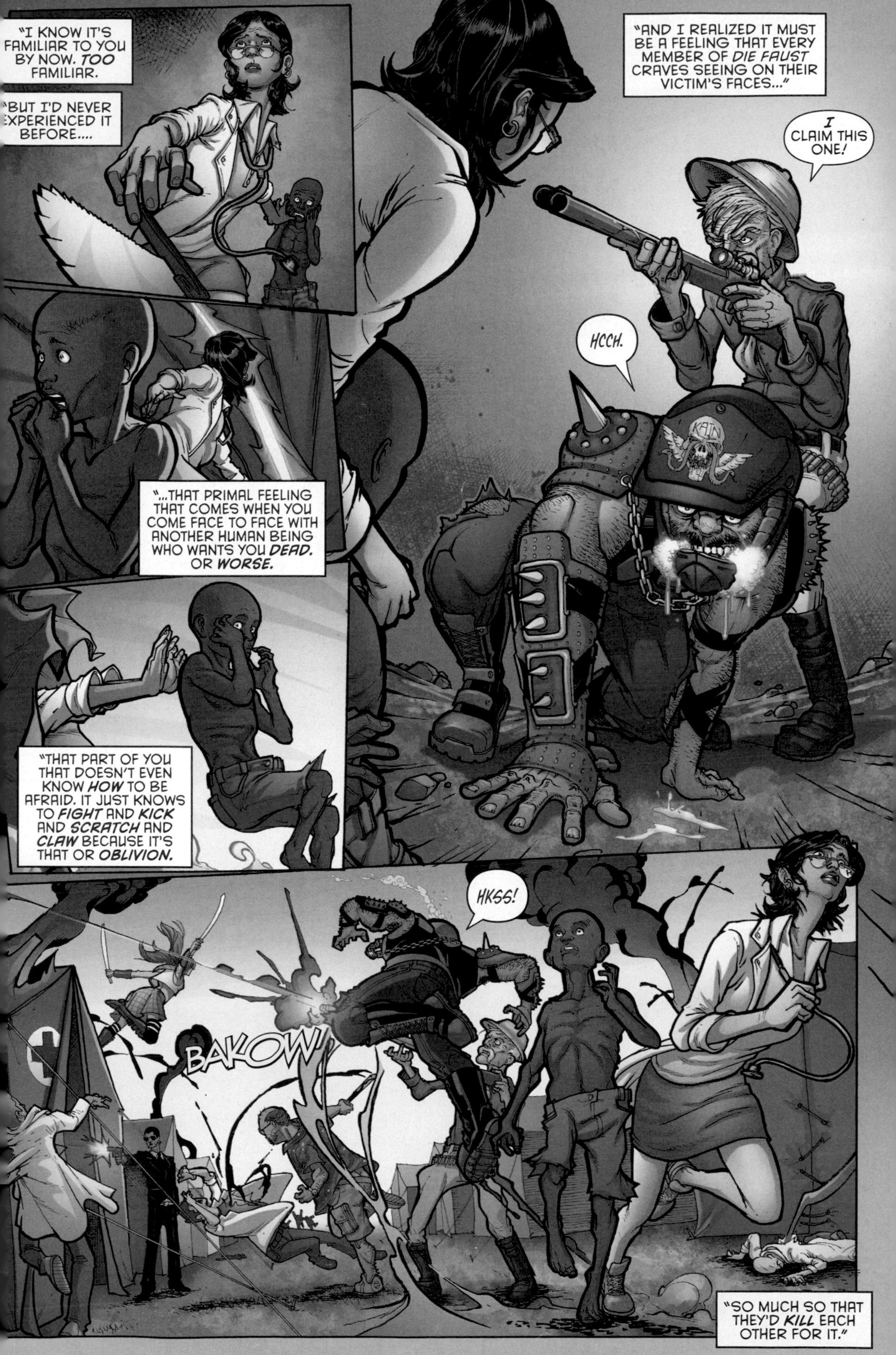
"I KNOW IT'S FAMILIAR TO YOU BY NOW. TOO FAMILIAR.
"BUT I'D NEVER EXPERIENCED IT BEFORE....
"...THAT PRIMAL FEELING THAT COMES WHEN YOU COME FACE TO FACE WITH ANOTHER HUMAN BEING WHO WANTS YOU DEAD. OR WORSE.
"THAT PART OF YOU THAT DOESN'T EVEN KNOW HOW TO BE AFRAID. IT JUST KNOWS TO FIGHT AND KICK AND SCRATCH AND CLAW BECAUSE IT'S THAT OR OBLIVION.
"AND I REALIZED IT MUST BE A FEELING THAT EVERY MEMBER OF DIE FAUST CRAVES SEEING ON THEIR VICTIM'S FACES..."
I CLAIM THIS ONE!
HCCH.
HKSS!
BAKOW!
"SO MUCH SO THAT THEY'D KILL EACH OTHER FOR IT."

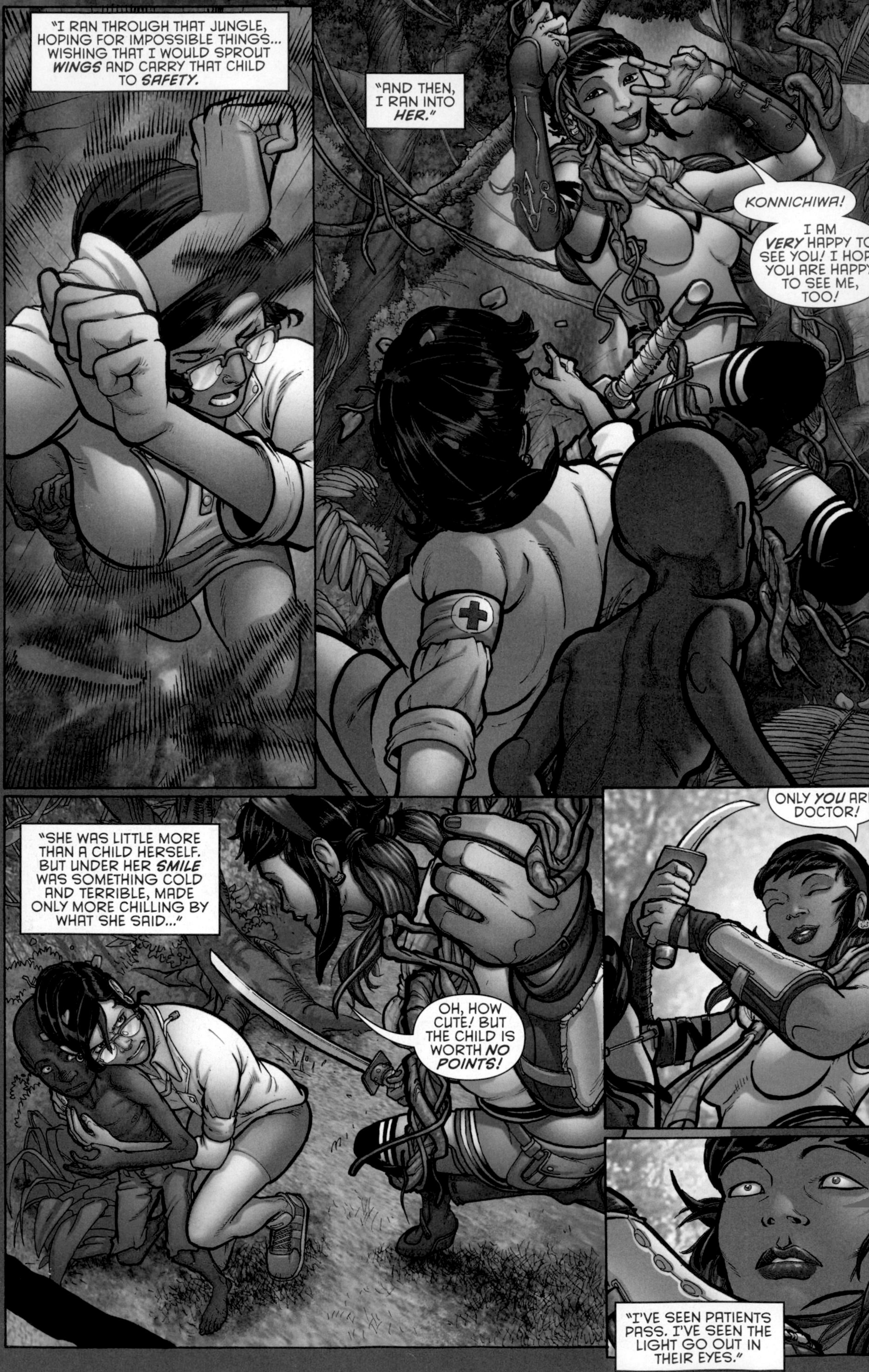
"I RAN THROUGH THAT JUNGLE, HOPING FOR IMPOSSIBLE THINGS... WISHING THAT I WOULD SPROUT WINGS AND CARRY THAT CHILD TO SAFETY.
"AND THEN, I RAN INTO HER."
KONNICHIWA!
I AM VERY HAPPY TO SEE YOU! I HOPE YOU ARE HAPPY TO SEE ME, TOO!
"SHE WAS LITTLE MORE THAN A CHILD HERSELF. BUT UNDER HER SMILE WAS SOMETHING COLD AND TERRIBLE, MADE ONLY MORE CHILLING BY WHAT SHE SAID..."
OH, HOW CUTE! BUT THE CHILD IS WORTH NO POINTS!
ONLY YOU ARE, DOCTOR!
"I'VE SEEN PATIENTS PASS. I'VE SEEN THE LIGHT GO OUT IN THEIR EYES."

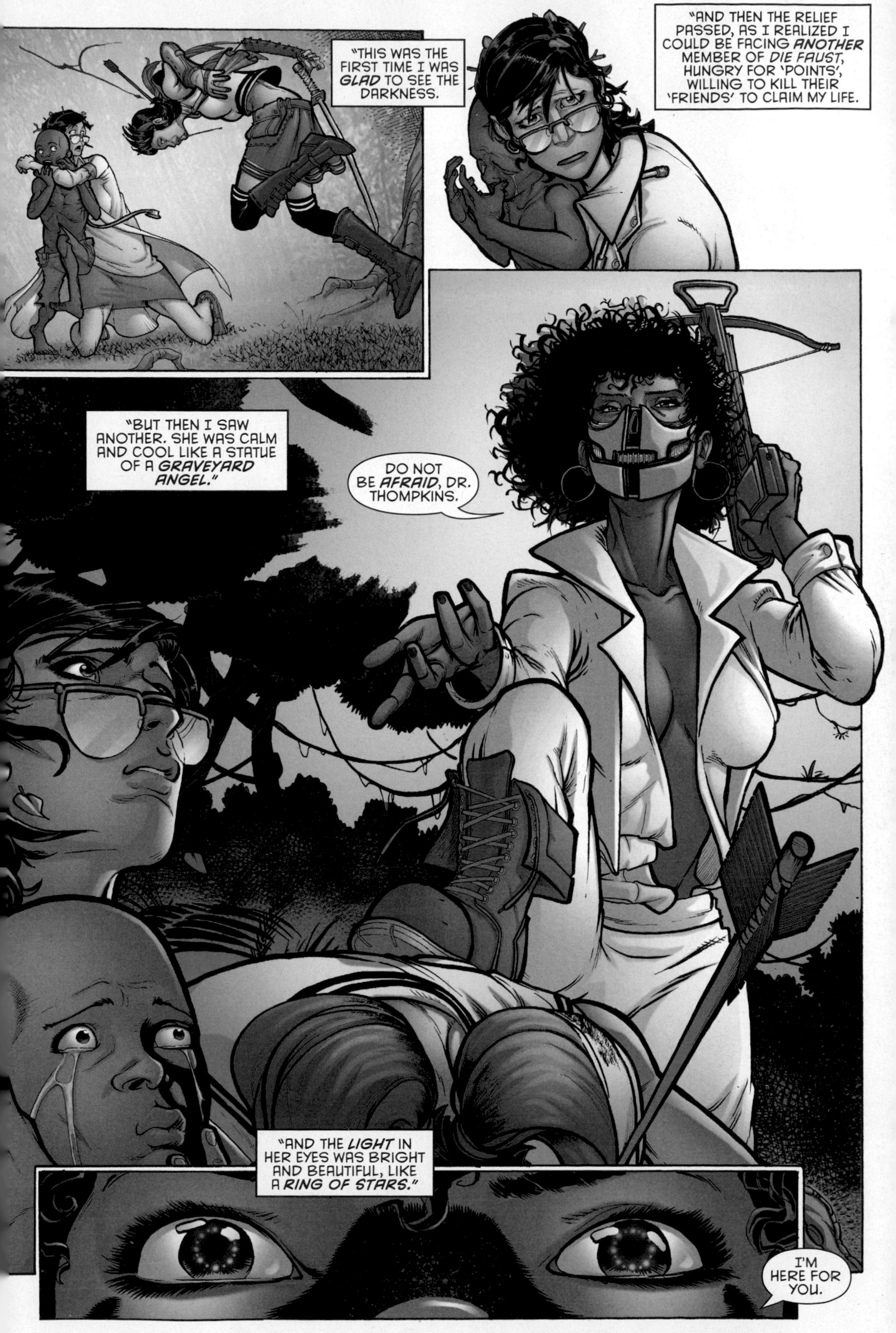
"THIS WAS THE FIRST TIME I WAS GLAD TO SEE THE DARKNESS.
"AND THEN THE RELIEF PASSED, AS I REALIZED I COULD BE FACING ANOTHER MEMBER OF DIE FAUST, HUNGRY FOR 'POINTS', WILLING TO KILL THEIR 'FRIENDS' TO CLAIM MY LIFE.
"BUT THEN I SAW ANOTHER. SHE WAS CALM AND COOL LIKE A STATUE OF A GRAVEYARD ANGEL."
DO NOT BE AFRAID, DR. THOMPKINS.
"AND THE LIGHT IN HER EYES WAS BRIGHT AND BEAUTIFUL, LIKE A RING OF STARS."
I'M HERE FOR YOU.

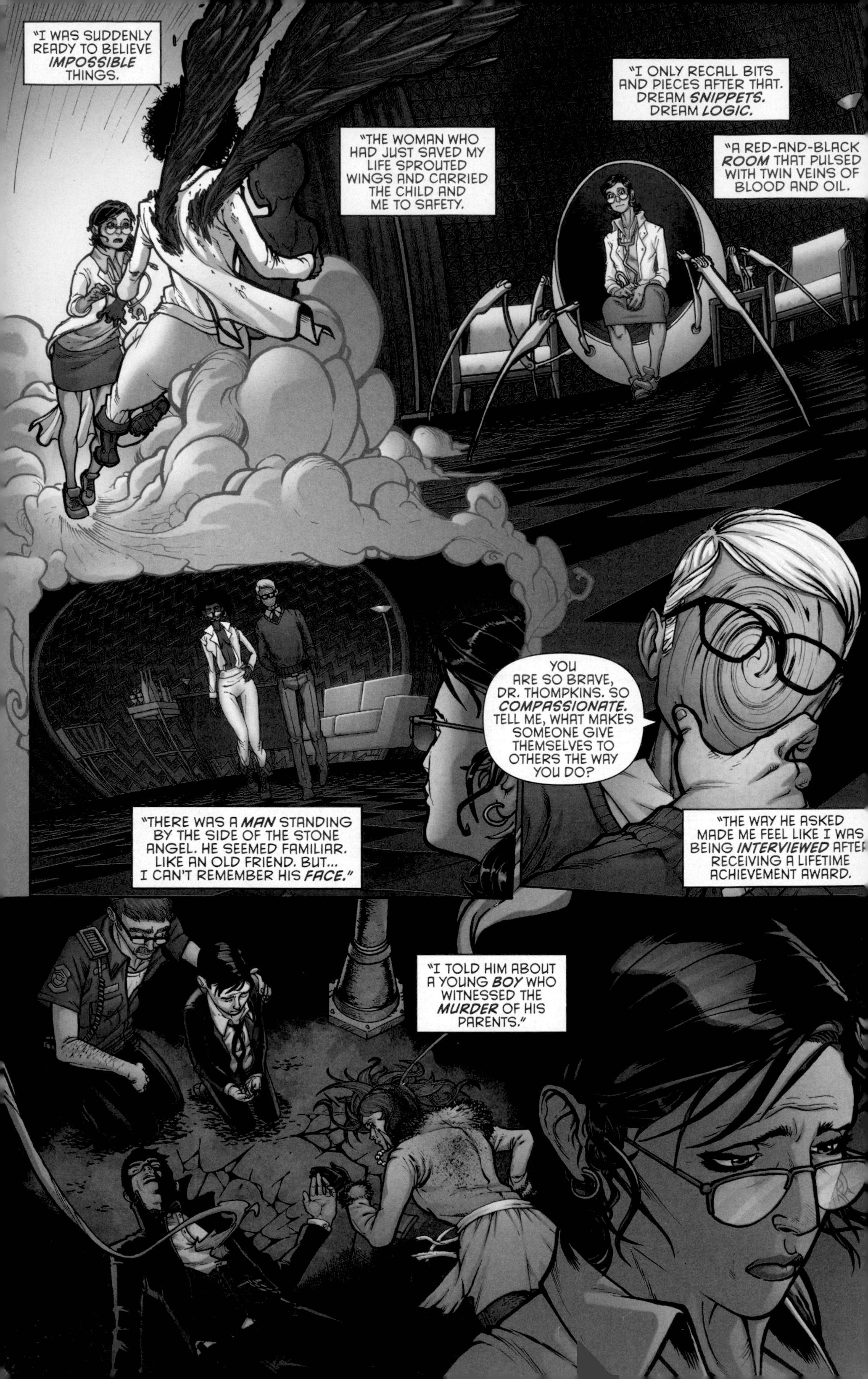
"I WAS SUDDENLY READY TO BELIEVE IMPOSSIBLE THINGS.
"THE WOMAN WHO HAD JUST SAVED MY LIFE SPROUTED WINGS AND CARRIED THE CHILD AND ME TO SAFETY.
"I ONLY RECALL BITS AND PIECES AFTER THAT. DREAM SNIPPETS. DREAM LOGIC.
"A RED-AND-BLACK ROOM THAT PULSED WITH TWIN VEINS OF BLOOD AND OIL.
"THERE WAS A MAN STANDING BY THE SIDE OF THE STONE ANGEL. HE SEEMED FAMILIAR. LIKE AN OLD FRIEND. BUT... I CAN'T REMEMBER HIS FACE."
YOU ARE SO BRAVE, DR. THOMPKINS. SO COMPASSIONATE. TELL ME, WHAT MAKES SOMEONE GIVE THEMSELVES TO OTHERS THE WAY YOU DO?
"THE WAY HE ASKED MADE ME FEEL LIKE I WAS BEING INTERVIEWED AFTER RECEIVING A LIFETIME ACHIEVEMENT AWARD.
"I TOLD HIM ABOUT A YOUNG BOY WHO WITNESSED THE MURDER OF HIS PARENTS."

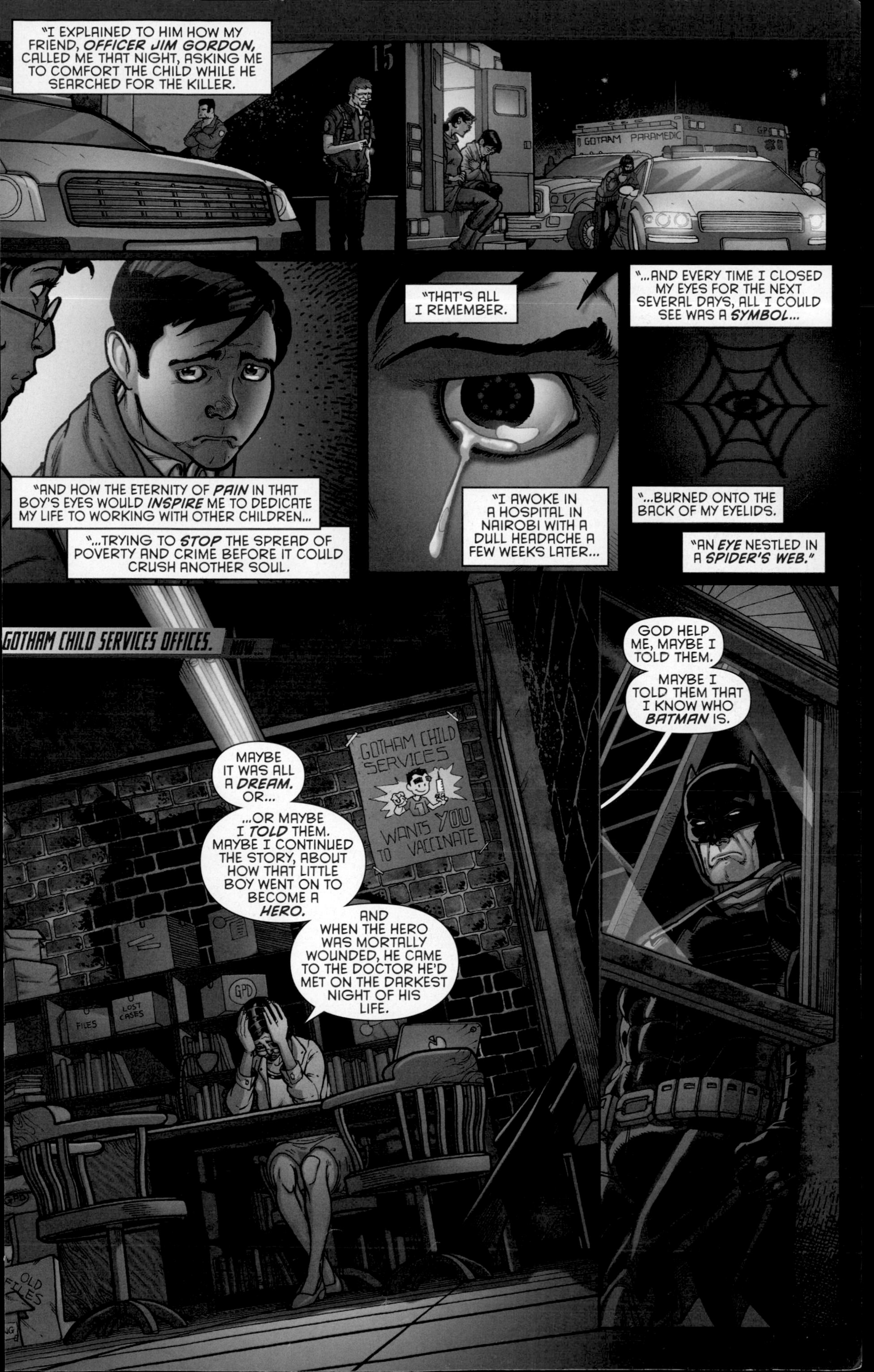

"I EXPLAINED TO HIM HOW MY FRIEND, OFFICER JIM GORDON, CALLED ME THAT NIGHT, ASKING ME TO COMFORT THE CHILD WHILE HE SEARCHED FOR THE KILLER.
15
GOTHAM PARAMEDIC
"AND HOW THE ETERNITY OF PAIN IN THAT BOY'S EYES WOULD INSPIRE ME TO DEDICATE MY LIFE TO WORKING WITH OTHER CHILDREN...
"...TRYING TO STOP THE SPREAD OF POVERTY AND CRIME BEFORE IT COULD CRUSH ANOTHER SOUL.
"THAT'S ALL I REMEMBER.
"I AWOKE IN A HOSPITAL IN NAIROBI WITH A DULL HEADACHE A FEW WEEKS LATER...
"...AND EVERY TIME I CLOSED MY EYES FOR THE NEXT SEVERAL DAYS, ALL I COULD SEE WAS A SYMBOL...
"...BURNED ONTO THE BACK OF MY EYELIDS.
"AN EYE NESTLED IN A SPIDER'S WEB."
GOTHAM CHILD SERVICES OFFICES. NOW
GOTHAM CHILD SERVICES WANTS YOU TO VACCINATE
MAYBE IT WAS ALL A DREAM. OR...
...OR MAYBE I TOLD THEM. MAYBE I CONTINUED THE STORY, ABOUT HOW THAT LITTLE BOY WENT ON TO BECOME A HERO.
AND WHEN THE HERO WAS MORTALLY WOUNDED, HE CAME TO THE DOCTOR HE'D MET ON THE DARKEST NIGHT OF HIS LIFE.
GPD
FILES
LOST CASES
OLD FILES
GOD HELP ME, MAYBE I TOLD THEM.
MAYBE I TOLD THEM THAT I KNOW WHO BATMAN IS.

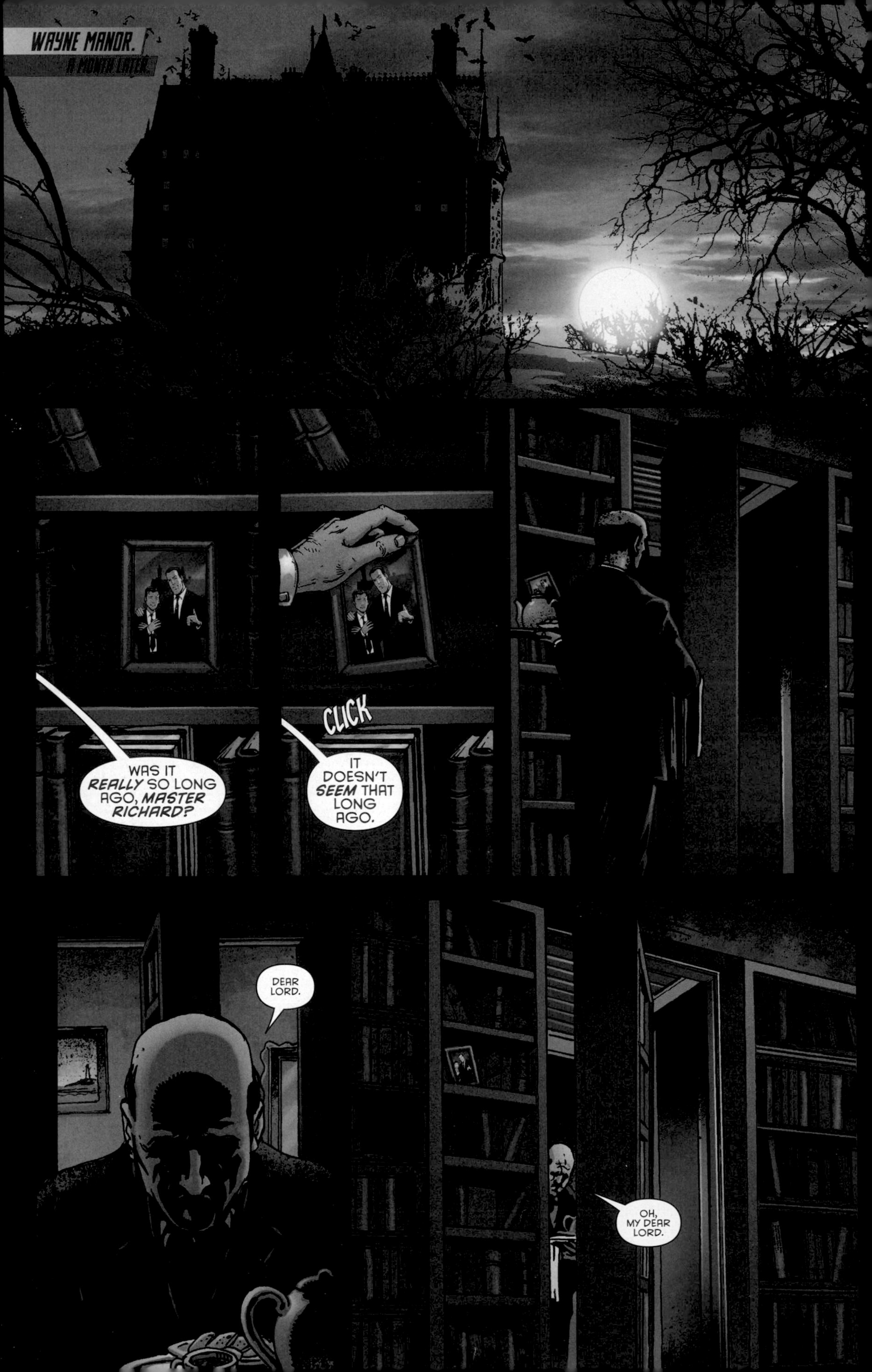
WAYNE MANOR.
A MONTH LATER.
WAS IT REALLY SO LONG AGO, MASTER RICHARD?
CLICK
IT DOESN'T SEEM THAT LONG AGO.
DEAR LORD.
OH, MY DEAR LORD.

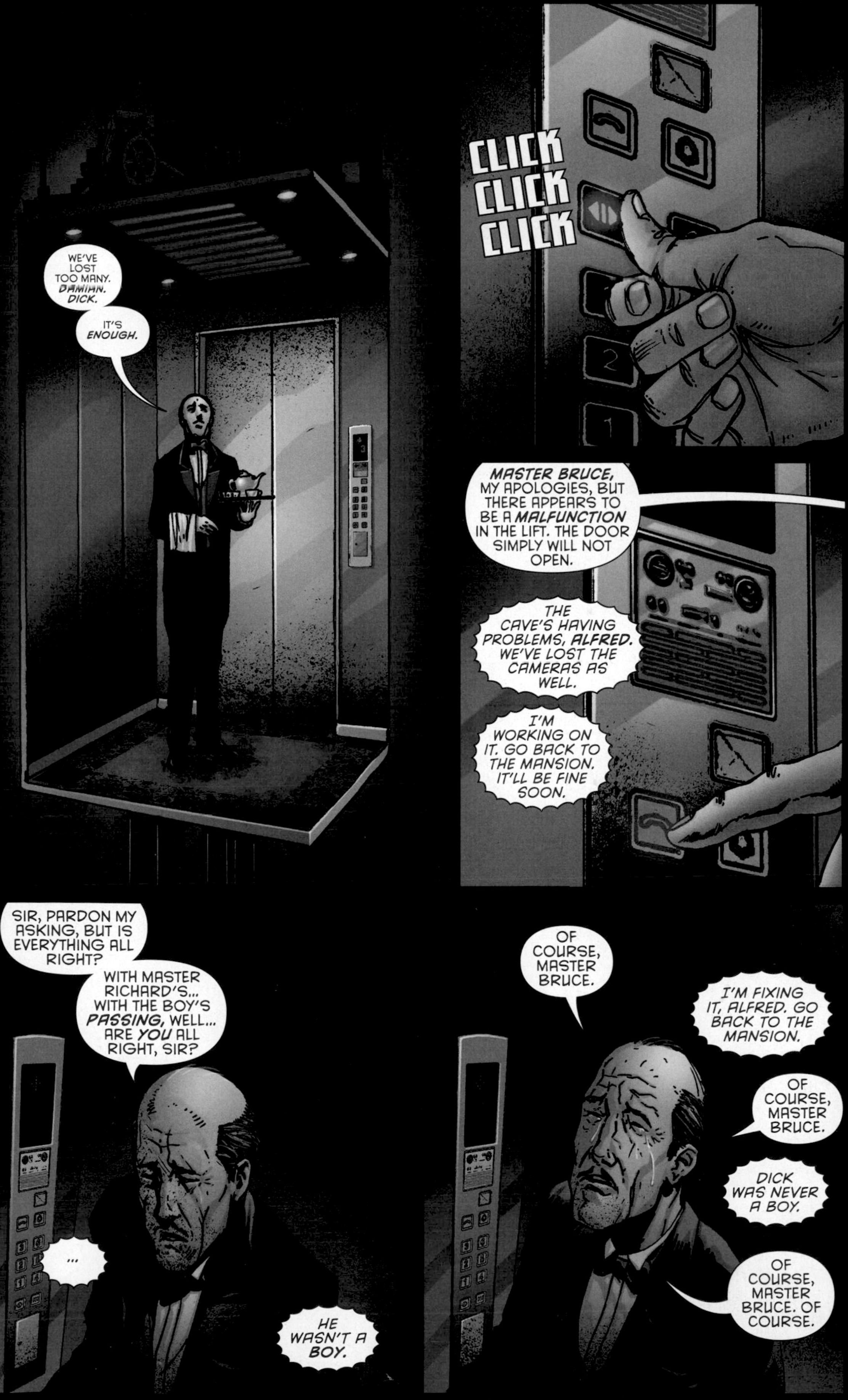
WE'VE LOST TOO MANY. DAMIAN. DICK.
IT'S ENOUGH.
CLICK CLICK CLICK
MASTER BRUCE, MY APOLOGIES, BUT THERE APPEARS TO BE A MALFUNCTION IN THE LIFT. THE DOOR SIMPLY WILL NOT OPEN.
THE CAVE'S HAVING PROBLEMS, ALFRED. WE'VE LOST THE CAMERAS AS WELL.
I'M WORKING ON IT. GO BACK TO THE MANSION. IT'LL BE FINE SOON.
SIR, PARDON MY ASKING, BUT IS EVERYTHING ALL RIGHT?
WITH MASTER RICHARD'S... WITH THE BOY'S PASSING, WELL... ARE YOU ALL RIGHT, SIR?
...
HE WASN'T A BOY.
OF COURSE, MASTER BRUCE.
I'M FIXING IT, ALFRED. GO BACK TO THE MANSION.
OF COURSE, MASTER BRUCE.
DICK WAS NEVER A BOY.
OF COURSE, MASTER BRUCE. OF COURSE.

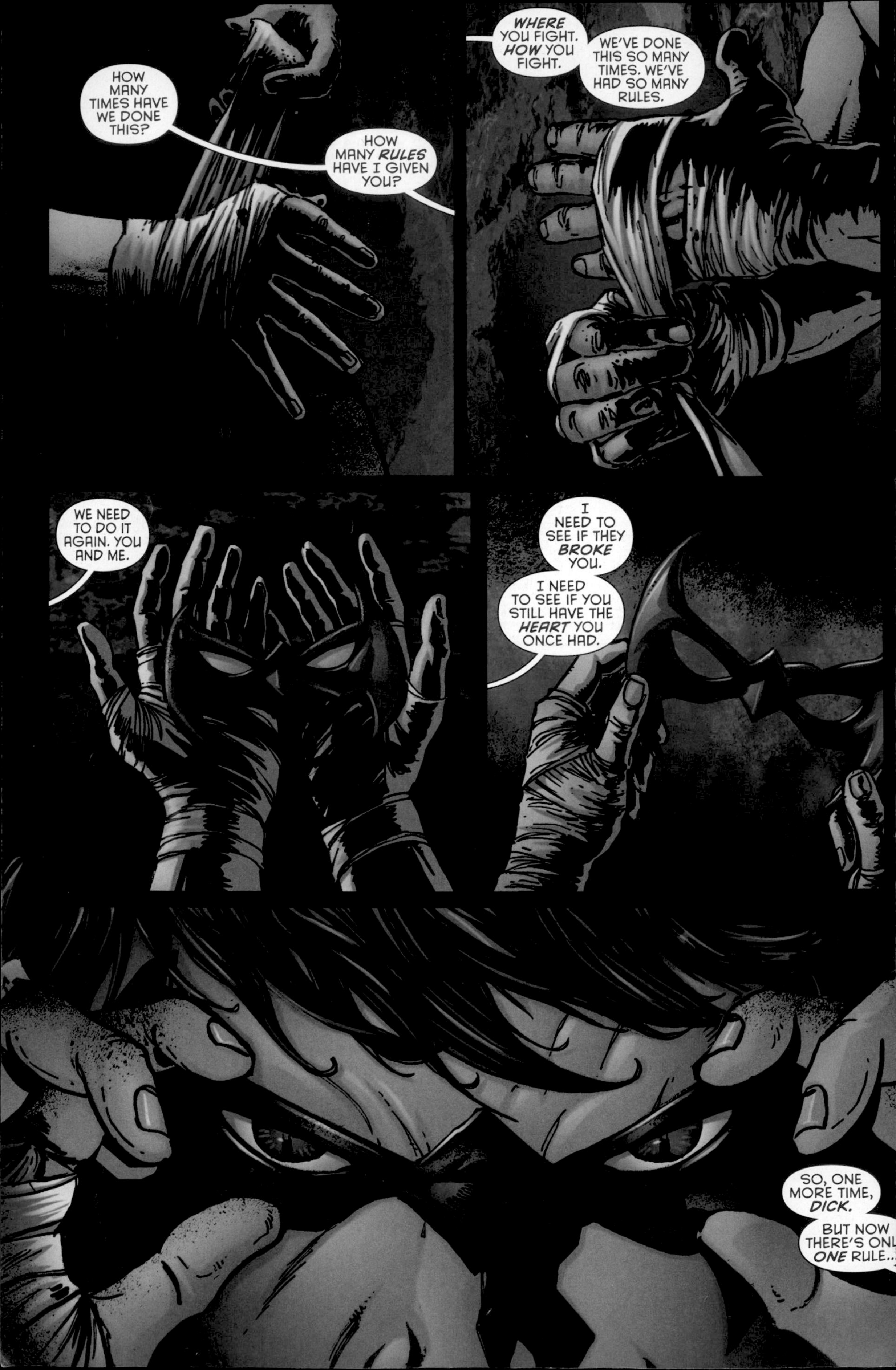
HOW MANY TIMES HAVE WE DONE THIS?
HOW MANY RULES HAVE I GIVEN YOU?
WHERE YOU FIGHT. HOW YOU FIGHT.
WE'VE DONE THIS SO MANY TIMES. WE'VE HAD SO MANY RULES.
WE NEED TO DO IT AGAIN. YOU AND ME.
I NEED TO SEE IF THEY BROKE YOU.
I NEED TO SEE IF YOU STILL HAVE THE HEART YOU ONCE HAD.
SO, ONE MORE TIME, DICK.
BUT NOW THERE'S ONL ONE RULE...

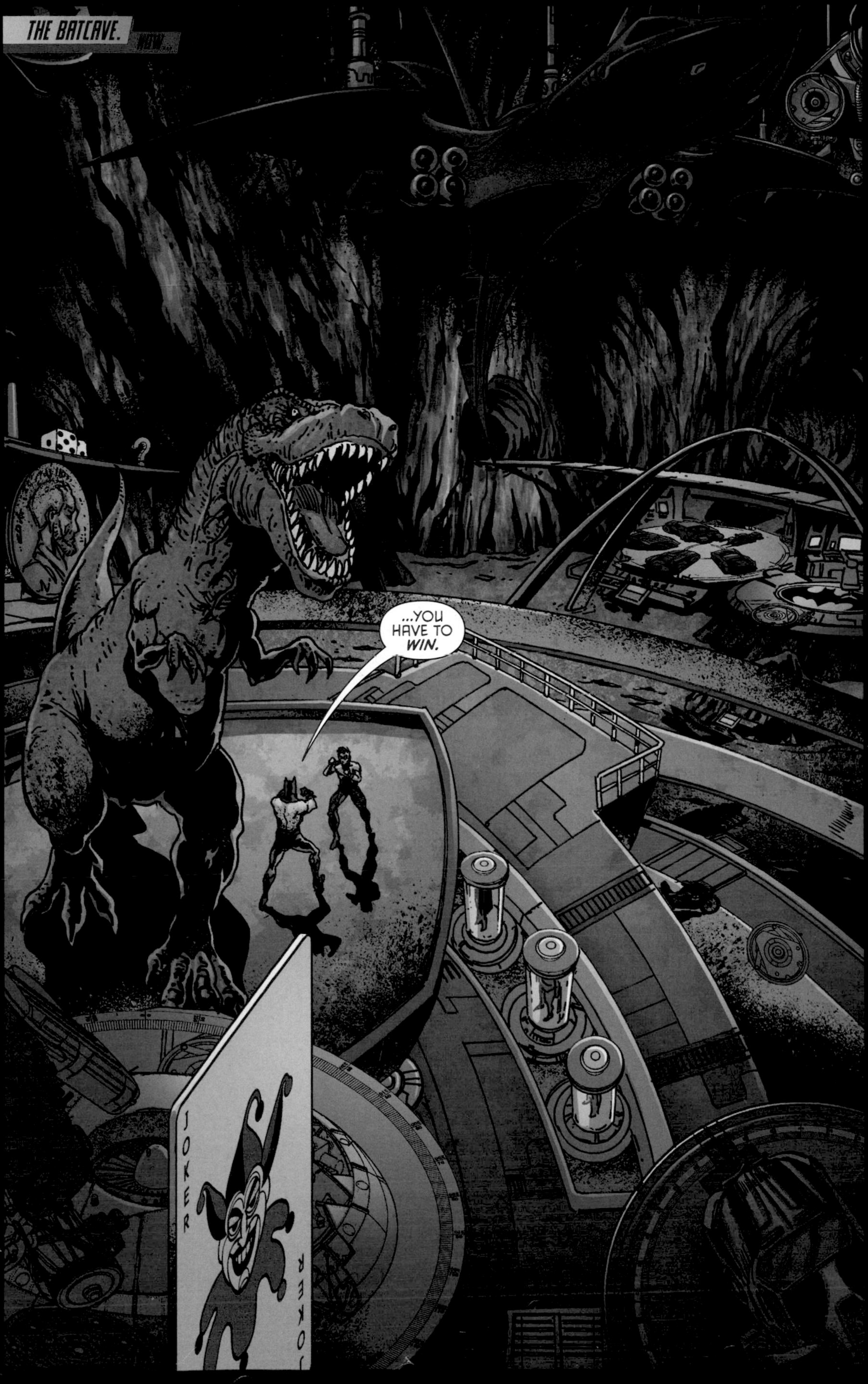
THE BATCAVE.
NOW...
...YOU HAVE TO WIN.
JOKER
JOKER

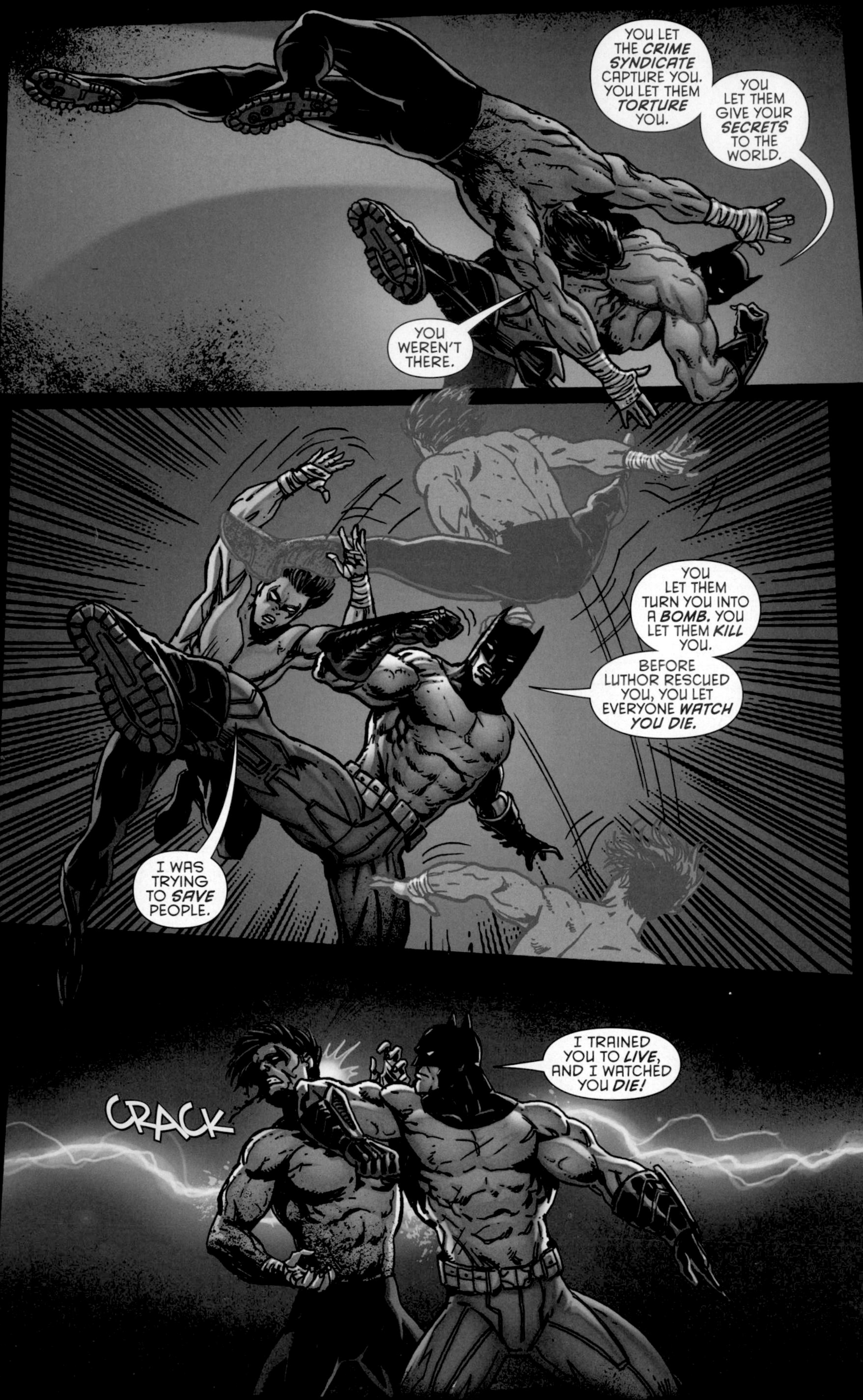
YOU LET THE CRIME SYNDICATE CAPTURE YOU. YOU LET THEM TORTURE YOU.
YOU LET THEM GIVE YOUR SECRETS TO THE WORLD.
YOU WEREN'T THERE.
YOU LET THEM TURN YOU INTO A BOMB. YOU LET THEM KILL YOU.
BEFORE LUTHOR RESCUED YOU, YOU LET EVERYONE WATCH YOU DIE.
I WAS TRYING TO SAVE PEOPLE.
I TRAINED YOU TO LIVE, AND I WATCHED YOU DIE!
CRACK

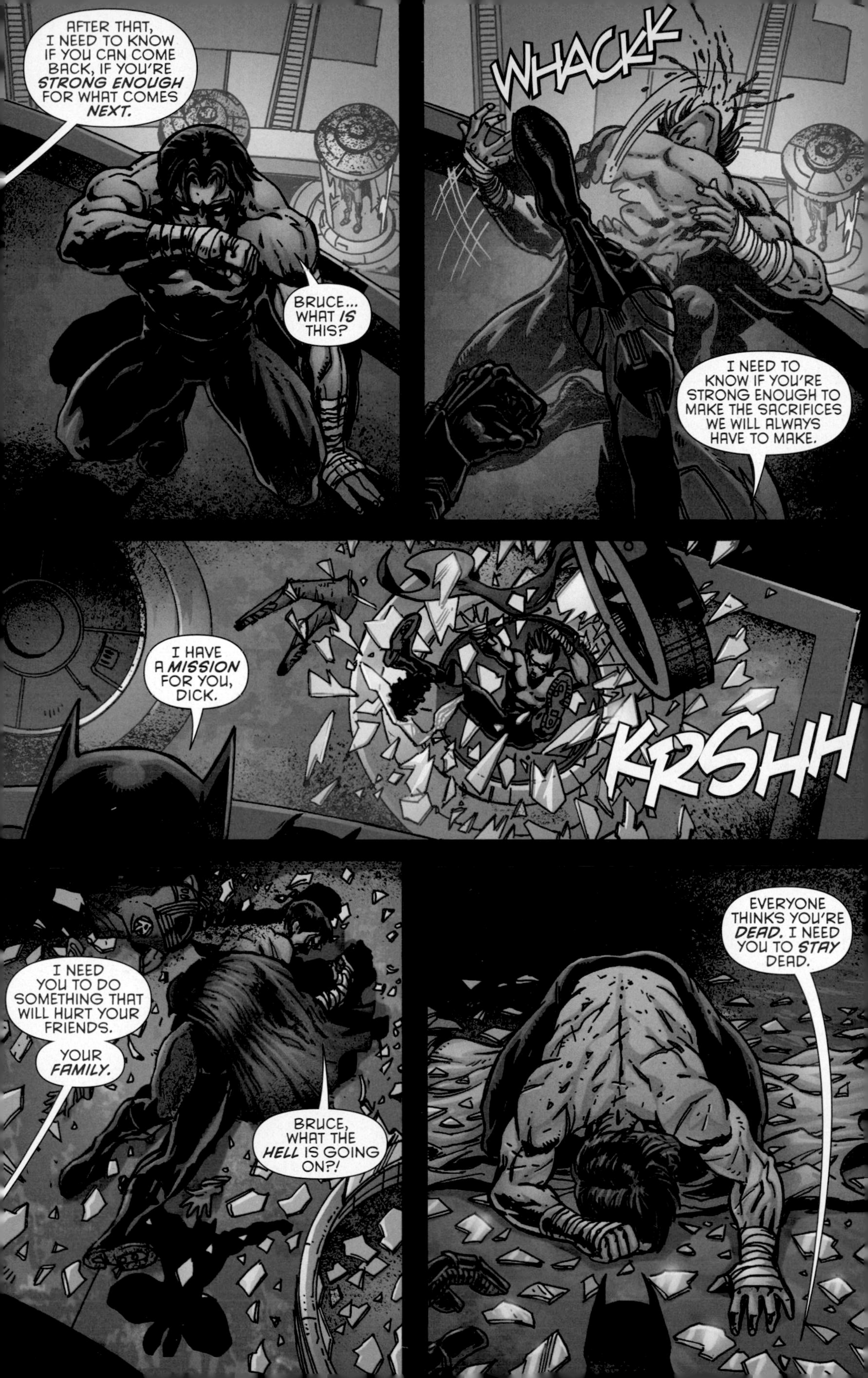
AFTER THAT, I NEED TO KNOW IF YOU CAN COME BACK, IF YOU'RE STRONG ENOUGH FOR WHAT COMES NEXT.
BRUCE... WHAT IS THIS?
WHACKK
I NEED TO KNOW IF YOU'RE STRONG ENOUGH TO MAKE THE SACRIFICES WE WILL ALWAYS HAVE TO MAKE.
I HAVE A MISSION FOR YOU, DICK.
KRSHH
I NEED YOU TO DO SOMETHING THAT WILL HURT YOUR FRIENDS.
YOUR FAMILY.
BRUCE, WHAT THE HELL IS GOING ON?!
EVERYONE THINKS YOU'RE DEAD. I NEED YOU TO STAY DEAD.

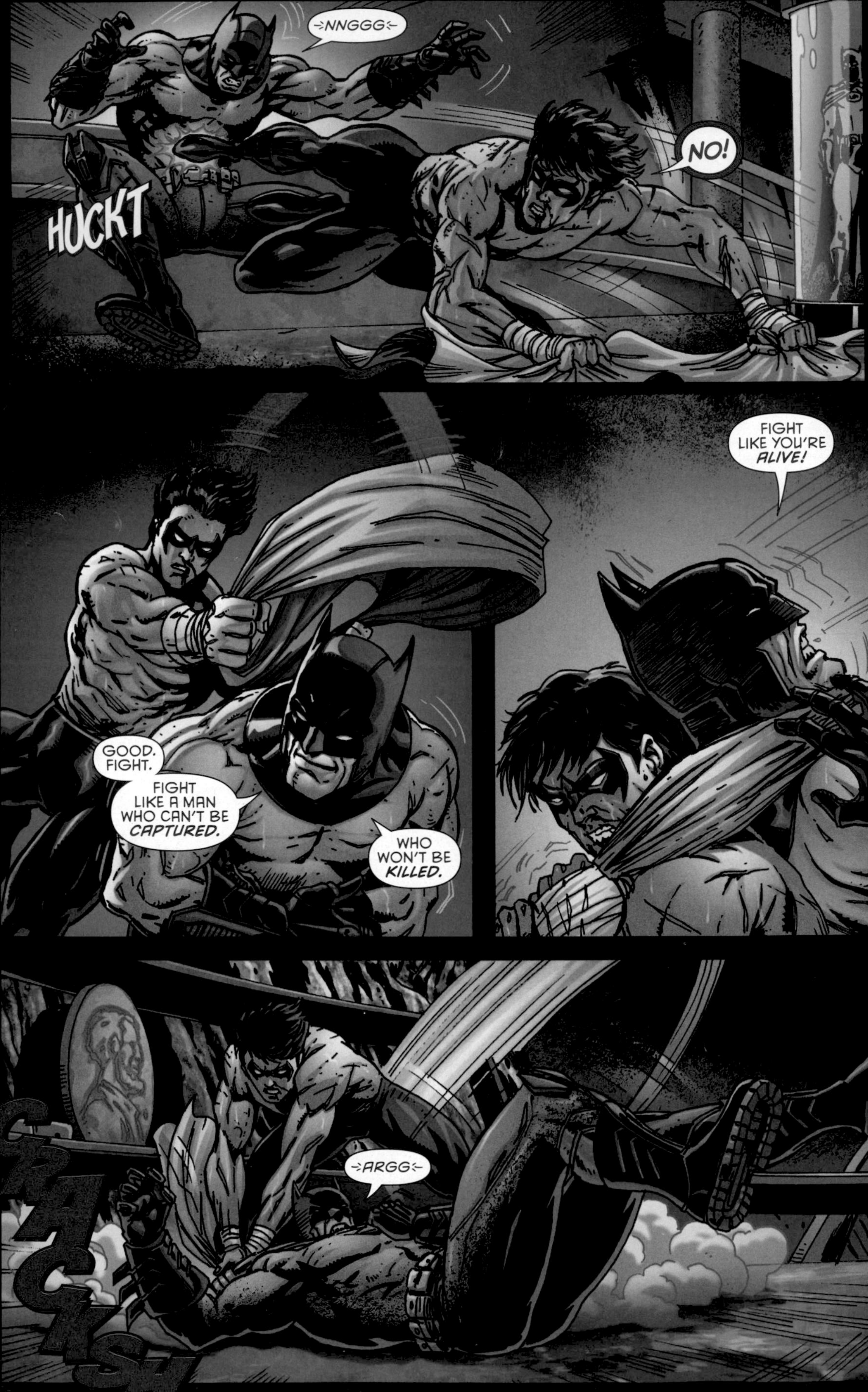
NNGGG
NO!
HUCKT
FIGHT LIKE YOU'RE ALIVE!
GOOD. FIGHT.
FIGHT LIKE A MAN WHO CAN'T BE CAPTURED.
WHO WON'T BE KILLED.
ARGG
CRACHSH

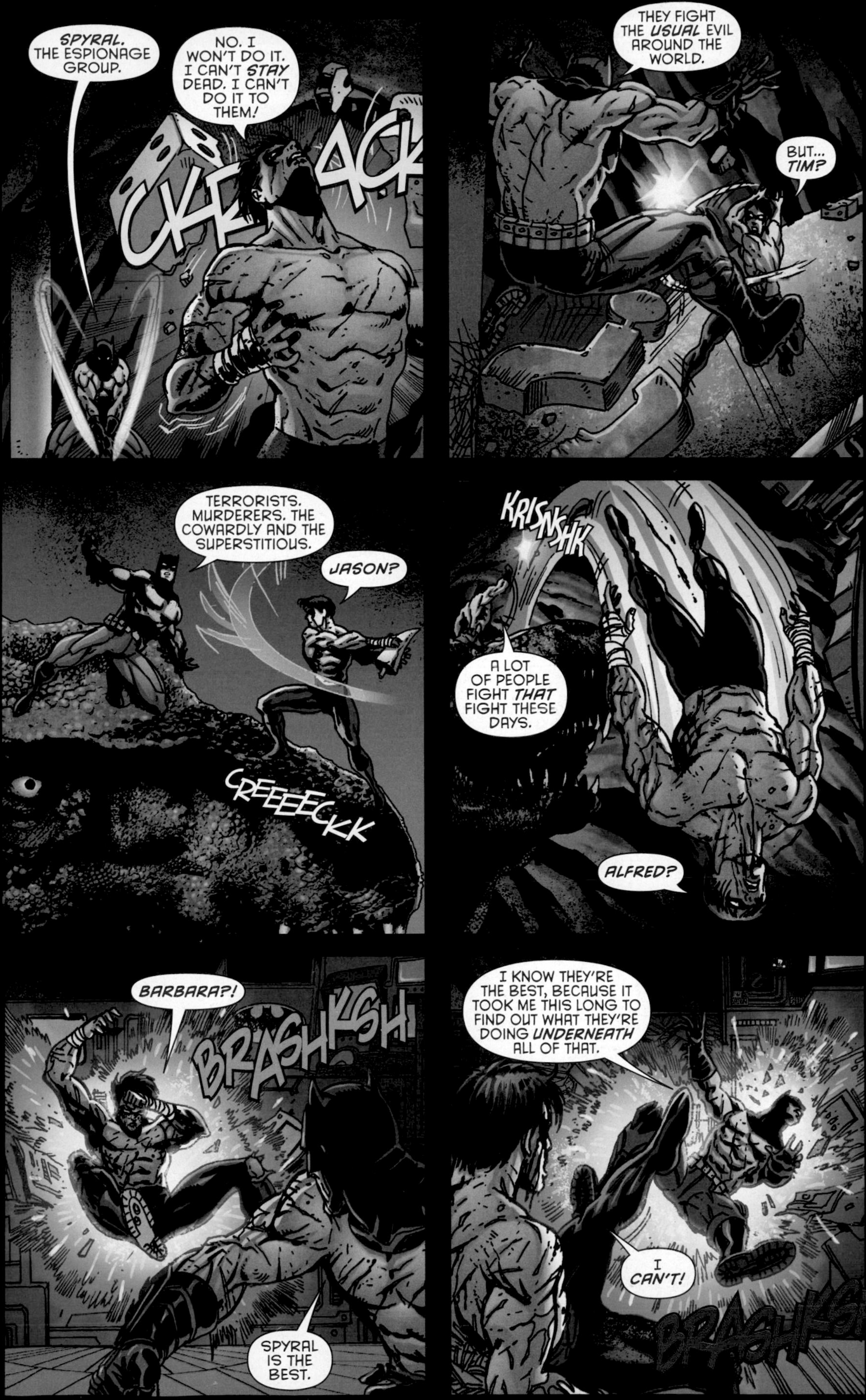
SPYRAL. THE ESPIONAGE GROUP.
NO. I WON'T DO IT. I CAN'T STAY DEAD. I CAN'T DO IT TO THEM!
CKRRACK
THEY FIGHT THE USUAL EVIL AROUND THE WORLD.
BUT... TIM?
TERRORISTS. MURDERERS. THE COWARDLY AND THE SUPERSTITIOUS.
JASON?
CREEEECKK
KRISNSHK
A LOT OF PEOPLE FIGHT THAT FIGHT THESE DAYS.
ALFRED?
BARBARA?!
BRASHKSH
SPYRAL IS THE BEST.
I KNOW THEY'RE THE BEST, BECAUSE IT TOOK ME THIS LONG TO FIND OUT WHAT THEY'RE DOING UNDERNEATH ALL OF THAT.
I CAN'T!
BRASHKSH

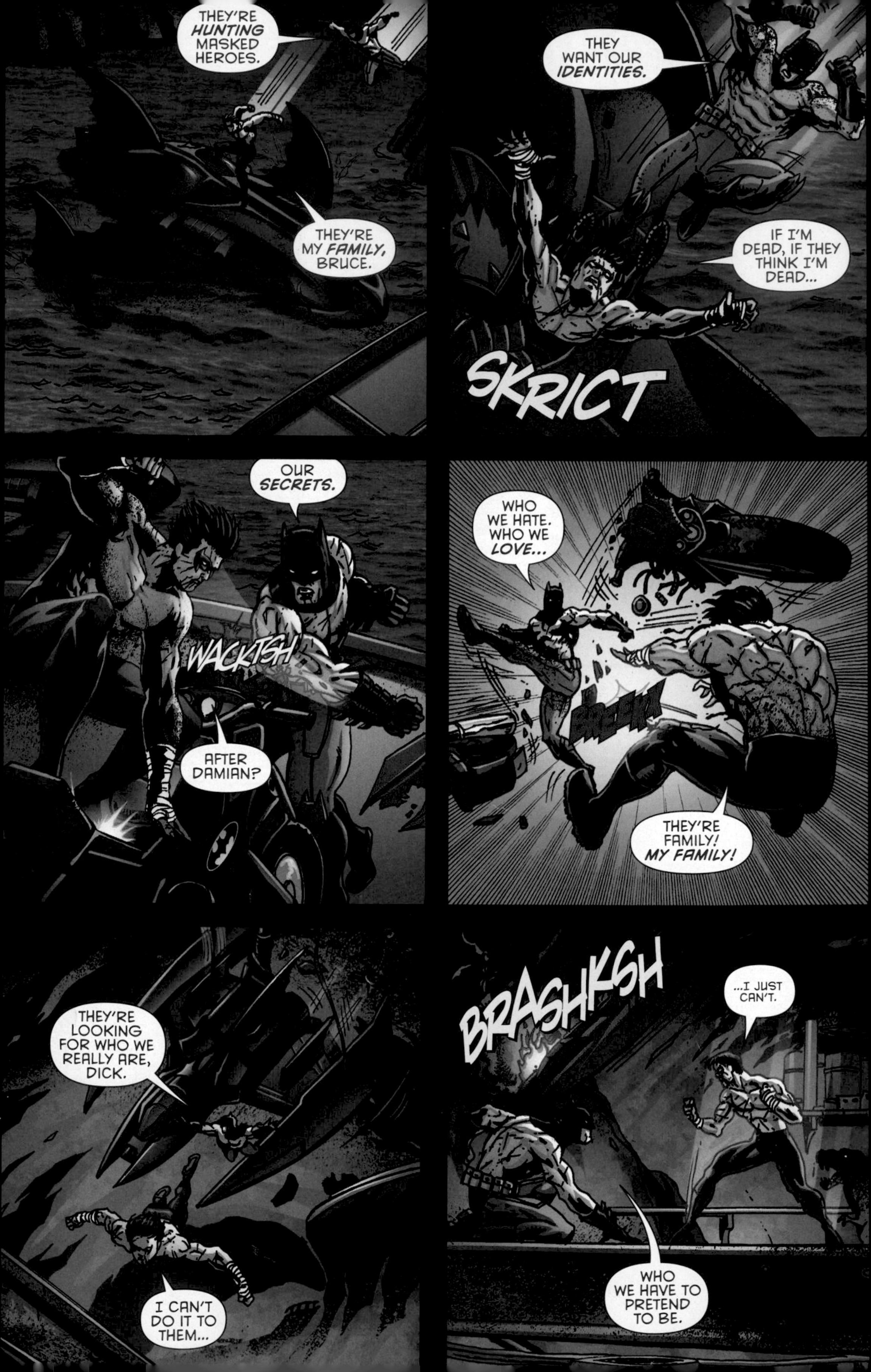
THEY'RE HUNTING MASKED HEROES.
THEY'RE MY FAMILY, BRUCE.
THEY WANT OUR IDENTITIES.
IF I'M DEAD, IF THEY THINK I'M DEAD...
SKRICT
OUR SECRETS.
WACKTSH
AFTER DAMIAN?
WHO WE HATE. WHO WE LOVE...
THEY'RE FAMILY! MY FAMILY!
THEY'RE LOOKING FOR WHO WE REALLY ARE, DICK.
I CAN'T DO IT TO THEM...
BRASHKSH
...I JUST CAN'T.
WHO WE HAVE TO PRETEND TO BE.

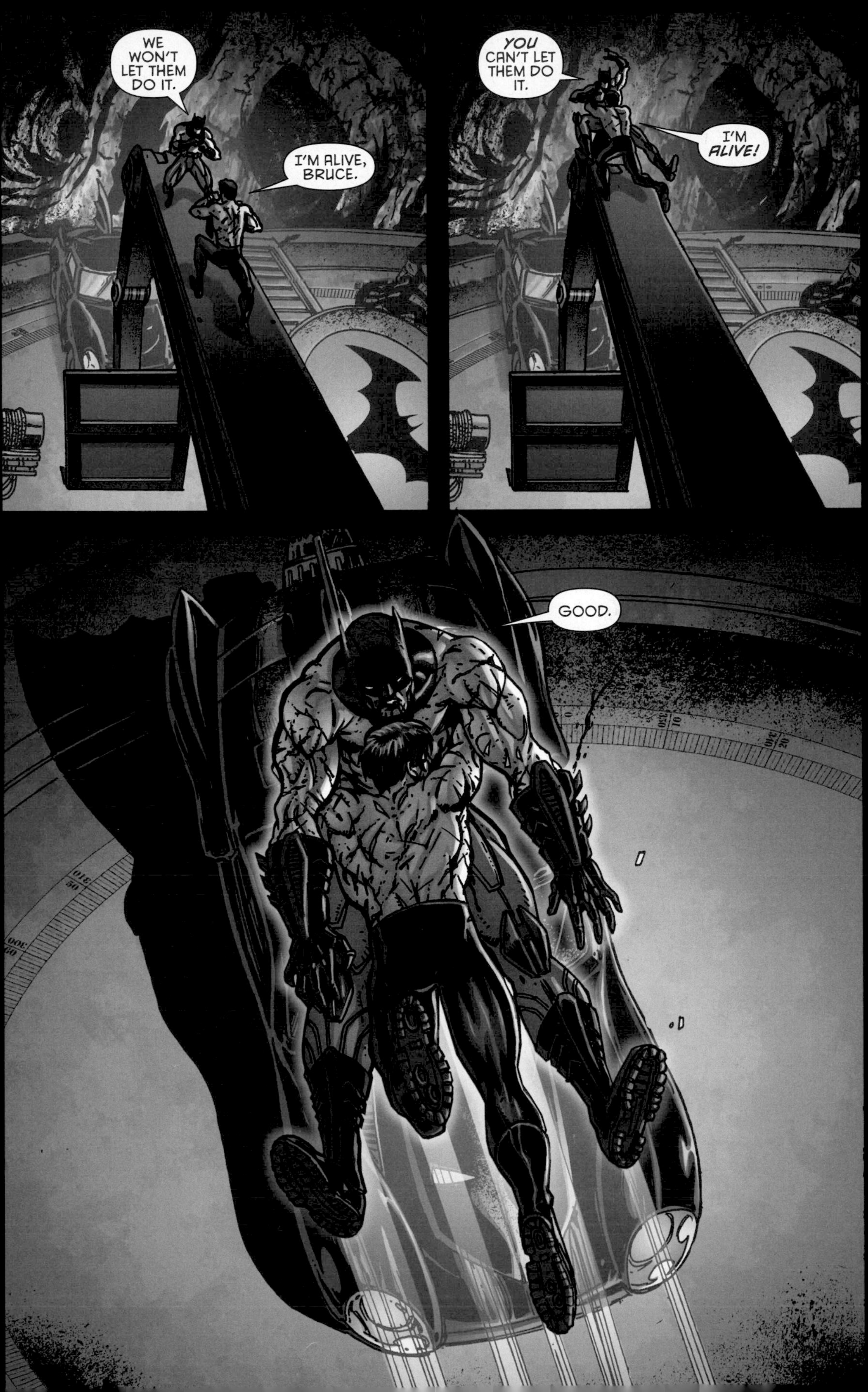
WE WON'T LET THEM DO IT.
I'M ALIVE, BRUCE.
YOU CAN'T LET THEM DO IT.
I'M ALIVE!
GOOD.

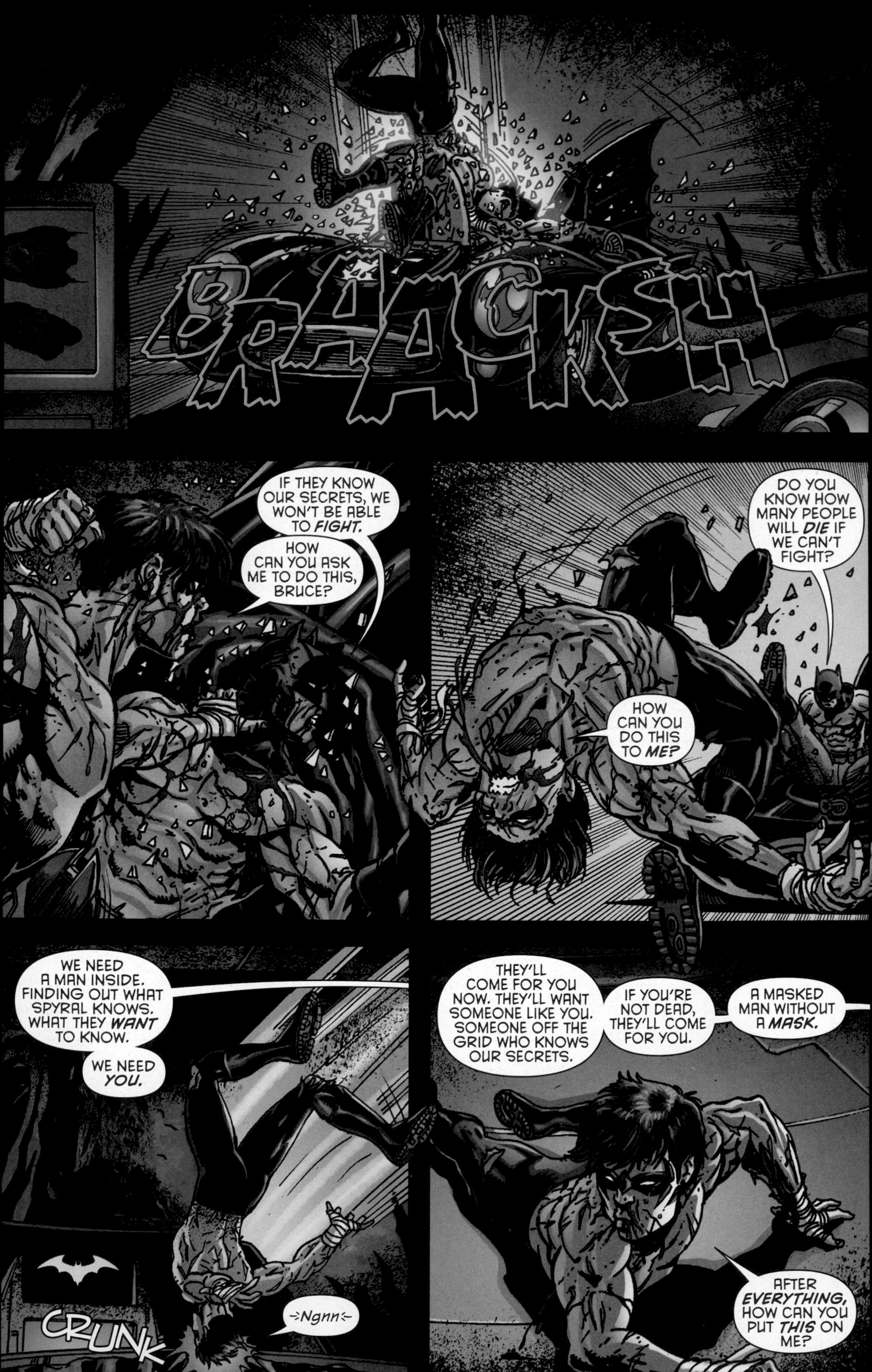
BRAACKSH
IF THEY KNOW OUR SECRETS, WE WON'T BE ABLE TO *FIGHT.*
HOW CAN YOU ASK ME TO DO THIS, BRUCE?
DO YOU KNOW HOW MANY PEOPLE WILL *DIE* IF WE CAN'T FIGHT?
HOW CAN YOU DO THIS TO *ME?*
WE NEED A MAN INSIDE. FINDING OUT WHAT SPYRAL KNOWS. WHAT THEY *WANT* TO KNOW.
WE NEED *YOU.*
CRUNK
Ngnn
THEY'LL COME FOR YOU NOW. THEY'LL WANT SOMEONE LIKE YOU. SOMEONE OFF THE GRID WHO KNOWS OUR SECRETS.
IF YOU'RE NOT DEAD, THEY'LL COME FOR YOU.
A MASKED MAN WITHOUT A *MASK.*
AFTER *EVERYTHING,* HOW CAN YOU PUT *THIS* ON ME?

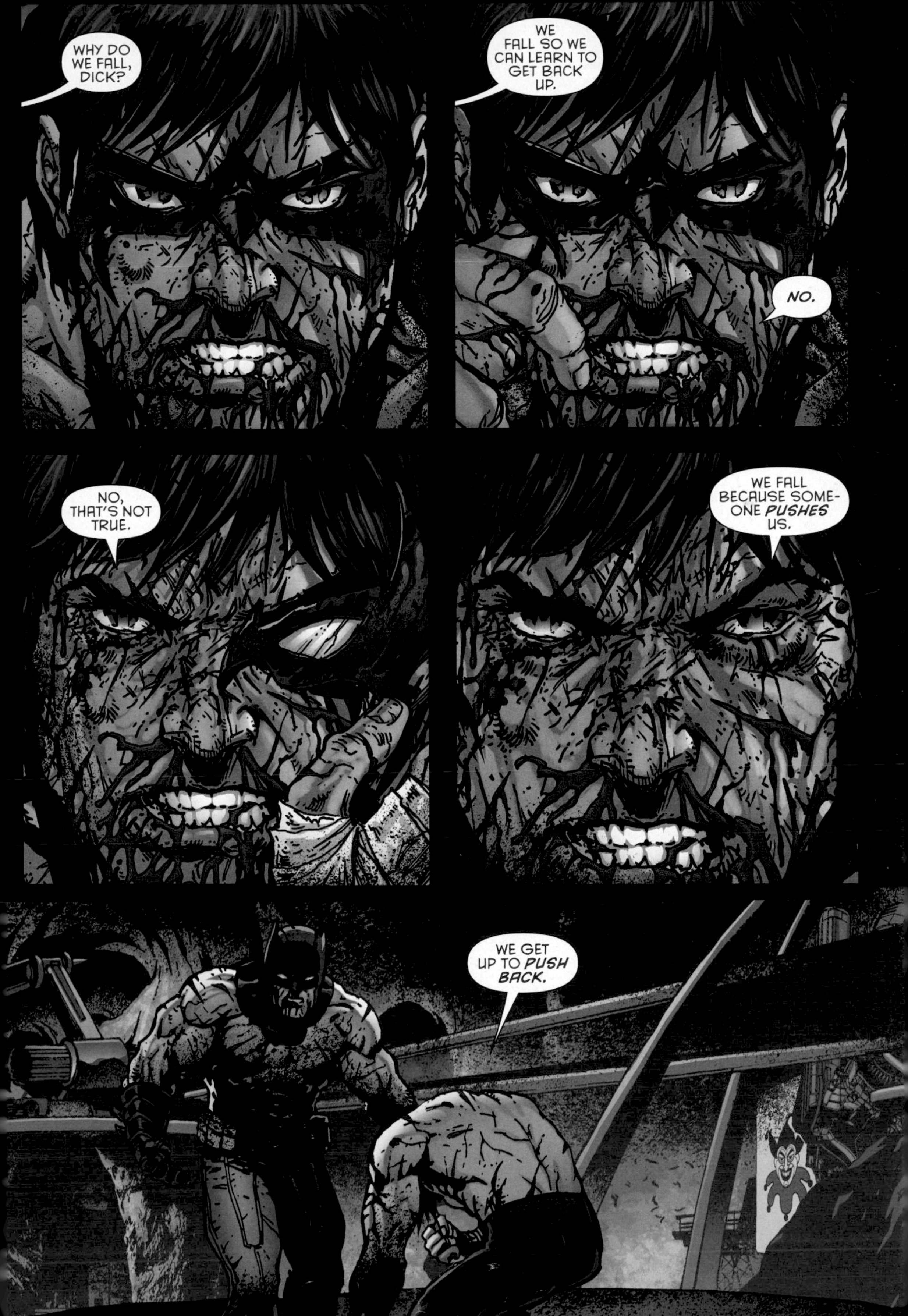
WHY DO WE FALL, DICK?
WE FALL SO WE CAN LEARN TO GET BACK UP.
NO.
NO, THAT'S NOT TRUE.
WE FALL BECAUSE SOME-ONE *PUSHES* US.
WE GET UP TO *PUSH BACK.*

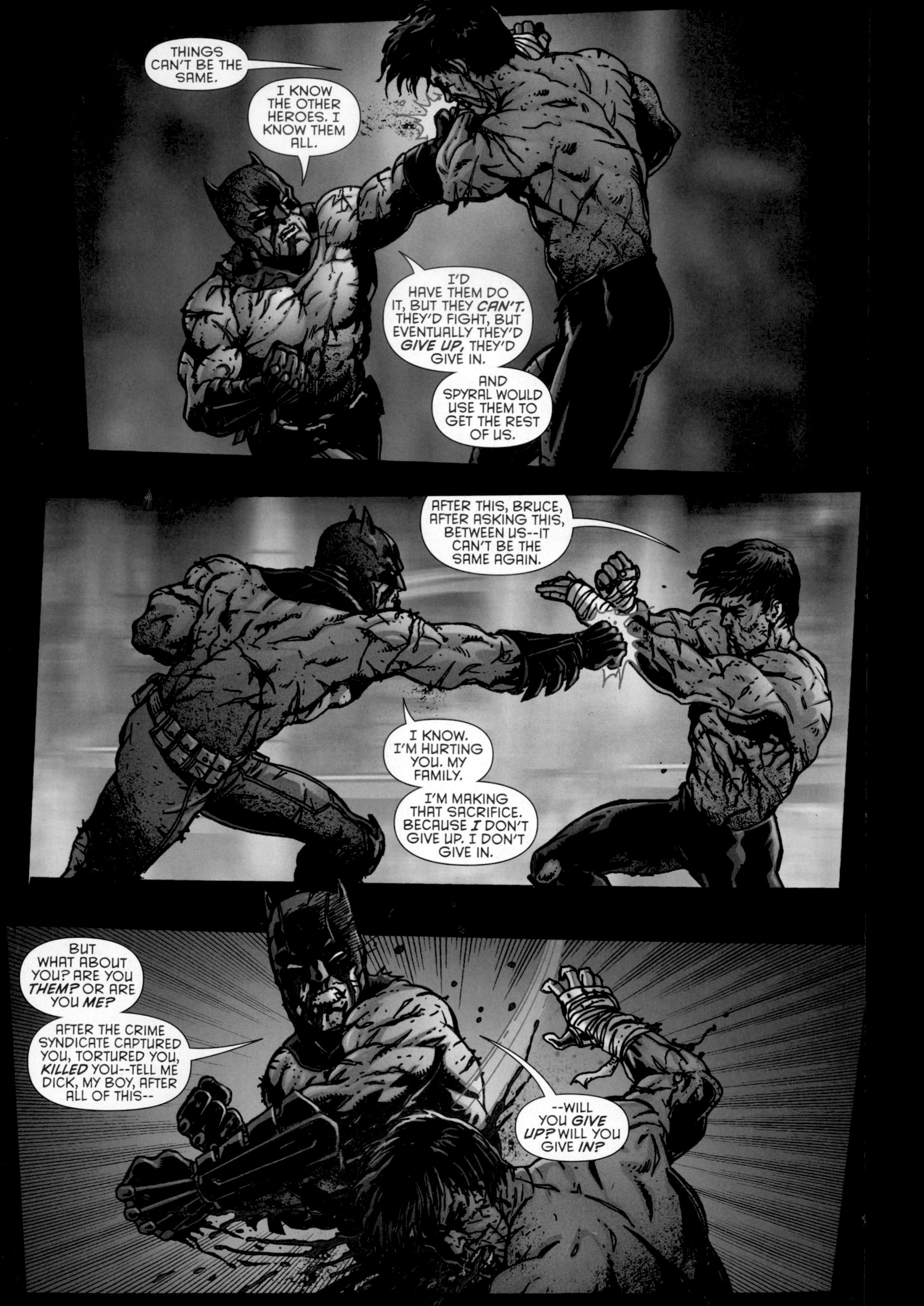
THINGS CAN'T BE THE SAME.
I KNOW THE OTHER HEROES. I KNOW THEM ALL.
I'D HAVE THEM DO IT, BUT THEY *CAN'T.* THEY'D FIGHT, BUT EVENTUALLY THEY'D *GIVE UP,* THEY'D GIVE IN.
AND SPYRAL WOULD USE THEM TO GET THE REST OF US.
AFTER THIS, BRUCE, AFTER ASKING THIS, BETWEEN US--IT CAN'T BE THE SAME AGAIN.
I KNOW. I'M HURTING YOU. MY FAMILY.
I'M MAKING THAT SACRIFICE. BECAUSE *I* DON'T GIVE UP. I DON'T GIVE IN.
BUT WHAT ABOUT YOU? ARE YOU *THEM?* OR ARE YOU *ME?*
AFTER THE CRIME SYNDICATE CAPTURED YOU, TORTURED YOU, *KILLED* YOU--TELL ME DICK, MY BOY, AFTER ALL OF THIS--
--WILL YOU *GIVE UP?* WILL YOU GIVE *IN?*

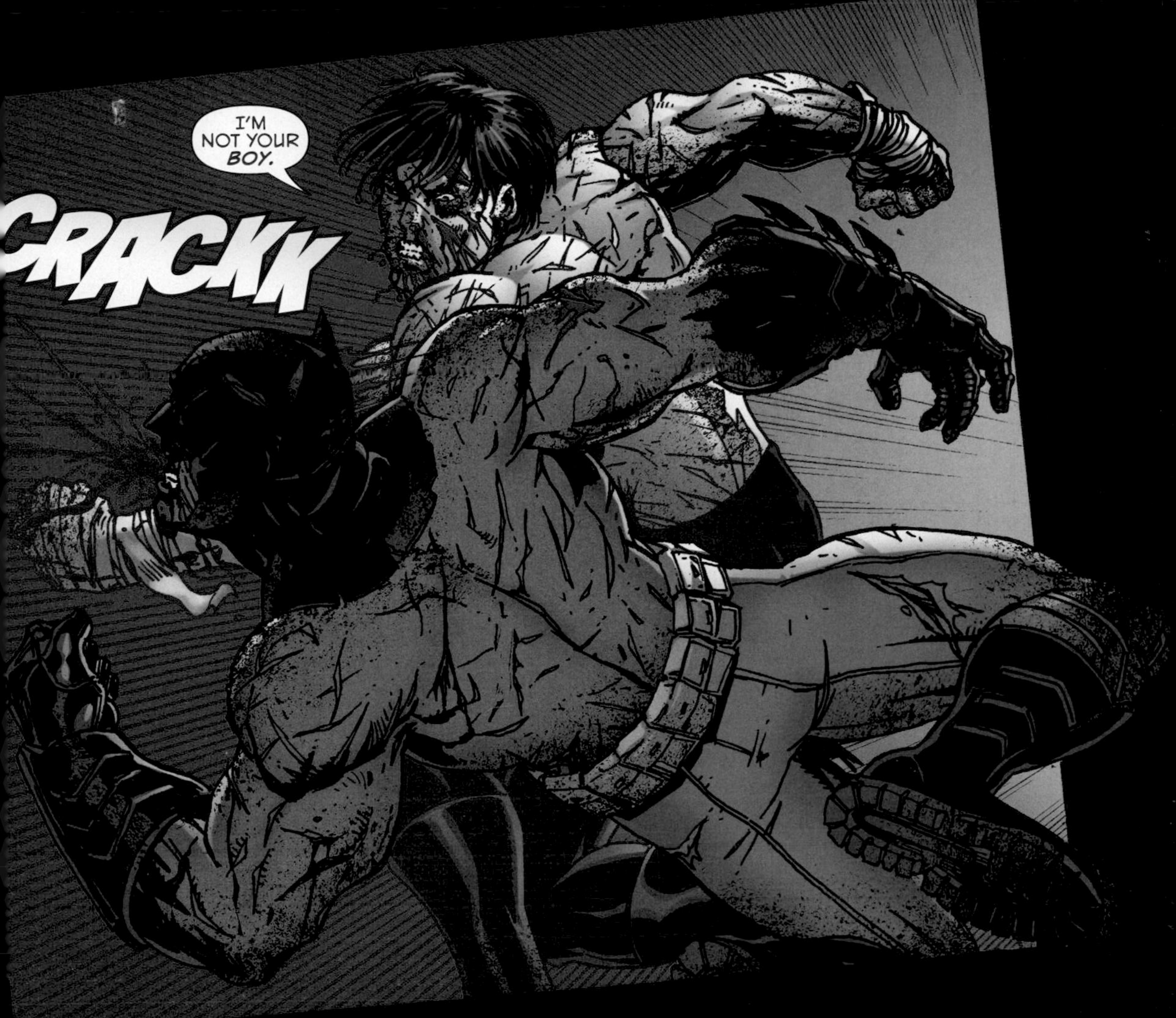
I'M NOT YOUR BOY.
CRACKK

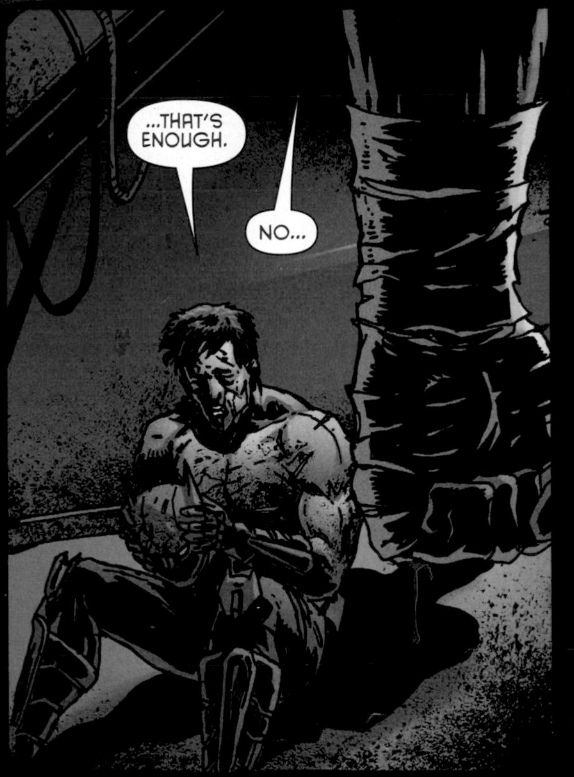
...THAT'S ENOUGH.
NO...

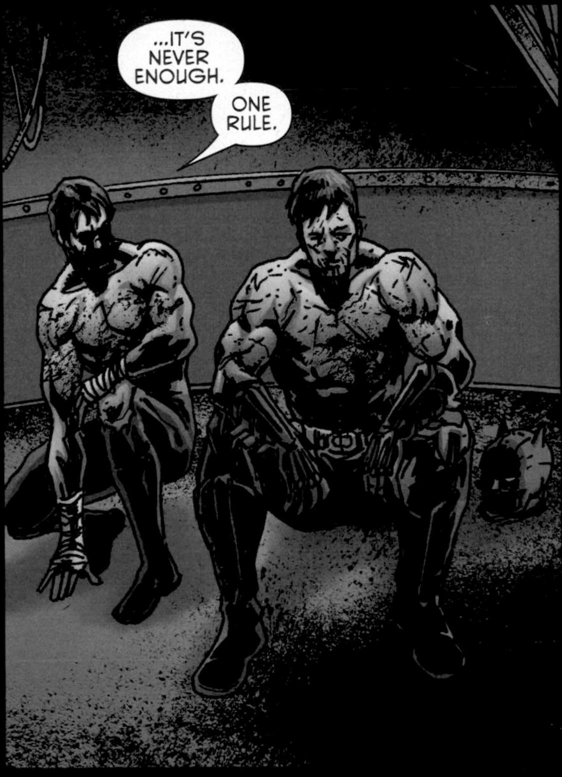
...IT'S NEVER ENOUGH.
ONE RULE.

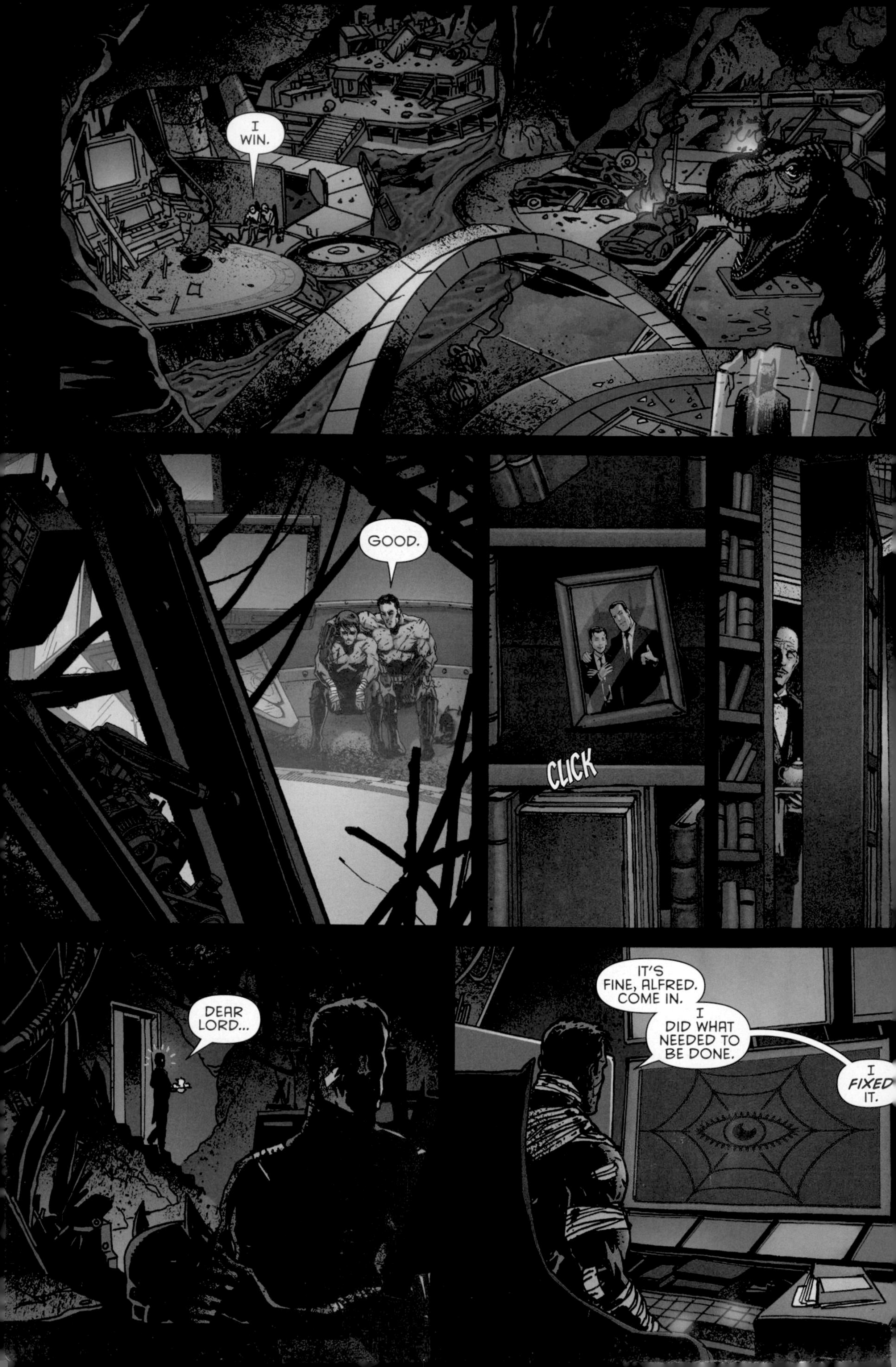
I WIN.
GOOD.
CLICK
DEAR LORD...
IT'S FINE, ALFRED. COME IN.
I DID WHAT NEEDED TO BE DONE.
I *FIXED* IT.

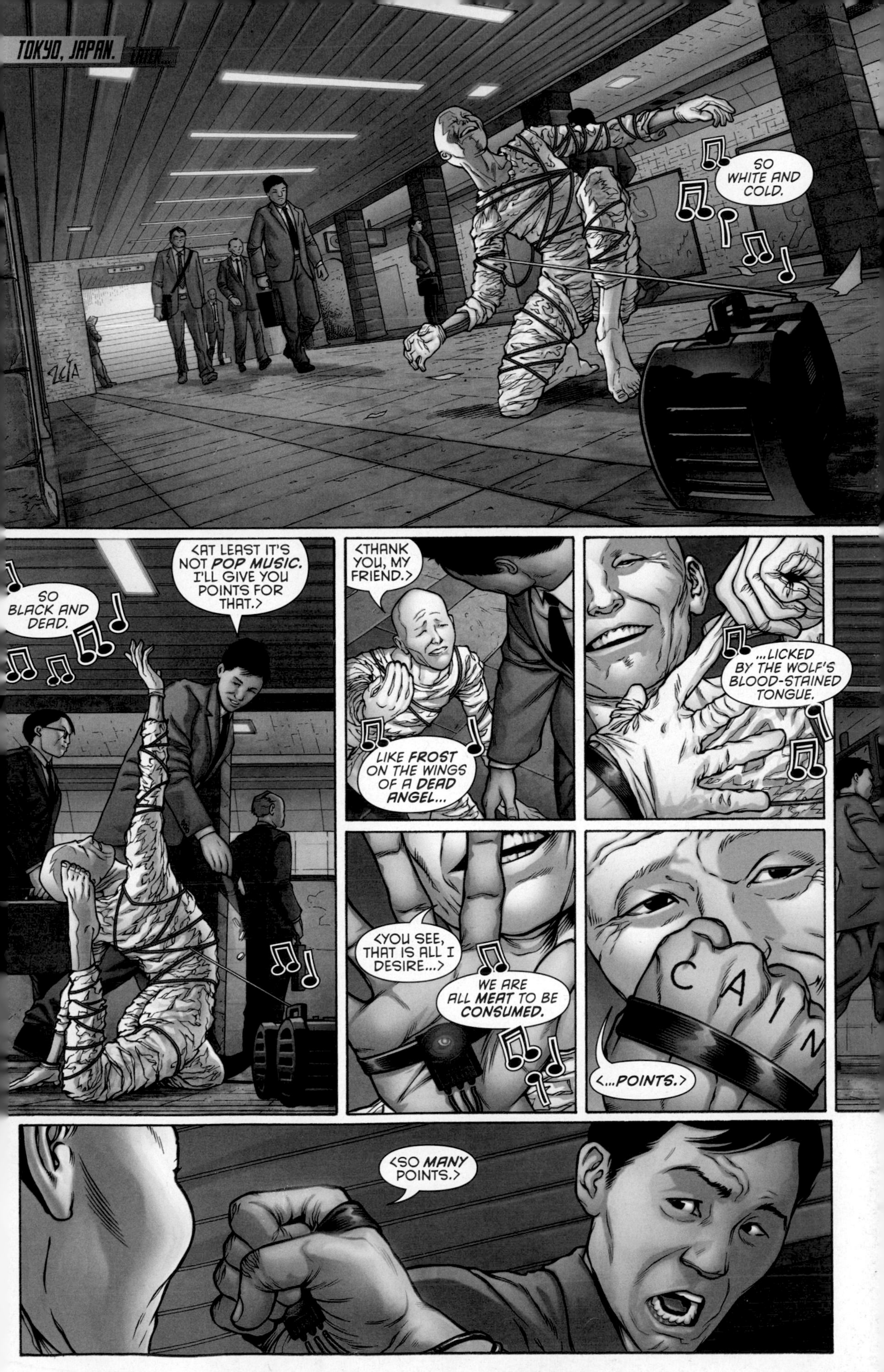
TOKYO, JAPAN. LATER...
SO WHITE AND COLD.
SO BLACK AND DEAD.
<AT LEAST IT'S NOT POP MUSIC. I'LL GIVE YOU POINTS FOR THAT.>
<THANK YOU, MY FRIEND.>
LIKE FROST ON THE WINGS OF A DEAD ANGEL...
...LICKED BY THE WOLF'S BLOOD-STAINED TONGUE.
<YOU SEE, THAT IS ALL I DESIRE...>
WE ARE ALL MEAT TO BE CONSUMED.
CAIN
<...POINTS.>
<SO MANY POINTS.>

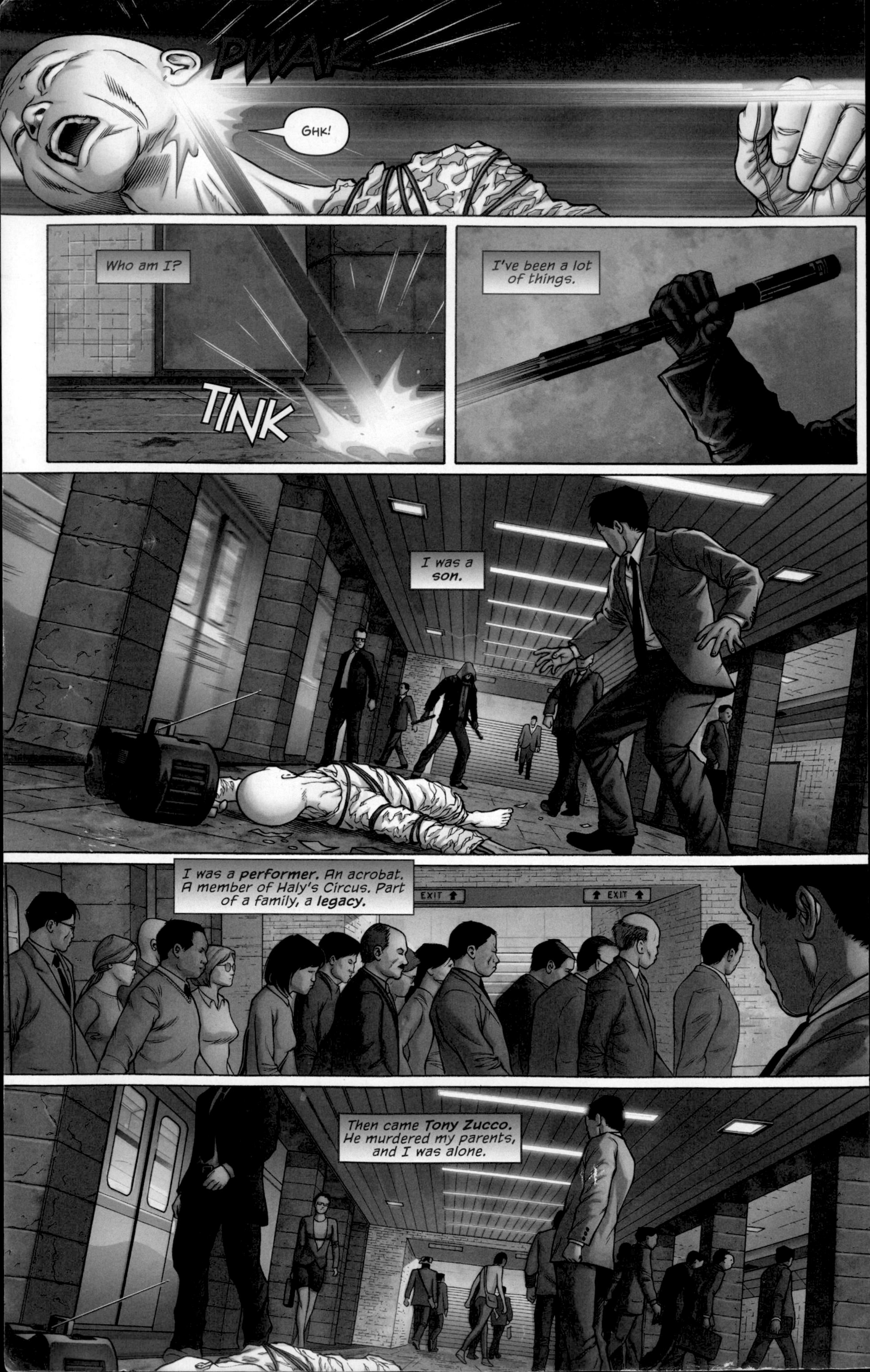
PWAK
GHK!
Who am I?
TINK
I've been a lot of things.
I was a son.
I was a performer. An acrobat. A member of Haly's Circus. Part of a family, a legacy.
EXIT
EXIT
Then came Tony Zucco. He murdered my parents, and I was alone.

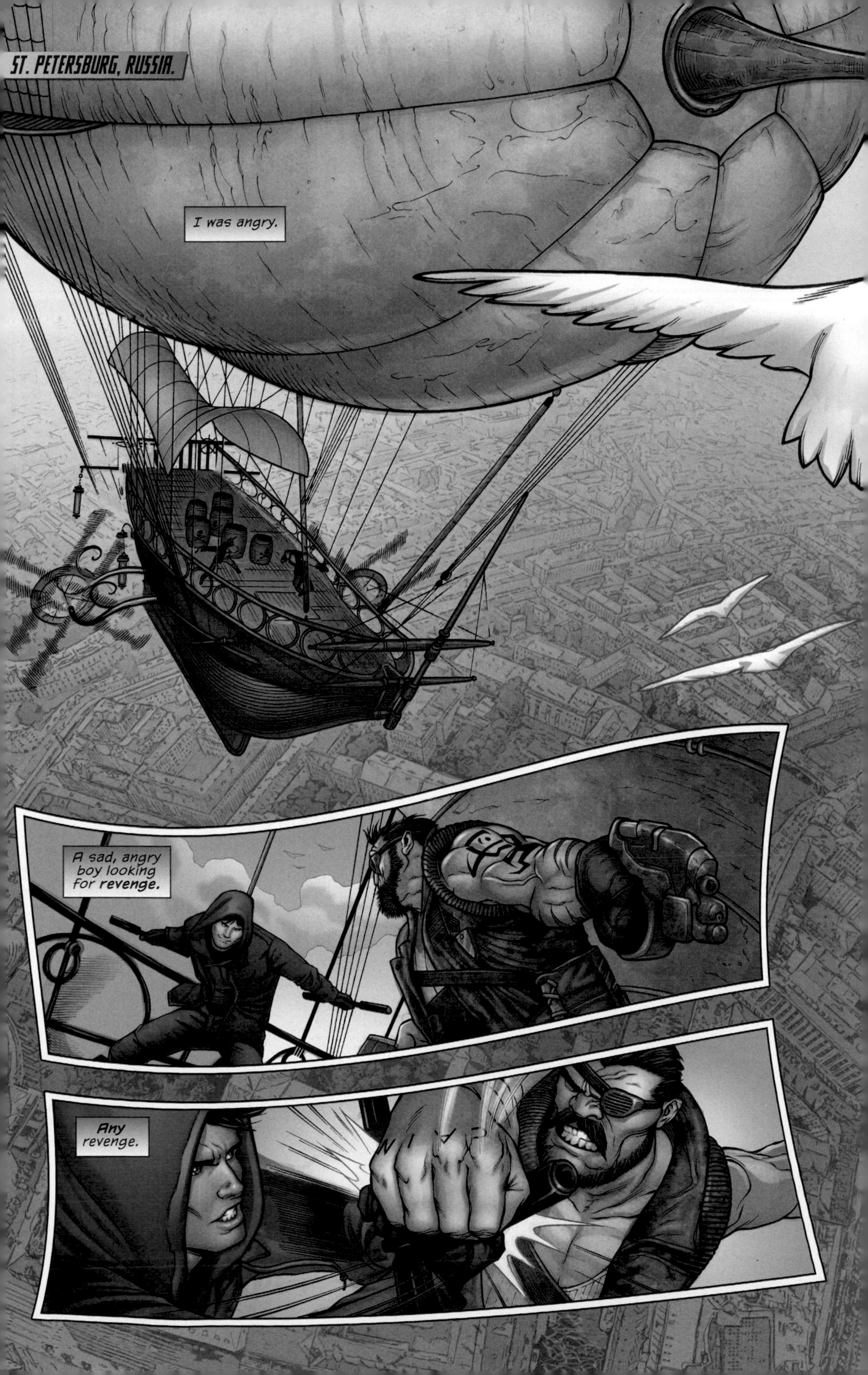
ST. PETERSBURG, RUSSIA.
I was angry.
A sad, angry boy looking for revenge.
Any revenge.

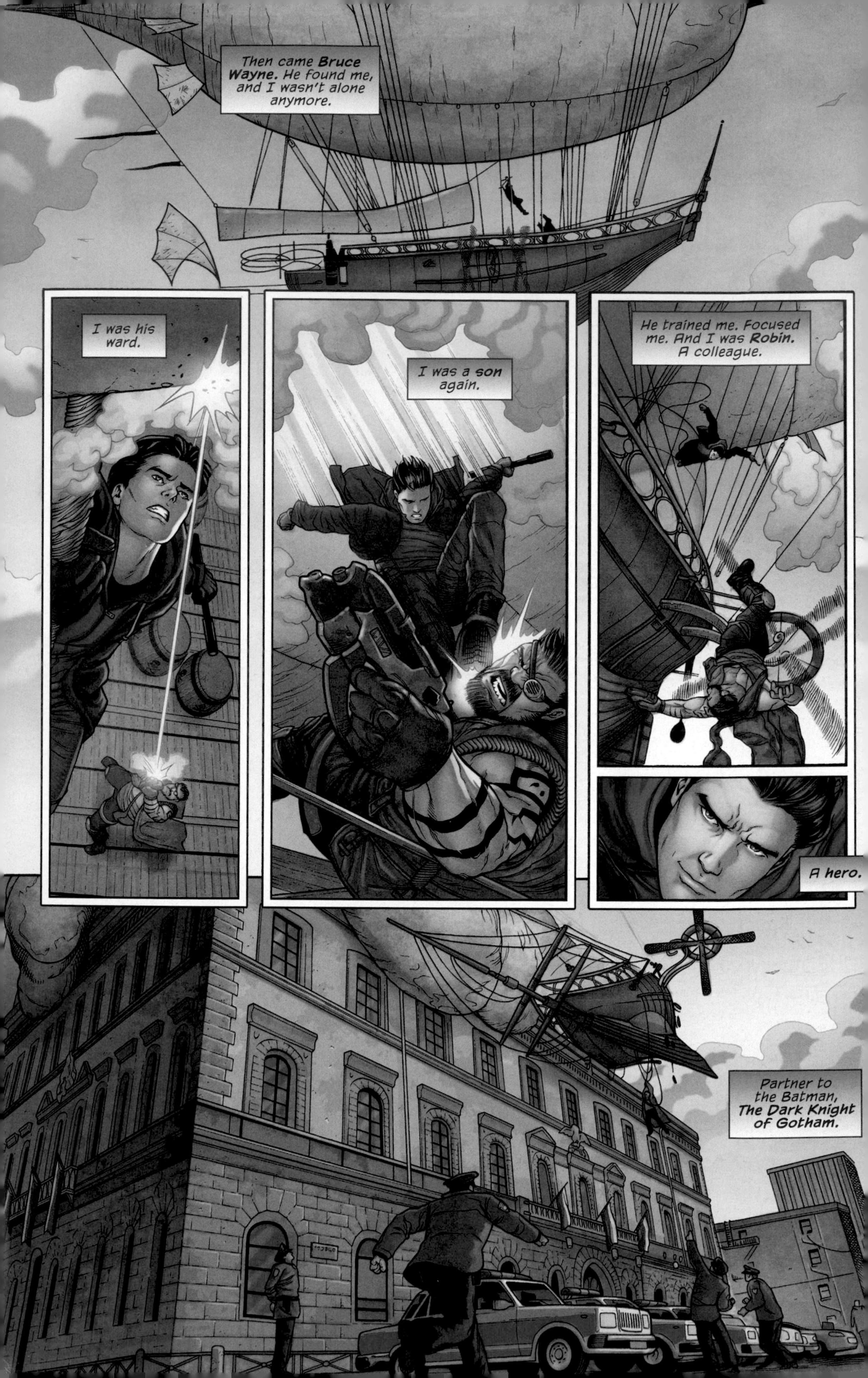
Then came Bruce Wayne. He found me, and I wasn't alone anymore.
I was his ward.
I was a son again.
He trained me. Focused me. And I was Robin. A colleague.
A hero.
Partner to the Batman, The Dark Knight of Gotham.

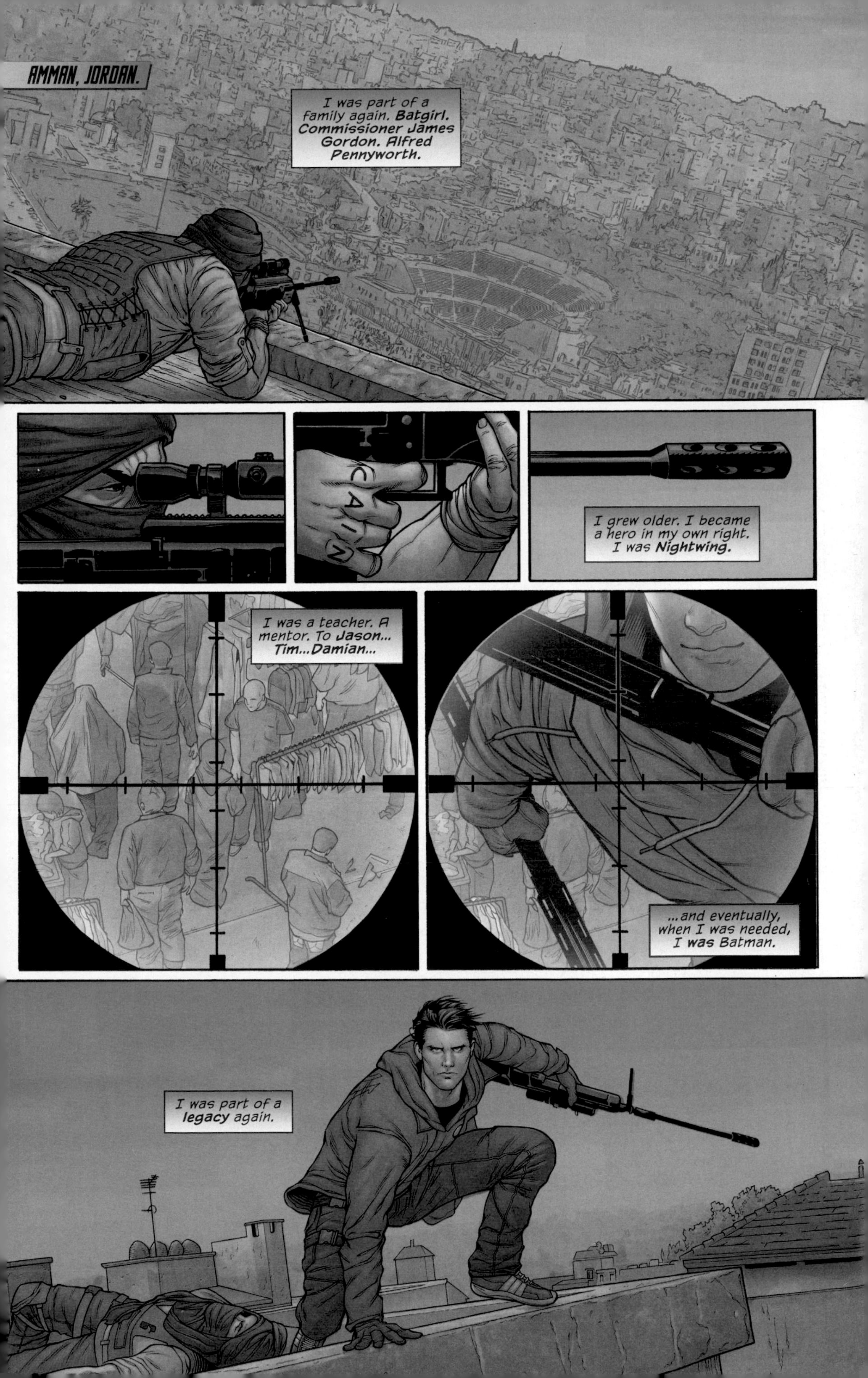
AMMAN, JORDAN.
I was part of a family again. Batgirl. Commissioner James Gordon. Alfred Pennyworth.
CAIN
I grew older. I became a hero in my own right. I was Nightwing.
I was a teacher. A mentor. To Jason... Tim...Damian...
...and eventually, when I was needed, I was Batman.
I was part of a legacy again.

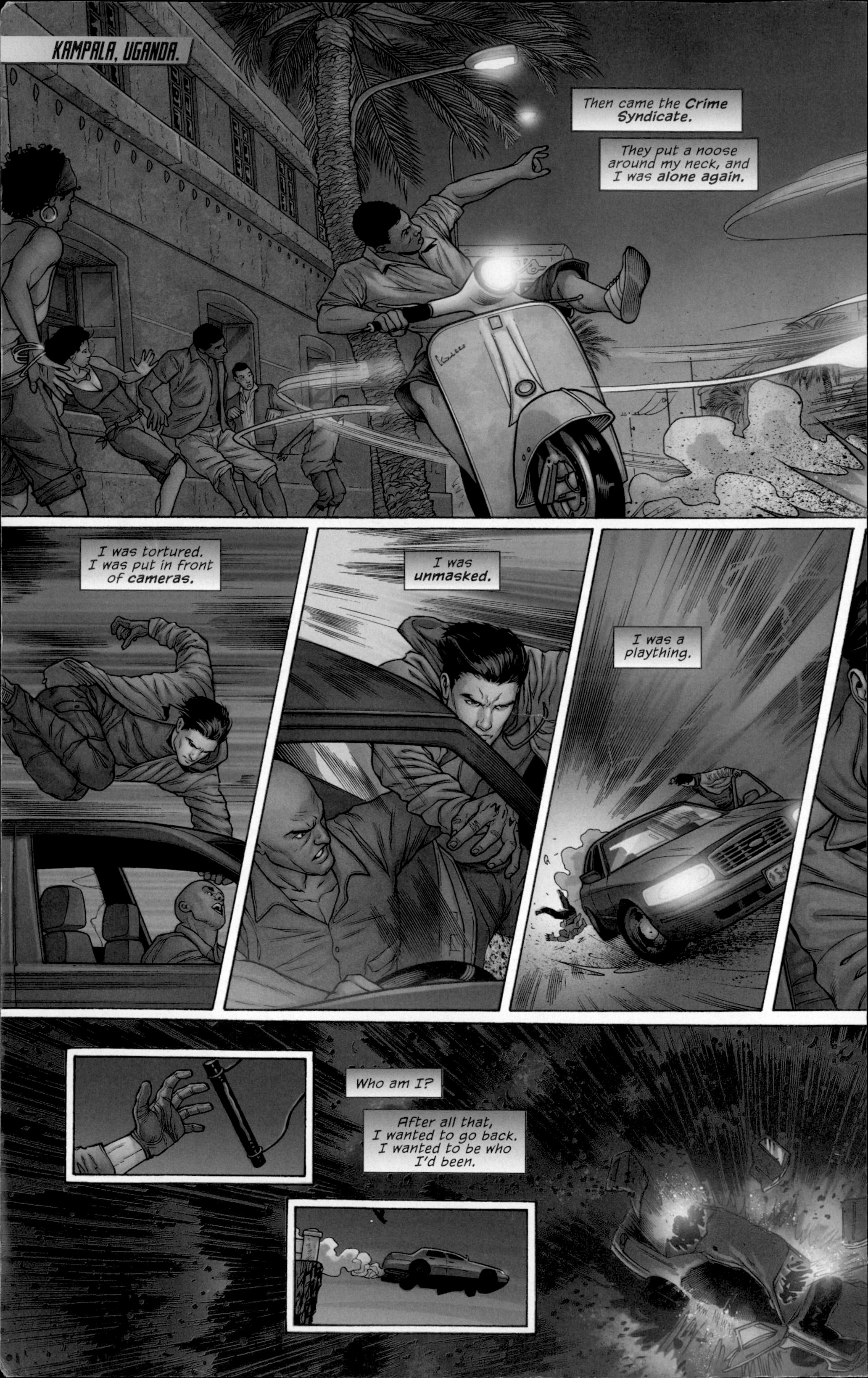
KAMPALA, UGANDA.
Then came the Crime Syndicate.
They put a noose around my neck, and I was alone again.
I was tortured. I was put in front of cameras.
I was unmasked.
I was a plaything.
Who am I?
After all that, I wanted to go back. I wanted to be who I'd been.

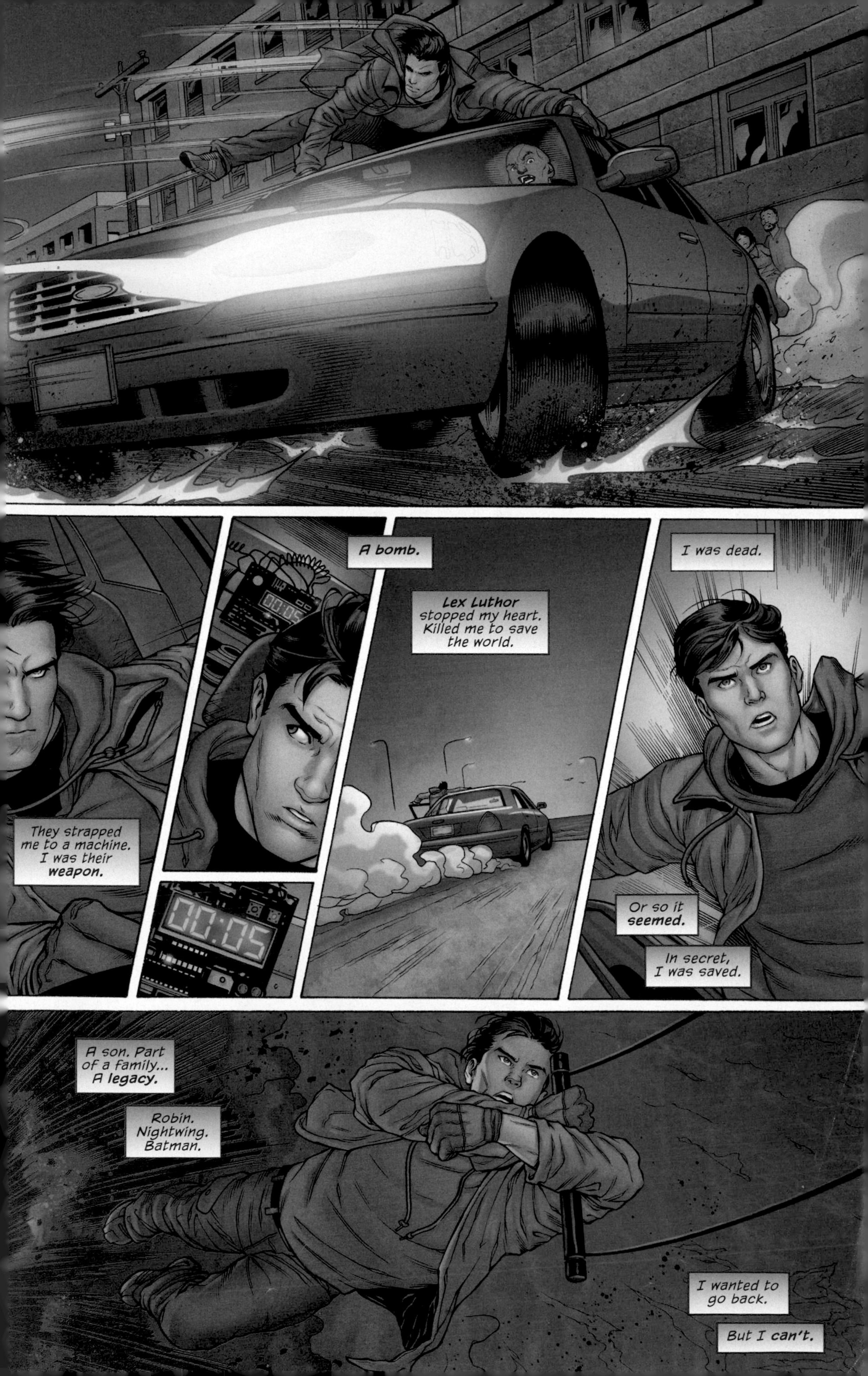
They strapped me to a machine. I was their **weapon.**
A bomb.
Lex Luthor stopped my heart. Killed me to save the world.
I was dead.
Or so it **seemed.**
In secret, I was saved.
A son. Part of a family... A **legacy.**
Robin. Nightwing. Batman.
I wanted to go back.
But I **can't.**

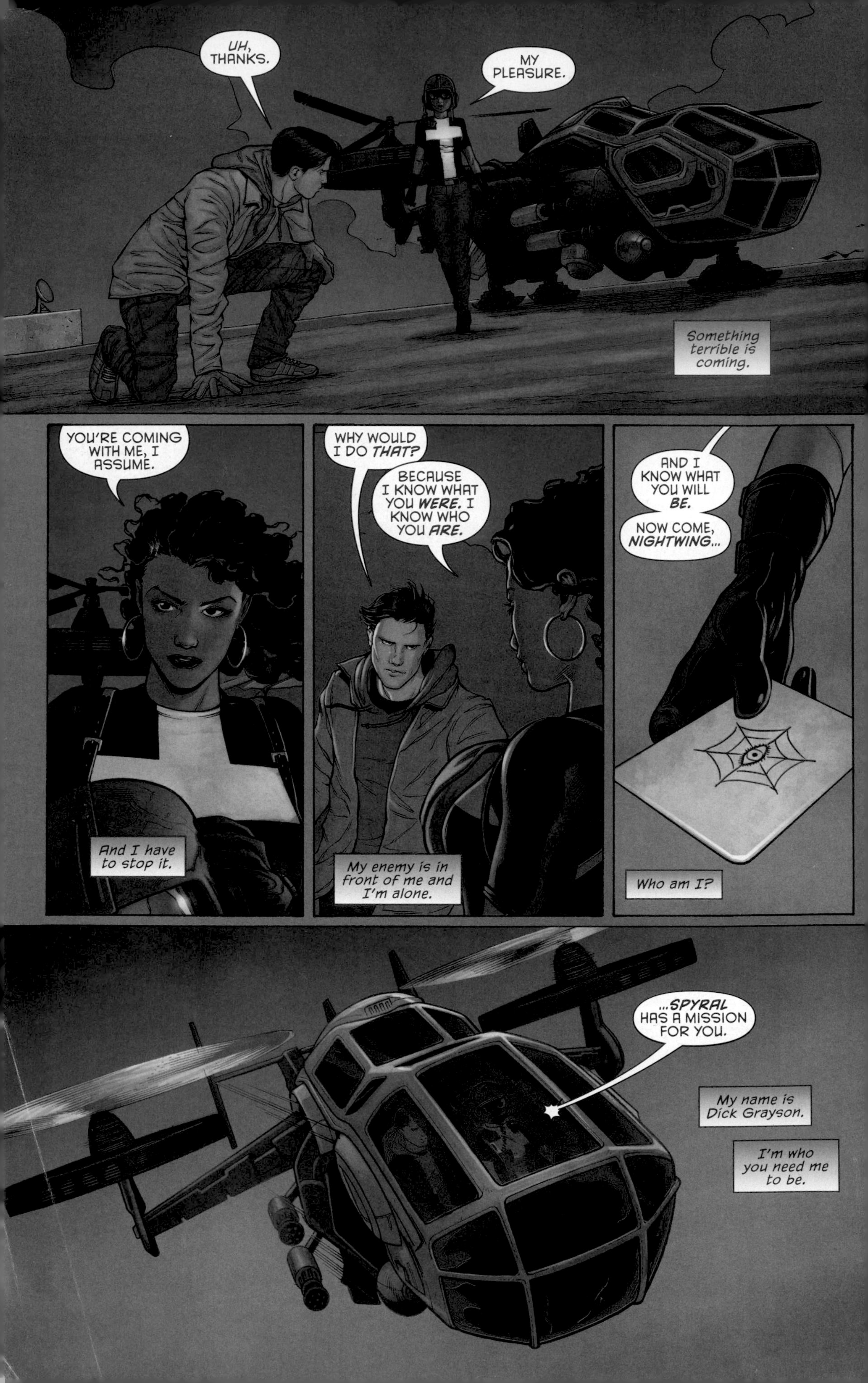
UH, THANKS.
MY PLEASURE.
Something terrible is coming.
YOU'RE COMING WITH ME, I ASSUME.
And I have to stop it.
WHY WOULD I DO *THAT?*
BECAUSE I KNOW WHAT YOU *WERE*. I KNOW WHO YOU *ARE*.
My enemy is in front of me and I'm alone.
AND I KNOW WHAT YOU WILL *BE*.
NOW COME, *NIGHTWING*...
Who am I?
...*SPYRAL* HAS A MISSION FOR YOU.
My name is Dick Grayson.
I'm who you need me to be.

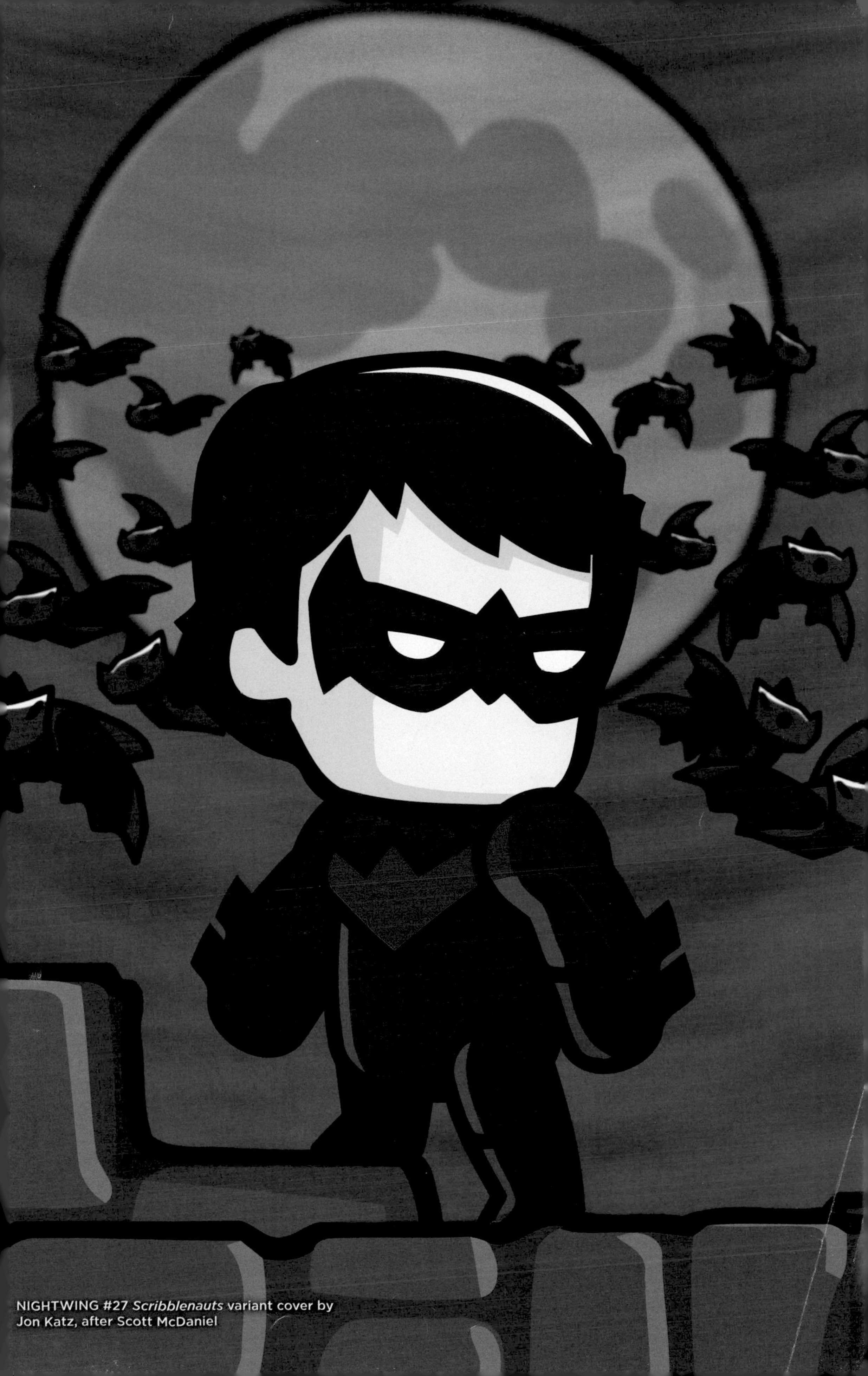

NIGHTWING #27 *Scribblenauts* variant cover by
Jon Katz, after Scott McDaniel

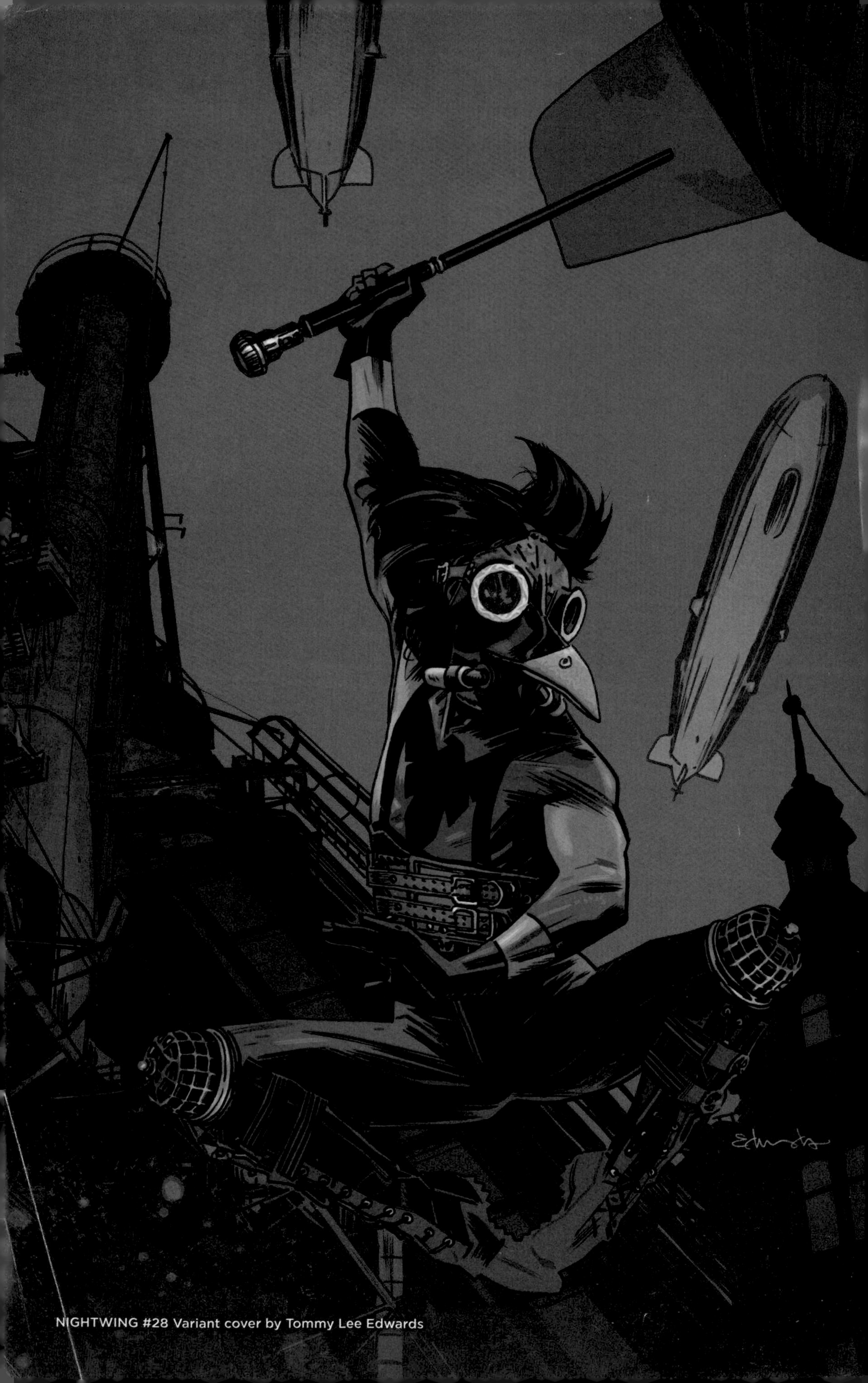

NIGHTWING #28 Variant cover by Tommy Lee Edwards

NIGHTWING #29 *Robot Chicken* variant cover by Scott McDaniel, Karl Story, Pete Pantazis and RC Stoodios

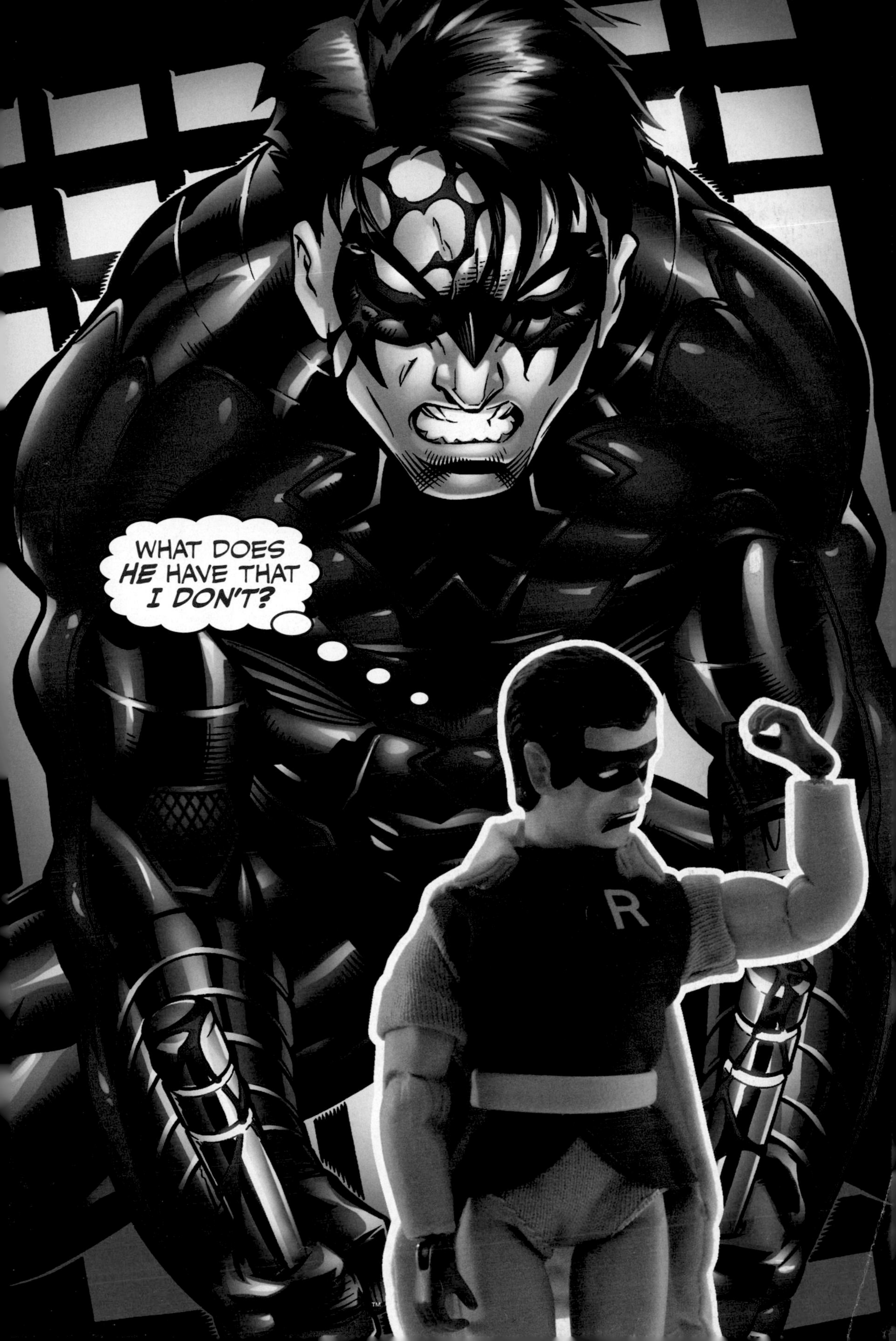
WHAT DOES *HE* HAVE THAT *I DON'T?*
R

NIGHTWING #30 MAD variant Cover by Sam Viviano

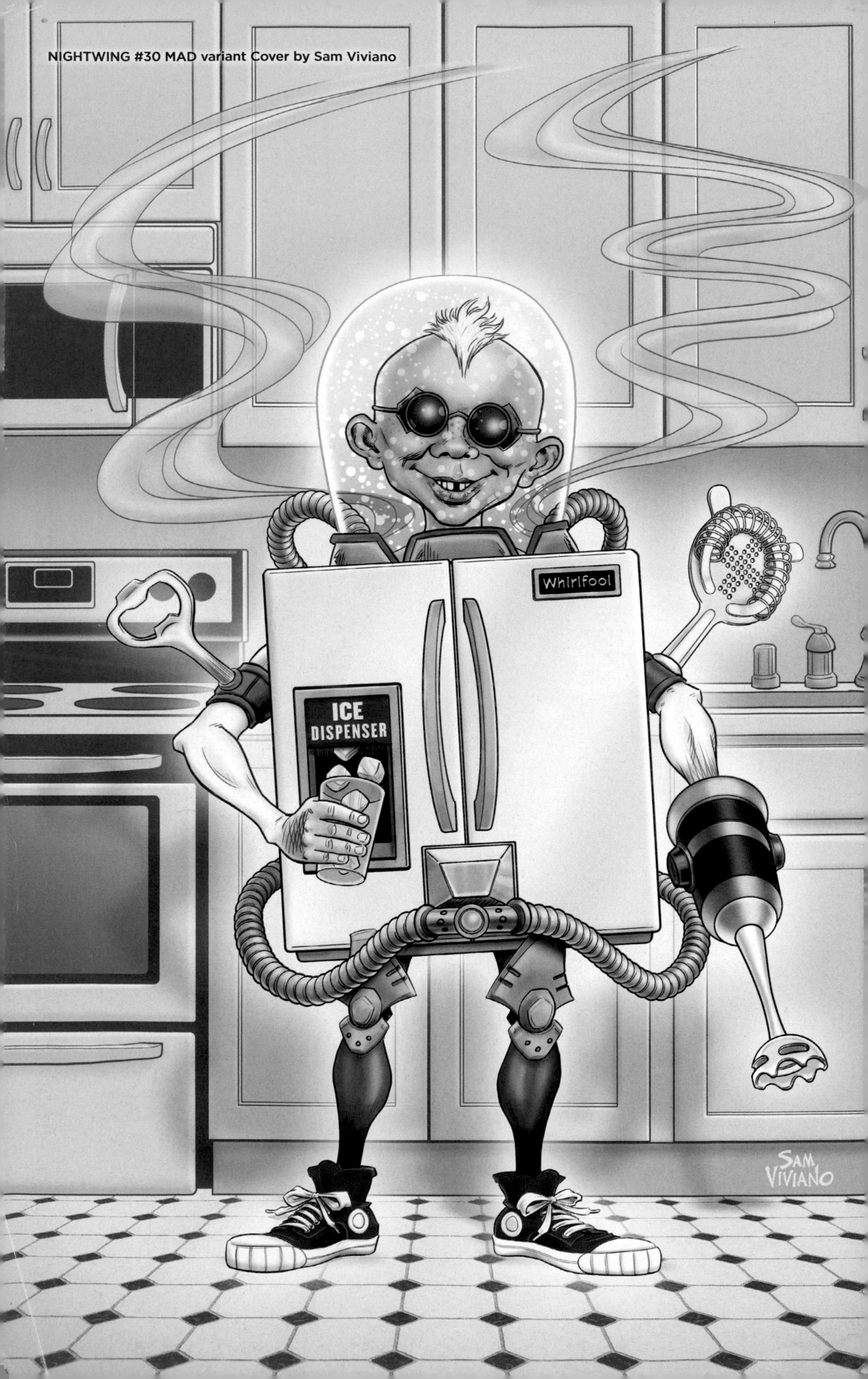
Whirlfool
ICE
DISPENSER
SAM
VIVIANO

DC COMICS™

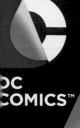

"Stellar. A solid yarn that roots itself in Grayson's past, with gorgeous artwork by artist Eddy Barrows."—IGN

"Dynamic."—The New York Times

"A new generation is going to fall in love with Nightwing."
—MTV Geek

START AT THE BEGINNING!

NIGHTWING
VOLUME 1: TRAPS AND TRAPEZES

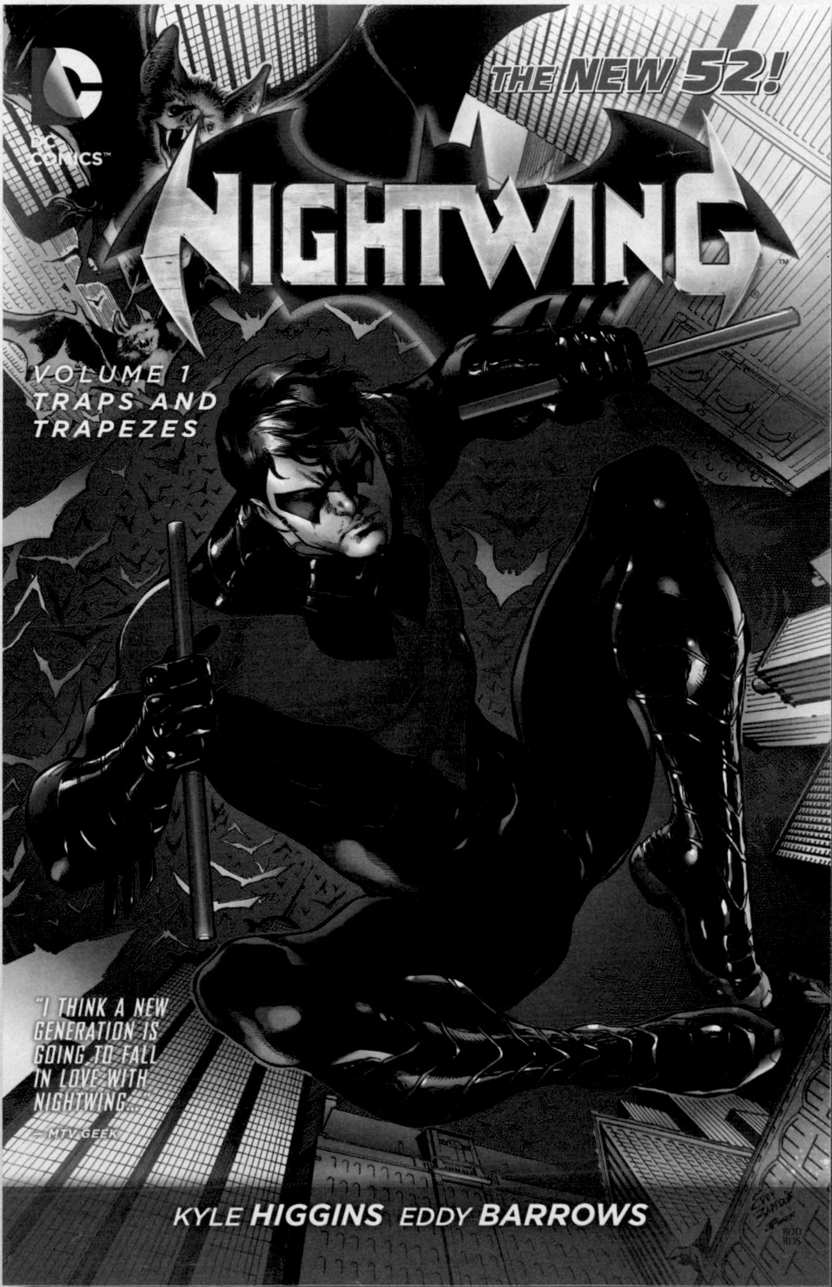
DC COMICS™
THE NEW 52!
NIGHTWING
VOLUME 1
TRAPS AND
TRAPEZES
"I THINK A NEW GENERATION IS GOING TO FALL IN LOVE WITH NIGHTWING."
—MTV GEEK
KYLE HIGGINS EDDY BARROWS

NIGHTWING VOL. 2:
NIGHT OF THE OWLS

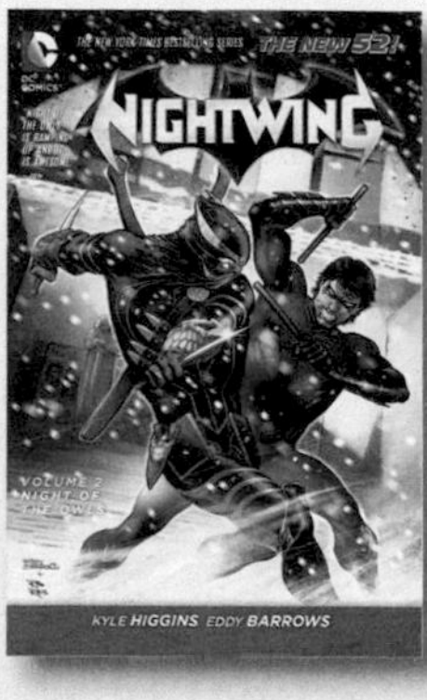
THE NEW 52!
NIGHTWING
KYLE HIGGINS EDDY BARROWS

NIGHTWING VOL. 3:
DEATH OF THE FAMILY

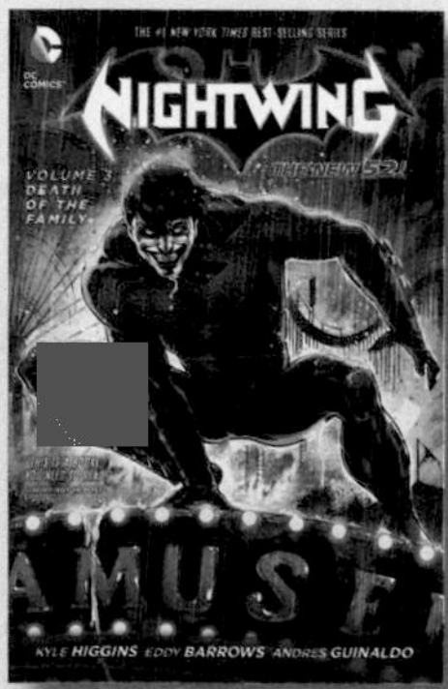
NIGHTWING
KYLE HIGGINS EDDY BARROWS ANDRES GUINALDO

BATMAN:
NIGHT OF THE OWLS

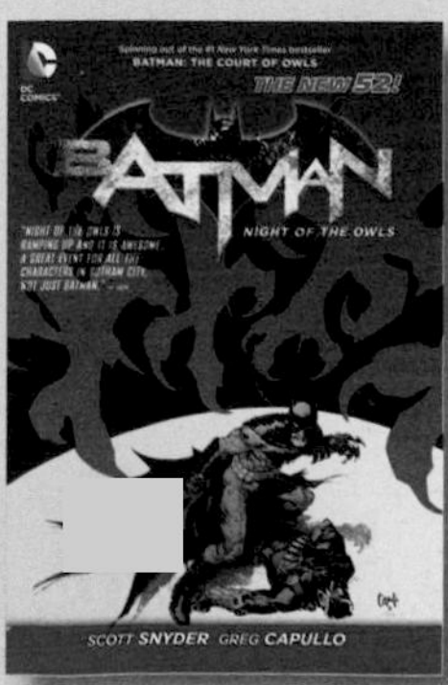
BATMAN: THE COURT OF OWLS
THE NEW 52!
BATMAN
NIGHT OF THE OWLS
SCOTT SNYDER GREG CAPULLO

DC COMICS™

START AT THE BEGINNING!

BATMAN VOLUME 1: THE COURT OF OWLS

BATMAN VOL. 2: THE CITY OF OWLS

with SCOTT SNYDER and GREG CAPULLO

BATMAN VOL. 3: DEATH OF THE FAMILY

with SCOTT SNYDER and GREG CAPULLO

BATMAN: NIGHT OF THE OWLS

with SCOTT SNYDER and GREG CAPULLO

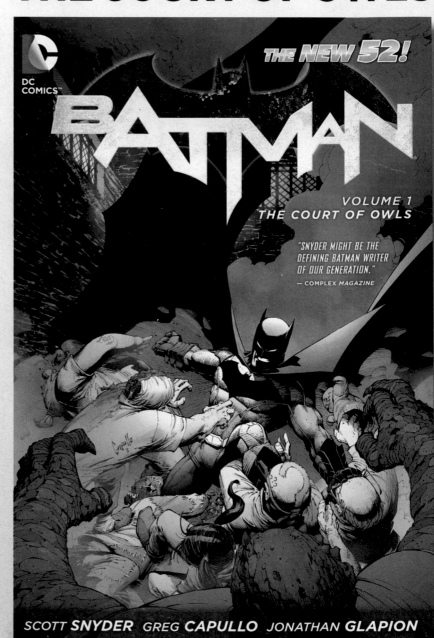

SCOTT **SNYDER**   Greg **CAPULLO**   Jonathan **GLAPION**